LATERALITY, 2010, 15 (1/2), 1–3

Introduction

The right hand and the left hand of history

On 10th April 1998, Tony Blair, the British Prime Minister, and Bertie Ahern, the Irish Taoiseach, signed the Belfast Agreement (the "Good Friday Agreement"), which, after three decades of what were known as, "The Troubles", resulted in peace in Northern Ireland, and began a period of economic growth and prosperity that has survived to this day. In signing the agreement, Tony Blair, in his typically felicitous way, said that, "I feel the hand of history upon our shoulders". The "hand of history" was a compelling phrase, and would seem to be originated by Blair himself, who later said, "it had just popped into his head".[1]

In signing the documents, Tony Blair and Bertie Ahern showed the hand of history in their own separate ways, for while Tony Blair signed with his right hand, it was with his left hand that Bertie Ahern signed.[2] It is only a small detail, but the fact of it being worth commenting on at all, reveals how left-handers are, to a large extent, a people without a history. Despite one in ten individuals nowadays being left-handed, there is little historical study of the role of left-handers in history, their treatment by right-handers, their problems, or even their prevalence. The occasional exceptions, such as Pierre-Michel Bertrand's *Histoire des Gaucheurs* (Bertrand, 2001), emphasise the scarcity of such studies.

Bertrand subtitled his book, "Des gens à l'envers"—a people who are back to front—a quotation from a French translation of *Los Sueños* (*Visions*), written between 1606 and 1622 by the Spanish writer Francisco de Quevedo (1580–1645). De Quevedo's book was first translated into English as *The Visions of Dom Francisco de Quevedo Villegas* in 1667 by Sir Roger L'Estrange (1616–1704).[3] The entire passage, from the Sixth Vision,

[1] http://www.guardian.co.uk/politics/2008/mar/19/northernireland.northernireland

[2] The image itself is distributed by Associated Press (www.apimages.com) as number AP98041001694. Unfortunately it is only available for distribution in North America, and can only be seen at the website by firstly registering as a user (which is free), when the serial number can then be entered.

[3] The full text is available at http://books.google.co.uk/books?id=csMPAAAAQAAJ&printsec=frontcover&dq=roger+l%27estrange+quevedo&client=firefox-a

ISBN: 978-1-84872-723-6 (hbk) ISBN: 978-1-03-292340-6 (pbk) DOI: 10.1080/13576500903201818

from which Bertrand took his excerpt, merits complete quotation, for it is little known in the literature of handedness and lateralisation, and shows well a particular historical view of left-handers. The narrator on a nocturnal walk finds two paths, the one being hard and difficult, whereas the other path, which is broad and easy, is that which leads to Hell. Not surprisingly it is, "the Left-hand way". The narrator describes how,

> ... my next Discovery was, of a great many People, Grumbling and Muttering, that there was no body lookt after them; no, not so much as to Torment them: *As if their Tails were not as well worth the Toasting as their Neighbours.* Answer was made, that being a kind of Devils themselves, they might put in for some sort of Authority in the Place, and execute the Office of *Tormentors.* This made me ask them what they were. And a Devil told me (with Respect) that they were a Company of Ungracious, *Left-handed* Wretches, that could do nothing Aright. And their Grievance was, that they were Quarter'd by themselves: But not knowing whether they were Men or no, or indeed what else to make of them, we did not know how to Match them, or in what company to put them. In the World they are lookt upon as *Ill-Omens*; and let any Man meet one of them upon a Journey in a Morning, Fasting; 'tis the same thing as if a Hare had cross'd the way upon them; he presently turns Head in a Discontent, and goes to Bed again. Ye know that *Scævola*, when he found his Mistake, in killing Another for *Porsenna*, (the Secretary, for the Prince) burnt his right Hand in Revenge of the Miscarriage. Now the Severity of the Vengeance, was not so much the Maiming or the Cripling of himself, but the Condemning of himself to be for ever *Left-handed.* And so 'tis with a Malefactor that suffers Justice; the Shame and Punishment does not lye so much in the Loss of his *Right Hand*, as that the other is *Left*. And it was the Curse of an old Bawd, to a Fellow that had vext her, *That he might go to the Devil by the stroke of a Left-handed Man.* If the Poets speak Truth, (as 'twere a wonder if they should not) the *Left* is the *Unlucky Side*; and there never came any Good from it. And for my last Argument against these Creatures; the *Goats* and *Reprobates* stand upon the *Left Hand*, and *Left-Handed Men* are, in Effect, a sort of Creature that's made to do Mischief; nay whether I should call them Men, or no, I know not. (L'Estrange, 1708, pp. 178–179)

It was clearly not always the case that left-handers such as Bertie Ahern, or for that matter, Barack Obama and his fellow left-handed American Presidents, could have risen to positions of power and status.

The papers in this special issue of *Laterality* are not a systematic review of the field, but instead are a group of studies that came together at the same time in the editorial offices, and it was realised that they would make more sense published as a group, to emphasise the general paucity of such material. Three of the papers in particular are by Lauren Harris, who is undoubtedly the doyen of historians of handedness and lateralisation, and we are particularly proud to publish these papers of his. Together we hope that the various studies will stimulate further research in this neglected but important area.

Chris McManus
Mike Nicholls
Giorgio Vallortigara

REFERENCES

Bertrand, P.-M. (2001). *Histoire des gauchers.* Paris: Imago.

L'Estrange, R. (1708). *The Visions of Dom Francisco de Quevedo Villegas, Knight of the Order of St. James (Tenth Edition, corrected).* London: Richard Sare.

LATERALITY, 2010, 15 (1/2), 4–14

On teaching infants "the right use of their hands": Advice and reassurance from Mary Palmer Tyler's *The Maternal Physician* (1811)

Lauren Julius Harris

Michigan State University, East Lansing, MI, USA

For parents anxious "lest their children should be left-handed", the American author Mary Palmer Tyler offered advice and reassurance in her 1811 child-care manual *The Maternal Physician*. This article provides a brief biography of Tyler and the text of her remarks, along with notes on the text and the author's sources.

What should parents do about their child's handedness, especially if the child shows signs of being left-handed? The question was of routine concern in the past and remains so today in certain communities and parts of the world, with experts of every stripe giving instructions and advice. In a prior article (Harris, 2003), I presented examples from five eighteenth-century European authors—three from England and two from France. They included the physicians William Cadogan (1772) and Nicholas Andry (1743), the philosopher Jean-Jacques Rousseau (1762), the writer John Hill (1754), and someone identified only as "An Eminent Physician" (1729)—all of them famous (if we accept the last one's nom de plume) and all of them men (if the last can be included here too). Recently I found yet another example, now from the early nineteenth century, that might be of interest to readers of this journal. It is notable on two counts: it appeared in a child-care manual that the historian Christina Gibbons (1983) called the first of its kind written by an American and published in the United States, and its author was a woman, Mary Palmer Tyler, who, while acknowledging that much had been written about child-care by "the most able physicians", declared that a child's best physician in all "ordinary cases" was its *mother.* Being a mother herself many times over, Tyler could also draw on personal experience, probably more than most if not all of her male counterparts. I begin this article with a brief biography of the author, followed by the full text of the

Address correspondence to: Lauren Julius Harris, Department of Psychology, Michigan State University, East Lansing, Michigan 48824, USA. E-mail: HARRISL@msu.edu

DOI: 10.1080/13576500701580777

section on handedness, along with my notes on the text and on the author's medical and other sources.

MARY PALMER TYLER

Mary Palmer Tyler was born in 1775 into a family of Boston-area revolutionary activists who "believed in their obligation to serve the public welfare as intellectual and social leaders."[1] Her father, Joseph Pearse Palmer, like his own father, served in the Massachusetts militia and the Massachusetts Provincial Congress and Committee of Safety, and her mother, Elizabeth Hunt Palmer, ministered to the troops during the wartime occupation of Boston. There were five daughters and four sons in the family, with Mary being the eldest daughter. In 1794, at age 18, Mary was wed to Royall Tyler, 18 years older, and a prominent playwright, lawyer, and later Chief Justice of Vermont, with a law practice in Guilford, Vermont. The couple moved there in 1796 and then in 1801 to a farm in Brattleboro. From 1794 to 1818, the family grew to include eleven children—two daughters and nine sons. Tyler lived the rest of her life in Vermont and died there in 1866 at the ripe old age of 91.

CHILD-CARE ADVICE IN THE LATE EIGHTEENTH AND EARLY NINETEENTH CENTURIES

In the late eighteenth century, as the historian Ruth H. Bloch (1978) has noted, writers began to dwell on the critical importance of proper maternal care during infancy, so that "What had earlier been left to custom for the first time became a matter of widespread written analysis and prescriptive advice" (p. 110), with medical experts instructing mothers on many aspects of child care, and with handbooks on child nurture and disease starting to be widely available. As Bloch went on to explain, most of these handbooks, or manuals, were American reprints of slightly earlier works by well-known English and Scottish obstetricians, but in the early nineteenth century "indigenous American publications" also began to appear. Most of the instructions "seem aimed toward increasing the amount of attention paid by mothers to small children", so that infant care came to be viewed as an "exacting occupation", requiring not only heightened concentration but also special expertise, with tasks previously "regulated by unwritten custom" now beginning to be matters for "extended analysis and deliberate, rational

[1] The biographical information provided here comes from Tyler's (1925) autobiography and from essays by Marilyn S. Blackwell (1992; reprinted in 1997) and Christina Gibbons (1983). The quotation is from Blackwell (1997, p. 33).

manipulation" (p. 111). Tyler's manual reflected these trends but at the same time, as we shall see, it told mothers that they could relax their guard just a bit, including where handedness is concerned.

The Maternal Physician

Child-care manuals in Tyler's time typically had long titles, and Tyler's was no exception: *The maternal physician; a treatise on the nurture and management of infants, from the birth until two years old. Being the result of sixteen years' experience in the nursery, illustrated by extracts from the most approved medical authors.* Tyler completed the manuscript in June 1810, when she was 35 years old, living in Brattleboro, and already the mother of eight children. The first publication, by Isaac Riley in New York, was in 1811, so that the "sixteen years' experience in the nursery" covered the period 1794–1810. Not coincidentally, Riley was Royall Tyler's publisher. The manual then was reprinted in a second edition and published in Philadelphia in 1818. The title page from that edition, the one used for this article, is reproduced in Figure 1.

In both editions, Tyler is identified only as "*an American matron*". That was her own decision (Burnham, 1880, p. 107), made to protect herself from "criticism from male professionals who might consider her book a deviation from traditional female deference" because "few women writers had claimed the authority to give child-care advice" (Blackwell, 1992/97, p. 35).[2] Both editions, some 291 pages long, are divided into five chapters each with several "Sections", most beginning with lines from so-called "pediatric poems" designed to instruct and inspire. The topics cover the broad range promised in the title, including, for example, "Mothers' Milk, the best and only proper Food for Infants", "the best Time and Method of setting Infants on their Feet", and the regulation of "Temper and Disposition". Brief descriptions of these and other sections can be found in Gibbons (1983). The material on handedness, which is not mentioned there, is presented under the heading "Observations relative to teaching Infants the right Use of their Hands" and comprises the whole of Section II of Chapter II (pp. 125–126). It begins with lines from William Stanley Roscoe's translation of the poem *La Balia* [*The Nurse*] by Luigi Tansillo (1798/1552), a Petrarchist poet active in Naples in the mid-sixteenth century

[2] If that was the reason, Tyler did not go so far as to adopt a male pseudonym, unlike certain other women writers, including Anne and Charlotte Bronte (Acton and Currier Bell), Mary Ann Evans (George Eliot), and Aurore Dupin (George Sand). The decision also cuts both ways, inasmuch as John Hill (1754), one of Tyler's European predecessors, published his manual under a *female* pseudonym (*the Honourable Juliana-Susannah Seymour*), presumably to trade on the common belief that women's feelings and intuitions about children were naturally stronger than men's.

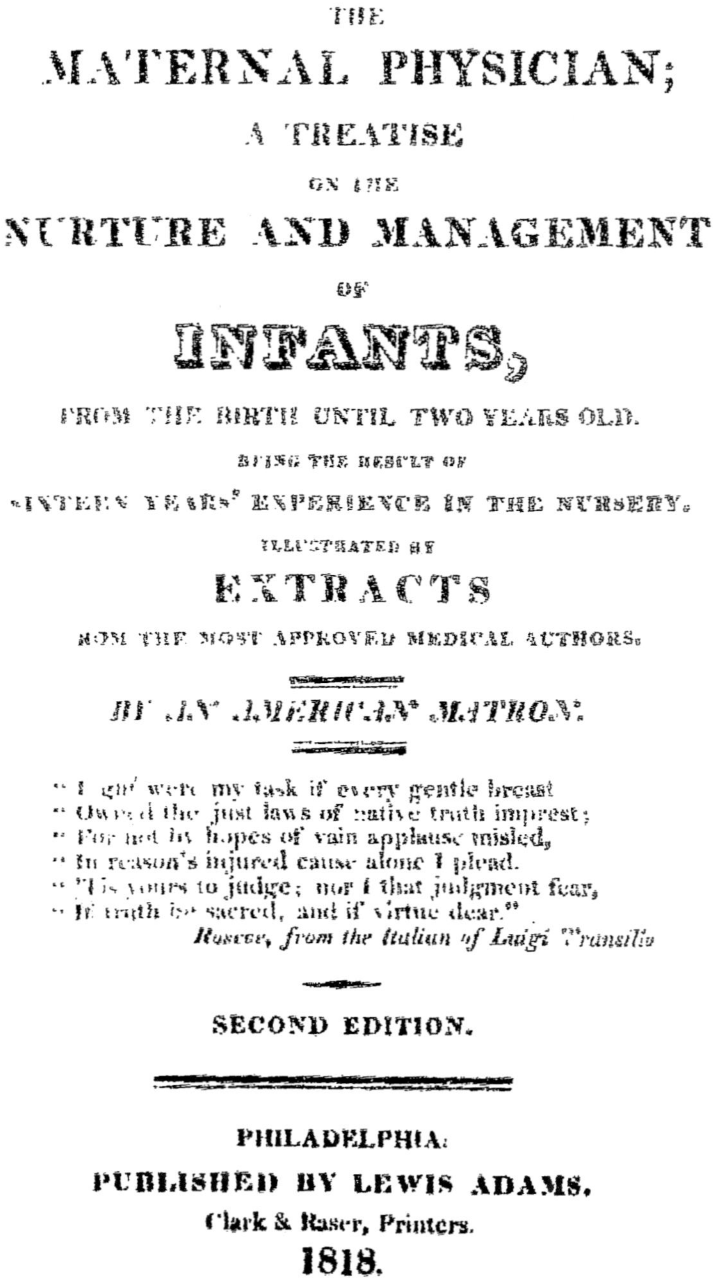

THE

MATERNAL PHYSICIAN;

A TREATISE

ON THE

NURTURE AND MANAGEMENT

OF

INFANTS,

FROM THE BIRTH UNTIL TWO YEARS OLD.

BEING THE RESULT OF

SIXTEEN YEARS' EXPERIENCE IN THE NURSERY.

ILLUSTRATED BY

EXTRACTS

FROM THE MOST APPROVED MEDICAL AUTHORS.

BY AN AMERICAN MATRON.

" Glad were my task if every gentle breast
" Owned the just laws of native truth imprest;
" For not by hopes of vain applause misled,
" In reason's injured cause alone I plead.
" 'Tis yours to judge; nor I that judgment fear,
" If truth be sacred, and if virtue dear."
Roscoe, from the Italian of Luigi Transillo

SECOND EDITION.

PHILADELPHIA:
PUBLISHED BY LEWIS ADAMS.
Clark & Raser, Printers.
1818.

Figure 1. The title page from the 1818 edition of *The Maternal Physician*, the one used for this article.

(Milburn, 2003). *La Balia* was among the first of the paediatric poems (Ruhräh, 1925), and the lines quoted stipulate that as soon as its hands are free to move, the child should be taught, but gently ("with reprehension light"), to use its right hand in preference to the left. Another translated passage from the poem appears on the title page of the manual but with the poet's name misspelled.

The instruction to teach right-hand preference was as common in Tyler's day as in Tansillo's, but not everyone endorsed Tansillo's gentle approach. For example, whereas Andry (1743) seemed to follow it in telling parents merely to "take care, that their Children employ the right Hand oftener than the other, and to this end [to] accustom them to present and receive everything with the right Hand" (Vol. 2, p. 208), others recommended harsher measures. Tyler, for her part, even while accepting the usual rationale, endorsed by Andry and Hill, among others, that left-handedness was a "defect", questioned whether any instruction was necessary in the first place. More than others, she also sympathised with the anxiety that she supposed parents would feel on discovering any tendency to left-handedness in their children and with their resolve to counteract it because of its "disagreeable" appearance and "inconvenient" effects. Recognising, however, that left-handedness was hereditary—that it ran in families—she pronounced it no less natural than right-handedness and saw this as a reason why counteraction, although well intended, could be effective only in part. She also reassured parents that a child without this "natural defect" will never acquire it after birth, so that "all anxiety upon the subject is superfluous". But even where it appeared in a child not "born" with it, Tyler regarded any censure of the mother or attendant to be unwarranted because in the absence of a family history, as she seems to have meant, they would have had no reason to pay special attention to the child's hand use. Finally, without providing any figures, Tyler noted the rarity of left-handedness in the general population and, relatedly, what she assumed was its equal rarity in members of the "labouring community" and in those in "more polished circles", and what that might signify. Unfortunately, although Tyler laced her discussion of other topics with personal anecdotes from her "experience in the nursery" along with illustrations "from the most approved medical authors" as promised in the title of her manual, the section on handedness had neither, leaving one to wonder which statements came from personal experience, and which from medical authorities. One exception would have been her calling left-handedness a defect, which, as already noted, was a common view of the time. Another would appear to be her "decided opinion" that left-handedness can never be entirely "overcome", which suggests that for at least one of her own children she had tried and failed.

Who were Tyler's readers, and in what numbers? Gibbons (1983, p. 34) quotes a passage from a letter (in Tanselle, 1967, p. 236) by Royall Tyler instructing Riley, his publisher, that the book "must be printed tastily as it is calculated for sale in cities". Also quoted is the author of a history of Brattleboro, Vermont, who wrote that the manual "was recommended by the best physicians of the time" (Burnham, 1880, p. 107). However, Gibbons (1983, p. 44) noted that there are no records of the number of copies sold, and very few surviving copies of the work, in contrast to "dozens of [extant] volumes by the physicians she [Tyler] quotes", which, Gibbons suggests, could mean that their voices were "major" and hers was "minor" (p. 44). Whatever their numbers, Tyler's readers were most likely city women from the middle classes, those who, according to Bloch (1978), were reading more and coming to depend on American manuals, like Tyler's, that offered practical advice and moral support in regard to child rearing.

Here, then, are Tyler's remarks on handedness, beginning with the lines from Roscoe's translation of Tansillo's poem, along with my further notes and comments.

Observations relative to teaching Infants the right Use of their Hands

– *Now*, when his little hands from bondage free,
– Restless expand in new-born liberty,[3]
– You teach the Child, with reprehension light,
– In preference to the *left* to use the *right*.
Roscoe.

The anxiety many parents discover, lest their children should be left-handed, may excuse my devoting a page or two of this book, in endeavouring to combat an idea pretty generally entertained, that it is necessary to watch an infant when it first begins to use its hands and direct it

"In preference to the left to use the right."

It is my decided opinion, that if a child is *left-handed*, it is a natural defect which it will be impossible ever entirely to overcome; and although the infant might, as it advanced in life, be taught to use the right hand so well as greatly to obviate the inconvenience and awkward appearance

[3] Tansillo was referring to the release from swaddling clothes, which, at least through the mid-1800s, were worn by most infants in Europe and America in order to shape the body and prevent distortion. During the first weeks, the clothes customarily remained in place except for cleaning and changing. After that, they were removed in stages, first from the upper body and limbs usually between the first and fourth months, then from the torso and legs by the eighth or ninth month or, at latest, by the end of the first year, with the order corresponding to when each body part had grown firm enough that there was no longer any fear of its being distorted. The hands and arms were freed first because they were ready first. Tansillo therefore evidently meant that instruction in hand use should begin at about 4 months.

arising from it,[4] yet the propensity would always predominate,[5] while a child which has not this natural defect, will never acquire it after birth, and therefore all anxiety upon the subject is superfluous. That this is as much an insurmountable defect as any other natural deformity, may be inferred from the rarity of its occurrence, and that, generally, whenever it does occur, it is observed to be hereditary, and often all the children of the same family will inherit it as a legacy from their parents.[6] Therefore,

---

[4] That left-handedness was inconvenient was so widely understood that Tyler evidently felt no need to elaborate. The many examples she might have offered pertained, among other things, to left-handers' being forced to use a host of right-handed tools and utensils, left-handed versions being unavailable. That also might have contributed to the left-hander's appearance of awkwardness, although Tyler might have seen something inherently clumsy in the very use of the left hand. That was Hill's (1754) impression: "when it is the left [that has the advantage of strength and activity] it communicates a great Awkwardness to the whole Deportment and Air; and though one does not see to what it is owing, yet it is strangely distasteful" (pp. 98–99). For other examples, see Harris (1989).

[5] Tyler did not elaborate, but she perhaps meant that some children persisted in using the left hand even for writing and for holding right-handed tools and utensils (see footnote 4), or that even when left-hand use for these acts was completely suppressed, it persisted and even predominated for other acts. That was Paul Broca's (1865) view, and his examples were such acts as throwing a stone, striking with the fists, and wielding a stick. Andry (1743) and Hill (1754), however, supposed that virtually all signs of left-handedness could be eliminated with proper exercise: "What is so difficult to be conquered in a grown Person . . . is very easily got the better of in a Child: nay, the Thing itself has nothing of Nature in it, but is merely Custom. Practice and more frequent Use give Strength and Activity, and they will give them to one Hand as well as the other" (Hill, 1754, p. 100). It seems fair to say that the weight of evidence today rests more with Tyler and Broca than with Andry and Hill.

[6] With eight children by 1810, it is not inconceivable that Tyler was drawn to a genetic explanation, at least in part, from personal experience, meaning that either she or her husband and one or more of their children were left-handed. If so, she did not give details, which makes it more likely that she had other families in mind. But which ones? Throughout history there have undoubtedly been instances of left-handedness in entire (or nearly entire) families, but I found no such reports in the medical books cited by Tyler (e.g., Buchan, 1798) or in those that, in Blackwell's (1997, p. 47, fn. 13) estimation, she is likely to have read (Cadogan, 1750; Smith, 1792; Underwood, 1797). In any case, so far as I know, any published accounts, along with other studies of the heritability of handedness based on family histories, did not appear until after Tyler's time (e.g., Darwin, 1877; Jordan, 1911; Ogle, 1871; Péré, 1900; Ramaley, 1913). The most remarkable report was of a right-handed father and left-handed mother with 14 children, all left-handed, as was the father's brother and his 5 children as well as the mother's 5 siblings and father (Péré, 1900). The only "report" that anyone in Tyler's time might have known about was based on legend—the famous rhyme about the left-handed Kerrs, the sixteenth-century Scottish border reivers, "the deadliest foes/That e'er to Englishmen were known/For they were all bred left-handed men/And fence against them there was none" (see Fraser, 1971, p. 51; McManus, 2002, pp. 302–303). However, according to Anthony Kerr (2007, Ch 4), a family descendant, the Kerrs' left-handedness was mostly acquired, not "bred", (i.e., born); only the patriarch Andrew Kerr was naturally left-handed and, after discovering its advantage for fencing, taught his sons and armed men-servants to wield the sword or axe with the left hand. The servants, in accord with custom, took the family name on joining the household.

although I would by no means wish to deter mothers or attendants from using every proper means[7] to counteract a defect so disagreeable in appearance, and inconvenient in its consequences, where they actually discover it to exist, yet I must believe no inattention whatever on their part can ever be censured as the cause of such a propensity in children who have it not born with them. If want of care and attention could produce this effect, we should probably more oftener discover this characteristic mark of the ancient Benjamites[8] among the labouring part of the community, who, from the necessity of constant occupation, seldom have time or inclination to attend to these little niceties in their children, and, provided they can procure them "food to eat and raiment to put on, therewith are content;"[9] and probably seldom think of the circumstance until the child has decided the point by evincing beyond dispute which hand it prefers to use: and yet I fancy the defect does not occur more frequently among that class than in the more polished circles.[10]

---

[7] Tyler offered no examples, but assuming that she agreed with Tansillo that one should proceed with "reprehension light", she presumably meant the sort of relatively gentle practices recommended by Andry (1743), as described earlier, rather than punitive measures like slapping and scolding.

[8] The reference was to the Benjaminite tribe in *Judges*: "And the children of Benjamin were numbered at that time out of the cities twenty and six thousand men that drew sword ... Among all this people there were seven hundred chosen men left-handed; every one could sling stones at a hair breadth, and not miss" (*King James Bible*, 0:15). Tyler perhaps mentioned the Benjaminites only to underscore her statement as to the "rarity" of occurrence of left-handedness—that is, that it was as uncommon in her day as it was in Biblical times—but she also perhaps meant to suggest that it matched the Biblical figure of 2.7% (700/26,000). That is well below today's estimates (e.g., Gilbert & Wysocki, 1992; Peters, Reimers, & Manning, 2006), although as Hardyck and Petrinovich (1977) noted, there is no evidence that all the remaining 25,300 Benjaminites were right-handed.

[9] The quotation is from Jacob's vow in *Genesis* (*King James Bible*, 28:20): "If God will be with me and keep me in this way that I go, and will give me bread [food] to eat and raiment to put on", except that the passage, instead of ending in Tyler's phrase "therewith are content," ends with "so that I come back to my father's house in peace, then shall the LORD be my God ..."

[10] Broca (1865) made the same comparison half a century later. However, unlike Tyler, who surmised that the similarly low incidence of left-handedness "between people in the "labouring class" and in "more polished circles" would mean that left-handedness was a *natural* defect rather than a product of lack of training, Broca used it to make the more general point that handedness in all forms, meaning right- as well as left-handedness, was natural and, in neither case, was a defect: if "this inequality [in hand use, i.e., handedness *per se*] existed only in manual laborers [*manouvriers*], one could suppose that it is a result of their occupation, and attribute it to the well-known fact that exercise develops muscular strength; but it also is pronounced in men devoted to the learned professions "[*les hommes voués à des professions intellectuelle*] (1865, p. 383). The question of whether there are social class differences in the incidence of left-handedness is largely unexamined, although what evidence there is does not show any relation. As McManus (2002, Ch. 7, Hypernotes) put it in summarising his own data (McManus, 1981), "there is simply no association between left-handedness and social class."

CONCLUSIONS

Like the other parts of her manual, Tyler intended her remarks on handedness to advise and to reassure. In particular, she wanted to relieve mothers from the burden of vigilantly watching the infant when it first begins using its hands, and then teaching it to use the proper, right hand in preference to the left. Instead she counselled letting nature take its course, since in most cases nature would favour the right, and to intervene only in the rare circumstance that the left is preferred and, in that case, to discourage its use gently and with "every proper means". Where left-handedness emerged nonetheless, mothers were also not to blame themselves for being insufficiently watchful. In sum, if Tyler did not reject the usual "sinistral" image of left-handedness or urge that the left-handed child be let alone, she at least could be seen as joining Tansillo and others in rejecting harsh treatment of the condition, and as counselling mothers to be relaxed in their style and realistic about their ability to effect change. As she explained, left-handedness, like "any other natural deformity", was an "insurmountable defect" and "impossible ever entirely to overcome". If, today, we can be confident that it is neither defect nor deformity, we can be no less confident that it is natural and "insurmountable".

REFERENCES

"An Eminent Physician." (1729). *The nurse's guide: or, the right method of bringing up young children, to which is added, An essay on preserving health, and prolonging life. With a treatise of the gout.* London: Printed for John Brotherton. [Reprinted in R. Trumbach, Ed. (1985), *Three treatises on child rearing*. In the series *Marriage, sex, and the family in England 1660–1800*. New York & London: Garland Publishing, Inc.]

Andry, N. [Andry de Bois-Regard] (1743). *Orthopaedia: or, the art of correcting and preventing deformities in children: by such means as may be easily put in practice by parents themselves, and all such as are employed in educating children.* [Translation (uncredited) from the French *L'orthopedie ou l'art de prevenir et de corriger dans les enfans.*] Two volumes. London: Printed for A. Miller. [First French publication, 1741. Facsimile reproduction of the first edition in English with an introduction by A. F. DePalma. Philadelphia & Montreal: J. B. Lippincott Co.]

Blackwell, M. S. (1997). The republican vision of Mary Palmer Tyler. In R. D. Apple & J. Golden (Eds.), *Mothers and motherhood: Readings in American history* (pp. 31–51). Columbus: Ohio State University Press. [Originally published in the *Journal of the Early Republic*, 1992, *12*, 11–35.]

Bloch, R. H. (1978). American feminine ideals in transition: The rise of the moral mother, 1785–1815. *Feminist Studies*, *4*, 100–126.

Broca, P. (1865). Sur le siège de la faculté du langage articulé. *Bulletins de la Société d'Anthropologie de Paris*, *6*, 377–393.

Buchan, W. (1798). *Domestic medicine: or, a treatise on the prevention and cure of diseases, by regimen and simple medicines: With an appendix, containing a dispensatory for the use of private practitioners*. Fairhaven, Vermont: Printed by and for James Lyon, at Voltaire's Head. [The first Vermont edition, containing all the improvements: Micro-opaque, Worcester, MA: American Antiquarian Society, 1955–1983; Early American imprints: First series; no. 33469; microform.]

Burnham, H. (1880). *Brattleboro: early history*. Brattleboro, Vermont: D. Leonard.

Cadogan, W. (1750). *An essay upon nursing, and the management of children, from their birth to three years of age* (4th ed., with additions). London: J. Roberts. [Reprinted in R. Trumbach, Ed. (1985), *Three treatises on child rearing*. In the series *Marriage, sex, and the family in England 1660–1800*. New York & London: Garland Publishing, Inc.]

Darwin, C. (1877). A biographical sketch of an infant. *Mind*, *2*, 285–294.

Fraser, G. M. (1971). *The Steel Bonnets: The story of the Anglo-Scottish border reivers*. London: Barrie & Jenkins Ltd.

Gibbons, C. (1983). Mary Tyler and *The maternal physician*. *Journal of Regional Cultures*, *3*, 33–45.

Gilbert, A. N., & Wysocki, C. J. (1992). Hand preference and age in the United States. *Neuropsychologia*, *30*, 601–608.

Hardyck, C., & Petrinovich, L. F. (1977). Left-handedness. *Psychological Bulletin*, *84*, 385–404.

Harris, L. J. (1989). Hand preference in gestures and signs in the deaf and hearing: Some notes on early evidence and theory. *Brain and Cognition*, *10*, 189–219.

Harris, L. J. (2003). What to do about your child's handedness? Advice from five eighteenth-century authors, and some questions for today. *Laterality*, *8*, 99–120.

Hill, J. (1754). *On the management and education of children: a series of letters written to a neice [sic] by the Honourable Juliana-Susannah Seymour* (i.e., John Hill). London: Printed for R. Baldwin. [Microfilm: Charlottesville, VA: Micrographics II, 1986, Part 1 of microfilm reel/ Eighteenth century sources for the study of English literature and culture; reel no. 598.]

Jordan, H. E. (1911). The inheritance of left-handedness. *American Breeder's Magazine*, *2*, 19–28; 113–124.

Kerr, A. (2007). *Ferniehurst Castle: Scotland's frontier stronghold*. Retrieved 4 March 2007 from http://www.electricscotland.com/history/ferniehurst

McManus, C. (2002). *Right hand, left hand. The origins of asymmetry in brains, bodies, atoms and cultures*. Cambridge, MA: Harvard University Press. Chapter 7, Hypernotes, retrieved 10 March 2007 from http://www.righthandlefthand.com/html/Notes7.htm

McManus, I. C. (1981). Handedness and birth stress. *Psychological Medicine*, *11*, 485–496.

Milburn, E. (2003). *Luigi Tansillo and lyric poetry in sixteenth-century Naples*. Leeds, UK: Maney Publications for the Modern Humanities Research Association.

Ogle, S. W. (1871). On dextral pre-eminence. *Transactions of the Royal Medical and Chirurgical Society*, *35*, 279–301.

Péré, A. (1900). *Les courbures latérales normales du rachis humain*. Inaugural Dissertation, Toulouse, France.

Peters, M., Reimers, S., & Manning, J. T. (2006). Hand preference for writing and associations with selected demographic and behavioral variables in 255,100 subjects: The BBC internet study. *Brain and Cognition*, *62*, 177–189.

Ramaley, F. (1913). Inheritance of left-handedness. *American Naturalist*, *47*, 730–738.

Rousseau, J. J. (1762). *Émile, ou, de l'éducation*. Paris: Éditions Garnier Frères, 1962.

Ruhräh, J. (1925). *Pediatrics of the past: An anthology* [foreword by Fielding H. Garrison]. New York: Paul B. Hoeber.

Smith, H. (1792). *Letters to married women, on nursing and the management of children* [first American edition, printed from the sixth London edition]. Philadelphia: Mathew Carey. [Original publication, 1767, London: printed for G. Keasly.]

Tanselle, G. T. (1967). *Royall Tyler*. Cambridge, MA: Harvard University Press.

Tansillo, L. (1798). *The nurse, a poem* [translation of *La balia* by William Stanley Roscoe]. Liverpool, UK: Printed by J. McCreery, for Cadell and Davies, London. [Original publication in Italian in 1552.]

[The Bible.] (1996). *King James Bible* "Authorized version". Alexandria, VA: Chadwyck-Healey. [First publication, 1611.]

Tyler, M. P. (1818). *The maternal physician; a treatise on the nurture and management of infants, from the birth until two years old. Being the result of sixteen years' experience in the nursery: illustrated by extracts from the most approved medical authors. By an American matron* (2nd ed.). Lewis Adams: Philadelphia: Clark & Raser. [Micro-opaque: New York: Readex Microprint, courtesy of A.A.S., 1979. Three micro-opaques: (Early American imprints. Second series; no. 44761). First publication, 1811, New York: Isaac Riley.]

Tyler, M. P. (1925). *Grandmother Tyler's book: The recollections of Mary Palmer Tyler (Mrs. Royall Tyler) 1775–1866* (F. Tupper & H. T. Brown Eds.). New York: G. P. Putnam.

Underwood, M. (1797). *A treatise on the disorders of childhood and management of infants from the birth: adapted to domestic use (three volumes)*. London: printed for J. Mathews.

LATERALITY, 2010, 15 (1/2), 15–55

In fencing, what gives left-handers the edge? Views from the present and the distant past

Lauren Julius Harris

Michigan State University, East Lansing, MI, USA

Recent studies show that in the sport of fencing left-handers have an advantage over right-handers. This was recognised by fencing masters as early as the sixteenth century. They also agreed that the advantage was due to left-handers' numbers—that being a minority gave them more opportunities to compete against right-handers than right-handers had against them. Fencing masters today have reached the same conclusion, as have laterality researchers, who see the advantage as an example of what is now called a "frequency-dependent" effect. However, some researchers have also suggested other possibilities that relate the advantage to natural differences in ability. This article presents a sampling of views of fencing masters from the past, along with a summary and analysis of explanations, old and new.

In recent times, the role of laterality in sports and athletics has been studied by scientists in a variety of disciplines, including neuropsychology, evolutionary biology and psychology, kinesiology, sports psychology, and anthropology, among others (e.g., Aggleton & Wood, 1990; Annett, 1985; Azémar, 2003; Edwards & Eaton, 1996; Faurie, Schiefenhövel, Le Bomin, Billiard, & Raymond, 2005; Guiard, 1981, 1982; Porac & Coren, 1981; Starosta, 2004). One of the questions driving this research is whether left-handers have an advantage over right-handers. In certain sports the numbers alone suggest that they do. For example, in major-league baseball, about 18% of all players are left-handed, meaning those who throw and bat with the left hand (Neft & Cohen, 1988; see also Grondin, Guiard, Ivry, & Koren, 1999; McLean & Ciurczak, 1982), compared to 10–12% in the general population (e.g., Gilbert & Wysocki, 1992; Peters, Reimers, & Manning, 2006; Raymond & Pontier, 2004). Similar differences are reported for cricket (Brooks, Bussière, Jennions, & Hunt, 2004; Dinakar, 2007; Wood & Aggleton, 1989), tennis (Holtzen, 2000), and table tennis

---

Address correspondence to: Lauren Julius Harris, Department of Psychology, Michigan State University, East Lansing, Michigan 48824, USA. E-mail: HARRISL@MSU.edu

---

DOI: 10.1080/13576500701650430

(Raymond, Pontier, Dufour, & Møller, 1996). The advantage also appears in performance. In baseball, left-handers hit for more power (Grondin et al., 1999) and in cricket for a higher average (Brooks et al., 2004). Left-handers also bring wins. In cricket, on the most successful teams in the 2003 World Cup, nearly 50% of batsmen were left-handed (Brooks et al., 2004), and in baseball, a survey for the years 1984–1989 showed that left-handed starters had better win–loss records and lower earned run averages (Shaughnessy, 1989, p. 52).

These are strong numbers, but they may be even stronger for the sport of fencing. In a survey of participants in the 1981 World Fencing Championship, 35% of the athletes in the foil competition were left-handed, with the figures even higher for those advancing in the competition (Azémar, Ripoll, Simonet, & Stein, 1983). In another survey, this one from 1979 to 1993, a remarkable 44.5% of tournament champions were left-handed (Azémar & Stein, 1994; cited in Raymond et al., 1996, Table 3), with left-handers taking the top eight places in the 1979 Pan American Games and the 1980 Olympics in 1980 (Hécaen, 1984; cited in Flor-Henry, 1990, p. 416). It was the same when the results included the 1996 Olympics (Azémar, 2003, Table XI, p. 100), with the percentage of left-handers again increasing as the competition advanced. For example, from the opening round to the round of 32 to the round of 8 to the medallist round of 4 to the championship round, the figures for épée were 25.8%, 30.2%, 44.4%, 47.2%, and 66.7%, respectively. Among left-handed champions, one worth special mention is Edoardo Mangiarotti (b. 1919), a natural right-hander who, after being changed into a left-handed fencer by his father Guiseppe Mangiarotti, himself 17 times the national (Italian) épée champion, went on to win 39 gold, silver, and bronze medals in Olympic and World Championships, the most in the history of the sport (Mangiarotti, 2006a, 2006b).[1]

For baseball, the first scientific analyses of left-handers' numbers and performance evidently appeared in the 1950s (Briglia, 1952; Lehman & Webb, 1951), but by then coaches and managers (and sports journalists) were already showing interest. By one account, the first interest was in the 1920s in the heyday of the left-handed Babe Ruth and Ty Cobb (Uhrbrock, 1970, p. 285), but it must have been even earlier, by the 1880s,

[1] Mangiarotti was reportedly converted to left-hand fencing sometime around his seventh birthday, when his father began teaching him the rudiments of the sport. By 11 he had won the national foil champion, and at 17 the gold medal in the 1936 Berlin Olympics, becoming the second-youngest fencing champion in Olympic history. Mangiarotti retired in 1961 after winning a silver medal at the Rome Olympics in 1960 (at 41 he was the oldest member of the Italian team), which means that he would not have been among the left-handers counted in Azémar et al.'s (1983) and Azémar and Stein's (1994) surveys.

because that is when left-handers' numbers first started to rise, presumably as their advantages in batting and pitching were becoming known (James, 1988, 112–123).[2] In the early days a few right-handed pitchers even became "switch-pitchers", throwing left-handed to left-handers and right-handed to right-handers, something that was easier to do in the days before pitchers began wearing gloves (James, 1998; Morris, 2006). Even more right-handers became switch-hitters. Like Edoardo Mangiarotti's father, some fathers—but now for baseball—began to appreciate the advantages and to train their sons accordingly: "Fathers are interested in the development of left-handers, of course. The southpaw has a start of six feet for first base, and seeing that most pitchers are right-handed, the old southpaws can slam that ball all over the lot" (Anon., quoted in Selzer, 1933, p. 77).

Compared to baseball, however long it took scientists to catch up with the sports professionals, the gap for fencing has been far longer. If, as it appears, the first scientific reports on fencing and handedness came in the 1970s, fencing masters were already taking notice centuries earlier, judging from the books and manuals they wrote for students in their academies and schools. So far as I can tell, except for three examples I included in a review of cultural influences on handedness (Harris, 1990), none of these writings has been mentioned in the laterality literature. Given recent developments it may be time for a closer look. In this article, I therefore present these and other examples in more detail. All come from fencing books and manuals from the sixteenth century to the early twentieth century in four countries: England, Scotland, Italy, and France, along with one by a French master who taught in the United States. The writings are of interest not only, as we shall see, because they foreshadow today's view as to the left-hander's advantage but also because they explain it in the same way as do most laterality researchers. Along with this consensus explanation, however, laterality researchers have also raised other possibilities, and these too will be considered.

FENCING MASTERS, ACADEMIES, STUDENTS, AND BOOKS

In the times we are surveying, fencing was "the passion of high and low" (Aylward, 1956, p. 17) and, throughout its history, it has been tied "inextricably to the duel" (Nye, 1990, p. 370). Its social role, especially

[2] A new analysis covering the period 1876 to 1985 shows that, for batters, the increase is a growth curve described by a logarithmic equation accounting for 52% of the variance (Goldstein & Young, 1996).

in the sixteenth and seventeenth centuries, is well expressed in two seminal English treatises on education: Richard Mulcaster's (1581) *Positions Concerning the Training Up of Children*, and John Locke's (1693) *Some Thoughts Concerning Education*. Mulcaster, in a chapter called "Of fensing, or the use of the weapon" (p. 85), recalled its benefits in "the olde time":

> *warlike* for valiauntnesse in armes, and activitie in the field, *gamelike* to winne garlandes and prices [prizes], and to please the people in solemne meetinges: Physicklike [healthful] to purchace therby a good haviour [property, or demeanour] of body and continuance of health.

In his own time, Mulcaster (p. 85) declared "armed fensing" to be "to [sic] vehement for our trade": "we scholers minde peace, as our muses professe that they will not medle, nor have to do with Mars." Even so, "none of [these sortes of fensing] is now to be refused, seeing the same effectes remaine, both for the health of our bodies, and the helpe of our countries ..."

Locke (1693, p. 254, paragraph 199), for his part, called fencing "dangerous to the Life" but acknowledged that it also "seems to be a good Exercise for Health" and that:

> A Man that cannot *Fence* will be more careful to keep out of Bullies and Gamesters Company, and will not be half so apt to stand upon Punctilio's [nice details of conduct], not to give Affronts ... since Fencing and Riding the great Horse, are so generally looked upon as necessary Qualifications in the breeding of a Gentleman, it will be hard wholly to deny any one of that rank these Marks of Distinction.[3]

For fencing (as for riding), in order to achieve this gentlemanly qualification many young men from the middle, upper, and noble classes

[3] Mulcaster's and Locke's sentiments about the dangers of fencing were hardly overstatements, given the body count. As Holmer (1994) noted, in the 1590s, even while Londoners enjoyed nonlethal prize playings or fencing "performances", "bloody sword-play" was common as it was in most of western Europe (p. 178). Turner and Soper (1990) estimated that in France, one third of the nobility—around 4000 men—were killed in private combats between 1590 and 1610, with nearly 2000 dying just between 1601 and 1609 (Aldi, 1943; cited in Turner & Soper, 1990, p. 6; see also Morsberger, 1974, pp. 67–71). They went on to suggest that England, by the early seventeenth century, probably resembled France in mortality rates from duels, and recalled this account: "Dead men, with holes in their breasts, were often found by the watchmen, with their pale faces resting on door stops of merchant's [sic] houses, or propped up and still bleeding, hid away in church porches" (Thornbury, 1856, p. 182; quoted in Turner & Soper, 1990, pp. 6–7). All this even though duelling had been banned in both countries since the mid-sixteenth century.

sought instruction from former soldiers and other masters of arms. The more famous instructors presided over, or were associated with, schools and academies, some autonomous, others connected to military academies, in major European cities.[4] Some taught under their own names, others under *noms de plume*. For example, the watercolour by Thomas Rowlandson (1787), reproduced (in black and white) in Figure 1, shows Henry Angelo's Fencing Academy in London, where Henry, following his father Domenico, taught generations of wealthy English youth (and, judging from the scene, men well past their youth). In the centre Henry, dressed in white, practices with a student while Domenico, the head master, stands at the right, holding three foils in his arms.

As in fencing academies today, instructional books and manuals were a normal adjunct to the curriculum. Egerton Castle (1885), in his classic work *Schools and Masters of Fence from the Middle Ages to the Eighteenth Century*, estimated that upwards of 400 books on fencing were published between 1474 and 1884. "Old books", however (he perhaps meant anything before 1800), were excessively difficult to find, probably because most were printed only in limited numbers for circulation among the master's students. For this reason, I was fortunate to have access to a remarkable collection of original works donated to the Michigan State University Library by Professor Charles Schmitter on the occasion of his 45th and final year as the fencing coach at Michigan State (Fiore, 1983) (see Figure 2). The title pages of three books from the collection are reproduced in Figures 3–5. I also examined reprinted editions of other works in the Michigan State collection along with digitised versions of still others, recently made available on the Internet.[5]

The books are all roughly similar in form. Their titles all incorporate one or another of the words "Treatise", "Science", "Art", or "School" of "Defence" or "Arms" or (in French) "Éscrime" (literally, touching without being touched). Domenico Angelo's (1763) own manual, one of the best known, is entitled *L'Ècole des Armes, avec l'Explication Générale des Principales Attitudes et Positions Concernant l'Éscrime*. As for content, many begin with brief accounts of the history of fencing along

[4] In sixteenth- and seventeenth-century France, when duelling was the "invariable method of resolving differences between gentlemen", all towns had fencing halls owned and staffed by a master of arms and governed by the guild's Academy of Arms. After the Academy was abolished in 1790, the number of halls diminished to about 10 in 1840 but increased again near the end of the Second Empire and then hugely after the Franco-Prussian war, so that in Paris alone, by 1890, there were over 100 masters of arms, and "salles d'armes sprouted in virtually every provincial city" (Nye, 1990, p. 370).

[5] See, for example, *Fencing Masters* (2006). The collection at Michigan State University also is beginning to be digitised and made available through *Project Gutenberg Ebook*.

Figure 1. "I shall conquer this". Watercolour by Thomas Rowlandson (1787) of Henry Angelo's Fencing Academy in London.

with statements attesting to its many virtues, including physical exercise and well-being (which, as we saw, even Mulcaster and Locke acknowledged). All give detailed instructions, many accompanied by drawings, for holding the weapon and for the correct positions and movements of the body and limbs (Figure 6 shows examples), and many refer occasionally to the opinions of other masters with whom they agreed or disagreed. Some also begin by explaining the social rules to be followed. As the Scottish master Sir William Hope (1707, p. 190) warned:

> All Cursing and Swearing, and obscene Language, should be discharged [i.e., eliminated] as much as possible; because, a Fencing School being a Place to which Persons of the best Quality do frequently resort, for their Exercise and Divertisement, all such Ungentlemanly, as well as Immoral Habits ought to be discountenanced; and that the Decorum and Civility observed and paid by the Scholars to one another, as it becomes Gentlemen, not only as they are Christians, but even as they pretend to be Men of True Generosity and Honour.

Figure 2. Coach Charles Schmitter. Photograph by Dan Waites. Reproduced with permission of Division of Special Collections, Michigan State University Library.

As for the weapons to be used, some manuals were unspecific; others focused on a certain kind—the foil (or fleuret), épée, saber, rapier, small and back swords, and for one manual the Scotch broad sword.[6]

[6] The foil, épée, and sabre are the three that survive in modern competitive fencing. The foil is a blunt weapon, resembling a small sword in the main, with a button at the point (originally developed in the mid-seventeenth century as a training weapon for the court sword, a light one-handed sword designed almost wholly for thrusting); the épée is the heaviest (nearly the weight of an actual court sword) and has a sharp-pointed blade without a cutting edge, and a bowl-shaped guard for the hand; the sabre has a curved guard and triangular blade and is used either as a cutting weapon or for both cutting and thrusting—descriptions from separate entries in Webster's *New International Dictionary of the English Language, Second Edition*, Unabridged (1957), and from the entry on fencing (2006) in *Wikipedia*.

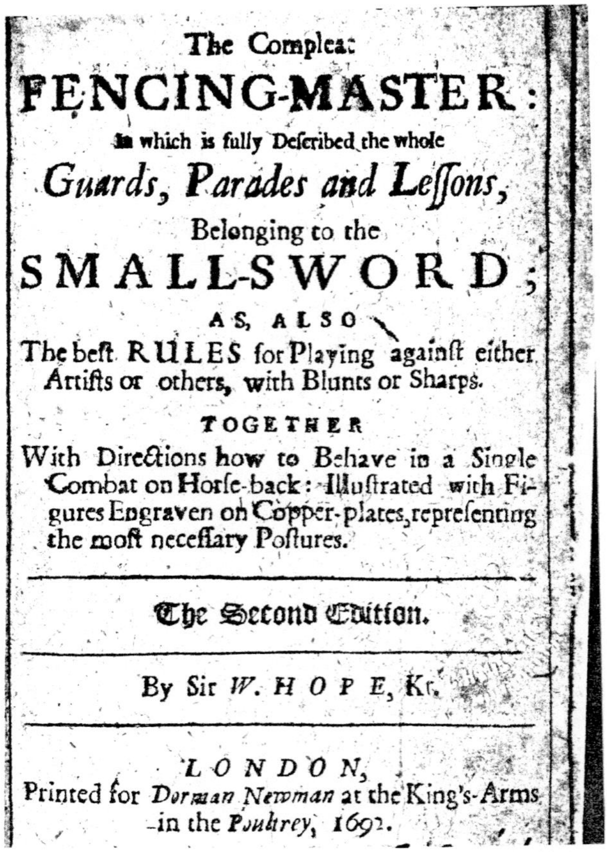

The Compleat
FENCING-MASTER:
In which is fully Deſcribed the whole
Guards, Parades and Leſſons,
Belonging to the
SMALL-SWORD;
AS, ALSO
The beſt RULES for Playing againſt either Artiſts or others, with Blunts or Sharps.
TOGETHER
With Directions how to Behave in a Single Combat on Horſe-back: Illuſtrated with Figures Engraven on Copper-plates, repreſenting the moſt neceſſary Poſtures.

The Second Edition.

By Sir *W. HOPE*, Kt.

LONDON,
Printed for *Dorman Newman* at the King's-Arms in the *Poultrey*, 1692.

Figure 3. Title page of Sir William Hope's *The Compleat Fencing Master* (1692). Reproduced with permission of Division of Special Collections, Michigan State University Library.

THE LEFT-HANDED FENCER: AN ACCEPTED MINORITY

The laterality literature is replete with accounts of customs pertaining to hand use, customs nearly always favouring right-handers, the majority, while conceding little or nothing to left-handers, the often disparaged minority. Thus, in Europe and most other parts of the world during the times under consideration here, it was and had long been the practice to require right-hand use for such acts as writing, eating with fingers or certain utensils, shaking hands and other acts of greeting, taking oaths, using tools, playing musical instruments, and even gesturing while speaking (e.g., Bulwer, 1644/1974; Clement, 1587/1966; reviewed in Harris, 1989, 1990, 2003). Certain objects, including knives, forks, and spoons, presented no physical barriers to left-hand use so that only custom was determinative. Other objects, however,

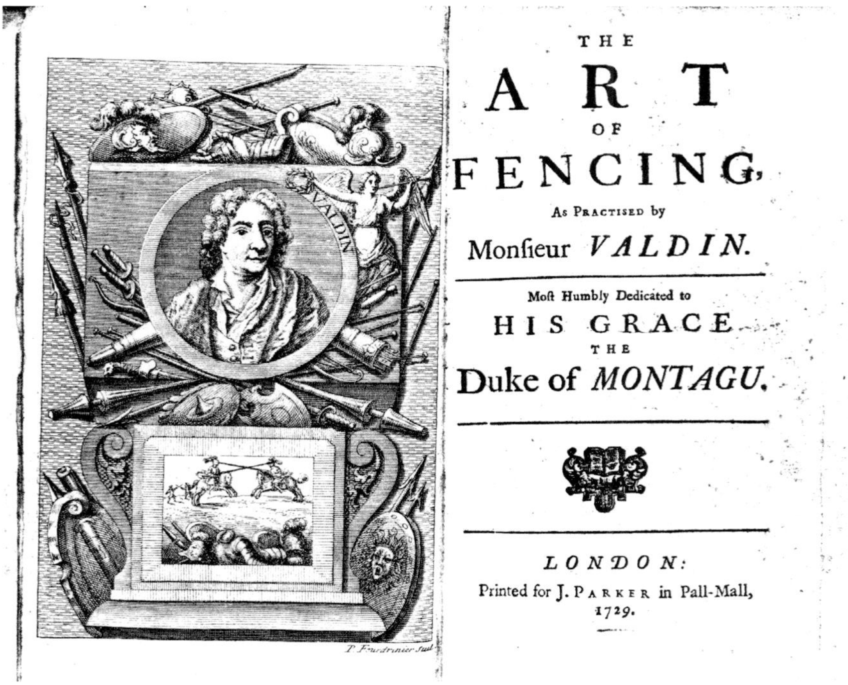

THE
ART
OF
FENCING,
As Practised by
Monſieur VALDIN.
Moſt Humbly Dedicated to
HIS GRACE
THE
Duke of MONTAGU.
LONDON:
Printed for J. PARKER in Pall-Mall,
1729.

Figure 4. Title page of Monsieur Valdin's *The Art of Fencing* (1729). Reproduced with permission of Division of Special Collections, Michigan State University Library.

were designed for the right hand, either for the principal act, such as opening and closing the crossing blades of the shears, or for one of the principal acts, such as plucking and bowing a stringed instrument, whether a violin, lute, or guitar. For stringed instruments, left-handers could play in reverse by switching the order of the strings and making other physical modifications, and if they were like their counterparts today, that may have been the solution for some, at least for solo playing if not for ensembles (Laeng & Park, 1999). Where modification was precluded, as it would have been for the shears, the left-hander's only recourse was to use the right hand or stay with the left and suffer loss of efficiency, not to mention blisters.

For asymmetrical objects the universal right-hand design could be rationalised on the grounds that it was uneconomical to make additional reverse-designed objects for a small minority. For violins and other stringed orchestral instruments uniformity also let right- and left-handers play side by side. The restrictions evidently succeeded totally for fiddling (at least for ensemble playing), and largely so for writing. For example, in the mid to late nineteenth century, left-handers were estimated to comprise only 2.5–5% of the population, based on observations of hand use for writing (e.g., van

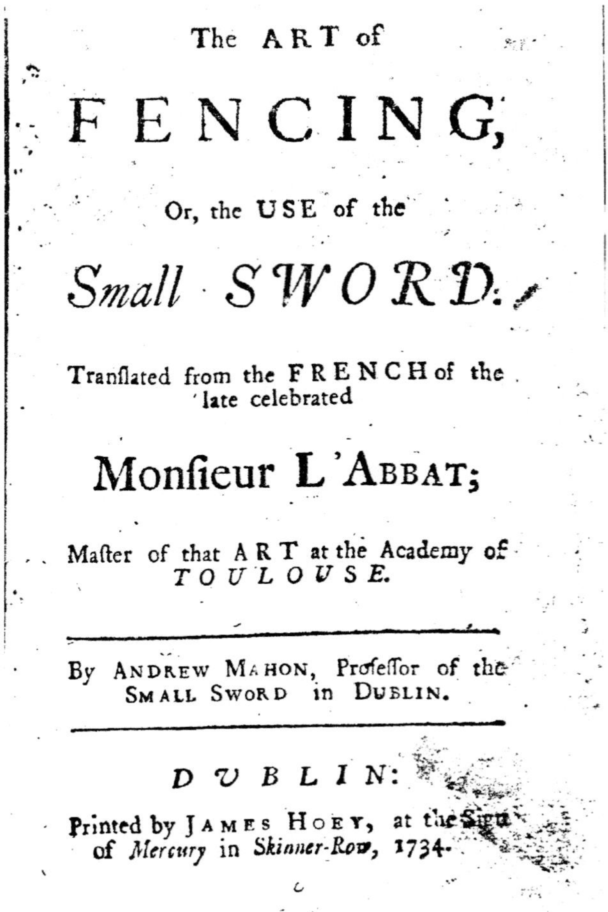

The ART of

FENCING,

Or, the USE of the

Small SWORD.

Tranſlated from the FRENCH of the late celebrated

Monſieur L'ABBAT;

Maſter of that ART at the Academy of *TOULOUSE.*

By ANDREW MAHON, Profeſſor of the SMALL SWORD in DUBLIN.

DUBLIN:

Printed by JAMES HOEY, at the Sign of *Mercury* in *Skinner-Row*, 1734.

Figure 5. Title page of Monsieur L'Abbat's *The Art of Fencing* (1734). Reproduced with permission of Division of Special Collections, Michigan State University Library.

Biervliet, 1901; Delaunay, 1874; Hyrtl, 1860; Jobert, 1885). Recognising the effects of custom and education, Paul Broca (1865) and others therefore surmised that the true percentage would be higher with non-biased measures (Broca's examples included the acts of throwing a stone, striking with the fists, and wielding a stick). They were right, and results from surveys using such measures are remarkably close to results today (e.g., Gilbert & Wysocki, 1992). For example, Joseph-François Malgaigne (1859) reported finding, in a sample of 182 men, 163 right-handers (89.6%), two "perfect ambidexters" (1.1%), and 17 left-handers (9.3%), or roughly 1 left-hander in every 11 or 12 persons. François Moutier (1908) reported a figure of 1 in 11 in 600 hospitalised patients (for details, see Harris, 1993a, pp. 114–115).

Figure 6. Illustration of fencing positions from Monsieur L'Abbat's *The Art of Fencing* (1734). Reproduced with permission of Division of Special Collections, Michigan State University Library.

There is no reason to suppose, and no evidence to suggest, that fencing masters endorsed right-hand customs any less than did teachers anywhere, so that for such acts as writing and eating, their left-handed students would have been as "right-handed" as students anywhere. After all, as Hope (1707) observed, they were "Gentlemen" and "Persons of the best Quality", of whom the highest standards of conduct were expected. However, judging from Hope's and others' books and manuals, fencing was exempt, with left-handers free to fence with the left hand just as they presumably would have done as children playing with wooden swords and sticks. And, like play swords, real swords were symmetrical, usable with either hand. The only asymmetrical features would have been such appurtenances as gauntlets, or protective gloves, and scabbards. These were not mentioned in the manuals I examined, but if gauntlets were worn, one assumes that left-handed gloves were generally available, if only because (like baseball batting gloves today) they would have been worn as pairs. As for scabbards, left-handers wore them on the right, right-handers on the left. That way, as the Italian master Angelo Viggiani (1575, para. 17) explained, both could draw out the sword with the dominant hand. There was, however, one concession not granted to left-handers, and that was the *name* for the dagger when it served as a secondary, or companion, weapon. Used mainly to assist in parrying incoming thrusts, it was held in the other hand, or off-hand. For right-handers, the off-hand was the left, so the dagger itself came to be called *la main gauche,* even though for left-handers, the off-hand was the right.

AN ADVANTAGE FOR THE LEFT-HANDER

In baseball, as we have seen, coaches and managers, along with the players themselves, have apparently seen an advantage of left-handedness for nearly as long as the game has been played. Likewise in fencing an advantage was known, or at least reputed, in the much earlier times under review here. The one example probably familiar to laterality researchers today is the legend of the Kerrs, sixteenth-century Scottish border reivers whom an anonymous poet famously called "the deadliest foes/That e'er to Englishmen were known/For they were all bred left-handed men/And fence against them there was none." However, according to Anthony Kerr (2007) a family descendant, only the patriarch Andrew Kerr was bred (i.e., born) left-handed, and that Andrew, after discovering its advantage for fencing, taught his sons and armed men-servants to wield the sword or axe with the left hand (the men-servants, in accord with custom, took the family name on joining the household). As the historian George McDonald Fraser (1971) and others have also noted, the Kerrs' legend was enhanced by the spiral staircases in the castles they built to defend their lands; some had an anti-clockwise spiral, with treads turned to the left, so that when a left-handed Kerr, from above, defended against a right-handed attacker from below, the staircase wall would leave his left arm free while constraining the right arm of the attacker.[7] In the Scottish Borderland the Kerrs even inspired left-handed sobriquets, including *ker-handed*, *car-handed*, and *corry-handed* (Fraser, 1971, p. 51).[8]

---

[7] Examples can be seen in Ferniehurst Castle, Jedburgh, in the County of Roxburgh; Pitreavie (also spelled Pittrevie) Castle in Dunfermline; and Smailholm Tower near Kelso. See Anthony Kerr (2007), especially Chapter 4, "The left-handed Kerrs", for an account of Ferniehurst Castle and the Kerr family.

[8] In 1971, the Kerrs were the subject of an editorial in a British medical journal seeking information for testing the implied link between left-handedness and the names Kerr and its variant Carr (Editorial, 1971), and subsequently in a series of articles on the same question (e.g., Keele, 1974; Research Unit, 1974; Shaw & McManus, 1993; for an account, see McManus, 2002, pp. 302–303).

Given their reputation, one could suppose that the Kerrs or their legend were known to the early fencing masters, or at least to those in England and Scotland. If so, there is no reference to them in the books and manuals I examined. Instead, fencing masters gave their personal impressions of left-handed fencers or stated what was generally known or believed. Based on these accounts left-handers were indeed believed to have an advantage. According to Malcolm Fare, in his foreword to William Gaugler's (1998) *The History of Fencing*, the first to take note was probably the sixteenth-century Italian master Camillo Palladini of Bologna, in his treatise *Discorso Sopra l'Arte Della Scherma* [Discourse on the art of fencing] (c. 1560). Gaugler himself did not address the question of priority but stated only that Palladini, in "touch[ing] on the subject of left-handed adversaries", observed that "many believe that a left-hander [*mancino*] has an advantage over a right-hander [*dritto*]" (p. 14). The words "many believe" suggest that Palladini was *not* the first, but Fare perhaps meant only that he was the first among *fencing masters*.[9] Whoever was first, if such a question even has an answer, there were many more to come. For example in England Captain John Godfrey (1747), author of *A Treatise Upon the Useful Science of Defence*, remarked, "I cannot help taking notice, that the left-handed Man has the Advantage over the right-handed, upon an equal Footing ..." (p. 16). Godfrey was sufficiently impressed that he confessed: "in both Small and Back-Sword, I would rather contend with the right-handed Man with more Judgment, than the other [the left-hander] with less" (p. 17). Joseph Roland (1809), fencing master of the Royal Military Academy, Woolrich (England), and author of *The Amateur of Fencing*, went so far as to declare (p. 162) that the left-hander had the advantage even with half the training:

> It sometimes happens that a fencer will meet with a left-handed one, who, perhaps, has not learnt half so long as himself, yet the left-handed one will have the

[9] By extending our time frame to include those periods before the rise of the class of fencing masters and the formalisation of rules for fencing, we could find still earlier accounts of left-handers' prowess and, by implication, of their advantage over right-handers. Most famously, there was the emperor *Commodus*, son of Marcus Aurelius, whose accomplishments, according to the Roman historian Cassius Dio (1914–1927, Book 73), included "Champion of secutores; only left-handed fighter to conquer twelve times (as I recall the number) one thousand men" (see also McManus, 2006; Small, 2006, p. 563). There also is the legend of *Muzio Cordo*, a Roman youth who, during the Etruscan siege of Rome (508 BCE), entered the enemy camp to kill Lars Porsenna, the Etruscan king but not knowing him by sight, drew his sword and mistakenly killed another. Captured and brought before Porsenna, Muzio showed that he was unafraid of the fiery punishment prepared for him by voluntarily thrusting his right hand into the fire and holding it there until the hand was consumed. Impressed, Porsenna spared his life and returned his sword, which Muzio received with his left hand. From then on he fought successfully with his left and became known as *Scevola*, from the Latin *scaeva* for "left", and *scaevola* for "left-handed" (Plutarch, 1962, Chapter 8, *Popicola*; see also Scevola, 2006).

advantage of the right-handed, supposing both to be of equal courage, and taught by masters of equal abilities.

Domenico Angelo (1763), in *L'Ècole des Armes*, described a right-hander who was greatly embarrassed [*fort embarassé*] when fighting a left-hander (p. xxib). Guillaume Danet (1766), author of *L'Art des Armes*, noted the left-hander's reputation for being dangerous (p. 219), and Gomard (A-J-J. Possellier) (1845), "Ancien Professeur d'escrime de l'École royale Polytechnique" and author of *La Théorie de l'Escrime*, noted the left-hander's "grand advantage" (p. 284), as did Augustin Grisier (1847), Fencing-Master at L'École Royale Polytechnique, Paris, and author of *Les Armes et le Duel*, who added that the advantage was "always known" [*de tous temps reconnu*] (p. 262).

Statements to the same effect appear in the works of the Jacobean fencing master Joseph Swetnam (1617); Monsieur Valdin (Salomon Negri) (1729), a professor of Syriac and Rome; Monsieur L'Abbat (1734), fencing master at the Academy of Toulouse; J. Olivier (1771), Professor of Fencing in St. Dunstan's Court, Fleet Street, London; Thomas Mathewson (1805), Lieutenant and Riding-Master in the Late Roxbrough [Roxborough, England] Fencible Academy; La Boëssière (1818);[10] George Roland (1824), Fencing-Master at the Royal Academy, Edinburgh; Florio Blasco (1844; cited in Gaugler, 1998, p. 123); the French master Cordelois (1862); Rosaroll Scorza and Pietro Grisetti (1871/1803), respectively Cavaliere delli Ordini reale della Due Sicilie and Capo di battaglione dell' Artigliera Italiana; Maître d'Armes Walter Pollock, F.C. Grove, and Camille Prevost (1890); Louis Rondelle (1892), French-trained Maître D'Armes at the Boston Athletic Association and the Harvard University Fencing Club; and the British jack-of-all-trades Sir Richard Burton (1911), fencing master, explorer, historian, linguist, scientist, and poet.

Although fencing masters are our focus, there is someone else with views worthy of note. It is Alexandre Dumas (père), whose many novels and dramatisations, such as *The Count of Monte Cristo*, *The Man in the Iron Mask*, and most famously *The Three Musketeers*, celebrated the fencer's life and art. In this last work, as many readers may recall, the youth d'Artagnan, while rushing after a thief, collides with the musketeer Athos, further hurting Athos's already wounded shoulder (his right, as we learn later on), and offers Athos satisfaction in a duel. When they meet Athos hesitates, saying "If I kill you, I shall be taken for a child-slaying ogre", and d'Artagnan replies "not so much, since you do me the honour of drawing with a wound that must be

[10] This was La Boëssière fils; his father, La Boëssière père, also a fencing master, is credited with inventing the face mask in 1780 (*A history of fencing*, 2006).

a great hindrance to you." (Dumas, 1844/2006, Ch. 5, p. 52; translation by Richard Pevear). Athos agrees:

> A great hindrance, on my word, and you caused me the devil's own pain, I must say: but I'll use my left hand, as is my habit in such circumstances. Don't think I'm doing you a kindness; I draw just as well with both hands; and there will even be a disadvantage for you: a left-handed man is very troublesome for people who are not forewarned. I regret not having informed you of this circumstance earlier.

That it would in fact be "very troublesome" for the right-handed d'Artagnan,[11] we never find out, because their duel is interrupted by the arrival of Cardinal Richelieu's guards. Where, though, might Dumas have learned of the left-hander's advantage? Dumas himself was a trained fencer, so he could have drawn on personal experience, but he also might have heard this from his own teacher, who was none other than Augustin Grisier, whose manual was among those attesting to the advantage. Dumas wrote a *Préface Anecdotique* for the manual, so we can assume that he knew it well.

TWO SCEPTICS

Among those, following Palladini, who mentioned left-handedness, I found only two who questioned the conventional view about the left-hander's advantage. One was a fencing master not yet cited: Palladini's near-contemporary Vincentio Saviolo. Saviolo came to England from Padua in 1590 and established himself as one of the premiere fencing masters of Elizabethan times. His two-part work, *Vincentio Saviolo His Practice with the Rapier and Dagger*, published in 1595, was the first original treatise on fencing ever published in England (Aylward, 1950) and is said to have been the source of the specific diction and general theory of fence that Shakespeare used for the duels in *Romeo and Juliet* (Holmer, 1994; see also Jackson, 1990). The work takes the form of a dialogue between Saviolo and the young scholar Luke. In the last chapter of book 1, entitled "Entreating how a lefte handed man, shall plaie with one that is right handed", Luke reported witnessing a contest between a right-hander and a left-hander, and asked (p. 1):

[11] We know, from context, that d'Artagnan was right-handed, even though he is never identified as such. He also is depicted as right-handed in Gustave Doré's monument to Alexandre Dumas, in the Place Malesherbes, Paris. On the reverse he is shown seated, wearing his scabbard on his left hip and holding his sword resting near his right hand (Doré, 2006/1880–1883).

> because I know many of opinion, that the left handed have great advantage of the right, yet I see both doe their uttermost this morning, without any hurt of either partie, and in beholding both the one and the other diligently I could not discerne anie jot of advantage betweene them: therefore you shall doe me the great favour, if you discourse unto me, whether the left hand can have any advantage of the right, or the right of the lefte: withall instructing me, both how to defende my self from such a one, and how to offend him.

To which Saviolo replied:

> Of this question, I have heard many times much reasoning, and many there are indeede which so think, but beleeve me, the left hand hath no advantage of the right hand, nor the right, of the lefte ...

The other sceptic, someone also not yet mentioned here, was Dumas's near-contemporary, Gustave Flaubert. Along with the many novels and essays that brought him fame, there is an odd and endearing work called *Le Dictionnaire des Idées Reçues.* It was compiled from Flaubert's notes taken from boyhood on (Flaubert was born in 1821) and first published posthumously in 1911 as an appendix to his unfinished satirical work *Bouvard et Pécuchet*, and then separately in 1913. In the first English translation by Edward J. Fluck, in 1954, the title is rendered as *A Dictionary of Platitudes*, and in 1994, by Geoffrey Wall, as *A Dictionary of Received Ideas.* As both translations imply, it was what Fluck (p. iii) called "a compendium of conversational clichés, blind beliefs, fashionable misconceptions, and fixed ideas" of the kind that Flaubert found to be common in bourgeois society. Among the entries there was this one on left-handers [*gauchers*]: "*Terribles à l'escrime. Plus adroits que ceux qui se servent de la main droite*", which Fluck translated as "redoubtable in fencing. More adroit than people who use the right hand" (p. 84). Unlike Dumas, Flaubert was not a fencer, but "swords abound" in his stories (Brown, 2006, p. 56) and "from his youth, he read the romantics"; in particular "Hugo and Dumas, Michelet and Balzac, he devoured and made his own" (Bart, 1967, p. 21). He was also a long-time friend of Dumas (Bart, 1967, p. 657). None of the entries in the dictionary is dated, but if the one on left-handers followed publication of *The Three Musketeers* (Dumas was 42 at the time, Flaubert just 23), might it have been inspired, at least in part, by the scene between Athos and d'Artagnan? If so, and if Dumas could have seen the entry (which he could not, since he also died before the dictionary was published), one could imagine him taking offence. After all, Flaubert was implying that the notion of the left-hander's special prowess was another of those "fashionable misconceptions", or one repeated too casually by persons without real knowledge of such matters.

WHY WAS THE LEFT-HANDER AT AN ADVANTAGE?

For fencing masters who held the conventional view, what did they think gave left-handers the edge—their Nature or their Nurture? The phrase was made popular by Francis Galton (1874, p. 12) as a way to frame debates about the roots of individual differences, but it was in use long before his time: Shakespeare's Prospero used it in *The Tempest (*Act 4, Scene 1) as did Mulcaster (1581) in his treatise on education, and so did the fencing masters, explicitly or implicitly. Among them was L'Abbat (1734), who wrote: "Most People imagine that a Left-handed Man has, by Nature, the Advantage of a Right-handed Man in Fencing" (p. 86). He did not identify "Most People" but probably did not mean other fencing masters who, as we shall see, did not endorse the Nature explanation. If he meant the general public, one wonders how they would have come to this view—from watching public exhibitions (or even duels), hearing stories about the Kerrs, or perhaps reading romantic accounts earlier than those of Dumas, if there were such? (One doubts that many knew of Commodus and Scevola; see footnote 9.) More likely, L'Abbat meant the academy students, and not just right-handers searching perhaps for a way to rationalise their defeats, but even the left-handers themselves on the possibility that winning gave them a sense of *natural* superiority. Nor is it clear whether, by "Nature", L'Abbat meant physical characteristics such as arm and leg speed, strength, balance, and quickness of reaction, or qualities of mind and spirit such as judgement, desire, and courage, all widely seen as important for success in fencing. Whatever he meant, L'Abbat himself favoured Nurture: the advantage was merely habit due to the left-hander's being in the minority and therefore "exercising oftener with Right-handed Men than a Right-handed Man with him" (p. 86; trans. by A. Mahon).

According to Gaugler (1998, p. 14), Palladini (c. 1560) reached the same conclusion nearly two centuries before. So did Joseph Roland (1809) 65 years after. Like L'Abbat (1734), Roland acknowledged the Nature explanation's appeal; he also named the *students* as the ones who believed it. Of the young right-handed fencer who is bested, presumably not once but repeatedly, by a left-hander, he wrote (Roland, 1809, pp. 162–163):

> This circumstance appears to the young practitioner as very *extraordinary*, and he thence concludes that the left-handed fencer has *naturally* the superiority over him; whereas if he reflected properly he would find that a *left-handed* man has only the advantage by the *habit* of practising continually with right-handed man, and that, on the contrary, the right-handed man seldom or ever has met with a left-handed one before, which is the reason of his being so much puzzled on this occasion.

Other explanations were variations on the same theme. Saviolo (1595) assured Luke that neither hand had the advantage "no otherwise than you your selfe finde your owne advantage" (p. 1); in other words, that "onelye use and knowledge giveth the better either to the right or the lefte ..." (p. 3). Godfrey (1747) supposed that "as there are more right-handed, than left-handed, the latter must be more used to the former, than the former to the latter" (p. 16). Danet (1766) explained that if left-handers are a danger to right-handers, it is because right-handers "are not accustomed to drawing their swords against them" [*derniers n'ont pas l'habitude de tirer contre les Gauchers*] (p. 219). Olivier (1771) observed that the reason was "as you are but seldom used to fence with them [left-handers]" (p. 187). Mathewson (1805) concluded, "Therefore a left-handed player has no advantage over one that plays with the right, only the right-handed players are, in general, not so much accustomed to play with them" (pp. 21–22). George Roland (1824) was sure that "nature has given the left-handed man no advantages in fencing which the right-handed man does not also possess" (p. 126). Grisier (1847, pp. 261–262) and Cordelois (1862) credited the advantage, in Cordelois's words, to "the relatively small number of left-handers" (p. 202) and, by implication, to right-handers' fewer opportunities to practise against them; so did Pollock et al. (1890), who added that if "right-handed fencers met left-handed fencers as often as the latter do the former, they would be on equal terms" (p. 108). Lastly, Burton (1911) put it to "our being more familiar with right-handed men. Change the conditions, and the pair are absolutely equal in their chances of victory" (p. 13).[12] Alone among the fencing masters, however, Cordelois (1862) saw another and different sort of negative effect for right-handers: he surmised that although the blows are the same for right-handers as for left-handers [*quoique les coups soient les memes pour uns come pour les autres, — par quelques* ...], the right-hander, "in striking unceasingly with his greatest force against the left-hander", would

[12] Is that what Athos (i.e., Dumas) meant when he told d'Artagnan that left-handers are "very troublesome for people who are not forewarned"? The uncertainty lies in the word "forewarned". In the original French text, the phrase is *qui ne sont pas prévenus*, and the translator Richard Pevear's (Dumas, 2006/1844) choice of "forewarned" for *prévenus* is the closest literal translation. What is unclear is how being "forewarned" would have helped d'Artagnan, because in the short period before their duel he would hardly have had time to acquire the necessary experience with left-handers. And in that case, how shall we understand Athos's expression of "regret" at not having informed him of this circumstance "earlier"? Was he implying that d'Artagnan then could have withdrawn from the duel? Alternatively, he may have meant only that if d'Artagnan had known earlier, he would have had time to adjust his plan of attack (perhaps along the lines described below in footnote 13). The phrase makes more sense psychologically—that is, it fits better with fencing masters', including Grisier's (1847), explanations of the left-hander's advantage—if it is translated less literally, either as "who are not used to them" or "who are unprepared for them".

ultimately reduce his effectiveness against other *right*-handers. Cordelais did not say why, but perhaps meant that the unceasing force of the right-hander's strikes, whether or not it strengthened him against left-handers, would weaken him against right-handers to the extent that force became his only weapon, replacing speed and guile.

If the fencing masters who acknowledged the left-hander's advantage agreed that the advantage lay in nurture, that is, in more opportunities for the right kind of practice, no one reported putting the matter to test, for example by directly comparing right- and left-handers on those physical and psychological qualities seen as important for success. In fairness, fencing masters—except for Burton (1911)—were not men of science and could not have been expected to perform such tests. Joseph Roland (1809), however, supposed that evidence for the role of practice could be gleaned simply from watching two left-handers compete against each other: both will be "more embarrassed than the right [-hander] with the left [-hander], and will, in general, fence in the most ridiculous manner imaginable" (p. 163). Likewise, Grisier (1847) observed that left-handers would be embarrassed when facing other left-handers (p. 262); as did Rondelle (1892), who in declaring that "Left-handed fencers really have no special advantage" remarked that "when two of them fence together they seldom exhibit grace or finish" (p. 189); and Burton (1911) noted that "Two first-rate left-handed fencers are never at home with each other ..." (p. 13).

INSTRUCTIONS FOR RIGHT-HANDERS

If the advantage came only from practice, then the way for right-handers to deal with left-handers was straightforward and, again beginning perhaps with Palladini (c. 1560), all masters gave their students much the same advice: get more practice against left-handers. As George Roland (1824) promised, "any difficulties, therefore, arising from the inverted [i.e., left-handed] positions will be easily overcome by practice" (p. 126).

To increase such opportunities Roland (1824) also recommended "occasionally getting lessons from your master with his left hand" (p. 126). So did Valdin (1729): "It is good that a Master knows how to shew fencing with his left Hand, to teach his Scholar, who is right-handed, to act against a left-handed Man ..." (p. 17), and Burton (1911): "The *maître d'armes* may always annul the incognito of the left-handed man by representing him at times in lessons to his pupils" (p. 14). La Boëssière (1818) called such lessons "indispensable" (p. 245), as did Domenico Angelo (1763) who, along with insisting that his pupils practise "various strokes left-handed", would himself "give some lessons left handed" (as stated by Czajkowski, 2005, p. 7).[13]

Along with recommending practice against left-handers, with the master himself occasionally serving as model, some masters advised the right-hander to practice with his own *left* hand. In that way, L'Abbat (1734) promised that one will not be "so much surprized when one meets with a Left-Handed Man, as they would otherwise be" (p. 87), and Angelo (1763), while acknowledging that the exercise would be difficult, promised that "with good will and hard work", a degree of skill will be achieved that is "advantageous for oneself and does honor to one's teacher" [*mais avec de la bonne volunté & en prenant peine on parvient a un dégré d'habileté, qui est avantageux pour foi & fait honneur a celui qui enseigne*] (p. xxiv). Hope (1707, p. 191), although not referring specifically to encounters against left-handers, advised allowing:

> use of the Left-hand ... that thereby a Man may become dexterous, at both Opposing and Parieing his Adversary's Sword with it; which it is impossible he can ever be, unless by frequently making use of it, both when taking a Lesson and Assaulting; And indeed it is too good and useful an assistance for a Man's Defence, to be wholly laid aside or neglected.

The advice of these three masters was clear—the rationale was not. L'Abbat perhaps meant that left-hand practice would help one think like a left-hander, so as to have a better plan of attack and defence when facing a left-hander, whereas Hope (1707) perhaps meant that *during* the match, whether against a right- or left-hander, one could switch to the left hand, thereby gaining the advantage of surprise by attacking from both sides. That was what Herger (quoted in Crichton, 1977, pp. 130–131), the swordsman of the Norse Myths, did with deadly effect:

> Then, Herger threw his own sword from one hand to the other, for these Northmen can fight as well with either hand, and equally strong. And quickly Herger turned and cut off Ragnar's head from behind with a single blow.

---

[13] For Roland (1824), "frequent practice" against left-handers was "the only useful advice" he could give right-handers (p. 125), but other masters had more to say. For example, Saviolo (1595) and Hope (1692) instructed right-handers to deal with left-handers by doing everything in reverse, or, as Hope put it, to "act quite contrary to what ye are to observe in playing against a Right-Handed Man" (Advertisement). Others were more specific. For example, Palladini (c. 1560) suggested opposing the left-hander's point thrust with a parry to the outside and riposte to the chest or face (Gaugler, 1998, p. 14); Olivier (1771) recommended engaging the left-hander "always on the outside of the arm, that you may perform small strokes or glizades along his blade, to thrust under the arm" (pp. 188–189); and Scorza and Grisetti (1871) recommended "keep[ing] your foil inside and push[ing] the [left-hander's] foil away [to the outside]" (p. 92).

If a switch during the match was what Hope had in mind, the only one I found who was explicit on this point was Edward Blackwell (1734), who saw it not as a tactic but only as a way to handle fatigue: "When your Right Hand is tired in the Engagement, you may flip your sword into your Left Hand" (p. 87). The musketeer Athos, we recall, could also switch, in his case following injury, as could the originally right-handed Edoardo Mangiarotti who, on being struck on his left index finger in the semi-finals at the 1951 Olympics, changed to his right hand and won his last two semi-final matches and the silver medal in the finals (Cohen, 2002, p. 382). There also was the Canadian archaeologist and ethnologist Daniel Wilson (1891), who wrote, "The fencer who can transfer his weapon to the left hand places his adversary at a disadvantage" (p. 206). Wilson was a left-hander who "became ambidextrous" (Wilson, 2006, p. 3); if he was a fencer too, he perhaps was reflecting on his own experience.

Of all the masters, Saviolo (1595) was perhaps the best equipped to model left-hand use and to convince his students of the benefits of left-hand practice because, according to his contemporary John Florio, Saviolo himself handled the sword equally well with either hand.[14] We learn this in Florio's (1591) *Second Frutes*, a guide to self-improvement, manual of topical journalism and polite conversation, and textbook for teaching English and Italian. In chapter 7 (pp. 117–119), Saviolo (V.S.) is portrayed in a conversation between two gentlemen, Geordano (G) and Edward (E):

G: … of whom doo you learne to plaie at your weapon?
E: Of master V.S.
G. Who, that Italian that lookes like Mars himselfe.
E. The verie same
…
G. I have heard him reported to be a notable talle man.
E. Hee will hit any man, bee it with a thrust or floccada, with an imbrocada or a charging blow, with a right or reverse blowe, be it with the edge, with the back, or with the flat, even as it liketh him.
G. Is he left or right handed?
E. Both, all is one to him.

When Saviolo (1595) reassured Luke that "onelye use and knowledge giveth the better either to the right or the lefte" it would appear, then, that he was speaking from experience.

[14] If, as has been proposed, Florio did the English translation of Saviolo's *Practice* (Aylward, 1950), then he probably knew Saviolo personally and might have seen for himself his either-handed prowess with the sword.

INSTRUCTIONS FOR LEFT-HANDERS

Unlike manuals on writing, etiquette, music performance, and public speaking, which barely took note of left-handers' existence, most fencing manuals not only acknowledged left-handers, they also included instructions for them. But unlike the often detailed instructions for right-handers (see footnote 13), those for left-handers were perfunctory, of the sort: use your left hand wherever instructions refer to the right, and vice versa. Thus, Valdin (1729) wrote that "if the Scholar is left-handed, his left Hand is to be conducted with the same Instructions as the right" (p. 17); and Scorza and Grisetti (1871) merely noted that the rules for left-handers facing right-handers were the same as for right-handers facing left-handers "and therefore will not be repeated here" (p. 95). As for two left-handers facing each other, "they should fence as would two right-handers" (p. 95). The one exception was Saviolo (1595). His student, Luke, after being assured that neither hand had any natural advantage, asked Saviolo, "Tell me therefore, if you would teach a [left-handed scholar], how would you begin?", and Saviolo answered with detailed instructions (see Hand, 2003, for examples and commentary). However, in the drawings accompanying the texts, even including Saviolo's, left-handers were overlooked altogether, since only right-handers were shown, as in Figure 6 from Andrew Mahon's English edition of L'Abbat's (1734) *The Art of Fencing*. Mahon acknowledged the absence: "Nor have I, in any of the Attitudes [positions] represented a Left-handed Figure", but he dismissed it as of no great matter because "by looking thro' the Paper on the Blank Side, they will appear reversed, and consequently Left-handed" (Preface, p. 4). Left-handed students could be forgiven for feeling short-changed.

If, as it appears, left-handers were given neither visual aids nor special tips for facing right-handers (for example, no one suggested that they practise with the *right* hand so that they too would be able to switch during a match), perhaps the fencing masters decided that they had advantage enough already. But neither were they advised to practise against other left-handers so that when competing against one another, they would *not*, as Roland (1809, p. 163) put it, fence in "the most ridiculous manner imaginable." However, Gomard (1845) did point out that left-handers and not just right-handers would profit if the fencing master used his left hand "because their [left-handers'] trouble is even greater [than right-handers'] when they encounter a left-hander" (p. 284). He presumably meant that left-handers had even fewer opportunities than right-handers for the recommended kind of practice.

INSTRUCTIONS FOR RIGHT-HANDERS AND LEFT-HANDERS IN ENSEMBLE

Alone among the authors whose works I examined, Angelo (1763) advised on how a right-hander and a left-hander could enhance their common attack and defence when fighting together, in ensemble, against right-handers. It should be with the left-hander on the left and the right-hander on the right. In that way, or so Angelo seems to have implied, their opponents would face sword-points from a wider angle than if facing only right-handers (or only left-handers). And, of course, in that way their own swords would not clash together.

DID FENCING MASTERS PRACTISE WHAT THEY PREACHED?

In sum, fencing masters advised right-handers to practise against left-handers and advised the masters to serve as models on occasion. Palladini (c. 1560), La Boëssière (1818), Danet (1766), and Angelo (1763) reportedly practised what they preached, but others did not. Danet (1766) noted that "if left-handers are a danger to right-handers", it is not just because right-handers have little or no experience fencing against them, but "because most masters do not from time to time use their left hand in giving lessons" (p. 219). Likewise, La Boëssière (1818), who deemed it "indispensable" (p. 245) for masters to model the left-hand style, complained that "The old masters were not sufficiently concerned" to offer this training [*ne se sont pas assez occupé de la manière d'exerciser les droitiers a tirer contre les gauchers*] (p. 244). Along with Palladini, it seems likely that the either-handed Saviolo (1595) was the exception.

A "SERIOUS DISADVANTAGE" FOR THE LEFT-HANDER

At least five masters, Roland (1824), Blasco (1844), Scorza and Grisetti (1871), and Burton (1911), while recognising the left-hander's advantage, observed that in one crucial respect it was not only nullified but reversed. As Roland (1824, p. 126) explained:

> In actual combat the left-handed person labours under a serious disadvantage, as many wounds of the lungs alone have been known to do well, which, if carried to an equal depth on the left side, would immediately have produced fatal consequences by wounding the heart.

In other words, the left-hander would tend to wound his right-handed opponent on the right side, striking the right lung, a non-mortal injury, whereas the same wound for the left-hander would be on the left, striking the heart. Still, none of these masters saw this as reason to recommend that left-handers fence with the *right* hand. Perhaps they assumed that by then it was too late to change or that the disadvantage was offset to the extent that left-handers were less likely to be injured in the first place.

Roland's (1824) and Blasco's (1844) statements antedate similar observations by the Scottish essayist Thomas Carlyle (1871; in Froude, 1898) and the English physician Philip H. Pye-Smith (1871). The difference is that Carlyle and Pye-Smith evidently saw no compensating advantage for the left-hander and instead invoked this structural feature in their "heart-shield" theories to explain the origins and ascendancy of right-handedness. Carlyle (June 15, quoted in Froude, 1898, pp. 348–349) wrote:

> Why [the right] hand was chosen is a question not to be settled, not worth asking except as a kind of riddle; probably arose in fighting; most important to protect your heart and its adjacencies, and to carry the shield in that [the left] hand.

Pye-Smith's (1871, p. 145) statement was similar except that it reflected the new ideas of the Darwinian era:

> If a hundred of our ambidextrous ancestors made the step in civilization of inventing a shield, we may suppose that half would carry it on the right arm and fight with the left, the other half on the left and fight with the right. The latter would certainly, in the long run, escape mortal wounds better than the former, and thus a race of men who fought with the right hand would gradually be developed by a process of natural selection.

DID FENCING MASTERS WELCOME LEFT-HANDERS OR MERELY ACCEPT THEM, AND WERE LEFT-HANDERS THEMSELVES DRAWN TO THE SPORT?

When baseball coaches and managers today welcome left-handers, they do so in hopes of making their teams more successful. If some fencing masters welcomed left-handers, it could have been for the same reason: that in matches against students from other academies, in tournaments open to the public or, if it came to that, in actual duels, their success would enhance their academies' reputations and help to ensure a steady supply of new students. And if some masters were welcoming, did they, like baseball coaches and managers, go further and actively recruit left-handers, and were left-handers drawn to the sport as they appear to be today so that their numbers came to exceed those in the general population? Finally, did any right-handers become left-handed fencers, like the twentieth-century champion Edoardo Mangiarotti? If any of these things happened, there are no signs in the books and manuals I examined. Instead, the only statements I found pertaining to the numbers of left-handed fencers suggest, in one case, that they were about as common as left-handers in the general population, using Malgaigne's (1859) and Moutier's (1908) estimates from non-biased measures, and in another case that they were less common. Thus, according to Gomard (1845), the right-hander "scarcely meets one left-hander in ten adversaries" (p. 284); and according to Swetnam (1617), "... a [right-handed] man may play with forty men, and not meete with too [two] left-handed men, except it be a great chance, ..." (p. 166).

DID ACCEPTING LEFT-HANDED FENCERS MEAN ACCEPTING LEFT-HANDEDNESS?

I have said that there is no reason to suppose, and no evidence to suggest, that fencing masters endorsed right-hand customs any less than did teachers anywhere. Still, inasmuch as they accepted left-handers into their academies, it is conceivable that they were more tolerant of left-handedness than was the general public. If they were, Godfrey (1747) was the exception. His contempt for the condition was unabashed: "I dare say no Body would chuse to be left-handed." He even digressed from his lessons to "propose a Way to put a stop to that undesired Race ..." It was to have the nurse hold the baby in her right arm. That way, its left arm would be pressed against her body, making that arm "confined and rendered inactive" (p. 17).[15] With such views, it is difficult to imagine Godfrey accepting, much less welcoming, left-handers into his academy. That may be why his manual was among the few *not* to include instructions for them, although that would not explain the absence of special instructions for right-handers who, even if shielded from left-handers in his academy, might still have to face them elsewhere. In any case, if Godfrey wanted to "put a stop" to left-handedness, left-handers could be grateful that he did not propose killing them outright!

[15] Godfrey (1747) noted that the nurse's usual practice was to carry "the Child in the left arm," thereby confining the child's right arm, and, for that reason, he was "confident most would be left-handed, if they were not by the Parent's Care broke of that habit after they are parted from the Nurse" (p. 17). Godfrey was not the first or the last to explain handedness in this fashion (Harris, 2002).

WHY IS THE LEFT-HANDER AT AN ADVANTAGE? THE VIEW TODAY

Frequency-dependency

Like their predecessors, fencing masters today routinely acknowledge the left-hander's advantage, now supported by impressive empirical evidence. To this extent, then, at least one of the clichés in Flaubert's *Dictionary of Platitudes* was not totally without merit. And like their predecessors, fencing masters today just as routinely credit the advantage to left-handers' smaller numbers (e.g., Crosnier, 1955, 1958, 1965; Deladrier, 1948; Manley, 1979). Recruiting advertisements do the same. For example, on its Internet site the Streatham Fencing Club, London (2005), posted this answer to the question of whether left-handers should join: "Fencing's a very good sport for left-handers – they learn to fence right-handers all the time, but the right-handers don't fence the left-handers nearly so often." Clearly, fencing masters today do not follow Godfrey (1747) in calling left-handers an "undesired Race". Like their predecessors, many also recommend left-hand practice (e.g., Czajkowski, 2005; Terrone, 1959), and some note left-handers' difficulties when facing other left-handers. As Manley (1979) put it, perhaps with some exaggeration, "About the worst panic scene in fencing occurs when two novice left-handers meet in competition" (p. 125).

The explanation that left-handers' advantage is a product of their smaller numbers is what, in evolutionary biology and ecology, is referred to as the "frequency-dependency" explanation (Ayala & Campbell, 1974) and, as it was for fencing masters in the past and for their modern-day counterparts, it appears to be the consensus explanation among laterality researchers today (e.g., Brooks et al., 2004; Grouios, Tsorbatzoudis, Alexandris, & Barkoukis, 2000). The explanation also has a powerful new kind of support from studies that take the kind of sport, the position, and the physical demands into account. Raymond et al. (1996) compared the numbers of left-handers in two kinds of sports: interactive and non-interactive. The former are adversarial, where one player directly opposes another, either exclusively, as in fencing, tennis, and boxing, or at key moments, such as during the pitcher-batter confrontation in baseball, and where the action of one depends directly on the action of the other. In the latter, such as swimming, gymnastics, and skiing, there is no direct opponent. By the frequency-dependency explanation, left-handers should be over-represented only in interactive sports, but in non-interactive sports should be no more common than in the general population, and this is what was found. Wood and Aggleton (1989) and Aggleton and Wood (1990) found the same in surveys of other non-interactive sports, such as snooker, ten-pin bowling, and darts. More recently, Faurie and

Raymond (2005) took the analysis a provocative step further by proposing that the left-hander's advantage in interactive, adversarial sports helps to explain why left-handedness has survived in the population despite certain purported fitness costs that, in extreme form, bring earlier death (e.g., Aggleton, Kentridge, & Neave, 1993; Coren & Halpern, 1991; but see Basso et al., 2000; Harris, 1993b; Steenhuis, Østbye, & Walton, 2001). The answer, they suggest, is that to the extent that interactive sports like fencing substitute for actual fighting, which in the past would normally have led to the death or maiming of one combatant, left-handers have had an evolutionary advantage sufficient to maintain their numbers. In support of this hypothesis, they offered their finding that the number of left-handers in traditional, or pre-industrial, societies increases as a function of the aggressivity, or violence, of those societies as reflected in their homicide rates. In this respect, their analysis could be seen as a variation on Carlyle's (1871) and Pye-Smith's (1871) heart-shield theories. The difference is that Carlyle and Pye-Smith, in focusing on the *disadvantage* of left-handedness, sought to explain only the ascendancy of right-handedness in the population, whereas Faurie and Ramond (2005), in focusing on the *advantage* of left-handedness, seek to explain only the persistence of left-handedness in the population.[16]

Other possibilities: Handedness-related differences in motor control and attention

To the extent that laterality researchers endorse the frequency-dependency explanation of left-handers' advantage in interactive sports, their views would be fundamentally the same as those of fencing masters past and present. Some researchers, however, have proposed that the advantage also reflects a real difference in ability, especially of the kind important for close interactive encounters. One possible difference lies in motor control, although that may depend on how it is defined and measured. For example, if, as Annett (1985) has proposed, left-handers tend to come from a group with random dominance for handedness, it raises the possibility that their

[16] The survival value of left-handedness has been reported in at least one other creature, snails. Crabs are major predators of two species of Atlantic snails, whelks and cones, but they are not always successful in killing their prey, with the signs of failed attacks appearing as jagged scars on the snail shells. From examination of scar patterns on the shells of morphologically similar pairs of right- and left-handed snail species, Dietl and Hendricks (2005) found evidence that the rarer form of left-handed coiling promotes survival from attacks by right-handed crab predators. The authors suggest one explanation that "parallels" the explanation for the left-handed advantage in sports or fights that involve dual confrontations, such as fencing, namely that "left-handed prey are less commonly encountered than right-handed prey" (p. 2).

axial motor control, on average, will be less strongly lateralised in one hemisphere compared to right-handers. This possibility is supported by evidence that in actual tests of skill, such as peg moving, left-handers, compared to right-handers, show smaller between-hands differences in performance (Kilshaw & Annett, 1983). If the smaller difference reflects more bilateral control then, as Geschwind and Galaburda (1987) proposed, it could enhance overall skill in bimanual tasks where each hand makes a significant contribution. That in turn would help to account in part for the elevated rate of left-handedness among athletes, "in contrast to the common view that this is entirely the result of an advantage in competing against righthanded opponents" (Geschwind & Galaburda, 1987, p. 79), in other words, in contrast to the frequency-dependency explanation. Geschwind and Galaburda (1987) did not identify the athletic endeavours for which increased bilateral control would give left-handers the advantage, but Grouios (2004) suggested that fencing would be among them. If it were, for what bilateral tasks would the advantage occur? The most direct, or so it would seem, would be for wielding the weapon with both hands, but while that might help in other sports for such bimanual "weapons" as baseball or cricket bats, the advantage for swordplay presumably would only be for earlier times than those under review, when heavier two-handed weapons were favoured. Other possibilities include blocking or seizing an opponent's weapon with one's hand or arm (as performed by the fencer on the right in the bottom panel of Figure 6), parrying incoming thrusts with an off-hand weapon, and *switching* hands, but here too it would depend on the historical period. For the periods reviewed here, blocking and grabbing were often permitted and the dagger was often used as an off-hand, or companion, weapon. Today, however, off-hand weapons are never used in competition, and use of the off-hand as a defensive measure is prohibited. As for hand switching, it is allowed only between, not during, matches (Rules, 2006), which is why, after injuring his left hand at the 1951 Olympics, Edoardo Mangiarotti had to wait for the next match before changing to his right.

If the implications of bilateral axial motor control for fencing, past or present, are uncertain, not to mention untested, the implications for another motor difference might be clearer. Along with showing smaller between-hand differences in motor performance, left-handers also show faster finger and hand speed overall as measured on peg-moving (Annett & Manning, 1989; Kilshaw & Annett, 1983) and finger-tapping tasks (Nalçaci, Kalaycioglu, Çiçek, & Genç, 2001). In fencing, arm and hand speed are essential for success, so if similar differences were found for thrusting, parrying, and other moves it would be further evidence for a motor advantage. So far such differences have not been found (e.g., Ketlinski & Pickens, 1973; Singer, 1968; see review in Harmenberg & Ceci, undated), but if they exist, how they are assessed may be important. For example, when world-class épée fencers and beginners were compared on a test of lunging in response to a light going on, no differences were found, but when a fencing-like starting procedure was used, the world-class fencers not only outperformed the beginners, their performance was also correlated with their success in competition (Harmenberg, Ceci, Barvestad, Hjerpe, & Nystrom, 1991). However, these studies did not take handedness into account, so it remains to be seen whether these measures would further differentiate right-handers from left-handers.

A second kind of difference might be in attention. In most persons, right- as well as left-handers, the cerebral hemispheres differ in the control and deployment of attention, with the right controlling attention across the entire extrapersonal space, while the left primarily controls contraversive orientation in the right hemispace (Mesulam, 1999; see also Gitelman, Nobre, Parrish, et al., 1999; Heilman & Van Den Abell, 1980). Bisiacchi, Ripoll, Stein, Simonet, and Azemar (1985) proposed that because fencing trains the individual to reduce errors in situations calling for spatial attention and cued recall, left-handers will have the advantage insofar as the right hemisphere also controls the left hand. To find out, they gave a cued reaction time test, modelled after Posner (1980; Posner, Snyder, & Davidson, 1980), to 12 fencers, including 6 right-handers and 6 left-handers, and 12 persons engaging in other sports, including judo and swimming. The targets were lights placed 8 or 24 degrees to the left and right of midline fixation, and the cues for each trial indicated whether the target would be to the left or right and whether at 8 or 24 degrees. On half the trials, participants were instructed to respond with their right hand, on the other half with their left. Overall, although fencers were not faster than other athletes, they were more accurate, with left-handed fencers best of all. The authors concluded that the left-handers' performance therefore best exemplifies "a good tradeoff for speed and accuracy" (Bisiacchi et al., 1985, p. 511). Comparison of the right- and left-hand scores also revealed a left-hand advantage in 10 of the 12 fencers, regardless of handedness, consistent according to the authors with the evidence, already noted, of the right hemisphere's predominant role in the control and deployment of attention. This further finding also suggests that the right-handed Edoardo Mangiarotti's remarkable success, after learning to fence with his left hand, may have been more than frequency-dependent.

Still a third difference that could help left-handers, especially in encounters calling for rapid, accurate responses from either side, while conceivably also contributing to any motor and attentional advantages, is in the speed of transfer of primary-level sensory and motor information across the cerebral hemispheres. In left-handers, transfer is generally faster than in right-handers (e.g., Cherbuin & Brinkman, 2006; Geffen, Rosa, & Luciano, 2000; Hellige et al., 1994; Potter & Graves, 1988). In this case, the relevant neural differences are proposed to lie not in the degree of cerebral lateralisation but in the size and/or fibre density of the corpus callosum (e.g., Westerhausen et al., 2004; Witelson, 1985; but see Morton & Rafto, 2006; Steinmetz et al., 1992).

Individual differences

The analyses so far have treated left-handers as a more or less uniform, or homogeneous, group behaviourally (in strength, or degree, of handedness) and neuropsychologically (in degree of lateralisation of speech, praxis, and/or visual/spatial/attentional functions, or speed of interhemispheric transfer), when in fact, compared with right-handers, left-handers are very heterogeneous and comprise what appear to be at least three neuropsychologically distinct subgroups (reviewed in Harris, 1992; Peters, 1996; see also Savage & Thomas, 1993). This raises the possibility that if any motor and attentional factors do prove to give left-handers an advantage for fencing and other close, interactive sports, the advantage will apply only to certain left-handers. For example, the extent that bilateral transfer of skill is faster and more accurate in left-handers than in right-handers may depend, among other things, on the combination of familial sinistrality and discordant hand and eye preference (Gorynia & Egenter, 2000; Kumar & Mandal, 2005). Consistency of left-hand preference may also be important. When consistent and inconsistent left-handers were compared on tests of strength and skill, they showed reliably different and distinct patterns of performance. For example, the stronger hand was the left in consistent left-handers, and the right in inconsistent left-handers. The two groups also differed in how they distributed attention to their hands when performing a difficult bimanual coordination task (Peters & Servos, 1989).

Fencing distances and kinds of movements

Whatever may be the left-handed fencer's natural motor and attentional advantages, they could also depend on the weapon used. This possibility is suggested by a further finding in Azémar and Stein's (1994) survey that, among elite fencers, the left-hander's advantage was greatest for foil competition, less for épée, and least for sabre (see Table 3 in Raymond et al., 1996; see also Table 1 in Azémar, 2003). Raymond et al. (1996) propose that the differences reflect the different rules and tactics for each weapon: opponents stand farther away when fencing with sabre than with épée or foil, despite the sabre's shorter length, because by convention the hand and arm are potential targets only for sabre competition (p. 1631). Boulinguez, Velay, and Nougier (2001) suggest instead that the advantage has to do not with the distance per se but with the spatial constraints of the movement being executed and that for certain movements, the advantage actually goes to *right-handers*, with left-handers favoured for movements requiring mostly sagittal and proactive control (foil and épée) and with right-handers favoured for movements requiring mostly lateral and retroactive control (sabre) (although this is not totally consistent with the pattern shown in Table 1 in Azémar, 2003). However the differences are explained, contemporary fencing masters have also remarked on the relation between the weapon and the left-hander's margin of advantage (e.g., Manley, 1979, p. 201), which prompts the question whether masters from the past said the same. At least from their manuals, I found no indications, keeping in mind that I examined only a small sample.

WHAT ABOUT WOMEN?

The focus of this article has been on men. Do left-handed female fencers have the same advantage over their right-handed counterparts? For fencing masters of the past the question never arose, or at least was never addressed in their manuals. This is understandable in as much as fencing was a male preserve, meaning among other things that the academies and schools were closed to women. However, as early as the eighteenth century that began to change as fencing became popular among upper-class women. The change is not reflected in the fencing manuals but rather by the growing number of challenges and duels involving women and the popularity of female duellists as subjects of news stories and art prints (Rizzo, 2002, pp. 88 ff.; see also Svinth, 2003). Three prominent female fencers are the French opera star Julie d'Aubigny, known as "La Maupin", who learned fencing from her father, a noted swordsman, and from her lover (Rogers, 1928, pp. 177–206; see also Cohen, 2002, pp. 79–82; Svinth, 2003, p. 7); the Duchess of Queensbury, who sent her servent Soubise to Henry Angelo's fencing academy to be trained so that he could train her, and where on at least one occasion in 1773 they fenced together, an event memorialised in a watercolour by William Austin (1773); and a Madame Collie of Rome, whose fencing prowess, also displayed on one occasion in Angelo's London academy, was depicted in another of Thomas Rowlandson's (1816) watercolours.

Today the sport of fencing is open to all, with women competing at all levels, and the record suggests that the left-handed advantage applies to them as well. In Azémar et al.'s (1983) survey of participants in the foil competition for the 1981 World Fencing Championship, left-handers were nearly as common among women as among men (32.3% vs 35%), with the percentage of left-handed women rising among those advancing in the competition by margins comparable to those for men. In Azémar's (2003) more comprehensive survey for Olympics competition for the years 1979–1998, left-handed women outperformed right-handers in all three events—foil, épée, and sabre—with the percentage of left-handers again rising among those advancing in the competition and again by margins comparable to the men, and also, like the men, more clearly for foil and épée than for sabre.

Because left-handed women are only marginally less common than left-handed men (approximately 10% vs 12%; Gilbert & Wysocki, 1992; Peters et al., 2006), their advantage should be comparable to left-handed men's based on the frequency-dependency effect alone. However, some studies also suggest sex by handedness interactions on certain tests of attention and motor control, although the interactions are inconsistent in size and direction, evidently depending on the task. For example, in one study of motor control in left-handers, women's left-hand speed was greater than men's on a peg-moving task, but their right-hand speeds were comparable (Tan, 1993); in another study, this time of visual reaction times in handball players, left-handers and men were faster overall, but the sex difference appeared only in right-handers, and the results depended on the combination of hand–eye dominance (Dane & Erzurumluoglu, 2003). As already noted, it remains to be seen whether performance on tasks like these can be related directly to performance in fencing, so until that can be shown I am not sure that these data can be used to predict handedness differences, much less handedness by sex interactions, in fencing prowess. We should also keep in mind that, collectively, studies comparing men and women on laterality tests indicate only weak population-level differences (e.g., Hiscock, Israelian, Inch, Jacek, & Hiscock-Kalil, 1995; Voyer, 1996). If similar studies were to be collected and assessed for sex by handedness effects, the differences will perhaps be larger, especially if the nature of the lateralised task were taken into account (see Boles, 2005). Even so, Azémar's (2003) survey of the rate of left-handedness in male and female fencers suggests that, like the handedness effect itself, any sex by handedness interactions would be outweighed by the frequency-dependency effect.

IN CONCLUSION

In conclusion, the evidence looks strong for the old view that left-handers' advantage in fencing comes from "Nurture"; that is, from their greater opportunities for the right kind of practice by virtue of their lower numbers in the population. At the same time, there are signs that at least some left-handers might have certain natural advantages. If they do, it would mean that those persons who, by L'Abbat's (1734) account, imagined that a "Left-handed Man" had an advantage "by Nature" were not completely off the mark. The lesson should be a familiar one for laterality researchers and all other neurobehavioural scientists: To understand individual differences in fencing as in virtually all other talents and skills, the reasons must be sought in that ever-complicated mix of Nature *and* Nurture, acting together as always. And, as always, the devil is in the details.

ACKNOWLEDGEMENTS

I have already expressed my indebtedness to Professor Charles Schmitter for his gift of books and manuals consulted for this article. He died before I could thank him in person, so I want to dedicate this article to his memory. I am also grateful to the other collectors who have made their copies of fencing manuals available on the Internet. Thanks go to Jeanine Fiore, Kristine Baclawski, Peter Berg, and other staff members of the Special Collections Division of the Michigan State University Library for their assistance; to my colleagues at Michigan State, Alessandra Passarotti (Department of Psychology), now at the University of Notre Dame, and Anne Meyering (Department of History), for help with Italian and French translation, respectively; to William Lee Martin (Department of Psychology, Universidade Federal da Paraíba, Joao Pessoa, Brasil), for bringing the story of Herger, the ambidextrous Norse swordsman, to my attention; and to Chris McManus and an anonymous reviewer for their comments and suggestions about the manuscript. My only regret is not starting this project while Charles Schmitter was still alive because, apart from the general advice he would generously have offered, he was a *left-handed* fencer whose sinistral experiences and reflections I would have been eager to hear about, from both the perspective of the student he had been and the *Maestro di Scherma* that he became. Luckily, Alessandra Passarotti, a fencer in her student days at the University of Padova, is left-handed (what are the odds!) and gave helpful accounts of her own experiences. With all this good advice, I should have got the story right. If I have failed in any ways, large or small, the fault is mine.

REFERENCES

A history of fencing. (2006). Retrieved 12 May 2006 from: http://library.thinkquest.org/15340/historyessay.html

Aggleton, J. P., Kentridge, R. W., & Neave, N. J. (1993). Evidence for longevity differences between left handed and right handed men: An archival study of cricketers. *Journal of Epidemiology and Community Health*, *47*, 206–209.

Aggleton, J. P., & Wood, C. J. (1990). Is there a left-handed advantage in 'ballistic' sports? *International Journal of Sport Psychology, 21*, 46–47.

Albert, B. (1989). Yanomami "violence": Inclusive fitness or ethnographer's representation? *Current Anthropology, 30*, 637–640.

Albert, B. (1990). On Yanomami warfare: Rejoinder. *Current Anthropology, 31*, 558–563.

Angelo, D. (1763). *L'école des armes, avec l'explication générale des principales attitudes et positions concernant l'éscrime.* London: R. & J. Dodsley, Pall-Mall. [2nd ed. In French and English, 1765.]

Annett, M., & Manning, M. (1989). The disadvantages of dexterity for intelligence. *British Journal of Psychology, 80*, 213–226.

Annett, M. A. (1985). *Left, right, hand and brain: The right shift theory.* Hove, UK: Lawrence Erlbaum Associates Ltd.

Austin, W. (1773). *Soubise and the Duchess of Queensbury.* Retrieved 9 July 2007 from http://www.martinez-destreza.com/prints/

Ayala, F. J., & Campbell, C. A. (1974). Frequency-dependent selection. *Annual Review of Ecology and Systematics, 5*, 115–138.

Aylward, R. D. (1950). Saviolo's ghost. *Notes and Queries, 195*, 226–229.

Aylward, R. D. (1956). *The English master of arms from the twelfth to the twentieth century.* London: Routledge & Kegan Paul.

Azémar, G. (2003). *L'homme asymmétrique: gauchers et droitiers face à face.* Paris: CNRS éditions.

Azémar, G., Ripoll, H., Simonet, P., & Stein, J-F. (1983). Etude neuropsychologique du comportement des gauchers en escrime. *Cinesiologie, 22*, 7–18.

Azémar, G., & Stein, J-F. (1994). *Surrepreséntation des gauchers, en fonction de l'arme, dans l'élite mondiale de l'escrime.* Paper presented at the Congrès International de la Société Française du Sport, Poitiers, September.

Bart, B. F. (1967). *Flaubert.* Syracuse, NY: Syracuse University Press.

Basso, O., Olsen, J., Holm, N. V., Skytthe, A., Vaupel, J. W., & Christensen, K. (2000). Handedness and mortality: A follow-up study of Danish twins born between 1900 and 1910. *Epidemiology, 11*, 576–580.

Bisiacchi, P. S., Ripoll, H., Stein, J. F., Simonet, P., & Azémar, G. (1985). Left-handedness in fencers: An attentional advantage? *Perceptual and Motor Skills, 61*, 507–513.

Blackwell, E. (1734). *A compleat system of fencing: or, The art of defence, in the use of the small-sword.* Williamsburg, VA: William Parks.

Blasco, F. (1844). *La scienza della scherma.* Catania, Italy: [No publisher given.]

Boles, D. B. (2005). A large-sample study of sex differences in functional cerebral lateralization. *Journal of Clinical and Experimental Neuropsychology, 27*, 759–768.

Boulinguez, P., Velay, J-L., & Nougier, V. (2001). Manual asymmetries in reaching movement control. II. Study of left-handers. *Cortex, 37*, 123–138.

Briglia, D.M. (1952). *Left-handed batting against left-handed pitching.* MS Thesis, Ohio University, Athens, OH, USA.

Broca, P. (1865). Sur le siège de la faculté du langage articulé. *Bulletins de la Société d'Anthropologie de Paris, 6*, 377–393.

Brooks, R., Bussière, L. F., Jennions, M. D., & Hunt, J. (2004). Sinister strategies succeed at the cricket World Cup. *Proceedings of the Royal Society London, 271*(Suppl. 3), S64–S66.

Brown, F. (2006). *Flaubert: A biography.* New York: Little, Brown & Co.

Bulwer, J. (1644/1974). *Chirologia: or the natural language of the hand, and Chironomia: or the art of manuall rhetoricke.* London: Tho. Harper. [Reprinted, with commentary and notes by J. W. Cleary, 1974, Carbondale & Edwardsville, IL: Southern Illinois University Press.]

Burton, R. (1911). *The sentiment of the sword: A country-house dialogue (Part VII).* London: Horace Cox. [Reprinted from *Journal of Non-Lethal Combat*, March 2000. Retrieved 11 November 2006 from http://jnc/jncart_burtonsentimentsword07_0300.htm

Carlyle, T. (1871). Cited in J. A. Froude, 1898, *Thomas Carlyle: A history of his life in London*. New York: Scribner.

Cassius Dio Cocceianus (1914–1927). *Dio's Roman History, with an English translation by Ernest Cary, on the basis of the version of Herbert Baldwin Foster. In nine volumes.* London: W. Heinemann; New York: The Macmillan Co.

Castle, E. (1885). *Schools and masters of fence, from the middle ages to the eighteenth century.* London: G. Bell & Sons.

Chagnon, N. A. (1990). On Yanomamö violence: Reply to Albert. *Current Anthropology, 31*, 49–53.

Cherbuin, N., & Brinkman, C. (2006). Hemispheric interactions are different in left-handed individuals. *Neuropsychology, 20*(6), 700–707.

Clement (1587/1966). *The petie schole with an English orthographie.* [Facsimile reproduction with an introduction by R. D. Pepper. Gainesville, FL: Scholars' Facsimiles & Reprints, 1966.]

Cohen, R. (2002). *By the sword: A history of gladiators, musketeers, samurai, swashbucklers, and Olympic champions.* New York: Random House.

Cordelois [no first name] (1862). *Leçons d'armes. Du duel et de l'assaut. Edition illustrée.* Paris: Chez l'auteur.

Coren, S., & Halpern, D.F. (1991). Left-handedness: A marker for decreased survival fitness. *Psychological Bulletin, 109*, 90–106.

Crichton, M. (1977). *Eaters of the dead (the manuscript of Ibn Fadlan, relating his experiences with the Northmen in A.D. 922)*. New York: Bantam Books.

Crosnier, R. (1955). *Fencing with the foil; instruction and technique.* New York: A. S. Barnes & Co.

Crosnier, R. (1958). *Fencing with the épée.* New York: A. S. Barnes & Co.

Crosnier, R. (1965). *Fencing with the sabre; instruction and technique.* London: Faber & Faber Ltd.

Czajkowski, Z. (2005). *Domenico Angelo – great fencing master of the XVIII century, champion of fencing as a sport.* Retrieved 15 May 2006 from http://www.fencing.ca/coaching/domenico_angelo_cza_eng.pdf

Dane, S., & Erzurumluoglu, A. (2003). Sex and handedness differences in eye–hand visual reaction times in handball players. *International Journal of Neuroscience, 113*(7), 923–929.

Danet, G. (1766). *L'art des armes, ou la maniere la plus certaine de se servir utilement de l'épée, ...* Paris: Chez Herissant, Fils, Libraire, rue S. Jacques.

Deladrier, C. (1948). *Modern fencing*. Annapolis, MD: United States Naval Institute.

Delaunay, C-G. (1874). *Biologie comparée du coté droit et du coté gauche chez l'homme et chez les êtres vivants.* Paris: N. Blanpain.

Dietl, G.P., & Hendricks, J. R. (2005). Crab scars reveal survival advantage of left-handed snails. *Biology Letters, 2*(3), 439–442.

Dinakar, S. (2007). Left could just be right. Retrieved 12 March 2007 from *The Hindu*: online edition of India's national newspaper: http://www.hindu.com/2007/03/11/stories/2007031102101900.htm

Doré, G. (2006). *Monument to Alexandre Dumas (1880–1883), Place Malesherbes, Paris.* Retrieved 24 December 2006 from http://www.artandarchitecture.org.uk/images/conway/e58bf710.html?ixsid=pn6Aja0QeXV

Dumas, A. (2006). *The three musketeers.* Translated with an introduction by Richard Pevear. New York: Viking. [Original title, *Les trois mousquetaires*, first published 1844.]

Editorial (1871). The handedness of Kerrs. *Journal of the Royal College of General Practitioners, 21*, 693–694.

Edwards, S., & Eaton, A. B. (1996). Howzat? Where is there an over-representation of left-handed bowlers in professional cricket in the UK? *Laterality, 1*, 45–50.

Erikson, P. (2005). Yanomamö handedness, homicide and alleged frequency-dependent selection. *Journal of the Royal Anthropological Institute (N.S., 11*, 837–840.

Faurie, C., & Raymond, M. (2005). Handedness, homicide and negative frequency-dependent selection. *Proceedings of the Royal Society, London B, 272*, 25–28.

Faurie, C., Schiefenhövel, W., Le Bomin, S., Billiard, S., & Raymond, M. (2005). Variation in the frequency of left-handedness in traditional societies. *Current Anthropology, 46*, 142–147.

Fencing. (2006). Retrieved 21 May 2006 from *Wikipedia, the free encyclopedia*. http://en.wikipedia.org/wiki/Fencing

Fencing masters. (2006). Retrieved 9 July 2007 from http://www2.nau.edu/~wew/fencing/masters.html

Ferguson, R. B. (2001). Materialist, cultural and biological theories on why Yanomami make war. *Anthropological Theory, 1*, 99–116.

Fiore, J. (1983). En garde: Coach Schmitter's grand gift. *The University Library (Newsletter of the Michigan State University Libraries), 15*, 1–2.

Flaubert, G. (1954/1913). *A dictionary of platitudes. Being a compendium of conversational cliches, blind beliefs, fashionable misconceptions, and fixed ideas.* [Translation with preface and notes by Edward J. Fluck of *Le dictionnaire des idées reçues.*] Emmaus, Pennsylvania, & London. Classic Firsts (first French publication, 1913, Paris: L.Conard).

Flaubert, G. (1994/1913). *The dictionary of received ideas.* [Translation by Geoffrey Wall of *Le dictionnaire des idées reçues*; preface by Julian Barnes.] London: Syrens; New York: Penguin Books (first French publication, 1913; edited by E. L. Ferrère, Paris: L.Conard).

Flor-Henry, P. (1990). Sinistrality and psychopathology. In S. Coren (Ed.), *Left-handedness: Behavioral implications and anomalies* (pp. 415–440). Amsterdam, The Netherlands: Elsevier Science Publishers B.V.

Florio, J. (1591). *Second frutes. to be gathered of twelve trees, of divers but delightful tastes to the tongues of Italians and Englishmen. To which is annexed his gardine of recreation yeelding six thousand Italian proverbs.* London: printed for Thomas Woodcock. [Facsimile reproduction, with an introduction by R. C. Simonini Jr. Gainesville, FL: Scholars' Facsimiles & Reprints, 1953.]

Fraser, G. M. (1971). *The Steel Bonnets: The story of the Anglo-Scottish border reivers.* London: Barrie & Jenkins Ltd.

Galton, F. (1874). *English men of science: Their nature and nurture.* London: Macmillan & Co.

Gaugler, W. M. (1998). *The history of fencing. Foundations of modern European swordplay. Foreword by Malcolm Fare.* Bangor, ME: Laureate Press.

Geffen, G., Rosa, V., & Luciano, M. (2000). Effects of preferred hand and sex on the perception of tactile simultaneity. *Journal of Clinical and Experimental Neuropsychology, 22*, 219–231.

Geschwind, N., & Galaburda, A. M. (1987). *Cerebral lateralization: biological mechanism, associations, and pathology.* Cambridge, MA: MIT Press.

Gilbert, A. N., & Wysocki, C. J. (1992). Hand preference and age in the United States. *Neuropsychologia, 30*, 601–608.

Gitelman, D. R., Nobre, A. C., Parrish, T. B., LaBar, K. S., Kim, Y-H., Meyer, J. R., et al. (1999). A large-scale distributed network for covert spatial attention: Further anatomical delineation based on stringent behavioural and cognitive controls. *Brain, 122*, 1093–1106.

Godfrey, J. (1747). *A treatise upon the useful science of defence, connecting the small and back-sword, and shewing the affinity between them.* London: T. Gardner.

Goldstein, S. R., & Young, C. A. (1996). Evolutionary" stable strategy of handedness in major league baseball. *Journal of Comparative Psychology, 110*, 164–169.

Gomard [A. J. J. Possellier]. (1845). *La théorie de l'escrime enseignée par une méthode simple basée sur l'observation de la nature. ...* Paris: Librarie Militaire de J. Dumaine.

Gorynia, I., & Egenter, D. (2000). Intermanual coordination in relation to handedness, familial sinistrality and lateral preferences. *Cortex, 36*, 1–18.

Grisier, A. E. (1847). *Les armes et le duel. Préface anecdotique by Alexandre Dumas.* Paris: Chez Garniers Frères, Libraires.

Grondin, S., Guiard, Y., Ivry, R. B., & Koren, S. (1999). Manual laterality and hitting performance in major league baseball. *Journal of Experimental Psychology: Human Perception & Performance*, *25*, 747–754.

Grouios, G. (2004). Motoric dominance and sporting excellence: Training versus heredity. *Perceptual and Motor Skills*, *98*, 53–66.

Grouios, G., Tsorbatzoudis, H., Alexandris, K., & Barkoukis, V. (2000). Do left-handed competitors have an innate superiority in sports? *Perceptual and Motor Skills*, *90*, 1273–1282.

Guiard, Y. (1981). Sport: les avantages des gauches. *La Recherche*, *124*, 894–896.

Guiard, Y. (1982). Left-handedness and performance: A review and a prospect. *Current Psychology of Cognition*, *2*, 271–289.

Hand, S. (2003). The practical Saviolo – Part 5. *Journal of Western Martial Art*. Retrieved 4 June 2007 from http://64.233.167.104/search?q=cache:40Kp7ZA-81sJ:ejmas.com/jwma/articles/2003/jwma.

Harmenberg, J., & Ceci, R. (19 pages, undated). *Fencing: biomedical; and psychological factors.* Retrieved 14 December 2006 from http:/www.tacomafencing.com/Fencingbiomed.pdf

Harmenberg, J., Ceci, R., Barvestad, P., Hjerpe, K., & Nystrom, J. (1991). Comparison of different tests of fencing performance. *International Journal of Sports Medicine*, *12*, 573–576.

Harris, L. J. (1989). Hand preference in gestures and signs in the deaf and hearing: Some notes on early evidence and theory. *Brain and Cognition*, *10*, 189–219.

Harris, L. J. (1990). Cultural influences on handedness: Historical and contemporary theory and evidence. In S. Coren (Ed.), *Left-handedness: Behavioral implications and anomalies* (pp. 195–258). Amsterdam, The Netherlands: Elsevier Science Publishers B.V.

Harris, L. J. (1992). Left-handedness. In I. Rapin & S.J. Segalowitz (Eds.), *Handbook of neuropsychology, child neuropsychology, Vol. 6, Section 10, Part 1* (pp. 145–208) (Series eds: F. Boller & J. Grafman). Amsterdam: Elsevier Science Publishers B.V.

Harris, L. J. (1993a). Broca on cerebral control for speech in right-handers and left-handers: A note on translation and some further comments. *Brain and Language*, *45*, 108–120.

Harris, L. J. (1993b). Do right-handers live longer than left-handers? A commentary on Coren and Halpern's "Left-handedness: A marker for decreased longevity". *Psychological Bulletin*, *114*, 203–234; 242–247.

Harris, L. J. (2002). Lateral biases for holding infants: Early observations, opinions, and explanations, with some possible lessons for theory and research today. [Abstract of poster presented at 2001 meetings of TENNET, Montreal, Quebec.] *Brain and Cognition*, *48*, 392–394.

Harris, L. J. (2003). What to do about your child's handedness? Advice from five eighteenth-century authors, and some questions for today. *Laterality*, *8*, 99–120.

Hécaen, H. (1984). *Les gauchers: Étude neuropsychologique.* Paris: Presses Universitaires de France.

Heilman, K. M., & Van Den Abell, T. (1980). Right hemisphere dominance for attention: The mechanism underlying hemispheric asymmetries of inattention (neglect). *Neurology*, *30*, 327–330.

Hellige, J. B., Bloch, M. I., Cowin, E. L., Eng, T. L., Eviatar, Z., & Sergent, V. (1994). Individual variation in hemispheric asymmetry: Multitask study of effects related to handedness and sex. *Journal of Experimental Psychology: General*, *123*, 235–256.

Hiscock, M., Israelian, M., Inch, R., Jacek, C., & Hiscock-Kalil, C. (1995). Is there a sex difference in human laterality? II. An exhaustive survey of visual laterality studies from six neuropsychology journals. *Journal of Clinical and Experimental Neuropsychology*, *17*(4), 590–610.

Holmer, J. O. (1994). Draw, if you be men": Saviolo's significance for Romeo and Juliet. *Shakespeare Quarterly*, *45*(2), 163–189.

Holtzen, D. W. (2000). Handedness and professional tennis. *International Journal of Neuroscience*, *105*, 101–119.

Hope, W. (1692). The compleat fencing-master; in which is fully described the whole guards, parades and lessons, belonging to the small sword ... (2nd ed.). London: Printed for D. Newman.

Hope, W. (1707). A new, short, and easy method of fencing: or the art of the broad and small sword rectified and compendiz'd. Edinburgh: James Watson. [Reprinted in M. Rector (Ed.). (2001). *Highland swordsmanship: Techniques of the Scottish swordmasters* (pp. 89–195). Union City, CA: Chivalry Bookshelf.]

Hyrtl, J. (1860). *Handbuch der topographischen Anatomie* (4th ed.). Vienna: Braumueller.

Jackson, J. L. (1990). "They catch one another's rapiers": The exchange of weapons in "Hamlet". *Shakespeare Quarterly, 41*(3), 281–298.

James, B. (1988). *The Bill James historical baseball abstract.* New York: Villard Books.

Jobert, L. (1885). *Les gauchers compares aux droitiers aux points de vue anthropologique et médico-legal.* Lyon, France (Pamphlet No. 5076, National Library of Medicine, Medical History Department).

Keele, G. (1974). The handedness of Kerrs. Letter to the editor. *Journal of the Royal College of General Practitioners, 24*, 712.

Kerr, A. (2007). *Ferniehurst Castle: Scotland's frontier stronghold.* Retrieved 4 March 2007 from: http://www.electricscotland.com/history/ferniehurst

Ketlinski, R., & Pickens, L. (1973). Characteristics of male fencers in the 28th Annual NCAA fencing championships. *Research Quarterly, 44*, 434–439.

Kilshaw, D., & Annett, M. (1983). Right- and left-hand skill 1: Effects of age, sex, and hand preference showing superior skill in left-handers. *British Journal of Psychology, 74*, 253–268.

Kumar, S., & Mandal, M. K. (2005). Bilateral transfer of skill in left- and right-handers. *Laterality, 10*, 337–344.

L'Abbat, Monsieur (1734). *The art of fencing, or, the use of the small sword. Trans. from the French by Andrew Mahon.* Dublin: James Hoey, Printer.

La, Boëssière (1818). *Traité de l'art des armes: à l'usage des professeurs et des amateurs.* Paris: De limprimiere de Didot, laîné.

Laeng, B., & Park, A. (1999). Handedness effects on playing a reversed or normal keyboard. *Laterality, 4*(4), 363–377.

Lehman, H. C., & Webb, F. E. (1951). Left-handedness among major league baseball players. *Motor Skills Research Exchange, 3*, 5–10.

Locke, J. (1693). *Some thoughts concerning education.* [Edited with introduction, notes, and critical apparatus by John and Jean S. Yolton. Oxford, UK: Clarendon Press, 1989.]

Malgaigne, J-F. (1859). *Traité d'anatomie chirurgicale et de chirurgie expérimentale* (2nd ed. Two vols.). Paris: J-B. Ballière et Fils.

Manley, A. (1979). *Complete fencing.* Garden City, NY: Doubleday & Co.

Mangiarotti, E. (2006a). Edoardo Mangiarotti. Retrieved 12 May 2006 from *Wikipedia, the Free Encyclopedia* http://en.wikipedia.org/wiki,Edoardo_Mangiarotti

Mangiarotti, E. (2006b). Edoardo Mangiarotti – Fencer extraordinaire. Retrieved 12 May 2006 from: *SifySports. Olympics 2004.* http://sify.com/sports/olympics/fullstory.php

Mathewson, T. (1805). *Fencing familiarized; or, A new treatise on the art of the Scotch broad sword: shewing the superiority of that weapon, when opposed to an enemy, armed with a spear, pike, or gun and bayonet.* London: printed by W. Cowdroy.

McLean, J. M., & Ciurczak, F. M. (1982). Bimanual dexterity in major league baseball players: A statistical study. *The New England Journal of Medicine, 307*, 1278–1279.

McManus, C. (2002). *Right hand, left hand. The origins of asymmetry in brains, bodies, atoms and cultures.* Cambridge, MA: Harvard University Press.

McManus, C. (2006). The modern mythology of the left-handedness of Alexander the Great. *Laterality, 11*, 566–572.

Mesulam, M-M. (1999). Spatial attention and neglect: Parietal, frontal and cingulate contributions to the mental representation and attentional targeting of salient extrapersonal events. *Philosophical Transactions of the Royal Society B/Biological Sciences, 354*(4), 1325–1346.
Morris, P. (2006). *A game of inches: The stories behind the innovations that shaped baseball. The game on the field.* Chicago: Ivan R. Dee.
Morsberger, R.E. (1974). Swordplay and the Elizabethan and Jacobean stage. *Jacobean Drama Series, 37* (Salzburg, Austria), 18–57.
Morton, B. E., & Rafto, S. E. (2006). Corpus callosum size is linked to dichotic deafness and hemisphericity, not sex or handedness. *Brain and Cognition, 62*, 1–8.
Moutier, F. (1908). *L'aphasie de Broca*. Paris: G. Steinheil.
Mulcaster, R. (1581). *Positions concerning the training up of children* [*original title, Positions wherein those primitive circumstances be examined, which are necessarie for the training up of children, either for skill in their booke, or health in their bodie*]. London: Thomas Vautrollier for Thomas Chare. [Edited by William Barker, with new introduction and some modernisations of spelling. Toronto, Canada: University of Toronto Press, 1994.]
Nadi, A. (1943). *On fencing*. New York: G. P. Putnam's Sons.
Nalçaci, E., Kalaycioglu, C., Çiçek, M., & Genç, Y. (2001). The relationship between handedness and fine motor performance. *Cortex, 37*, 493–500.
Neft, D. S., & Cohen, R. M. (1988). *The sports encyclopedia: Baseball 8th ed.* New York: St. Martin's Press.
Nye, R. A. (1990). Fencing, the duel and Republican manhood in the Third Republic. *Journal of Contemporary History, 25*(2/3), 365–377.
Olivier, J. (1771). *Fencing familiarized: or, A new treatise on the art of sword play.* London: Printed for John Bell, near Exeter Change in the Strand, and C. Etherington, at York.
Palladini, C. (undated, c. 1560). *Discorso sopra l'arte della scherma*. Publisher unnamed.
Peters, M. (1996). Hand preference and performance in left-handers. In D. Elliott & R. Roy (Eds.), *Manual asymmetries in motor performance* (pp. 123–142). Boca Raton: FL: CRF Press.
Peters, M., Reimers, S., & Manning, J. T. (2006). Hand preference for writing and associations with selected demographic and behavioral variables in 255,100 subjects: The BBC internet study. *Brain and Cognition, 62*, 177–189.
Peters, M., & Servos, P. (1989). Performance of subgroups of left-handers and right-handers. *Canadian Journal of Psychology, 43*, 341–358.
Plutarch (1962). *The lives of the noble Grecians and Romans.* Translated by John Dryden; revised with an introduction by Arthur Hugh Clough. London: Dent; New York: Dutton.
Pollock, W. H., Grove, F. C., & Prevost, C. (1890). *Fencing*. London: Longmans, Green, and Co. [bound with *Boxing*, by E.B. Michell, and *Wrestling*, by W. Armstrong].
Porac, C., & Coren, S. (1981). *Lateral preferences and human behavior.* New York: Springer-Verlag.
Posner, M. I. (1980). Orienting of attention. *Quarterly Journal of Experimental Psychology, 32*, 3–25.
Posner, M. I., Snyder, C. R., & Davidson, B. J. (1980). Attention and the detection of signals. *Journal of Experimental Psychology: General, 109*, 160–174.
Potter, S. M., & Graves, R. E. (1989). Is interhemispheric transfer related to handedness and gender? *Neuropsychologia, 26*, 319–325.
Project Gutenberg Ebook. Retrieved 9 July 2007 from: http://www.gutenberg.org/catalog/
Pye-Smith, P. H. (1871). Left-handedness. *Guy's Hospital Reports (3rd Series), 16*, 141–146.
Raymond, M., & Pontier, D. (2004). Is there geographical variation in human handedness? *Laterality, 9*, 35–51.
Raymond, M., Pontier, D., Dufour, A-B., & Møller, A. P. (1996). Frequency-dependent maintenance of left handedness in humans. *Proceedings of the Royal Society, London B, 263*, 1627–1633.

Research Unit. (1974). The Handedness of Kerrs – a surname study. Family studies. *Journal of the Royal College of General Practitioners, 24*, 437–439.

Rizzo, B. (2002). Equivocations of gender and rank: Eighteenth-century sporting women. *Eighteenth-Century Life*, Winter, Number 1, 70–93 [with 32 figures for Rizzo and an accompanying article, pp. 95–118].

Rogers, C. (1928). *Gallant ladies* (with illustrations by Charles O. Naef). New York: Harcourt, Brace & company.

Roland, G. (1824). *A treatise on the theory and practice of the art of fencing*. London: William Sams, and Edinburgh: Archibald Constable & Co.

Roland, J. (1809). *The amateur of fencing, or a treatise, on the art of sword-defence theoretically and experimentally explained, upon new principles, designed chiefly for persons who have only acquired a superficial knowledge of the subject.* London: Printed by the author.

Rondelle, L. (1892). *Foil and sabre; a grammar of fencing in detailed lessons for professor and pupil.* Boston: Estes & Lauriat.

Rowlandson, T. (1787). Angelo's fencing academy. Retrieved 10 November 2006 from: *Georgian Index* (2006). http://www.georgianindex.net/Sport/Angelo/Henry_Angelo.html

Rowlandson, T. (1816). *Madame Collie of Rome fencing at Henry Angelo's London Academy.* Retrieved 9 July 2007 from: http://www.martinez-destreza.com/prints

Rules (2006). Retrieved 15 November 2006 from: http://www/abc.au/olympics/2000/FENCING/about/rules.htm

Savage, C. R., & Thomas, D. G. (1993). Information processing and interhemispheric transfer in left- and right-handed adults. *International Journal of Neuroscience, 71*, 201–219.

Saviolo, V. (1595). *Vincentio Saviolo his practice: In two bookes. The first entreating of the use of the rapier and dagger. The second, of honor and honorable quarrels.* London: John Wolfe. Retrieved 22 May 2006 from: http://www.cs.unc.edu/%7Ehudson/saviolo/firstbook.html1

Scevola, M. (2006). Retrieved 10 December 2006 from: *Wikipedia*. http://it.wikipedia.org/wiki/Muzio_Scevola

Scorza, R., & Grisetti, P. (1871). *La scienza della schermalespostia dai due amici Rosaroll Scorza e Pietro Grisetti e Pietro Grisetti.* Nocera Inferiore: Tippgrafoa Agrocola G. Orlando. [First published, 1803.]

Selzer, C. A. (1933). *Lateral dominance and visual fusion.* (Harvard Monographs in Education, No. 12: Studies in educational psychology and educational measurement.) Cambridge, MA: Harvard University Press.

Shakespeare, W. (undated). *The Tempest*. In *The works of William Shakespeare gathered into one volume* (pp. 1135–1159). New York: The Shakespeare Head Press Edition, Oxford University Press.

Shaughnessy, D. (1989). Baseball '89: The invaluable lefty. *The Boston Globe, March, 31, 52*, 55–56.

Shaw, D., & McManus, I. C. (1993). The handedness of Kerrs and Carrs. *British Journal of Psychology, 84*, 545–551.

Singer, R. N. (1968). Speed and accuracy of movement as related to fencing success. *Research Quarterly, 39*, 1080–1083.

Small, J. P. (2006). Was Alexander the Great left-handed? *Laterality, 11*, 562–563.

Starosta, W. (2004). Types and effects of motor adaptation [in] left-handed persons in daily life and in contemporary sport training. *The Sport Journal, 7*, No. 1. Retrieved 21 May 2006 from: http://www.thesportjournal.org/2004Journal/Vol7-No1/starosta.asp

Steenhuis, R. E., Østbye, T., & Walton, R. (2001). An examination of the hypothesis that left-handers die earlier: The Canadian Study of Health and Aging. *Laterality, 6*, 69–75.

Steinmetz, H., Jancke, L., Kleinschmidt, A., Schlaug, G., Volkmann, J., & Huang, Y. (1992). Sex but no hand difference in the isthmus of the corpus callosum. *Neurology, 42*, 749–752.

Streatham Fencing Club, London. (2005). Retrieved 18 June 2005 from: http://www.streathamfencing.org

Svinth, J. R. (2003). Women's martial arts: A chronological history, 479 BCE– 1896 CE. *Proceedings: Electronic Journals of Martial Arts and Sciences* (17 pages). Retrieved 13 November 2006 from: http://ejmas.com/proceedings/GSJSA03svinth.htm

Swetnam, J. (1617). *The schoole of the noble and worthy science of defence. (Part 2).* A facsimile copy transcribed by Steve Hick and scanned by Stuart Huntley, May 2000, from the original provided by Patri Pugliese. Retrieved 13 November 2006 from: http://www.stoccata.org/stoccata.nsf/

Tan, U. (1993). Speed and accuracy of aimed hand movements in left-handed human subjects: Sex-related differences in motor control. *International Journal of Neuroscience, 72*(3–4), 235–243.

Terrone, L. F. (1959). *Right and left hand fencing* (with a biographical preface by L. M. Fleisher). New York: Dodd, Mead, & Company.

Thornbury, G. W. (Ed.). (1856). *Shakespeare's England; or sketches of our social history in the reign of Elizabeth* (2 vols.). London: Londman, Brown, Green & Longmans.

Turner, C., & Soper, T. (1990). *Methods and practice of Elizabethan swordplay.* Carbondale and Edwardsville, IL: Southern Illinois University Press.

Uhrbrock, R. S. (1970). Laterality of champion athletes. *Journal of Motor Behavior, 2*, 285–291.

Valdin, Monsieur [Salomon Negri]. (1729). *The art of fencing, as practiced by Monsieur Valdin.* London: Printed for J. Parker in Pall-Mall.

van Biervliet, J. J. (1901). *Etudes de psychologie: L'homme droit et l'homme gauche.* [Publisher unnamed.]

Viggiani, A. (1575). *Lo schermo d'Angelo Viggiani.* Venice: Giorgo Angelieri, printer. [English translation byWilliam Jherek Swanger, 2002.] Retrieved 15 September 2006 from: http://www.drizzle.com/ ~ celyn/jherek/Schermo.Pdf

Voyer, D. (1996). On the magnitude of laterality effects and sex diferences in functional lateralities. *Laterality, 1*(1), 51–84.

Webster's new international dictionary of the English language (2nd ed.). Springfield, MA: G. & C. Merriam Company.

Westerhausen, R., Kreuder, F., Dos Santos Sequeira, S., Walter, C., Woerner, W., Wittling, R. A., et al. (2004). Effects of handedness and gender on macro- and microstructure of the corpus callosum and its subregions: A combined high-resolution and diffusion-tensor MRI study. *Cognitive Brain Research, 21*(3), 418–426.

Wilson, D. (1891). *The right hand: left-handedness.* London: Macmillan and Co.

Wilson, Sir Daniel. (2006). *Dictionary of Canadian biography online* (p. 3). Retrieved 16 May 2006 from: http://www.biographi.ca/EN/ShowBio.asp?Biold=90625

Witelson, S. F. (1985). The brain connection: The corpus callosum is larger in left-handers. *Science, 16*, 665–668.

Wood, C. J., & Aggleton, J. P. (1989). Handedness in 'fast ball' sports: Do left-handers have an innate advantage? *British Journal of Psychology, 80*, 227–240.

LATERALITY, 2010, 15 (1/2), 56–135

Side biases for holding and carrying infants: Reports from the past and possible lessons for today

Lauren Julius Harris

Michigan State University, East Lansing, MI, USA

Most adults hold human infants on the left side, with the infant's head to the left of their own body midline. The discovery of this bias is credited to Lee Salk, who first reported it in 1960, but the same was reported at least 300 years earlier and many times again through the early decades of the twentieth century. Along with the left-side reports, however, others named the right as the preferred side. Authors on each side explained the preference and foresaw consequences for the infant: different ones in each case. This article describes the two kinds of reports, asks whether and how they might be reconciled, and discusses their possible lessons for theory and research today.

Keywords: Infants; Cradling; Side of holding and carrying; Handedness; Laterality; History.

INTRODUCTION

Nearly half a century ago, the child psychologist Lee Salk (1960) reported seeing something curious during a visit to the Central Park Zoo in New York City. Watching a rhesus monkey (*Macaca mulatta*) with her newborn, he noticed "a marked tendency" to hold the infant on her left side (p. 169). It perhaps resembled the hold shown in Figure 1, except that this infant is older. Over the next few weeks, Salk counted 39 holds on the left, only 2 on the right, for a 95% bias overall.

Salk never mentioned whether other monkey mothers did the same (perhaps there were no others to observe), but it led him to wonder what *human* mothers would do. To find out, he made observations in the maternity

Address correspondence to: Lauren Julius Harris, Department of Psychology, Michigan State University, East Lansing, Michigan 48824, USA. E-mail: HARRISL@msu.edu

Accounts of parts of this article were presented at the 1997 meeting of TENNET, for the M. Philip Bryden Memorial Symposium "Laterality: Hands, feet, eyes, and ears", Montreal, Quebec; and at the 2001 meetings of TENNET, Montreal, and the Society for the Study of Human Development, Ann Arbor, Michigan.

DOI: 10.1080/13576500802584371

Figure 1. Rhesus monkey mother with infant (courtesy Harlow Primate Laboratory, University of Wisconsin-Madison).

ward of a local hospital. Holding the newborn from behind, he presented it for the mother to take and hold. Eighty-three percent (236 of 287) held on the left, either against the chest or over the shoulder. Figures 2A and 2B show Salk with one of the mothers (from Salk, 1973). Salk (1961, 1970) later found nearly the same bias (80%) in works of art, including Renaissance-era portraits of the Madonna and Child and sculptures by the twentieth-century artist Henry Moore.

These reports inspired many new studies, over 50 by my count through 2007, in a variety of settings including hospitals, laboratories, private homes, and public places ("field" studies), along with new studies of works of art.[1] They confirm Salk's results in showing the left bias in mothers as well as other women, usually by a roughly 2:1 margin (de Château, 1983; Harris, Spradlin, & Almerigi, 2007). They also find the bias whether the infant is held against the chest and shoulder, cradled in the arms, or seated on one arm with its back against the holder's body (Harris et al., 2007; Rheingold & Keene,

[1] The reports cited in this introduction are only examples. For further citations, along with more extensive accounts and assessments of the proposed explanations of the bias as presented below, several reviews are now available (Damerose & Vauclair, 2002; Donnot & Vauclair, 2005; Harris, 2007; Turnbull & Lucas, 2000).

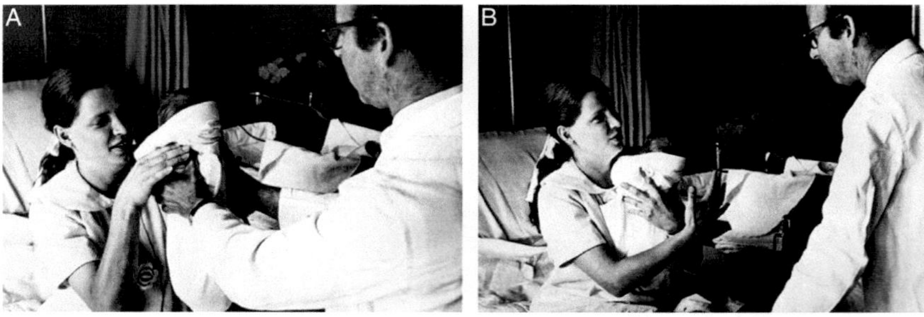

Figure 2. Lee Salk testing one of the mothers in his 1960 study (from Salk, 1973, p. 26; Courtesy, Globe Photos, Inc., New York). (A) Salk offering the infant to its mother. (B) After the mother has taken her infant.

1965); whether it is only being held or also being nursed (Trevathan, 1982); and whether the holder sits, stands, or walks about (de Château, 1983).

Three other details of the bias bear mention: it often peaks for holding newborns and young infants (Dagenbach, Harris, & Fitzgerald, 1988; Trevathan, 1982) and then declines and by 3 or 4 years reverses (Lockard, Daley, & Gunderson, 1979); it occurs when adults hold a doll (Saling & Tyson, 1981) or a ball that they are asked to pretend is an infant (Sperber & Weiland, 1973) and even when they imagine holding an infant in the absence of any physical object (Harris, Almerigi, & Kirsch, 2000); and however it is measured, it is often stronger and more reliable in women than in men (Manning, 1991).

The bias has been found in people around the world, from Europe and the Americas to Africa and Asia. The one known exception is the Malagasey, the indigenous people of Madagascar, the island nation off the southeast coast of Africa, where most adults, women and men alike, hold on the right (Nakamichi, 1996). There also is a report that among the Tanka, boat people living in the coastal waters and rivers of Southern China, women nurse from only the right breast (Ing, Ho, & Petrakis, 1977a). Nothing was said of how infants were held at other times, but if it was on the right, the Tanka would be a second exception.

The new reports include studies of other primate species and, for some at least, with similar results, although most samples are small and only females have been observed. So far, the left bias is strongest (near 75%) in chimpanzees and gorillas, and weaker or absent in orangutans, gibbons, and baboons (Manning & Chamberlain, 1990; Manning, Heaton, & Chamberlain, 1994; Nishida, 1993; but see Dienske, Hopkins, & Reid, 1995). As for monkeys, one study found the bias for carrying but not for cradling or retrieval (Tomaszycki, Cline, Griffin, Mastripieri, & Hopkins, 1998); another only when the mother was frightened and used her left hand to scoop up her infant (Hatta & Koike, 1991); and another in individuals but not in the population (Tanaka, 1989). In one of the chimpanzee studies, infants also preferred the left nipple for suckling, which the author suggested was from their being held on the left side (Nishida, 1993).

Finally, for humans the bias looks selective: robust for holding infants and their representations but weaker, absent, or reversed for books, packages, and other inanimate objects (Alley & Kolker, 1988; Almerigi, Carbary, & Harris, 2002). For other primates, no such evidence has been reported. As it does for humans, it would have to be shown that species that carry infants on the left carry other objects, such as food items, on the right. Alternatively, if they carry food items on the left, as reported in bonobos (Hopkins & de Waal, 1995), and they are selective, they would carry infants on the right, contrary to the usual direction.

Explanations of the Bias

The bias's modal direction is clear. Less clear is why it exists at all, why it is to the left, and what its benefits might be and for whom. According to Salk's own *heartbeat explanation*, the key factor has to do with what Salk called the "anatomy of emotion". Observing that when the newborn monkey was held on the left, it was "frequently" pressed against the mother's heart, he proposed that the heartbeat was responsible—that, being more detectible on the left side of the chest, it makes the left hold more soothing, for the infant directly, and for the mother by its reflection back from the infant. The *handedness explanation* supposes instead that because most people are right-handed, they hold on the left to keep their right, or dominant, hand free for acts of care, feeding being a prime example. The *infant-posture explanation* credits the bias to the holder's accommodating to the infant's usual tendency to turn right while lying supine, therefore away from the holder when held over the shoulder, facilitating exploration of its environment, and towards the holder when cradled, facilitating nursing and social exchange. The *attention* or *emotional monitoring explanation* supposes that it reflects the state of "action–approach" in which most people respond to infants. Because its associated pattern of cortical arousal is hypothesised to be higher left-anterior, right-posterior, the left hold is to the side to which the holder's attention is directed. That lets them better monitor the infant's needs, and lets the infant better see the normally more expressive left side of the holder's face. These four explanations all focus on the infant's needs and imply that the left hold is more nurturing, the right more utilitarian. The *holder-posture explanation* focuses instead on the holder and supposes that the left hold is favoured, at least for the standing position, because it is compatible with the direction to which most people shift their weight to find a comfortable position.

Most of these explanations also seek to account for the left bias decline with age. As one example, by what we might call the *strength* version of the handedness explanation, as infants grow older, bigger, and heavier, and holding comes to be less for feeding and social exchange and more for transport, the bias declines as the normally stronger right arm takes over, especially for carrying for long durations and distances. As another example, by the heartbeat explanation, it declines as infants come to need less soothing and help with arousal control. As for the bias's selectivity, by the attention-emotional monitoring and handedness explanations, books and packages neither elicit emotional responses of the kind associated with infants nor require the kind of care provided by the dominant hand.

So far, the explanations have accounted for the bias only in part or under certain conditions. For example, when adults are asked to give a bottle to a doll, the majority use the dominant hand and hold the doll on the non-dominant side—right-handers on the left, left-handers on the right (Van der Meer & Husby, 2006)—but otherwise left-handers are nearly as likely as right-handers to hold on the left (Salk, 1960). For other primates, the handedness explanation also assumes what is still in dispute—that they show handedness at the population level (Lonsdorf & Hopkins, 2005; McGrew & Marchant, 1997; Schmitt, Melchisedech, Hammerschmidt, & Fischer, 2008). Direction of attention likewise accounts for only part of the effect, depending, among other things, on the sex of the holder and type of hold (Bourne & Todd, 2004; Donnot & Vauclair, 2007; Harris, Almerigi, Carbary, & Fogel, 2001). As for the heartbeat explanation, if the left hold is more soothing, direct evidence is lacking. The right-holding Malagasey, along with the Tanka if they qualify, also remain to be explained.

In sum, probably no one explanation (there are still others) will suffice, and many factors are involved. But whatever accounts for the bias, it is noteworthy that the 2:1 ratio of left to right holds matches the ratio found, as Previc (1991) observed, in "most 'natural' forms of auditory and motoric lateralisation" (p. 299), which may be another sign that the bias is a natural phenomenon. Collectively, the explanations also illustrate a main theme of Vallortigara and Rogers' (2005) essay on the advantages and disadvantages of cerebral lateralisation—how "a dynamic relationship might be established between lateralised behaviors in interacting asymmetric organisms" (p. 578).

A Bias Rediscovered

The emergence of this field of laterality research owes much to Lee Salk. His work spurred new studies of the bias, and he is widely credited with its discovery. In the sciences, however, assigning priority is difficult because most discoveries come in what the sociologist Robert Merton (1957, 1961) called "multiples"—discoveries or hypotheses conceived by two or more individuals independently and often in different places and times. The discovery of the left bias for holding infants is no exception. The same was reported at least 300 years before Salk and many times again through the early decades of the twentieth century, so it would be more accurate to credit Salk with its *rediscovery*. Like current reports, the early reports come from different countries—nine by my latest count—with all but one from the West, including Canada, the United States, and countries in Western Europe. The difference is that where investigators today agree that the modal bias is to the left, with reversals, at least for women, being rare exceptions, many early reports also named the right side as preferred. Not only, then, has the left bias been rediscovered, so has its reversal, which prompts the question whether other exceptions will be found. Most authors on both sides—I shall call them *right-siders* and *left-siders*—also sought to explain why "their side" was preferred, and most foresaw consequences for the infant, some they thought beneficial, others not.

Overview of Current Article

In the 1980s and early 1990s, when many of the new studies were under way, I mentioned a few of the early reports in essays on laterality (e.g., Harris, 1991). Now, with research more developed, it may be time for a more comprehensive look. So far I have found 13 early right-side and 18 left-side reports (or 12 and 16, depending on how three reports are interpreted, as we shall see). All are of interest for their explanations of the bias, or rather *biases*, with some identical or similar to current explanations, others not; for their accounts of child-rearing practices pertaining to laterality; and for their possible lessons for theory and research today. In seeking to reconcile the early right- and left-side reports, I also hope that light might be shed not only on the phenomenon generally but on the exceptions today in particular. To help track the two kinds of reports, I have listed them in separate tables.[2]

GENERAL COMMENTS ON EARLY REPORTS AND THEIR OTHER DIFFERENCES FROM CURRENT REPORTS

Before going further, some general comments about the reports and certain other differences from current studies are in order.

[2] The tables show a total of 31 reports, but they come from only 30 different published accounts because one author, who reported right as well as left biases in different groups, appears in both tables.

Lines of work and level of detail

To begin with, whereas most current authors are psychologists, most of their predecessors followed other lines of work: medicine, surgery, physiology, philosophy, religion, anthropology, archaeology, art education, Greek and Roman history, physical education, home economics, literature and *belles lettres*, and even the military and the teaching of fencing and duelling. There are further differences in the reports' level of detail. Current reports describe the settings, methods of observation, sample sizes, and ages (or approximate ages) of the infants; most early reports lacked such details, some doing little more than attesting to the bias rather than reporting it in the usual sense. Many, however, did offer clues about settings and infants' ages, as I shall explain later. Current reports also cite and build on prior evidence and identify the preferred holding-side directly, whereas most early reports stood alone, with some identifying the preferred side indirectly by naming only the non-preferred side or by their account of consequences foreseen for the infant.

The debate on the origins of handedness

Reasons for interest in the bias also differ. Many researchers today see it as a window into the origins and development of the mother–infant relationship and, having concluded that it depends on the holder's handedness only under special conditions, relate it to other lateralised perceptual and motor functions. Most of their predecessors took the handedness explanation for granted and were interested in the bias for another reason, but still pertaining to handedness. In their time, as in ours, there was lively debate about the origins of handedness, why it takes two forms, right-handedness and left-handedness, and why the former is far more common. Some thought it had to do with the side on which people were held as infants. They therefore saw handedness not only as the cause of the bias but also as its effect.

To show more clearly how these ideas about holding side were rooted in the handedness debate, it will help to identify that debate's main features and players. Like most debates about the origins of behaviour, the question was about the roles of "Nature and Nurture", in Galton's famous phrase (1874, p. 12).

Blood and balance: The role of nature

Blood. Starting with Aristotle (384–322 B.C.E.) if not before, naturists, or nativists, called handedness a natural, useful state, with many supposing that it was caused by an asymmetry in blood supply. For Aristotle, the heart's three "cavities" were the key: the right-most, being largest and highest, concocted the hottest, most abundant blood, so that all motion began on the right, giving the right hand the lead (*De Animalium Incessu*, 1912a, 705–706a,b; *De Partibus Animalium*, 1912b, 666–667a,b).[3] By the early 1800s, the focus turned to the arteries—first to the subclavian, with the right, reputedly because it was larger, assumed to send more blood to the right arm (e.g., Anon., 1810; Magendie, 1827), and then to the internal carotid, after Paul Broca (1865) named the cerebral hemisphere opposite the dominant hand as the controlling organ, with the left carotid, because it was closer to the aorta, assumed to send more blood to the left hemisphere (e.g., Ogle, 1871). By whatever means, the modal result would be right-handedness, and left-handedness when the asymmetry was reversed.

Not all blood supply explanations linked the difference in supply to asymmetries in the heart or arteries. In 1828, a French physician, Joseph Comte, related it to the infant's intrauterine position in the last trimester, which he estimated from the infant's birth presentation position. After observing hundreds of deliveries at the Maternité de Paris, Comte inferred that the most common intrauterine position was what he called the "*première position du sommet*" or "first position of the crown of the head", where the infant's left arm is wedged against the mother's back and spine, its right arm against her abdomen, as shown in Figure 3A. Reasoning that this position compressed the left side, reducing its blood supply and weakening its development (Comte did not name the artery affected, but his emphasis on arm position suggests that he had the subclavian in mind), Comte predicted right-handedness as the outcome, and left-handedness for the less common "*deuxième position*," as shown in Figure 3B.

Balance. For blood supply theorists it was all about physiology. For Andrew Buchanan (1862a), a University of Glasgow physician, it was mechanics and balance. Noting that the liver and lungs were larger and heavier on the right, he argued that the body centre of gravity shifted right and that balance was restored by leaning left. That put more weight on the left leg, leaving the right arm and leg "freer for action" (p. 152) and facilitating right-handedness (and right-leggedness). Again a reversal, now through visceral transposition, supposedly led to left-handedness.

"Maimed by the folly of nurses and mothers": The role of nurture

Whatever their disagreements about means, nativists agreed that handedness was inborn, with education and child-rearing only secondary.

[3] The cavities refer to the chambers of the heart, but their identity is uncertain. According to Lloyd (1973, p. 184, fn. 32), the possibility that best fits Aristotle's account is that offered by D'Arcy Thompson who, in his translation of *Historia Animalium* (Aristotle, 1910), supposed that the right-most, largest chamber referred to the right auricle and ventricle combined, which would account for the other chambers being "far smaller."

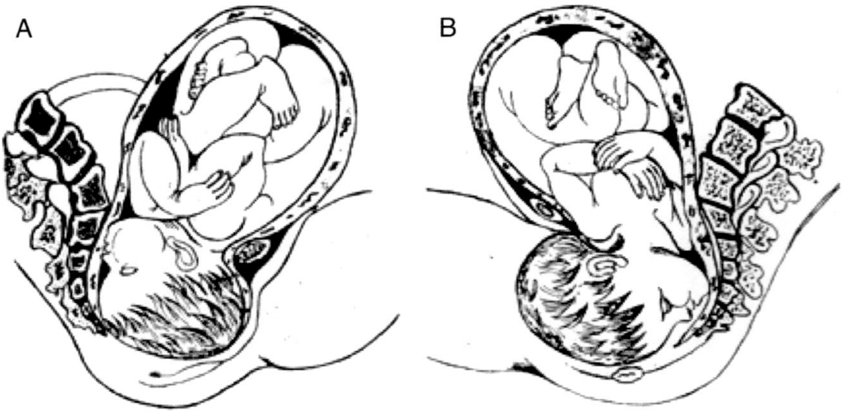

Figure 3. Birth positions (from Comte, 1828). (A) "*Première position du sommet*" (facing p. 48). (B) "*Deuxieme position du sommet*" (facing p. 48).

For nurturists, they were primary. Like nativists, many saw handedness as useful, but they usually endorsed only right-handedness, with some calling left-handedness unnatural, maladaptive, even a kind of deformity. Others felt the same about handedness per se. In classical times, Plato (c. 427–347 B.C.E.) led the way and laid the blame: "we are, as it were, maimed by the folly of nurses and mothers; for although our several limbs are by nature balanced, we create a difference in them by bad habit" (Plato, 1937, *Dialogues*, *Laws* 7, 794). "Several limbs" presumably included feet and legs as well as hands and arms.

Lessons in table manners and writing. Plato did not name the "folly" or "bad habit" that unbalanced the limbs. For the hands, he could have meant how nurses and mothers taught table manners (see *Laws*, 7, 795; see also Blümner, 1895, ch. 2), for example letting the child hold food or utensils only in the right hand while restricting or even punishing use of the left. It would have been the same for lessons in writing, although once the child entered school, men took over. Judging from images on Greek painted steles, terracottas, and figurines, the lessons worked: the child always holds the stylus in the right hand, the tablet in the left or on the lap (Klein, 1932).

Side-of-holding. These and other practices continued to be endorsed long after Plato's era (Harris, 2003, 2010b this issue), and then some time before or after, depending on how the texts are read, the effect of side-of-hold was first proposed. Noting that when the infant was held on one side, one hand was pinned against the holder's body, leaving the other free to move, reach, and grasp, a number of authors surmised that the free hand became dominant. Some credited handedness to side-of-hold entirely; others saw it as one of several contributing factors.[4]

Holding vs carrying

Along with the differences already mentioned, early and current reports differ in two other ways. One is whether the infant is described as being held or carried. Current reports are split, with holding predominating in laboratory and hospital studies because that is what is usually requested or observed, whereas carrying predominates in field studies because most holders are observed while walking or just before or after. Early reports are more like current field studies, with "carrying" predominating, and "holding" and other styles well behind.

Of the 20 "carrying" reports, in 1 the infant was described only as being "carried", in 2 more as carried "in the arms", presumably meaning cradled, and in the rest as carried "on the arm", suggesting that the infant was seated on the forearm. The in-arms/on-arm distinction may be a clue to the infant's age. Any infant can be cradled, or carried *in* the arms, but to be carried *on* the arm it must be at least 3 months old because of the upper-body strength required. In their *Encyclopedia of Domestic Economy*, Webster and Parkes (1848) alluded to this difference when they advised carrying the infant "always in a recumbent posture" for "the first six weeks or two months" and then, at 3 months, "in an upright position" (p. 1168). That infants carried "on the arm" were older is also consistent with their often being described as using their free hand to "take things" offered them.[5]

---

[4] In some reports the infant's *hand* was said to be constrained, in others it was the *arm*, and in still others it was both. My descriptions follow the original reports. Although no report pointed this out, it is possible that the outside hand (or arm), instead of being completely free, was partly constrained by the holder's arm, making it free only relative to the inside hand, that is, the one pressed directly against the holder's body. Likewise, the inside hand might not be completely constrained by the holder's body, or it might not be constrained at all by the holder's body but rather by the infant putting that hand around the holder's neck for support. These variations are illustrated in drawings and photographs reproduced in this article.

[5] It is also consistent with age differences in swaddling. Through at least the mid-nineteenth century, most infants in Western countries were swaddled. The Greek physician Soranus (fl. early second century C.E.) set the standard: wrap the newborn in soft cloths from the head "to the very tip of the toes" (1956, Book II, p. 85), which restrained movement and kept the infant from scratching or otherwise injuring itself. The main goal was to guide its physical development so that it would not grow "Crooked, Awry, or Lame" (Mauriceau, 1710, p. 367). During the first weeks, the infant was kept swaddled except for cleaning and changing. After that, the cloths were removed in stages, first from the upper body, arms, and hands usually between the first and fourth months, then from the torso and legs by the eighth or ninth month or at latest by the end of the first year

(Continued overleaf)

Of the "hold" reports, four in all, in one the infant was described only as being "held", in one more as "held on the arm", and in two more as held "in the arm" (or "arms").

In three more reports the infant was, respectively, "placed on the arm", "seated on the forearm", and "supported" by the arm.

The last three reports referred to nursing. In one the holder was described as lying on her side, with the infant beside her. In the others the infant was held "in the arms". Like infants "carried in the arms", these infants most likely were young and were observed indoors.

Nurses and mothers

The other difference is in the identity of the holders. Many current reports include both sexes, with nearly all holders being parents observed in maternity hospitals, at home, or out in public, or college students tested in laboratories. In early reports, only women were observed (or at least only women were mentioned), none were college students, only a few were mothers, and all the rest were nurses.[6]

Later, I shall suggest that their training as nurses may help reconcile the right- and left-side reports. But first, who were these nurses, where were they observed, and why were they usually the focus and not the mothers themselves?

Hospital nurses

Reports by physicians may well have been of nurses observed at work in maternity or paediatric hospitals, such as the Maternité de Paris, where Comte (1828) recorded birth-presentation positions. In maternity hospitals, of course, mothers could have been observed too, although the

(Nelson, 1756, p. 105), the order corresponding to when each body part had presumably become firm enough that "there is no longer any fear" of its "being distorted" (Soranus, 1956, Book II, p. 114). The upper limbs were freed first because they were ready first. Then, "having his arms and hands at liberty, [the child] may use and stirre them" (Guillemeau, 1612, p. 22). For the hypothesis linking side-of-holding to infant handedness, side-of-hold would have been less of a factor for fully "wrapped" infants because *both* hands and *both* arms were constrained. For holding side to affect hand use asymmetrically, at least the upper limbs would have to have been freed, meaning that the infants were at least 1 to 4 months old, with 3 months as the more likely lower bound (see Harris, 2003, for further details).

[6] It is safe to assume that all the nurses were female. In the historical periods under review, nursing was overwhelmingly women's work, and male nurses, in any case, were not in charge of infants and young children. A census in 1901 for England and Wales estimated 63,500 female nurses and 5700 male nurses, with 3000 of the men working in mental institutions and with most of the rest in their patients' homes. The ratios had not changed much by 1931 (Abel-Smith, 1975, p. 52 and Appendix I).

infants generally were the nurses' responsibility.[7] It was the same in paediatric hospitals. As was said of the paediatric ward at the Great Ormond Street Hospital in London, the infant patients, "even when recovering, because they could not feed or entertain themselves, quite often cried all night unless carried around by a *nurse*" (Lomax, 1996, p. 43; emphasis added).

Private nurses

Observations in hospitals could have comprised at most only a small fraction of the total because most settings appear to have been either in private homes or, like "field" studies today, in neighbourhoods, parks, or other outdoor places. In two reports, the locations were identified—"public gardens" in one, outside the author's home in another—but the main clue is the holder's identification as "the child's nurse" or occasionally as a "nursemaid", in either case meaning someone hired to care for someone else's child. As Webster and Parkes (1848) explained, "the nurse washes, dresses, feeds, ... and in every way ... attends to the development of all [the infant's] powers" (p. 1174), but what is important for our story is that her "chief duties" "consist in holding the infant in her arms, carrying it out into the open air for exercise, and accompanying the mother in visiting, so as to relieve her from the fatigue of attention to the child" (p. 1175). The reference to "the open air" provides, along with the accounts of the "seated-on-arm" style, another clue to the infants' ages because, as one physician advised, only when infants were 3 months old "[shall] the Nurse ... begin to carry him abroad, so that it be faire weather, to sport and exercise him" (Guillemeau, 1612, p. 22).

So, at least until the late nineteenth century, when baby carriages came into fashion, the nurse was the main vehicle for transport.[8] We see her at work in Figure 4, Louis-Leopold Boilly's painting (c. 1803) of a man demanding payment from a family for using the wood planks he has laid on

[7] Infants in maternity hospitals most likely would have been children of the very poor because, in Europe and the United States until about the mid-nineteenth century, most maternity hospitals were charitable institutions for indigents. These were dangerous places—many infants and mothers died from contagious disease (childbed fever, or puerperal sepsis)—so women who could afford to were delivered at home by physicians or midwives. In the United States a significant shift to hospital births for all social classes began only in the 1920s (Thoms, 1960; Wertz & Wertz, 1989, esp. chs. 4 & 5).

[8] The baby carriage was invented in 1733 but not commonly used until the 1870s and 1880s (Bellis, 2004; Brown, 2004). It brought the nurse some relief from carrying the infant when outdoors, but she still had to lift and carry it back and forth from carriage to house. In one report cited in this article, the nurse was observed while performing these acts.

Figure 4. Louis-Leopold Boilly, "*Passer Payez*" (c. 1803), oil painting. Retrieved 10 August 2004 from http://www.pemberley.com/janeinfo/passpaye

the muddy street. The title is *Passer Payez* [*To Pass, Pay*]. Note that while the nurse holds the baby, the baby's mother holds a pet dog.

Private nurses and nursemaids were prominent in every era covered in this review. In Jaques's speech on the "seven ages of man" from Shakespeare's *As You Like It*, set in Elizabethan times, the infant is described as "mewling and puking in the *nurse's* arms" (Act 2, Scene 7, emphasis added). The nurse also saw to the infant's exercise, as in this line from a "paediatric poem" from this same period: "cease you [the nurse] not to dance him in your arms, For exercise will best preserve from harms" (Saint-Marthe, 1584, p. 96, verse 555). In late-Victorian England a writer called the nurse's "dominion in the matter of babies" "necessarily large" (J.S., 1881, p. 546), and an American psychologist even equated the "replacement of mothers by nurses" with living in a civilised country (Baldwin, 1894, p. 607). Civilisation, of course, had its price, meaning that private nurses served middle- and upper-class families, like the one in Figure 4 or in Figure 5, from Robert Smirke's illustration (c. 1798–1801) of the "first" of the "seven ages of man".

Figure 5. Robert Smirke, c. 1798–1801, "Seven ages of man" (Act Two: Scene Seven: The First Age). Engraved by Peltro William Tomkins and designed by Robert Smirke for John Boydell's "Shakespeare Gallery". Retrieved 10 October 2007 from http://shakespeare.emory.edu/illustrated_showimage.cfm?imageid =269

Given their occupations, the early authors most likely were from the same classes, so at least some private nurses could have been in their employ and observed in the authors' own homes or neighbourhoods.[9]

Education, reputation, and treatment of nurses

Wherever they worked, most private and hospital nurses came from the domestic servant class (Abel-Smith, 1975, p. 5), few had schooling beyond the secondary level, and most, fairly or not, were held in low regard. As a

[9] Private nurses should be distinguished from wet-nurses: women who, through the late-eighteenth century, were employed by most middle- and upper-class families to suckle their infants. Ordinarily, infants were "farmed out" to women in the country. For wealthy families, the wet-nurse more often lived in the employer's home (Still, 1965; Sussman, 1982, especially ch. 2), thus putting her within the purview of the authors of these early reports. But since only three holding-side reports referred to nursing, one involving mothers, if wet-nurses figured in any of the remaining reports, they evidently were not observed while performing their primary duties.

physician said of nurses at St. Bartholomew's Hospital, London, in the early 1800s, the "best" were "kindly, and careful, and attentive in doing what they were told," but as a group they were "dull, unobservant, and untaught" (Paget, 1914, quoted in Abel-Smith, 1975, pp. 5–6). In their defence, one writer laid their faults mostly to "the want of proper treatment" (Anon., 1857; quoted in Nutting & Dock, 1907, p. 505). For example, Florence Nightingale (1854) described how hospital nurses slept in "wooden cages on the landing places outside the doors of the wards, ... where it was impossible ... to sleep at all owing to the noise, where there was not light or air" (quoted in Woodham-Smith, 1951, p. 51).

Private nurses' treatment and reputations were hardly better, so those seeking their services often looked to child-care books for advice about qualifications. Along with cleanliness, sobriety, and good character, the books routinely mentioned strength and endurance, which, as explained by Simon de Vallambert (1565), author of the first French work on paediatrics, were needed "for carrying the child on her [the nurse's] arms for long periods" (p. 6).

Eventually, thanks to Nightingale and other reformers, training programmes began and stricter standards were set. For example, in London in 1856 the Great Ormond Street Hospital started programmes for teaching "privately employed nursery maids the art of handling sick children" and, beginning in 1875, did the same for hospital nurses. Schools were also established for training nursemaids and other young women "in the day to day management of small children to maintain and promote good health" (Lomax, 1996, pp. 152–153).

Anticipations, not foundations

There is no reason to suppose that Salk was influenced by or even knew of any of the early reports when he gave his own account. They *anticipate*, or foreshadow, his work but are not *foundational* to it (see Sarup, 1978). In compiling this list of "anticipations", however, I have also tried to steer clear of what Merton (1961) called "the pointless practice" of "adumbrationism"—"claiming to find dim anticipations of current scientific discoveries in older, and preferably ancient, work by the expedient of excessively liberal interpretations of what is being said now and what was said then" (p. 485). Of course, the line between conservative and liberal is not always bright, but where I thought I might be treading the line or, especially, crossing into "excessively liberal" territory, I have tried to draw back with properly qualified language.

RIGHT-SIDE REPORTS

We are ready now to start our review. We begin with the right-siders (Table 1), those calling right-side holding the norm and right-handedness the effect, or what I shall call the "right-side hypothesis".

TABLE 1
Right hold reports ("right-siders")

Author	*Year of report*	*Holder's identity &, if nurse or nursemaid, her employment status*	*Holder's presumed nationality*	*Kind & function of hold*	*Proposed effect on infant's handedness*
Plato*	c. 427–347 B.C.E.	Nurse (P)	Greek	carry on arm (T)	promote RH (*i*)
Wurtz	1656**	Mother, Nurse (P)	Dutch	carry on arm (T)	promote RH (*i*)
Andry	1741	Nurse (P)	French	carry on arm (T)	promote RH (*i*)
Rousseau	1762	Nurse (P)	French	carry on arm (T)	promote RH
Comte	1828	Nurse (P)	French	carry on arm (T) (forearm)	promote RH
Reade	1878	Nurse (P)	English	carry on arm (T)	promote RH
Hall & Hartwell	1884	Nurse (H?)	American	carry on arm (T)	promote RH
Cosmovici	1889	Nurse (P)	French	carry on arm (T)	promote RH (*i*)
Hughes	1890	Mother	American	recline, infant on arm (N)	promote RH
Ballin	1896	Nurse (P)	American	carry on arm (T)	promote RH
Lydon	1907	Mother, Nurse (P)	English	carry on arm (N)	promote RH
Watson & Watson	1921	Mother? Nurse (H?)	American	carry in arms (T)	promote RH (*i*)
Burt	1937	Mother, Nurse (P)	English	carry on arm (T?)	promote RH

Notes: (P)=private; (H)=hospital; (N)=nursing (always stated); (T)=transport (usually only implied); RH=right-handedness (*i* if only implied).
*according to Blau (1946) and others.
**Based on date publication;1563 if based on date of writing.

Was Plato the first?

I said that the side-of-hold effect was first proposed either before or after Plato's era, depending on how the texts are read. This applies to both the *left*- and *right*-side versions. For the latter, the American psychiatrist Abram Blau (1946) dated the first instance to the classical era and to Plato himself: "It was Plato who advanced [the right-side hypothesis] when he said that handedness might unconsciously be developed in the infant by the way the mother held it in her arms," and that the right hold was preferred. "[T]he child's right arm would thus be free to exercise while the left was restricted by the mother's body" (p. 20). In the example in Figure 6, of a woman holding her sleeping infant after breast-feeding it, the infant's right arm, although constrained by the mother's shawl, is still freer than the left (see Footnote 4).

Was Blau right about Plato? Plato did blame handedness on the "folly of nurses and mothers" but as I said, he never named the "folly", and I suggested lessons in table manners and writing as possibilities. In supposing that Plato was referring to how the infant was held or carried, Blau perhaps was alluding to another passage in *Laws*, where Plato instructed nurses to carry infants "to the temples, or into the country, or to their relations' houses" until they are "well able to stand" but "to take care that their limbs are not distorted by leaning on them when they are too young" (1937, *Laws*

Figure 6. "The Amiable Mother", mezzotint. Published by Robert Sayer, London, 4 December 1790. (Courtesy The Wellcome Trust, London.)

7, 789). In the conventional reading, "limbs" means the legs, so Plato meant that making infants stand before they were "well able" would distort, or deform, their legs. Blau, however, presumably would have understood "limbs" to refer to the arms and would have read the passage to mean that *carrying* the infant always on the same side made it lean to that side, deforming the arm pressed against the nurse's body. Held on the nurse's right, it would lean on its left arm.

Along with Blau (1946), others naming Plato as the author of the right-side hypothesis include Fritsch (1968), Ingalls (1928), Schiller (1936), and Wile (1934). Of these, only Fritsch and Schiller named a source, and it was the same section in *Laws* (and, for Schiller, from the same Jowett translation) from which I quoted earlier. Given what Plato actually wrote, it is a mystery how any of these writers came to name Plato as the author. Some, perhaps all, could merely have been repeating, without attribution, a statement first made by someone else. Of those listed here, the first would be Ingalls (1928), except that in his account of Plato's views, the child is held in the mother's *left* arm (p. 309), which Ingalls nonetheless linked to the development of *right*-handedness. Whoever was first perhaps had conflated the two parts of the text from *Laws* that I cited above, that pertaining to handedness and that pertaining to holding and carrying infants.

Seventeenth century

If Plato was not the first to report a right-hold bias or to have originated the right-side *hypothesis* as I defined it, who might have been? Keeping in mind the problem in assigning priority, the first unambiguous report I have found of the right-hold bias came much later. The author was Felix Wurtz, a Dutch physician and surgeon. In 1656, in *The Childrens Book*,[10] he declared (p. 363):

> Children commonly are carried on one arm, as those usually do, which are wont to carry onely on the right arm, and never change the child from the right to the left side, or arm, and again from that [left arm] to the right arm...

Like Plato, if indeed he was referring to holding and carrying, Wurtz warned that the practice of carrying always on the same side was "hurtfull also unto children" (p. 363), except that Wurtz noted only its effects on the legs: that the leg that "lyeth closer to the body ... is caused to grow crooked" and that the holding side therefore should alternate from day to day (p. 363).

[10] This was the English translation of a German work written nearly a century earlier, in 1563. The translation, however, marked its first appearance in any form, and then only as an addendum to another translated work, Wurtz's (1656) *An Experimental Treatise of Surgerie, in Four Parts.*

If Wurtz was the first to report the right-hold bias, he still cannot have originated the right-side hypothesis because he never mentioned its effect on handedness. Who else, then, might have been first?

Eighteenth century

The next possible candidate I found came along nearly a century later. It was the French surgeon Nicholas Andry, often called the father of orthopaedic medicine. For Andry, handedness was a product of nurture, but of the wrong kind in the case of left-handedness. In *L'Orthopedie*, first published in French in 1741 (Figure 7) and then in 1743 in English translation, he wrote (Vol. 1, p. 206):

> . . . they who have this Defect, and for this reason are called Left-handed, make use of the left Hand more readily and more freely than of the right. This is commonly owing to a fault in Nurses, some of whom carry the Children always upon the left Arm, by which means the [child's] left Arm is only at liberty, and so they employ it upon all Occasions; whence the left Hand becomes stronger, and the other weaker.

In stating that "some" nurses carry children "always upon the left Arm", making those children left-handed, if Andry meant that *most* nurses carry on

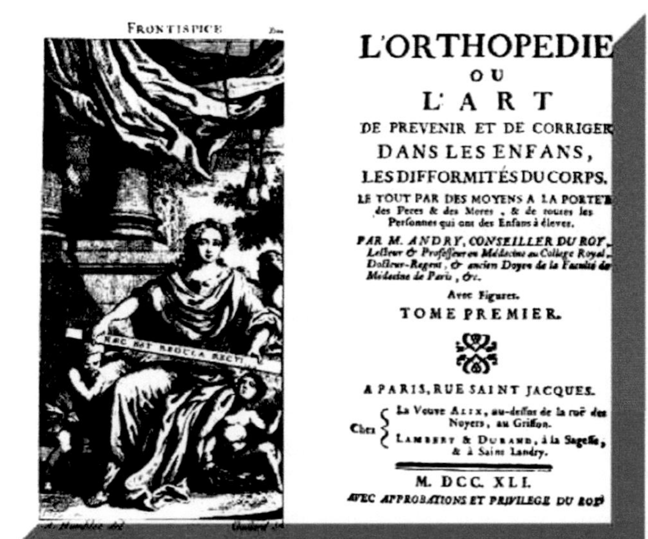

Figure 7. Title page from Nicholas Andry's (1741) *L'Orthopedie.*

the right, making *most* children *right*-handed, that would be a statement, although indirect, of the right-side hypothesis.

In 1762, another indirect statement, or at least intimation, of the hypothesis came from the philosopher Jean Jacques Rousseau. It was in a passage from *Émile*, Rousseau's paean to the natural life, one unencumbered by the habits of the civilised world. The passage implies that those habits included handedness, which Rousseau evidently disparaged in any form and to which he saw side-of-hold as contributing: "The only habit the child should be allowed to contract is that of having no habits; let him not be carried on one arm more than the other; let him not become accustomed to offer one hand more than the other, or to use one more than the other" (1762/1962, p. 42).

To whatever extent Rousseau credited handedness to side-of-hold, he would have meant the *right hold*, since right-handedness was the norm. Other passages show that he blamed nurses for handedness and most other (in his view) bad habits.

Nineteenth century

In the nineteenth century, the right-side hypothesis was stated at least six times, again sometimes directly, sometimes indirectly. Perhaps the first direct statement was by Joseph Comte (1828). Comte, however, did not suppose that right holding created right-handedness *de novo*; instead, it maintained a tendency first established by intrauterine position (1828, p. 45):

> I have said that education from the outset tends to maintain this unbalance and this native disproportionate use of the two arms; one will be convinced, as I have been, by the truth of this remark, if one watches how nurses carry their infants: ... the infant, seated on his nurse's right forearm has the free use of his right arm, whereas his left arm, caught by his side, is held nearly totally immobile against the nurse's chest.

According to Comte, the right hold was nurses' usual practice [*cette habitude des nourrices est générale*], and because he saw the first intrauterine position as promoting right-handedness pre-natally through its effect on blood supply, he presumably saw the right hold as having the same effect post-natally (see again Figures 3A & 3B).

Unlike Andry and Rousseau, Comte was unconcerned about the practice or its effect, probably because he saw handedness as a natural state. The English writer Charles Reade disagreed. Reade opposed nativist explanations and championed ambidexterity, and in 1878, in a letter to the *London*

Daily Telegraph,[11] declared that all mankind would be "even-handed" if not for the "pagan prejudices against the left hand" (19 January, p. 51). In another letter he gave these examples and recommendations (18 May, p. 394):

> Infants are overhandled ... More floor and less lap; more safety-chair, with both arms free, and less hugging, cuddling, and carrying, with one little arm crippled against a nurse's body. Children *must* be carried *out-of-doors* for air, but even there the nurse must carry them an equal time on each arm. It is necessary to her own body, and to the child it is vital. Nothing will require more parental vigilance and determination than this. Carrying for an hour on one arm and five minutes on the other makes the nurse lop-sided and the infant lop-handed.

Again, with right-handedness as the norm, Reade presumably meant that the "one little arm crippled against a nurse's body" was usually the *left*, meaning that the infant was usually carried on the right. His remark about "parental vigilance and determination" shows that he saw parents as guardians against one-sided carrying, and his remark about the nurse's becoming "lop-sided" shows that he saw it as crippling her as well.

Reade's statement of the right-side hypothesis was indirect, like Andry's. Another direct statement, like Comte's, came in 1884 from the American psychologists G. Stanley Hall and E. M. Hartwell. In an essay on bilateral asymmetry of function, they wrote: "Nurses carry children on their own right arm, leaving the child's right arm a freer field of motion" (p. 101). As for the physiological consequences, whereas Comte (1828) at most only implied that right holding affected the *postnatal* blood supply, Hall and Hartwell (1884) were specific: it was "disturbing" for "the equilibrium of blood-pressure" (p. 101).

Another statement of the hypothesis, again indirect, appeared in 1889 in a letter to the French periodical *Revue Scientifique*. The author, C. Cosmovici, recalled how his son became *left*-handed from being reared by a nurse who carried him constantly on her *left* side, so that he could take things offered him only with his left hand. Likewise, the author's brother-in-law (the boy's uncle) was left-handed and *his* nurse held him the same way. With no other left-handers in the family, Cosmovici concluded that the left-handedness in both cases was "easily explained" (p. 572) without needing to invoke "inborn mechanisms" and, like Andry (1743), implied that an infant normally became *right*-handed by being carried on the nurse's *right* side.

Plato named nurses and mothers as the principal agents of handedness training, but so far his successors, except for Rousseau, had mentioned only

[11] The 1878 date is to the American magazine *Harper's Weekly*, where the letters also appeared. I have not seen the *Daily Telegraph* letters.

nurses. In 1890, C. H. Hughes, an American professor of psychiatry and neurology, focused on the mother, and now not on her position while standing and carrying, but on her recumbent position for nursing. According to Hughes she preferred to lie on her right side, with her infant on her right arm. In that position, its left arm would be "confined against her breast", so that the "first effective hand movement" towards her breast would be with the right hand. "It is thus that the habit of right-handedness is initiated and established" (all quotations from p. 147). Figure 8 shows the position, from a contemporary manual on breastfeeding.

In 1896, there was another indirect statement of the hypothesis, with nurses again the focus. In an essay entitled "Symmetry in Education," the American educator Hans Ballin accepted the blood-supply explanation of handedness but, going beyond Comte (1828), saw child-rearing practices as enhancing and not just maintaining the effect, so that "in ninety-eight cases out of a hundred, children at the age of six have already established well-working mechanical systems of circulation which destine them to be right-handed" (pp. 306–307). (The figure "ninety-eight cases out of a hundred" exceeds what by consensus today is the true figure for right-handedness, but it is close to the figure given in late nineteenth-century reports that used writing hand as the measure; Harris, 1991.) Like Plato and Reade, Ballin called handedness maladaptive and promised "symmetrical physiological training" as the cure (1896, p. 308):

> All activities of the young child should be so guided that both sides receive at least equal attention. If carried on the arm by its nurse, it should be as often on one

Figure 8. Illustration of reclining position for nursing (from LaCerva, 1981, p. 98; courtesy Victor LaCerva).

> arm as the other. As nurses are generally one-sided in actions themselves, it should be made one of their duties to fulfil.

With nurses "generally one-sided" in their actions, and with right-handedness as the norm, we can infer that Ballin, like Rousseau and Reade, meant that the usual carrying side was the right.

Twentieth century

In the early twentieth century, the right-side hypothesis appeared at least three more times. The first, in 1907, came from Frederick Lydon, a British art teacher and champion of ambidexterity. In his book, *Ambidextrous and Free-Arm Blackboard Drawing and Design,* Lydon wrote (p. 12):

> when being carried by its mother or nurse [the infant] is most usually held on the right arm . . . This position . . . will give it more freedom to reach and handle with the right hand, which is farthest from the person who is nursing it. Thus a slight advantage is gained by the right arm from the very start.

In the 1920s, the American psychologist John B. Watson weighed in. In his laboratory at The Johns Hopkins University, Watson sought evidence on the origins of handedness from physical and behavioural tests on infants. Finding no reliable lateral differences, he concluded that handedness was a product of training, and in an essay with Rosalie Rayner Watson, his wife and former student, he called it "natural to suppose that we would try to instill in youngsters almost from the beginning the dominance of the right hand," among other ways by "leaving its right hand free in carrying it in our arms" (Watson & Watson, 1921, p. 500), meaning presumably on the right side. Elsewhere, Watson (1924, p. 101) put it this way: "We hold the infant so that it will wave 'bye-bye' with the right hand." It is unclear whether he meant himself, his wife, the nurses who brought the infants to his laboratory (next door to the maternity hospital), the infants' mothers, or people in general.

Finally, in 1937, the British psychologist Cyril Burt remarked that for nurses, "right-side holding seems certainly looked upon as orthodox", and acknowledged its possible contribution to right-handedness by leaving the right hand "free for active movement" (p. 299). But he implied that the effect would appear only when the child "is old enough to sit up in [the holder's] arms", or "just about the time that most children develop a preference for one hand rather than the other" (p. 299). Citing the psychologist Arnold Gesell's (1925) norms for tests of visually directed reaching, Burt identified that time as 6 to 15 months (p. 272). That would fit his description of the infant's left-arm position during a right hold: "round the [holder's] neck" instead of "pressed against the holder's chest", a position only an older infant could attain.

Explanations of preference for right-side holding

Not counting Plato, we have 11 statements of the right-side hypothesis, 6 direct and 5 indirect, with Rousseau's being perhaps only an intimation of a statement, and one more (Wurtz's) that attested to the right-hold bias without mentioning handedness. But what accounted for the bias itself?

To favour the right side because it is stronger

The most frequent explanation was what I called the "strength" version of the handedness explanation or, as Comte (1828) put it, "the need to support the child with the stronger arm" (p. 45). That meant the right arm for most persons. Others agreed, including Blau (1946), Burt (1937), and Lydon (1907). Burt (1937) wrote, "Every mother, it might be supposed, would regularly use her stronger hand to support her baby. Hence, if she is right-handed she will naturally hold him on her right side", whereas a "great many left-handed mothers undoubtedly assume the opposite [left-side] position". Therefore, just as right holding could contribute to right-handedness, left holding could do the same for left-handedness, so that the child will use "his left hand to pick up his toys or to wave 'Good-bye'" (all quotes from p. 299). By such means, Burt concluded, the child's hand preference should follow the mother's. Likewise, Cosmovici (1889) assumed that the nurses who made his son and brother-in-law left-handed by left-side holding were themselves left-handed, and from that he surmised that right holders were right-handed.

To follow instructions

When Burt (1937) remarked that right-side holding was "looked upon as orthodox" for nurses, he evidently meant that it was seen as the *correct* style, and consistent with that reading added that it was "taught in several institutions where nurses are trained, and occasionally in classes where younger girls are instructed in infant management" (p. 299). Burt did not name the institutions or classes, but such instructions would have contravened Wurtz's (1656) and others' warnings *against* holding on only one side, right or left. Nor did he explain the rationale, although given the strength needed "for carrying the child ... for long periods" (de Vallambert, 1565) and his own surmise that the mother or nurse would hold on her stronger side, perhaps the right hold was seen as safer because, for right-handers, the right side was stronger. If so, was an exception made for left-handers? Burt did not say.

To achieve the most restful, comfortable position

The "strength" and perhaps the "instruction" explanations credited the right-hold bias to the right side's normally greater strength. For Hughes (1890), who described how the mother lies on her right side and nurses the infant from that position, the reason was rest and comfort: the right side "is the most restful position" because the liver, "the largest of [the] viscera after the womb is emptied, lies on the right side" (p. 147). Hughes thus related right holding to an asymmetry of the same organ that figured in Buchanan's (1862a) balance theory of handedness.

To accommodate the infant's preference for the right breast

So far, the explanations have referred only to the holder's dispositions and characteristics. Without saying so explicitly, Hall and Hartwell (1884) mentioned something that could suggest a role for the infant—that infants preferred nursing from the right breast because it gave "the best and richest milk" (p. 96).[12] In that case, mothers (or wet-nurses) would have to hold on the right—and perhaps do the same on other occasions.

LEFT-SIDE REPORTS

The right-side reports obviously fall short of today's methodological and reportorial standards. Still, their numbers are impressive, and they gain credibility from the current, albeit exceptional, right-side reports. If the bias was for the left, that would nullify all explanations of a right bias, at least at the population level. Moreover, since left holding constrains the infant's *right* hand and *frees* the left, side-of-hold could not be the cause of handedness because *right*-handedness was the norm. Some left-siders acknowledged this, but others maintained that side-of-hold was still influential, now by promoting early *left*-handedness (as two right-siders,

[12] This was one of over 40 examples given by Hall and Hartwell in support of the then-common idea that growth was more vigorous on the right side of the body. Other examples included growth of the teeth, hair and beard, and nails. By contrast, many diseases and congenital defects were believed to be more common on the left side, including fever and resulting weakness, pneumonia, cancer, epilepsy, and deformities of the lung, kidney, eye, and ear. All such differences were seen as evidence of the superiority of the right side of the body and, correspondingly, of the left side of the brain. Most of the examples, including the one for breast milk, were undocumented in Hall and Hartwell's article, although some were among those reported and documented by the French neurologist Armand Trousseau (1868) in his *Clinique Médicale* (Volume 2).

Andry, 1743, and Cosmovici, 1889, also concluded), and that most infants become right-handed only because their early left-handedness is countermanded. Because not all left-siders made this argument, only those who did could be said to have posited the "left-side" version of the right-side hypothesis. But all at least reported, or attested to, the left-hold bias itself. Again, like the right-siders, most left-siders (see Table 2) referred to nurses rather than mothers and, again, to *private* rather than to hospital nurses.

Was Alexander the first?

Who was the first left-sider? Again, keeping in mind the problem in assigning priority, a possible candidate might be none other than Aristotle's most famous pupil, the young Macedonian prince who became Alexander the Great (356–323 B.C.E.). According to legend, Alexander asked, "Which one is better, the right or the left side?" and answered his own question, "The left, because the woman nurses her son on the left side first" (quoted in Flusser, 1980, p. 474; trans. by Wout van Bekkum; cited in McManus, 2006, p. 570). Figure 9 shows a Roman woman nursing on the left side.[13]

According to tenth-century Jewish texts, as noted by Michele Klein (1998, p. 161, n. 14, and p. 256), rabbis described the same practice, now for mothers and nurses alike. But the rabbis went further: they not only described the practice, they recommended it. All such accounts of nursing practices, however, would qualify as statements of a left-hold preference only if Alexander and the rabbis meant that women nursed first on the left because that was their preferred side for holding the infant even when it was not nursing. But if that is not what was meant, then who else might have been first?

Seventeenth century

The earliest alternative candidate I have found did not appear until the mid-seventeenth century (perhaps coincidentally around the same time as Felix Wurtz, 1656, the first *right-sider*). It was the English churchman Christopher Wren, Dean of Windsor and father of the architect by the same name, and the statement was in the notes (transcribed and reprinted by Wilkin, 1852) he had written in his copy of a famous book. The book, published in 1646, was Sir Thomas Browne's *Pseudodoxia Epidemica, or Enquiries into Very*

[13] This image is from the website VRoma (2008). The editor, Barbara McManus, notes that the temple in the background suggests that the standing woman might be a priestess, who may have just given the child to the mother. The man is perhaps the father.

TABLE 2
Left hold reports ("left-siders")

Author	*Year of report*	*Holder's identity &, if nurse or nursemaid, her employment status, stated or implied*	*Holder's presumed nationality*	*Kind & function of hold*	*Proposed effect on infant's handedness*
Alexander	c. 356–323 B.C.E.	Mother	Greek	no description of kind (N)	
Rabbis	c. 900	Mothers, Nurses	European	no description of kind (N)	
Wren	c. 1648–1658	Nurses (P) Servants (P)	English	carry on arm (T)	promote LH
Godfrey	1747	Nurse (P)	English	carry in arm (T)	promote LH
Webster & Parkes	1848	Nurse (P)	American	carry on arm (T)	
Buchanan	1862	Nurse (P)	Scottish	carry on arm (T)	
Wyeth	1880	Nurse (H?; P?)	American	hold (N) carry on arm (T)	promote LH
J.H.	1889	Author	French	place on arm	
H.M.	1889	Parent, Nurse (P)	French	carry on arm	
Wilson	1891	Nurse (P)	Canadian	carry on arm (T)	
MacPhail	1891–1894	Nurse (P)	Irish	hold in arms	
Baldwin	1894	Author, Nurse (P)	Canadian	carry (T)	
Girdwood	1908	Mother	Canadian	carry on arm (T)	promote LH
Woolley	1910	Nurse (P)	American	carry on arm (T)	promote LH
Kenealy	1920	Mother	Irish	"arm for supporting" (C)	
Klein	1923	Mother	Greek*	hold on arm (N; C?)	
Schiller	1936	Mother	American	hold in arm	
Burt**	1937	Mother	English	carry on arm (T)	
Mead	1942	Mother, Child–Nurse (P)	Balinese	carry on hip (T) carry on arm (T)	promote LH

Notes: (P)=private; (H)=hospital; (N)=nursing (always stated); (T)=transport (usually only implied); (C)=comforting; LH=left-handedness.

*Greek terracottas and painted steles of mother and child.

**also in paintings of Madonna and Child.

Figure 9. Mother nursing an infant; marble relief, Roman, imperial period; Rome, Chiaramonti Corridor, Vatican Museum. Credits: Barbara McManus. Retrieved 2 April 2008 from http://www.vroma.org/images/mcmanus_nursingwoman.jpg

Many Received Tenents, and Commonly Preserved Truths.[14] Also called *Vulgar Errors*, it was dedicated to "disproving a number of common errors and misconceptions about the natural world and those arising from human society and culture". Among them was the belief that *right*-handedness is natural—that there is "in men a naturall prepotency in the right" (p. 186)—and that left-handedness is a defect, or anomaly. This, Browne (1646, p. 186) declared,

> we cannot with constancy affirme, if we make observations in children, who permitted the freedom of bothe [hands], do ofttimes confine unto the left, and are not without great difficulty restrained from it, and therefore this prevalency [of right-handedness] is either uncertainly placed in the laterality, or custome determines its differency.

[14] Wren's notes are undated, but given the publication date of the book, they would have been written between 1646 and 1658, the year of his death.

For Browne, then, left-handedness was no defect, and both forms of handedness could be natural *or* learned or both. Although Wren himself took no position on right-handedness, he believed that left-handedness *was* a defect—a "vitiosity"—and that side-of-holding was to blame (Wren, n.d.):

> This vitiosity proceeds from the manner of Gestation; servants and nurses usually carry them on their left arme, so that the children cannot use it [the right hand] right [i.e., properly, correctly], and being accustomed to the left, become left-handed.

Wren did not say how he came to this view. Could his architect son have been left-handed, and had he seen him held that way by a servant or nurse? But whatever it was, his words would qualify as a statement of the left-hold bias and even of the left-side hypothesis as it pertains to the effect on handedness only if, in stating that "servants and nurses usually carry [infants] on their left arme", he meant servants and nurses in general, and that *all* children so treated became left-handed but that most revert to their native right-handedness when no longer carried or when their parents intervened. His meaning can perhaps also be gleaned from the statement that directly followed: "but among the Irish who carry their children astride their neckes, you shall rarely see one left-handed, of either Sex." In other words if, unlike the English, the Irish carried their children in a way that kept them from favouring either hand, then Wren meant that right-handedness predominates in Ireland and England because it is the natural, normative state, but that in England it is inadvertently suppressed in favour of left-handedness, permanently in some children, temporarily in the rest.

Eighteenth century

Wren's statements about servants' and nurses' practices are open to interpretation, but my reading is not incompatible with statements by later authors. One appeared in, of all places, an eighteenth-century fencing manual by Captain John Godfrey (1747), an English master of arms. Like the authors of many such manuals, Godfrey described the difficulties that left-handed fencers posed for right-handers and gave advice for those occasions (Harris, 2010a this issue). He then went on to opine about the origins of left-handedness (1747, p. 17):

> The nurse carries the child in the left arm; the consequence of that is, it's [sic] right arm is confined and the left at liberty to play and exercise; and I believe it will be allowed that the child, in its Infancy, is most of the day in the nurse's arms. If accustomed to that habit, so long as till it can go alone, no wonder of it's continuing to use the left arm.

Like Wren, Godfrey did not say how he knew this about nurses, but he was clear, where Wren was not, that left-side carrying was the mode and that, as he went on to say, most children would be left-handed "if they were not by the Parent's Care broke of that Habit after they are parted from the Nurse", or "till [the child] can go alone" (p. 17), that is, when either no longer under the nurse's care or old enough to walk unassisted. Godfrey evidently regretted that more parents did not intervene because, like Wren, he regarded left-handedness as a defect, calling it "odious" and adding, "I dare say no Body would chuse to be left-handed" (p. 17). He even proposed a way to "put a stop to that undesired Race" (p. 17):

> But let the Child be carried in the right Arm, I engage he will scarcely turn left-handed; for that [left] Arm next to the Nurse's Body is certainly in a great Measure confined and rendered inactive.

Nineteenth century

For the eighteenth century, Godfrey is the only left-sider I have found. For the nineteenth century, the count is higher—seven so far. Webster and Parkes (1848) were the first. Recall that they advised carrying the infant "always in a recumbent position" for the first 6 weeks or 2 months, and then at 3 months in an "upright position". Like Nicholas Andry (1743), they described the dangers of always holding on the same side, but where Andry implied that the modal side was the right, they implied that it was the left (p. 1168):

> ... it is often very distressing to those who have maternal feelings to see fine children carried about for hours together, *on the left arm generally*, their bodies bent forward, their backs forming a bow; unnoticed by their nurses, their countenances are overcast, and the benefit the air and exercise might afford them is lessened by the weariness they evidently experience from this continued, painful position on the same arm. (emphasis added)

Webster and Parkes warned that constant left holding could cause deformity but, unlike Wren, Andry, and Godfrey, did not include left-handedness among its effects. Neither did another left-sider, Andrew Buchanan (1862a), the dynamic balance theorist, who stated that "The nurserymaid carries an infant on her left arm" (p. 162) but that handedness developed only later, when the child was old enough to walk. The reason was that only then could the child exert enough effort to fully expand its lungs and, because the right lung was larger, to shift the centre of gravity far enough to the right to produce the necessary shift in balance.

Godfrey (1747) and Webster and Parke (1848) described left holding in nurses with no mention of mothers. Buchanan (1862a) added that the bias also appeared in mothers "in the humble ranks of society" (p. 162). So did John Wyeth (1880), an American physician and surgeon: "A right-handed mother or nurse holding an infant to the breast, or carrying it when it is not nursing, will almost invariably carry the child on the left arm" (p. 129). Like Godfrey, Wyeth evidently saw left-handedness as the effect (p. 129):

> In this position [the infant's] right arm for a considerable portion of the first year of its extra-uterine existence, is pressed helplessly between its body and that of its attendant, while the left arm is free to be used, and is, as I have observed, more freely exercised than the right.

And like Godfrey he implied that the effect was temporary because the child's right arm "is preferred when the upright position is assumed" (p. 129), meaning when the child was old enough to walk and, therefore, no longer carried about.

Two more left-side statements came in 1889, in letters to *Revue Scientifique* in response to Cosmovici's letter that same year. Recall that Cosmovici supposed that left-handers held on the left, right-handers on the right, resulting in left- and right-handedness respectively. Two correspondents disagreed. J.H. (1889) told how, although right-handed ("my right arm is notably stronger than my left"), when taking a child "to examine or to caress [*pour examiner ou le caresser*], I place him on my left arm" (p. 701). H.M. (1889, p. 764), also right-handed, carried "on the *right* arm" but reported:

> [having] never met *a single* person — servant-maid, nurse, or parent — who, in taking the child from me, fails to remark that she could not carry it on the right arm. Struck by this detail, I have observed in public gardens how people carry their children, and I have become convinced that those who carry them on the right arm are the exception. (emphasis in original)

H.M. thus affirmed what J.H. had only implied: "this [left-arm] style is the rule" (p. 764) but then added, "If the arm that carries the child influenced the [future] dexterity of [the child's] movements, nearly everyone would be left-handed" (p. 764). H.M. therefore rejected side-of-holding as the cause of handedness and concluded that handedness was inborn.

In the 1890s, three more authors drew the same conclusion. In 1891, Daniel Wilson, a prominent archaeologist and President of the University of Toronto, wrote (p. 127):

> The nurse naturally carries the child on the left arm, with its right side toward her breast. All objects presented to it are thus offered to the free left hand; and it is accordingly no uncommon remark that all children are at first left-handed.

The words "no uncommon remark" would seem to attest to the frequency with which initial left-handedness was reported or assumed, but if Wilson himself accepted the possibility that "all children are at first left-handed", then like H.M. he rejected side-of-holding as the cause of handedness and for the same reason: since left holding was the norm, nearly everyone would be left-handed. Wilson saw another implausible implication in the explanation: "the left-handed nurses of the next generation would reverse the process" (p. 127), meaning that they would hold on the right, making the succeeding generation right-handed.

Soon after, the left hold bias was mentioned by S. Rutherford MacPhail (1891–1894), medical superintendent for the Derby Borough Asylum, a hospital (now the Kingsway) in Derbyshire, UK (p. 56):

> From the way a child is held in its nurse's arms, it naturally uses its free left arm, and the tendency of children is undoubtedly to be left-handed if the training they receive in their nurse's arms has anything to do with it.

MacPhail then added, "but if so, the left-handed nurses of the next generation would reverse the process" (p. 56). This last statement is identical to Wilson's, so it is unclear that MacPhail made an independent observation, although his hospital position would have given him opportunity.

Independence is certain for the next author, Wilson's colleague the American psychologist James Mark Baldwin. It was his observation about nurses and living in a civilised country that I quoted earlier. In an article published in 1894 while he was teaching at the University of Toronto, Baldwin remarked that left holding was "an invariable tendency with myself and with nurses and mothers whom I have observed" and that this kept the child's left arm free. But he dismissed the idea that this was the cause of handedness for the same reasons given by Wilson (1891)—and for one reason more: To test the hypothesis along with certain other explanations of handedness, Baldwin had reared his own daughter during her first year so as to preclude all postnatal influences on hand preference (1894, p. 607):

> She was never carried about in arms at all — never walked with when crying or sleepless . . .; she was frequently turned over in her sleep; she was not allowed to balance herself on her feet until a later period than that covered by the experiments [a reference to Buchanan's (1862a) balance hypothesis]. Thus the conditions of the rise of the right-handed era were made as simple and uniform as possible.

Baldwin then assessed her hand preference for reaching for objects. The result, as described in a prior report, was that by 7 and 8 months she had a "distinct preference for the right hand" and by 13 months was a "confirmed right-hander" (1890, pp. 247–248), leading Baldwin (1894) to conclude that the true cause of handedness lay in brain physiology, not in side-of-holding or any other postnatal experience.

Twentieth century

In the early twentieth century, there were at least six more left-hold statements. One was in a 1908 article on handedness by G. Prout Girdwood, an emeritus professor of medical chemistry at McGill University in Montreal. Girdwood was among those who assumed that left holding promoted left-handedness, at least initially (1908, p. 181):

> In man, in very early childhood, the mother carries her infant on her left arm and thus the child's right arm is compressed against the mother's breast, this would leave the child's left hand and arm free to move and would give the child the earliest tendency to use its left hand most.

The next statement, in 1910, was not, strictly speaking, a statement of the bias because it did not call left holding the norm. Like Girdwood's, however, it did describe its initial effect on left-hand use. The author was the American psychologist Helen Thompson Woolley. Soon after her daughter's eighth month, Woolley observed that the nurse, in taking her out for a carriage ride, "always carried her on the left arm, leaving the child's left hand free, and as a result, she learned to wave 'Bye-Bye' with the left hand." A few days later, when her left hand was held, "she refused to wave, but did so joyfully" as soon as it was released. By 9 months, she waved with her right hand if the left was held but used the left if it was free. By 15 months, she no longer used her left and now waved "habitually with the right". Left-hand preference was restricted to this one act because "long before her right-handedness had conquered habit in the matter of waving 'Bye-Bye,' it was perfectly evident in other activities, such as throwing a ball" (all quotations from 1910, p. 39). For Woolley, like Baldwin, the roots of handedness thus lay in brain physiology, not side-of-holding or other post-natal experiences.

In 1920, there was a clearer statement of the bias by the Irish writer and physician Arabella Kenealy, who wrote that the mother's left arm was preferred for "supporting her infant for hours together" (p. 63).

In 1932, Anita Klein, an American scholar of Greek and Latin, offered a different kind of evidence. Her monograph, *Child Life in Greek Art*, included this account of images of mothers and infants on painted steles and terracottas from Ancient Greece: "One often sees the mother either standing or seated, nursing her child at the breast, or simply holding it on her left arm while the baby turns its face toward hers, or nestles its head close to her neck" (p. 2). Recall that Salk (1961) also found a left bias in works of art, so perhaps Klein was the first to use this resource. Klein, however, mentioned the side-of-hold only in passing.

In 1936, the question of the preferred side-of-hold was addressed by the American psychologist Avner Schiller. Schiller was among those naming Plato as author of the right-side hypothesis (see earlier), but for Schiller the answer "more reasonable" and "more highly confirmed by experience" was that "the mother would hold her child in her left arm" (p. 697).

In 1937, Cyril Burt weighed in again, but now as a *left-sider*. Despite having said that every mother "might be supposed" to hold "naturally" on the stronger side (meaning the right for right-handers), that right holding for nurses was the "orthodox" method "taught in several institutions", and that the infant's handedness could be affected, he cautioned that to attribute handedness always to the side-of-hold was "to fly in the face of the facts" (p. 299). The reason, he seems to have implied, was that the right hold was not the norm when *not* formally taught, meaning that it might not be natural after all. Here Burt cited his own "peripatetic census in the streets of poorer districts [of London], where mothers take their infants with them when they shop" (p. 299). Of 100 mothers observed, 73 carried their infants on their left arms, only 27 on their right. Even more telling were Burt's own records of family handedness histories, which showed no relation between the predominant side-of-hold and the child's eventual handedness. They included "at least a score of cases where a right-handed mother has habitually carried the child on her left arm, and the child nevertheless has in the end become right-handed, as if his own right-handedness rested on an inherited tendency that reappeared and slowly ripened, irrespective of the freer opportunity for exercise thus afforded to the left" [Burt here cited Woolley's 1910 study in support] (1937, p. 300).

There were also "a dozen more [cases] where the child of a left-handed mother was never carried by the mother at all, but by a right-handed nurse who adopted the orthodox right-handed method, and still the child developed a left-handed habit", and finally "another dozen, where a left-handed mother with a family of several children adopted the same method for every one, and yet some turned out right-handed and others left-handed" (p. 300).

Like Klein (1932), Burt (1937) also found a left bias in works of art, except that Burt examined images of the Madonna and Child, just as Salk (1961) would do later. However, the bias in Burt's sample, 56%, was smaller than in Salk's, 80%.

The last report (this was the only one from a non-Western culture) came in 1942. The author was the anthropologist Margaret Mead. In *Balinese*

Character (Bateson & Mead, 1942), Mead (1942) noted that the Balinese mother "carries a child" on her left side. Mead mentioned only the hip (p. 13), which the book's photographs bear out, but it was the same for all styles, including in-the-arms (cradling) and on-the-arm, and for a range of activities, including nursing and feeding (Harris, Jentoft, & Almerigi, 2002). Figure 10 shows an example for nursing.

Like Godfrey (1747) and others, Mead (1942) remarked on how the left hold facilitated the infant's use of its left hand: the "*left* arm is free, while the right is frequently pinioned in against the breast, or at best extended behind the mother's back" (p. 13, emphasis in original).

All together, then, not counting Alexander or the medieval rabbis, we have 16, and counting Wren, 17 statements of the left bias, now all but one direct.

Explanations of preference for left-side holding

To free the right hand for skilled tasks

The most common explanation for left-side holding was the complement of the one for right holding: whereas right holding was seen as drawing on that side's normally greater strength, left holding was seen as *freeing* it for

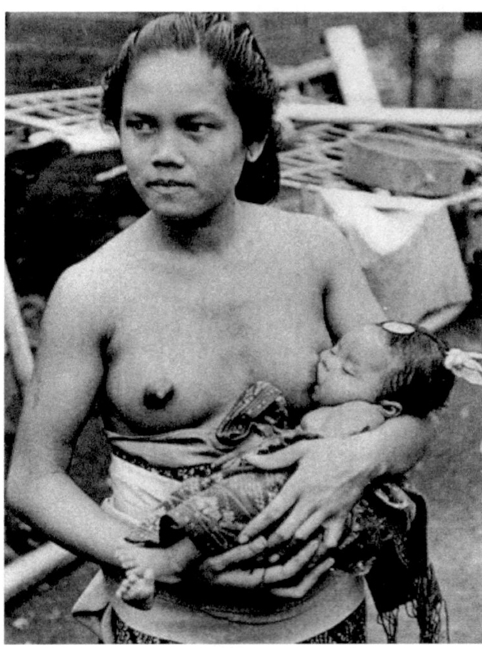

Figure 10. Balinese mother nursing her infant (from Bateson & Mead, 1942, *Balinese Character*, plate 35, p. 124; courtesy New York Academy of Sciences).

other tasks, especially those requiring its greater skill. For example, according to Buchanan (1862a), "an intelligent mother in the humble ranks of society" would say that she "must keep her right arm free for the older children, and for her various household duties", or, in the words of J.H. (1889), the *Revue Scientifique* correspondent, "for routine needs to perform at a moment's notice [*a tout instant*]" (p. 701). The same was implied in the medieval rabbis' advise about nursing: "a right-handed woman would nurse her infant from the left breast more comfortably than from the other, leaving the right hand free for use" (Weisberg, 1986, vol. 1, p. 199, note 1; cited in Klein, 1998, p. 256, note 14). The nurse in Figure 11 shows how—using her free hand to tend to an older child.

Curiously, no left-sider mentioned dry-nursing: giving the infant cow's milk mixed with water and sugar or other ingredients. For this, a "baby-feeder" was used, like the one in Figure 12, a polished cow's horn fitted with a cloth nipple. Such horns were in common use at least through the eighteenth century (Armstrong, 1777).

In the thirteenth-century scene depicted in Figure 13, the mother, attended by one nurse, watches from her bed while a second nurse pours milk into the wide end of the horn and a third holds the infant while guiding the nipple into its mouth. Because cows' horns were symmetrical, nothing in their design favoured one hand over the other, so to the extent that the dominant hand was better at guiding the nipple, a right-handed nurse could

Figure 11. Nurse suckling infant while attending to older child (from a 15th-century manuscript reproduced in Wright, 1862, p. 402).

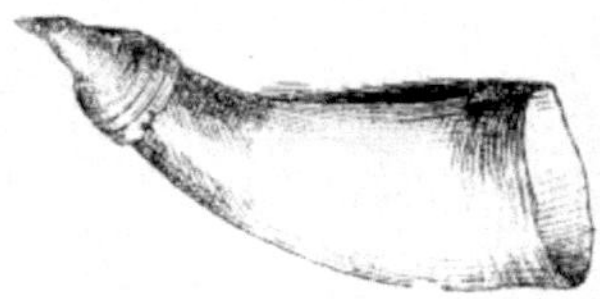

Figure 12. Cow's horn used as baby-feeder (from Auvard & Pingat, 1889, p. 66).

hold the horn in her right hand while supporting the infant with her left, as shown in Figure 13, and a left-hander could do the reverse.

It would be the same for symmetrical feeders with handles, that is, with handles opposite the spouts, like those in Figure 14A–C. However, there were also feeders with handles placed asymmetrically, at a right angle to the spout, and judging from those shown in a variety of sources (e.g., Auvard & Pingat, 1889, part 3; Still, 1965), all were designed for the *right* hand, like those in Figure 15A–C.

If, as this suggests, left-handed feeders were unavailable, as was generally the case for other asymmetrical tools and implements, then everyone whatever their handedness would have to hold the infant on the left for feeding, which might have encouraged left holding on other occasions. For dry-nursing, however, any such effect should have waned by the nineteenth

Figure 13. A thirteenth-century nurse using a cow's horn as a baby-feeder while the mother watches from her bed (courtesy The Wellcome Trust, London).

Figure 14. Symmetrical (either-handed) feeding vessels (from Auvard & Pingat, 1889): (A) porcelain feeding-cup (p. 67); (B) glass feeding-cup (p. 64); (C) clay feeding-cup (p. 66).

century. By then, feeders with handles had largely been replaced by sucking bottles (Dewees, 1826, pp. 82–84) which, being symmetrical, did not favour a particular hand. Even so, to the extent that the dominant hand would continue to be preferred for holding and guiding the bottle, we would expect most right-handers to continue to hold the infant on the left, and most left-handers to hold on the right. We can assume, then, that the mother in Figure 16 bottle-feeding her 7-month-old daughter is right-handed (from Gesell, 1934, p. 42). The infant's hand movements, incidentally, suggest why it was not unreasonable for early authors to suppose that left holding encouraged left-handedness. In frame A the infant's left hand and arm are free; in B she reaches for the bottle with her left hand; in C she grasps the bottle in her left hand and takes the nipple into her mouth; in D the bottle is withdrawn, and she sucks her (left) thumb; in E apparently asleep she sucks while holding the bottle with both hands; in F she takes the nipple once again into her mouth but without sucking (descriptions based on Gesell's text). Note also that in frames D, E, and F the mother's own left hand supports the infant's left arm, seemingly facilitating her left-hand grasp of the bottle.

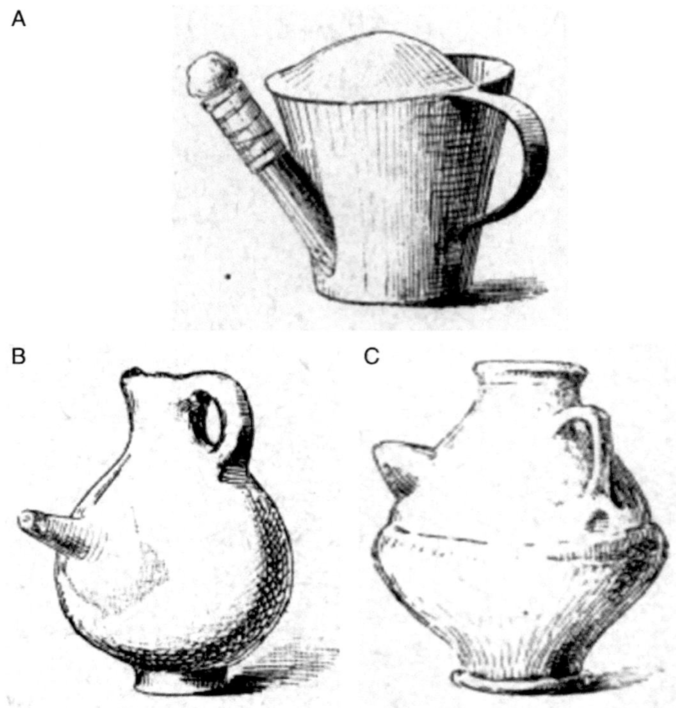

Figure 15. Asymmetrical (right-handed) feeding vessels (from Auvard & Pingat, 1889): (A) clay feeding cup (p. 63); (B) glass feeding cup (p. 64); (C) clay feeding cup (p. 66).

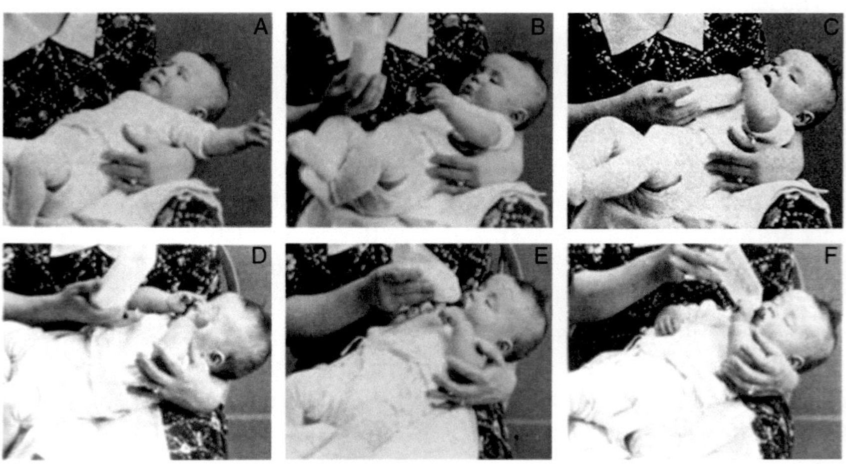

Figure 16. Bottle feeding (from Gesell, 1934, Vol. 2, p. 595).

To prevent food-handling and other acts forbidden for the left hand

The free-the-right-hand explanation focuses on what, at least for right-handers, the right hand normally *can* do better. In societies throughout the world there are also things that only the right hand is *permitted* to do, whatever one's handedness (Needham, 1973; Wile, 1934). The most prominent of the acts prescribed for the right and proscribed for the left is the handling of food, so that when an infant is fed, it again would have to be held on the left.

Although no European or North American reports mentioned these beliefs and practices as further reasons for left holding, they are implicit in Mead's (1942) account of the Balinese: "the right hand touches food and the right thumb may be used in pointing", whereas the left hand is "for cleaning oneself or protecting one's genitals in bathing" and "must *never* be used to touch food, to point, or to receive a gift" (p. 13, emphasis added). When mothers fed their infants or fed themselves while holding their infants, as shown in Figure 17, the left hold therefore would have been all but guaranteed, which is what we found (Harris et al., 2002).

If left holding facilitated the infant's use of its left hand, especially for the "wrong" acts such as reaching for food as also shown in Figure 17, Balinese custom would have made correction all the more urgent. Unlike the English, then—who, Godfrey (1747) said, began right-hand training to break the "[left-handed] Habit" only after the infant was "parted from the Nurse"—the Balinese, according to Mead (1942), began "as soon as the child is able to grasp at a proffered object", and discontinued it "usually when the child is off the hip" (p. 13) or no longer routinely carried because it was old enough to walk. By then, Mead perhaps meant that the child's native right-handedness would have emerged, just as Woolley (1910) assumed about her daughter, or that the training had taken effect. Mead also noted that when the infant used its left hand inappropriately, the mother not only restrained the left hand but also facilitated use of the right (1942, p. 13):

> Naturally, when a baby is offered a flower or a bit of cake, it reaches for it with the free left hand, and the mother ... invariably pulls the left hand back, extricates the baby's right hand — usually limp and motiveless under this interference with the free gesture — and extends the right hand to receive the gift.

To follow instructions

Given their near-perfect left bias for holding infants and the strict prohibitions against handling food with the left hand, could the Balinese also have been *taught* to hold infants on the left? Mead did not say, but that is what Andrew Buchanan (1862a), the dynamic balance theorist,

Figure 17. Balinese mother feeding herself while holding her infant (from Bateson & Mead, 1942, *Balinese Character*, plate 36, p. 126; courtesy New York Academy of Sciences).

implied about the left-hold in his own time: "an intelligent mother in the humble ranks of society" would explain that she held on the left to "keep her right hand free", but a nurserymaid "can probably only reply that she was instructed to do so, or that all other nurserymaids do the same" (p. 162). Buchanan did not name the instructor, but perhaps it was the mother herself. After all, if an intelligent mother in the *humble* ranks could explain the left hold's benefits, her wealthier counterpart could surely do the same for nurses and nursemaids in her employ.

For nurses and nursemaids who had been to school, the question of left-side instruction is more problematic given Burt's (1937) report that *right* holding was "orthodox" and was taught in nursing schools and institutions and in classes in infant management. Burt, however, used the qualifiers "some" for the former and "occasionally" for the latter, so perhaps other places taught *left* holding. In Ireland, one such place may have been the Dublin Lying-In Hospital. A photograph, reproduced in Figure 18 (from Kirkpatrick, 1913) and dated 1912, shows the head nurse, dressed in black, surrounded by 42 hospital "probationers", or student nurses, all women and all dressed in white. Except for the three in the top row, all are holding infants, all in the cradle position and, except for the

Figure 18. Head nurse and "probationers" at Dublin Lying-In Hospital (from Kirkpatrick, 1913, "The Probationers of the Hospital, 1912", facing p. 180).

second student from the right in row 2, all on the *left* side (the head nurse is holding two infants, one on each side). The percentage of left holders (38 of 39, or 97%) exceeds that in any study today. Such uniformity of style and near-uniformity of side surely could reflect instructions given *and* taken.

The indications here are indirect. There are more direct signs in early twentieth-century books on child care. In *The Mothercraft Manual*, Mary Read (1916) advised that for "lifting a young baby, the left hand and arm are slipped under the lower back, the right hand under the lower back", so that the infant "may be carried in one arm by supporting the head in the crook of the elbow" (p. 86). William and Lena Sadler (1919, p. 228) gave similar advice in *The Mother and Her Child*:

> A very young baby should be lifted from his bed by grasping the clothing below the feet with the right hand, while the left hand slips underneath the back and with spreading fingers supports the neck and head. It is then raised upon the left arm. During the early months the entire spine must be supported in this manner.

In both cases, the result would be a left-cradle, which the Sadlers (1919) illustrated with a photograph (Figure 19) entitled "How to Hold the Baby".

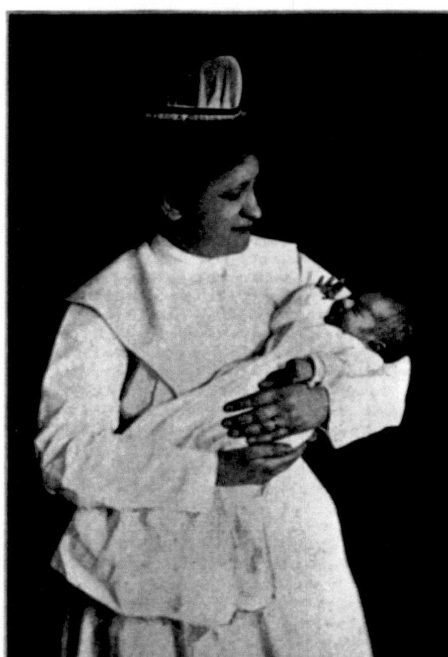

Figure 19. "How To Hold the Baby" (from Sadler & Sadler, 1919, facing p. 110).

In a later book, Lena Sadler (1925) included another photograph, also showing a left-cradle, entitled "Correct Position, if Baby is Held, While Taking Bottle Feeding". Although none of these books explained why the left hold was correct, the first two implied that it gave better support while the last implied that it was to free the right hand, whether for holding the bottle or for grasping the infant in preparation for lifting.

To favour the gentler, more delicate side

By the free-the-right-hand explanation, holding the infant on the left freed the right hand for feeding and other skilled acts; by the prohibition explanation, the left hold was required because only the right hand was allowed to perform these acts. Neither explanation therefore linked the left hold to any *positive* quality of the left side. One explanation, Kenealy's (1920), did just that. From ancient times the left and right sides were everywhere likened to the sexes—the left gentle, delicate, and female, drawing inward for acts of nurturance and care; the right strong, active, and male, projecting outward for acts of force and combat (Forbes, 1959; Hertz, 1909; Needham, 1973). In Kenealy's words (1920, p. 63):

> The left arm of woman is essentially the woman-member. In its half-passive action of supporting her infant for hours together, it is stronger for this maternal ministration than is the more active and doughty right arm of the male. Her left hand is more delicate of form, gentler and more soothing of motion than her right hand is. It is the hand she caresses with. While for direct, strong action — masculine action, that is — the paternal right half of her is dominant, as in the male.

Kenealy evidently meant that while the mother holds the infant on her left arm, and while also perhaps feeding the infant with her right hand, she caresses and soothes with her left. Because the left hold would constrain her left hand's range of motion, her caresses presumably would be mostly on the side or underside of the infant's body and limbs. In emphasising the left hold's soothing effect, Kenealy can be seen as anticipating Salk's explanation except for the agent of the effect: for Kenealy the hand, for Salk the heart.

To restore balance or body equilibrium

Buchanan (1862a) had yet another way to explain the left-hold bias. In keeping with his dynamic balance theory, it was that the left hold helped to restore balance, or equilibrium. The centre of gravity being on the right because of visceral asymmetry, "less inclination of the body to that side is required when the weight is appended to the left", which means "less interference with the natural play of the limbs in walking" (p. 163). With the right hold, however, "the body must be thrown very much to the opposite side to keep the equilibrium stable, and the motion of the limbs will be proportionately constrained" (p. 163). By this analysis, the left hold was well adapted for what Webster and Parkes (1848) called the nurse's "chief duties": "holding the infant in her arms" and carrying it about.

Note that the left-sider Buchanan (1862a) and the right-sider Hughes (1890) both used visceral asymmetry to explain side-of-hold. For Hughes, however, it predisposed lying on the right for *comfort*, with *right* holding as a by-product, whereas for Buchanan, for the standing position, it shifted the balance to the right, which right holding would exacerbate but left holding would help to correct.

To accommodate to the style of dress

Two authors also stated or implied a role for the style of dress. In Ancient Greece, a common article of clothing was the *himation*, or mantle, a long piece of cloth that was draped over one shoulder, wrapped around the body, and then gathered at the waist and, as Klein (1932, p. 35) explained, worn so as to leave only the right side free. She presumably meant that it was draped over the left shoulder, which is how it normally appears in statues and other images. For acts of infant care for which the right hand was more skilled, the infant would therefore have to be held on the left. Figure 20 shows an example.

Like nurses and mothers in the post-classical era (or at least until baby carriages became popular), the Greeks and Romans carried infants in their arms. So did the Balinese except that for carrying for long periods or while working in the fields they also used slings. As the photographs in Bateson and Mead (1942) showed, the sling, unlike the himation, was always worn over the *right* shoulder but now with the base, or pocket, securing the infant on the holder's left side. Although the result in this case was to leave both of the holder's limbs free, the left was positioned behind the infant where it could be used for further support and only the right was used for attending to the infant, as shown in the photograph in Figure 21 of a mother using her right hand to help her infant suckle. In analysing the photographs, we therefore focused on *non-sling* holds on the view that they would more accurately reflect any bias freely expressed. The results were virtually the same: nearly all were on the left (Harris et al., 2002). Note that the nurse in Boilly's painting (Figure 4) also wears a sling over her right shoulder and holds the infant on her left.

Figure 20. Woman wearing *himation* and feeding infant (from Klein, 1932, plate IIIA; courtesy The Metropolitan Museum of Art, New York).

To hold near the soulful heart

Finally, with respect to the practice of nursing first on the left, as described by Alexander and recommended by the rabbis of medieval times, the reason, as the rabbis explained, was the left breast's closeness to the heart. But whereas for Salk it was the heart's soothing beat that mattered, for the rabbis it was its soulfulness—its being the seat of the soul, meaning the mind, wisdom, and life itself. In ancient times, many others believed the same, including Aristotle (1912b: 655b). If Aristotle, for this reason, also recommended nursing first on the left, could that be how his student Alexander learned of the practice? As Klein (1998) notes, the same link between heart, soul, and the left breast can be found in The Talmud, the record of rabbinic discussions on Jewish law, ethics, customs, and history, compiled from 200–500 B.C.E.

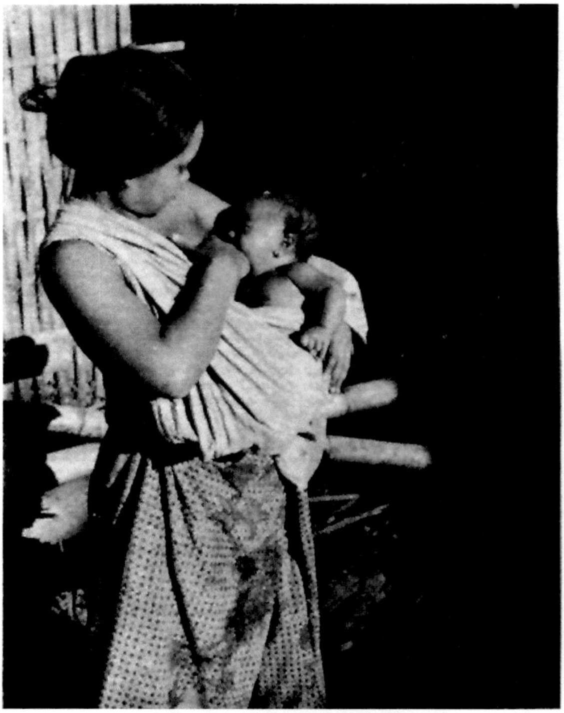

Figure 21. Balinese mother suckling her infant (photograph by Gregory Bateson; from Mead & Macgregor, 1951, Plate XIII – I Ngendon, #2, facing p. 88; courtesy The Institute for Intercultural Studies, New York)

HOLDING BOYS VS HOLDING GIRLS

In Klein's (1998) account, there is a tantalising hint that any left-hold preference might also have varied with the sex of the child. The reason pertains to men's and women's different obligations for studying Torah, the narrative of Jewish religious teachings and principles of law and ethics. Because Torah study was required only for men, for whom learning and wisdom were seen as more important, some rabbis confined their advice about nursing first on the left to the nursing of *sons*. If we can suppose that mothers who followed their advice came to *prefer* the left side, it is conceivable that they showed this preference more strongly when holding their sons than their daughters. Similar beliefs about male primacy and duty, of course, can be found in other times and places. Consider the engraving in Figure 22. Made in France in 1776 by J. J. Moreau the younger, it shows a nurse holding the master's newborn son (and on the left side). The title "*C'est un fils, Monsieur!*" and the father's response speak for themselves.

Figure 22. *"C'est un fils, Monsieur!"* Engraving, 1776, by Jean Charles Baquoy (1721–1777), from a drawing by Jean Michael Moreau, the younger, 1776 (reproduced in Abt, 1965, p. 83).

Ancient Greece was another bastion of male primacy, in which case Alexander's reference to the nursing of *sons* may be significant.

If more boys were nursed first on the left and held preferentially on that side, then by the left-side hypothesis more boys should be left-handed. One wonders whether Christopher Wren had this in mind when he wrote, "but among the Irish who carry their children astride their neckes, you shall rarely see one left-handed, *of either Sex*" (emphasis added). Recall that Wren believed that left-handedness was unnatural and found only, as in England, where infants are carried on the left. If more boys *were* left-handed, and if Wren thought that was why, was he underscoring the point by noting that left-handedness in Ireland is rare in children of "either Sex", meaning even in boys?

WHAT ABOUT MEN?

When Kenealy (1920) called the woman's left arm "more delicate of form, gentler and more soothing in motion", she presumably did not mean that only the *woman's* left arm had those qualities. They belonged to the limb itself and to both sexes. Still, in focusing on mothers, was she implying that more women held on the left or that men even preferred the right? If so, then except perhaps for Burt (1937), as I shall explain later, she would have been the only early author to allude to, much less mention, *men's* preferences or even to stipulate that the reference group was women rather than people generally. That men were overlooked is understandable, since infant-care was *women's* work. This is shown in the literature of the time, including books and manuals on child-rearing, as well as in drawings and photographs of people holding infants, like those reproduced in this article, where nearly all holders are women. In a survey of early Renaissance to contemporary-era paintings of people holding infants, Finger (1975) estimated that the holder was a man in less than 4%.[15]

In public, men occasionally held and carried infants, but the men and the occasions were usually special. Pictorial examples include men in nurturing, protective roles, such as St. Vincent de Paul rescuing children abandoned in the streets of nineteenth-century Paris (Figure 23A), and in patriarchal roles, such as monarchs presenting their male heirs to the people, whether it is Napoleon holding the King of Rome after his baptism (Figure 23B) or Louis XII holding the Dauphin (Figure 23C). Some images of St. Paul show him with one infant, others with two, but the holds are always tender and close with most, perhaps not coincidentally, on the left; the monarchs, by contrast, hold their sons aloft and facing away for display. The latter images further illustrate male primacy, since daughters are never shown. A few images from classical times also show fathers holding infants, and the holds are also on the left (e.g., VRoma, 2008). In Greece and Rome, the male costume for citizens was the toga which, like the himation, was worn so as to leave the right hand less encumbered (Wilson, 1924, p. 126).[16] The intent again was to free the right hand and arm for public acts including, for men, their use for gesturing according to the rules of rhetoric (Harris, 1989). For men, style of dress therefore would have favoured holding on the left.

One more example—a second photograph from the Dublin Lying-In Hospital (Kirkpatrick, 1913)—bears special mention. The first photograph (Figure 18), from 1912, showed student nurses, all of them women, holding infants. This one, from 1911 (Figure 24), shows student midwives, now with men greatly outnumbering women (29 to 7). The difference reflects the extent to which, by the early twentieth century, men had come to

[15] Times have changed, but even today direct observations as well as family portraits and photographs show that the woman more often holds the child, especially if it is an infant (Harris et al., 2007; Lockard et al., 1979; Manning, 1991; Rheingold & Keene, 1965; Roopnarine, Talukder, Jain, Joshi, & Srivastava, 1990).

[16] In putting on the toga it was first thrown over the left shoulder so that about 6 feet hung in front and about 12 feet behind. The longer portion was then carried under the right arm and then diagonally across the chest and over the left shoulder again. A fold of this portion hanging in front formed the "sinus" (notes by Butler, in Quintilian, 1936, p. 318).

Figure 23. Men holding infants. (A) Saint Vincent de Paul rescuing children abandoned in the streets of Paris. Drawing made from a statue by Alexandre Falguière, in the Pantheon, Paris (reproduced in Abt, 1965, p. 70). (B) "A L'émpereur les bonnes villes de l'empire"; medal struck to mark the occasion of the baptism of the King of Rome (reproduced in Witkowski, 1890, p. 371). (C) Louis XIII presenting his son, the Dauphin, to the people, 1638 (reproduced in Witkowski, 1890, p. 176).

dominate the "new obstetrics", that part of midwifery concerned with difficult labours requiring access to and training in the use of new medical instruments such as forceps. Many of these men went on to become general practitioners while women were relegated to the practice of normal births (Donnison, 1988).

Unlike the student nurses, so uniform in their style and side of hold, the student midwives show a mix of styles, with left holds barely more frequent than right holds: 15 vs 14 for the men, 4 vs 2 for the women. If the student

Figure 24. Student midwives at Dublin Lying-In Hospital (from Kirkpatrick, 1913, "A Group of Students, 1911", facing p. 132).

nurses' uniformity reflected instructions in style and side, that cannot be said for the student midwives, but they were being trained to deliver babies, not to hold, feed, or carry them about. Posing them holding infants may have been *pro forma*, which may be why, at least for the men, several look as if they have not done it before. The men's near-equal numbers of left and right holds also fit with those current reports showing a weaker left bias in men.

For the historical periods covered in this article, these are, for the most part, the only kinds of images I found of men holding infants. One notable exception is Balinese men, who hold infants "tenderly and skillfully" (Mead, 1942, p. 24) and, like the women, predominantly on the left for sling- and non-sling holds alike (Harris et al., 2002). The difference is that men held and carried only their own kin, whereas women made no distinction.[17]

That holding and carrying infants was women's work may explain not only why men were almost always overlooked in the early reports, but also why Burt (1937), after citing evidence from his records against the side-of-hold explanation of handedness, could add one more example where the explanation "must plainly break down altogether". These were cases where "not the mother, but the father is the left-handed parent of the left-handed child" (p. 300), the implication being that fathers could not have made their children left-handed from left-side holding because they did not hold them enough to make a difference.

HOLDING INFANTS VS HOLDING INANIMATE OBJECTS

In my introduction, I noted that the left bias was robust for holding infants, but weaker, absent, or even reversed for inanimate objects. Did early authors make this distinction?

Right-siders

Among the right-siders, no one did. Nor would it fit their explanations of the bias. For example, if right-handers prefer the right because it is stronger, and if stronger meant safer—important for holding a precious, vulnerable infant—the same could be said for holding anything with these qualities. The exception would be an explanation built on Hall and Hartwell's (1884)

[17] There is one other kind of image that I have not included: men holding infants they have killed or are about to kill. Needless to say, their holds were not for giving comfort. For example, in Raphael's fresco *The Judgment of Solomon* (1509–1511; 1518–1519), the infant is held or swung roughly by one limb. In that instance, of course, the infant was spared.

observation that infants prefer to feed from the right breast. Of course, inanimate objects have no "preferences" of this or any kind.

Left-siders

No left-sider made the distinction either, although it was implicit in Kenealy's (1920) explanation that left holding favoured the "more delicate, gentler" *left* hand. I mean that these qualities would be irrelevant for inanimate objects except for those that can easily break. The distinction was also implicit in the free-the-right-hand explanation, since inanimate objects would not need the skilled ministrations of the right hand. For Buchanan's (1862a) dynamic-balance theory, however, there was no rationale for a distinction because an infant held on the left and a package held on the left, of the same size and weight, should restore balance or equilibrium equally well. In accord with this view, after describing the nurserymaid who "carries an infant on her left arm", Buchanan added, "Look at the women who go along with baskets of eggs or vegetables. They all carry the baskets on their left arms" (p. 162). "[C]arrying or supporting burdens" thus was the "special function of the left side" (p. 163). In this connection, in a different printing of his article, Buchanan (1862b, p. 29) quoted Aristotle who, in support of his thesis that movement begins on the right, stated that "all [men] throw the burden on the left side; for that which supports the weight must be moved, while that which moves is free."[18]

There were at least three others whose views Buchanan should have found compatible with his own. One was the physician George Sigerson (1884), who, after examining casts of warriors with shields in the Irish National Gallery, concluded that "in peace, the left hand carries, whilst the right is extended" (p. 39). Another was the anthropologist Frank Hamilton Cushing (1892). Drawing on the then-popular "heart-shield" theory of handedness (Pye-Smith, 1871), he observed that inasmuch as the left hand carries the shield over the heart while the right hand wields the sword, man has "*acted* constantly with the right hand; *carried* as constantly with the left" (p. 290). For Cushing, it was therefore natural for the Zuñi Indians of the American southwest to call "the right hand the 'Taker,' the left hand the 'Holder'" (p. 290). The third was the anthropologist Robert Hertz (1909), cited earlier, who was the first to document the universality of the different meanings of left and right. In his essay "The pre-eminence of the right hand: A study in religious polarity" he wrote: "To the right hand go honors, flattering

[18] Buchanan did not identify the translation. In the Farquharson translation (Aristotle, 1912a, 705b, 30), the passage reads: "all men carry burdens on the left shoulder; in this way they set free the side which initiates movement and enable the side which bears the weight to be moved."

designations, prerogatives: it acts, orders, and *takes*. The left hand, on the contrary, is despised and reduced to the role of a humble auxiliary: by itself it can do nothing; it helps, it supports, it *holds*" (translated from the French by Rodney Needham; in Needham, 1973, p. 3).

In linking the left hold (like right-handedness itself) to a visceral asymmetry, Buchanan (1862a) implied that exceptions would be as rare as visceral transposition. In that case, as Daniel Wilson (1891) predicted, "the great majority of mankind should instinctively use the same side in bearing a burden" (p. 170). To find out, he observed deck-porters loading freight onto a Mississippi steamboat (p. 171):

> Watching them closely, I observed that some gave the preference to the right and some to the left shoulder in bearing their burdens; and this whether, as with bale and sack, they had it placed on their shoulders by others, or, as with cordwood, they took up the load themselves.

For three series of 218, 121, and 101 observations, the percentages of left holds were 64%, 62%, and 64%, respectively. Wilson set the results against Buchanan's theory, seeing correctly that it predicted far higher figures. At the same time, he made nothing of the fact that the results showed a left bias. Because Wilson did not report how many deck-porters he had observed, his figures cannot be statistically evaluated. We probably cannot assume that each observation represented an individual deck-porter, but if it did, all three percentages would be significantly different from chance ($p < .05$) based on the binomial distribution.

HOLDING LIGHTER VS HEAVIER WEIGHTS

Finally, in my introduction, I noted the possibility that, at least for right-handers, the left bias decline with age is related to the infant's increasing size and weight, along with the change from holding for the purpose of feeding and comforting to holding for the purpose of transport. Given the nurse's "chief duties" to hold and carry the infant for long periods, and based on the "strength" explanation of the right hold, one would expect at least some early authors to have distinguished between holding younger, lighter vs older, heavier infants. None did, but among those who saw no difference between holding infants and holding inanimate objects, three authors, all left-siders, said that weight would *not* make a difference.

The first was the right-handed J.H. (1889). After stating that he held an infant on his left arm, he added that he did the same for any "load to carry", including his briefcase, "even when it is heavy and laden with books" (p. 701).

Figure 25. Engraving (from Buchanan, 1862a, p. 163).

The second was Buchanan (1862a), who supposed that an object's weight would affect the type of hold but not the side—the left side was for "light weights swung upon the arm" (p. 163) as well as for "heavier weights borne upon the shoulder". He illustrated the latter in an engraving (Figure 25) and explained that different factors governed the two types of hold (p. 163).

> Whereas the lighter weight is held on the left for maintaining equilibrium, [the heavier] burden is in reality supported, not by the left, but by the right lower limb. The body is inclined to the right side [as it is for the act of throwing a stone], so that the mechanical axis passes from the left shoulder to the right foot, and the load is placed right upon the top of it, the whole force of the right arm being employed to place it there. In this way the muscles exert their full force effectively in sustaining the load, while the body is so disposed that it can revolve freely on its mechanical axis, which is of great service in adjusting and throwing off the load.

Buchanan concluded by comparing the right side to a horse, "prompt, rapid, powerful, and graceful in its movements", and the left side to a camel, a "beast of burden", "less ready, and more slow and awkward, but bearing its burden indefatigably, and stooping to receive and to be released from its load" (pp. 163–164).

The third was Burt (1937). Referring to the strength explanation of the right hold, which he himself had entertained, he noted: "On the contrary, the left hand is very generally used for carrying heavy objects" (p. 299), and even when a mother clasps her child against her right shoulder, "she often uses her

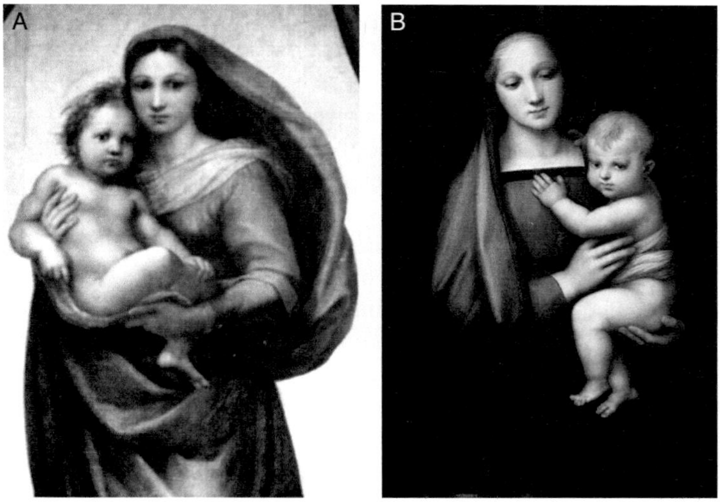

Figure 26. Madonnas by Raphael. (a) *Sistine Madonna*, 1513–1514 (detail). Oil on canvas. Original in Gemäldegalerie Alte Meister, Dresden, Germany. Retrieved 15 November 2007, from http://en.wikipedia.org/wiki/Sistine_Madonna__(Raphael) (b) *Madonna del Granduca*, probably 1505. Oil on wood. Original in Palazzo Pitti, Florence. Retrieved 15 November 2007, from http://en.wikipedia.org/wiki/Madonna_Madonna_del_Granduca

left hand to support him, leaving to the right hand, as the more delicate and agile member, the task of supplying any additional adjustment or aid" (p. 299). To illustrate, Burt referred to two portraits by Raphael of the Madonna and Child from his survey. In the *Sistine Madonna* (Figure 26A) the child is on the right, in the *Madonna del Granduca* (Figure 26B) the child is on the left, but in each the Madonna's left hand bears most of the weight so that, in effect, both are left holds.[19] That would fit with what the child-rearing books had implied (Read, 1916; Sadler & Sadler, 1919)—that the left hold gives better support.

POSSIBLE LESSONS FOR CURRENT THEORY AND RESEARCH

This concludes my survey of the early reports. Now, what of their possible lessons for theory and research today? I mean the explanations as well as the observations themselves.

[19] In describing the right hand as "delicate" in the sense of "agile", Burt was evidently referring to a different quality from what Kenealy (1920) meant when she called the *left* hand more "delicate". Thus Burt, while identifying the left hand as the weight-bearer, also incorporated the free-the-right-hand explanation into his account.

A closer look at the explanations

Handedness

Let us begin with the two versions of the handedness explanation. Researchers today reject the free-the-dominant-hand version because right- and left-handers both hold preferentially on the left. Early proponents of this version never compared right- and left-handers directly, but they were correct at least to the extent that among the majority of right-handers who hold on the left, and the minority of left-handers who hold on the right, some do *say* that it frees their dominant hand for other acts (Cárdenas, Almerigi, Puts, & Harris, 2007), and correct to an even greater extent when, as I noted, the holder gives the infant (or doll) a bottle. But this version of the handedness explanation needs more comprehensive testing, especially by controlling the skill demands of the concurrent act. For example, to cut an infant's nails one can normally use *only* the dominant hand, so that virtually all right- and left-handers would be expected to hold the infant on the side opposite that hand, whereas bottle-feeding or hair-brushing can be performed more nearly equally well by either hand, even if the dominant hand is normally favoured.

The strength version deserves consideration as well. For one thing, some right- and left-handers who hold on the dominant-hand side do say it is because it is stronger (Cárdenas et al., 2007); for another, questionnaire studies show that right-handers hold heavy burdens on the right, including a "heavy suitcase" and a "briefcase full of books" (e.g., Grimshaw & Bryden, 1994; Kang, 1992), or at least use either hand (Steenhuis & Bryden, 1989). The strength version, however, conflicts with Burt's (1937) remark that the left hand is "very generally used for carrying heavy objects" (p. 299), with Wilson's (1891) observations of deck-porters, and with Buchanan's (1862a) calling the left side a "beast of burden" for light and heavy weights alike.

For light weights that can be carried "upon the arm", or "swung", to use Buchanan's word, I see no simple resolution of the conflict, but for heavier weights "borne upon the shoulder" the key perhaps is the kind of hold. For example, as infants grow older and heavier and are shifted from left cradling to right-arm-holding, perhaps for shoulder holds the *left* remains the preferred side. Even so, by Buchanan's (1862a) balance hypothesis the right, or dominant, arm would take the lead because lifting a heavy burden is predominantly by action of the right side (hand and arm), and then if the burden is to be "borne upon the shoulder" it is transferred to the left (see again Figure 25). Buchanan thus can be said to have distinguished between *left*-side dominance for *passive holding* and *right*-side dominance for *active lifting*. His analysis suggests that we analyse the movements leading to picking up, holding, and carrying infants and other burdens, taking their size and weight into account. The holder's strength and handedness should be considered too, along with the hold duration to find out whether the side changes over time, even for light burdens. Burt's (1937) statement that the left hand bears the weight even for right-side holding also deserves testing and raises the question whether, for right- as well as left-handers, left- and right-side holds are true mirror-reversals in position and action of the body and limbs. Burt's statement suggests that they are not. The strength version of the handedness explanation also implies an interaction of handedness, side-of-hold, and infant age; namely, the left bias will weaken for right-handers as the infant grows bigger and heavier, but *strengthen* for *left-handers*, who are already holding on their stronger side.

When all is said and done, adequate tests of the two versions of the handedness explanation are lacking. A further complication is left-handers' greater heterogeneity as a group (Peters, 1996) and the dissociation in some individuals between strength and skill (Peters & Servos, 1989).

Social rules pertaining to use of the hands

Also worth further study is the relation between side-of-hold and social customs for hand-use, especially the prohibitions against using the left hand for food-handling and other social acts. So far, among current authors, only Nakamichi (1996) has mentioned these customs but in his case to explain the *right-hold* bias among the Malagasey. Noting that such prohibitions are common on the African mainland (e.g., Wieschhoff, 1973), he suggested that they might also be common in Madagascar, even for holding an infant. But if they are, they could apply only to carrying and transport (the only acts Nakamichi observed), not to feeding. Otherwise, the food must be offered with the *left* hand. In Bali, as already mentioned, all photographs of mothers holding infants while feeding them or feeding themselves show left holds (Harris et al., 2002), but more cross-cultural studies are needed, along with a closer look at Madagascar itself because Nakamichi (1996) did not assess such prohibitions directly.

Delicacy of form and movement

Kenealy (1920) supposed that the left side is preferred because the left hand is more "delicate of form" and "soothing of motion"—that it is "the hand [the mother] caresses with". These too are possibilities worth testing. But if left-hand movements *are* more delicate and soothing, could the reason also lie in differences in *sensory acuity*? Such differences favouring the left hand and arm were first reported by Ernst Weber (1834) for warmth and weight (see Mollon, 1978) and later for pressure sensitivity and point localisation (e.g., Weinstein, 1968; Wolff & Jarvik, 1964). The reliability of the reports has been questioned (e.g., Corkin, 1978; Kaplan-Solms & Saling,

1988), but they are supported by new evidence that the right hemisphere leads in somatosensory processing (Coghill, Gilron, & Iadarola, 2001; Fagot, Lacreuse, & Vauclair, 1997), although the matter remains unsettled (e.g., Long, 1994). Possibly, even a small difference in acuity could predispose a left hold by enhancing the holder's sensitivity to the infant's needs as expressed in its body tonus, thereby helping the holder adjust to and soothe the infant more effectively. And if, as Kenealy (1920) implied, these movement styles and sensory qualities are more common in women, perhaps they even contribute to the sex difference in strength of the left bias.

The cosmology of the body

Kenealy's (1920) calling the left arm "essentially the women member" suggests yet another approach to studying the laterality of holding and carrying. As already noted, many indigenous societies describe human laterality in gendered terms – the feminine left limb drawing inward for acts of nurturance and care, the masculine right limb projecting outward for acts of force and combat. These societies include Bali, where the relation between left and right is said to be not merely of dual opposites but of the enveloping of the intimate and feminine in a protective cloak of the social and the masculine:

> Consequently, in magical practices the right side becomes the side for "male" magic such as the invulnerability to weapons. It is associated with aggressiveness and combativeness as well as rectitude. The left side on the contrary, is the side of "female" magic associated with health and caring as well as deviousness. (Ottino, 2000, p. 259; see also Tcherkézoff, 1987)

In this light, and putting aside the association with deviousness, holding infants on the left could be seen to exemplify this drawing inward for nurturance and care, so that whatever might be the role of lateral sensory differences, the left hold would be enhanced by the cosmology of the body itself—the meanings associated with its different parts. Such associations presumably cannot explain the right-hold bias in Madagascar, but they could have further strengthened the left-hold bias in Bali. The near-total left bias shown in the Balinese photographs suggests as much, but independent evidence is lacking. As for people in industrialised societies, they show some of the same associations, although muted, or disguised. For example, Domhoff (1969–1970) found what he saw as evidence of the male–female (but also the good–bad) dichotomy in the psychoanalytic literature on dreams and in his own studies of American college students and schoolchildren using the semantic differential. The left was female, unclean, curved, limp, and weak (among other attributes); the right was just the opposite. Unfortunately, Domhoff did not test for the positive qualities of nurturance, health, and caring, but if they were found to be associated with leftness and femaleness sufficient to outweigh the negative qualities, it is conceivable that the associations, collectively, could predict the preferred side for holding an infant, especially where nurturing and care are needed.

Balance and equilibrium and their effects on comfort and restfulness

Buchanan's (1862a) dynamic balance theory has failed as an explanation of handedness, but balance and equilibrium might still contribute to side-of-hold biases. Among left holders in our studies, right- and left-handers alike, many (about 40% in Cárdenas et al., 2007) say that the left hold "just feels right" or "more comfortable". These feelings may reflect what Buchanan called "balance", and what Burt (1937) meant in calling the left hold more "natural" (another term used by many of our participants). The problem is that all these terms are poorly defined. For example, comfort and discomfort are often used as reciprocals of the same dimension even though ergonomic studies show them to be affected by different variables, meaning that different criteria should be used in their assessment (Helander & Zhang, 1997). For the acts of holding and carrying, the acts themselves need to be closely examined along with the different but complementary roles of the left and right hands and arms.

Comfort and the centre of gravity. Buchanan's (1862a) analysis hinged on his conception of the body centre of gravity, now more commonly called the body centre of mass (BMOC). He was correct that it is not the geometric centre (Duggar, 1962); it would be only if the body were of uniform density and/or the weight were evenly distributed. Today, the BMOC is the subject of much research by human factors specialists, especially those studying the biomechanics of movement, including lifting, standing, and walking (e.g., Benda, Riley, & Krebs, 1994; Gard, Miff, & Kuo, 2004). It also figures in research on the energy costs of holding and carrying infants and even in their hypothesised role in the evolution of the sexually dimorphic human pelvis (Pawlowski & Grabarczyk, 2003; Wall-Scheffler, Geiger, & Steudel-Numbers, 2007). The BMOC also has been applied to the functional analysis of asymmetric lifting (Danneels et al., 2001) but not yet to lifting, holding, and carrying an infant.

Comfort and posture. Buchanan's (1862a, 1862b) and Burt's (1937) focus on balance, comfort, and doing what feels "natural" is also consonant with Saling and Cooke's (1984) description of the act of holding as "a tonic postural configuration" (p. 335). They meant how one arranges the parts of the body—neck, arms, shoulders, trunk, and hips—to produce an agreeable feeling of tonus, or muscular tension. In contrast to precision finger and hand movements, whose control lies in the pyramidal motor system, postural acts depend more on extrapyramidal structures. Unlike pyramidal structures, which mediate the most voluntary, least automatic movements, extrapyramidal structures serve less voluntary, more automatic movements, just the kind involved in the act of cradling and arm-holding, and just the kind that could make some positions feel more comfortable, balanced, or natural.

For the upper limbs, this analysis fits with evidence that handedness is multidimensional, with some tasks, such as targeted ball-throwing, dependent on inter-joint coordination and control of inter-segmental dynamics, whereas other tasks, such as holding a piece of paper while cutting it with scissors or orienting a hand in space for catching a ball, are more spatial-postural. The former tasks are performed almost exclusively by the dominant hand and arm, the latter more often by the non-dominant side (e.g., Sainburg, 2002; Sainburg, Ghez, & Kalalanis, 1999). Unlike inanimate objects, infants squirm, twist, and change positions so that, at least for the right-hander, frequent and fluent adjustments of the holder's arm might be among the tasks favouring the non-dominant, or left, side. As for the lower limbs, the analysis fits with the comfort-posture hypothesis mentioned in the introduction, which relates the preferred side-of-hold to the preferred direction of shifting one's weight (e.g., Erber, Almerigi, Carbary, & Harris, 2002).

Comfort, posture, and achieving the most restful position. If comfort and posture are important for the sense of restfulness, they should figure in Hughes' (1890) analysis of the mother's recumbent position for nursing—that she prefers to lie on her right side, with the infant on her right arm, because it is the "more restful" position. Other than Hughes's account, however, there are evidently no side-of-hold studies for the recumbent position, so the question is open. But if lying on the right side is more restful, it is presumably not because it restores the balance and equilibrium disturbed by the asymmetrical position of the viscera, as it would, according to Buchanan (1862a), for the standing position. Nonetheless, it may still have to do with visceral position. Recall that Hughes focused on the liver, which "lies on the right side" (p. 147), so that the mother, in effect, lies on her heavier side. The stomach might be critical too because of the asymmetrical positions of the oesophagus and pylorus as they enter and leave the stomach, respectively. Especially after eating, lying on the right side would use gravity to promote digestion and gastric drainage, which is the rationale for placing the infant, post-prandially, on its right side with head slightly elevated (e.g., Miller & Stark, 2007). But if the mother lies on her right side during nursing, the infant would have to lie on its left (see Figure 8), so that the position would favour the mother's comfort over the infant's. That prompts the question whether, for nursing, women who prefer to hold on the right while lying supine, prefer to hold on the left while sitting or standing.

Accommodating to the style of dress

What of the possible link between side-of-hold and style of dress? The question has not come up in current studies, but it too may be worth considering. For example, baby slings are ubiquitous in traditional societies and are becoming so in the industrialised world, judging from advertising, sales figures, and new patents (e.g., Carmichael, 2007). To the extent that in Bali and other traditional societies, custom continues to dictate right-hand use for food handling, it would imply that the sling will be worn with the base, or pocket, on the left, so that all sling-holds should be on the left as they were in Bali in the 1930s. In many industrialised societies, however, where restrictions on left-hand use for food handling are no longer imposed and where slings can be worn on either side, the left bias for sling-holds should be lower, closer to that found in the absence of slings.

In Ing et al.'s (1977a) report of right-side nursing among the Tanka, there also is a suggestion that the practice was required by the design of the women's dresses, which opened only on the right. Unfortunately, no reasons or details were given. For example, did the design reflect body cosmology but now the good–bad rather than masculine–feminine dimension? If so, perhaps the Tanka believed that the right breast, as Hall and Hartwell (1884) supposed, gave "the best and richest milk" (p. 96).[20] In that case, breast preference could have dictated the dress design rather than the other way round. In a further communication the authors noted that "most Tanka women", when asked why they nursed only from the right breast, "said that it was more convenient" (Ing et al., 1977b, p. 657), which sounds like a reference to dress design. However, the practice was "now being abandoned, especially by young Tanka mothers", more of whom were being delivered in hospitals and were attending maternal and child health clinics, "where they are being advised to breast-feed from both breasts" (p. 657). If, as this suggests, the right-breast preference is a thing of the past, we may never learn why it was preferred or whether there was an associated right-side preference for holding or carrying.

[20] In that case, the belief presumably would override actual physiological differences, since the authors noted that the milk supply has been "abundant on both sides", making it unlikely that Tanka women have "a poor milk secretion from the left breast owing to a genetic predisposition" (Ing et al., 1977b, p. 657).

Instructions and training

For the early reports, the role of instructions and training remains a puzzle because so far, for right-side instructions, we have only Burt's (1937) and Buchanan's (1862a) statements, and for left-side instructions only Read's (1916) and Sadler and Sadler's (1919). The last two, as I said, were the only ones specifically addressed to mothers and nurses and the only instances of direct instructions that I found. The one other instance was indirect: the near-perfect left bias in the photograph of student nurses in the Dublin Lying-In Hospital (Figure 18). For our own time, when I checked a sample of books on obstetrics, midwifery, nursing, and infant-care (Biancuzzo, 1999; Brennan & Heilman, 1977; Kenner, Amlung, & Flandermeyer, 1998; LaCerva, 1981; Moore, 1972, 1981; Sweet, 1982; Wong & Perry, 1998), I found only one—a nurse's manual on teaching mothers to breast-feed—that mentioned side-of-hold but only to note that most women prefer nursing on the *left*, probably because they "are more comfortable holding on this side" (Biancuzzo, 1999, p. 118). The author, however, did not recommend that nurses teach this to mothers. As in any occupation, though, many details of nurses' training are learned on-the-job, although from what I have been told about current training in Great Britain and the United States these details do not include instructions about side-of-holding. But whether or not it is taught, nurses today evidently show the same left-hold bias as do mothers and other women. For example, in our photographic survey (Harris et al., 2007), although mothers holding their newborns were the primary focus of interest, nurses occasionally were shown holding the infant, and they too more often held on the left. Of course, none of this means that left- *or* right-holding was *not* taught in the past.

Today the role of instruction, like that of the cosmology of the body, has hardly been raised, but it too may be worth studying. Instructions need not be explicit: they could be conveyed through modelling and imitation, both known to be effective for motor learning (e.g., Iacoboni et al., 1999). Instructions might help to explain why, except for fathers holding their newborns, the modal left bias is often weaker in men. The mother being the first to hold the infant, the father might be inclined to imitate. She also could teach him the "correct" way" by placing the infant in his arms.

The soulful heart

What of the ancient belief in the heart as the seat of the soul? In an essay "The matter of the (thoughtful) heart" the anthropologist Jay Miller (1980) traced its persistence in traditional societies throughout the world. His examples include the Delaware people from the eastern United States, for whom the heart is the source of thought and emotion (Miller, 1977); the people of the western plains culture area, who point to the heart and then bring the hand forward "to gesture thought coming forth from the heart" (Sebeok & Umiker-Sebeok, 1978, p. 120); and the people of the northwest, whose widely used trade pidgin called *Chinook jargon* expresses the word for thinking as literally "to use the heart" (Gill, 1933, p. 34). Indigenous peoples in these same parts of the world and elsewhere also hold infants preferentially on the left. Could a belief in the soulful heart have guided their choice, and could a similar belief, at least in the figurative sense, even affect people in the industrialised world?

Holding boys vs holding girls

The possibility that such beliefs could influence the side-of-hold, along with the rabbinic argument that nursing from the left breast is more important for sons, prompts other questions: Do mothers, or parents generally, use the left hold more often for sons, and has this anything to do with male primacy? One way to find out might be to compare side-of-hold figures in regions of the world where sons are strongly favoured, as in East and South Asia (e.g., Gupta, 1987; Gupta et al., 2002), with regions where both sexes are valued more nearly equally, as in Europe, Canada, and the United States (e.g., Hank & Kohler, 2000). But if differences occur, other factors also might be at play. One reason is that in the one study reporting differences (Lockard et al., 1979), where 70% of women held boys on the left versus 58% for girls (estimated from authors' bar graph, Fig. 1, p. 239), the observations were made in the United States, where some evidence suggests that women prefer *daughters*, whereas it is *men* who prefer sons (e.g., Pooler, 1991). The nature of the preference should also be considered. For example, in a Canadian study of new parents, fathers and mothers both expressed more "pride" at the birth of sons but more "happiness" at the birth of daughters. The authors suggested that parents unconsciously categorised boys and girls into different motivational systems: status and attachment, respectively (Gonzalez & Koestner, 2005). However, the most compelling indication that other factors are at work is that differences like those found in human mothers (Lockard et al., 1979) were found in two of the studies, cited earlier, of non-human primates. In Manning et al. (1994), in all four species—chimpanzees, gorillas, orangutans, and gibbons—proportionately more male than female infants were held on the left, although the difference was significant only in gorillas; and in Nishida (1993), the left-side nipple preference in chimpanzee suckling, which as we recall the author credited to left-side holding, was stronger in males. On the premise that the left hold signifies closer attention and care, Manning et al. (1994) suggest that the sex difference in humans and non-humans alike may have originated as an adaptation to males' higher neonatal mortality (Clutton-Brock, 1991; see also Kraemer, 2008).

Reconciliation of the right- and left-side reports

There is still the matter of the conflicting right- and left-side reports and their possible reconciliation. Putting aside the unlikely possibility that the differences are products of differences in the infants' age and weight, with older, heavier infants over-represented in right-side reports and therefore more often held on the normally stronger side, and putting aside the seemingly even more remote possibility that right-holders' garments were designed for right-side holding, there are two explanations that may be worth considering.

Role of instruction and training

The more straightforward would credit the roles of natural preference along with instruction and training. If, as Burt (1937) and others surmised, the left hold was *naturally* preferred, whereas the right hold was taught, and recalling that "holding" and "carrying" were the nurse's "chief duties" (Webster & Parke, 1848), the reports could be reconciled if *right-side* instructions were only for the *on-arm hold*, to be used for holding and carrying, especially for long periods and distances requiring strength and endurance. In that case, *left*-side instructions would have been only for nursing, feeding, and other acts requiring use of the right hand, and for which the cradle position would be the mode, and would have served mainly to reinforce the *natural* left-hold preference. This explanation fits with another photograph from the past, now from the United States (Figure 27). Dated 1918, it shows three hospital nurses, each holding an infant, one on the left side, two on the right. (A fourth infant lies in a stroller.) The infant held on the left is cradled; the two held on the right are seated upright on the nurse's arm.

Role of the holder's emotional state

The other explanation involves something not yet mentioned: the holder's emotional state. Recall that 83% of the mothers in Salk's hospital study held on the left. All had normal deliveries and contact with their infants immediately after birth. In another group, this one of mothers initially separated from their infants because of prematurity or illness, only 52% held on the left (Salk, 1970). Salk offered no explanation. Later studies, however, show a bias decline, or even reversal, in adults of both sexes in certain psychological states—in depressed, anxious, stressed, or "emotionally uninvolved" mothers of newborns (de Château, 1991) and older infants (Weatherill et al., 2004), in nulliparous women whose stress was experimentally induced (Suter, Huggenberger, & Schächinger, 2007), and in expectant

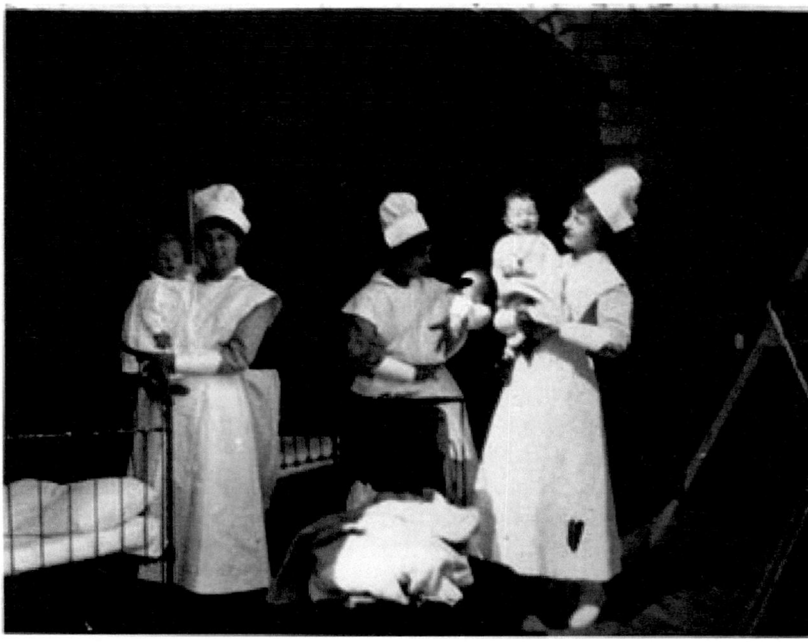

Figure 27. "Nurses holding babies," 1918, Beth El Hospital, Colorado Springs, Colorado (courtesy Special Collections, Pikes Peak Library District, Colorado Springs, CO). Retrieved 25 February 2008, from http://library.ppld.org/SpecialCollections/Project/admin/FullDisplay.asp?ID=2172

fathers diagnosed with the couvade syndrome, with symptoms including depression and dysphoria (Bogren, 1985).

These reports suggest that stress and related emotional states may have contributed to Salk's results for separation, prematurity, and illness. By the attention, or emotional-monitoring, explanation, the mothers in his study would have been in states of "inaction–withdrawal", whose associated states of cortical arousal are hypothesised to be the reverse of the pattern associated with action–approach, and resulting in a *reduction* of left-side attention as well as left-side holding, along with other more direct signs of disturbances in holding and care. In this connection, it is noteworthy that in Salk's time mothers were still being routinely excluded from the majority of premature newborn nurseries in the United States. In effect, they were isolated from their infants, allowed to look at them but not to touch or hold them. The practice dated from the work of the Alsatian physician Martin Cooney from the 1890s through the 1930s, first in Berlin, then in England and the United States (for reviews, see Klaus & Kennell, 1970, 1982).

Relatedly, there is evidence of lateralisation of somatic symptoms associated with emotional disturbances, with the chief symptoms including pain presenting more often on the left side (e.g., Galin, Diamond, & Braff, 1977; Min & Lee, 1997). The reliability of the effect has been questioned (Stone et al., 2002; Stone, Smyth, Carson, Warlow, & Sharpe, 2006), but if confirmed it would strengthen the possibility that at least some early instances of right-holding by nurses reflected stress and emotional disengagement. After all, even the most devoted nurses must have been sorely tested by their low pay, poor treatment, and long hours, and by the fatigue and even pain from routinely lifting and carrying infants and small children (see Lin, Tsauo, & Wang, 1996). Add to this the likely effect of the nurses' stress on the infants themselves—recall Webster and Parke's (1848, p. 1168) description of children "carried about for hours together", "their countenances ... overcast", "unnoticed by their nurses"—and we have the ingredients for a vicious circle of unhappiness. But if right holding could reflect stress and disengagement, the majority of reports, including Webster and Parke's, did name the *left* side as the norm. Not all left holds, whether in early or current reports, therefore would signify nurturance and solicitude, just as not all right holds would be strictly utilitarian, much less signify stress and disengagement (cf. Figure 6). A further complication is the possibility that for the somatic symptom of fatigue the lateralisation effect is reversed, with the left side *less* affected. For example, in a hand-dynamometer study, anxious, depressed women showed significantly less *left*-hand fatigue than did non-anxious, non-depressed women, which the authors interpreted as a product of higher right-hemisphere arousal in the anxious–depressed group (Crews, Harrison, Rhodes, & Demaree, 1995). Thus any effects on side-of-hold would presumably make the left hold *more*, not less, likely. If, therefore, the holder's "emotional state" did figure in any of the early reports, the right- and left-side reports can be reconciled only in part.

Influence on the infant's handedness

Finally, whatever may be the causes of side biases for holding infants, there is the question whether side-of-hold itself can affect the infant's handedness, as Comte (1828), Ballin (1896), and others declared. Wilson (1891), Baldwin (1894), Woolley (1910), and others dismissed it as the fundamental agent, and justly so, but they were open to the possibility that it could encourage early preference for the free hand, at least temporarily if it were the left, as Woolley (1910), Mead (1942), and others supposed. These authors were not the only ones to report a temporary period of left-handedness in the first year. Since the early 1900s there have been several more (Anderson & McDonald, 1979; Carlson & Harris, 1985; Dearborn, 1910; Lederer, 1939; Meyer, 1911, 1913; Myers, 1908), with one author even stating that a normal human being is "at first left-handed and then changes into being right-handed" (Meyer, 1911,

p. 179). However, none of these authors supposed that the effect was due to side-of-holding, and only two offered any explanations at all. One was that initial left-handedness reflects earlier maturation of the right hemisphere (Meyer, 1911; see Chiron et al., 1997; Corballis & Morgan, 1978, and commentaries); another was that certain left-hand movements serve a localising rather than motor-manipulative function and, as such, are early expressions of right-hemisphere specialisation for spatial localisation (Bresson, Maury, Pieraut-le-Bonniec, & de Schonen, 1977). Although the reliability of an initial period of left-handedness has been questioned (Young, Segalowitz, Misek, Alp, & Boulet, 1983), many infants *do* change their direction and degree of hand preference (e.g., Carlson & Harris, 1985; Michel, Sheu, & Bromley, 2002) and, as I said about the infant's hand use in the sequence of images in Figure 16, one can see why left-holding was believed to encourage left-handedness. So far, there is no evidence for human infants, but there is for chimpanzees. Of 12 mothers observed with their infants, 7 held mostly on the left, 5 on the right, and when hand preference for 9 of the infants was independently measured, it was in the reverse direction in every case (Hopkins, Bard, Jones, & Bales, 1993; see also Hopkins, 1999). However, in another study, now with monkeys, infants preferred the left nipple for suckling, but it was unrelated to their mothers' preferred side-of-cradling (Zhao, Gao, Li, & Watanabe, 2008).

THE REAL MERIT OF SALK'S REDISCOVERY OF THE LEFT-SIDE BIAS

As we have seen, opinions, observations, and explanations of lateral biases for holding and carrying infants have a long history. By 1942, with Mead's report, the totality of evidence favoured the left-siders, consistent with the view today, but with no agreement on the cause of the bias or its effect on the infant. The explanation that, for right-handers, it freed the holder's right hand for other tasks could be endorsed only by showing a reverse bias in left-handers, and not only when another task was performed but even when not. However, neither the handedness explanation nor any others were pursued, and no one tried to resolve the discrepancy between the left- and right-side reports. (At most Burt, 1937, implied that the answer lay in differences between natural preference for the left and formal instruction for the right.) The reason may be that most of the early authors were interested in side-of-holding only on the possibility that it *was* the cause of handedness, so that when Wilson (1891) and others noted the implausibility of that hypothesis, and when Baldwin (1890) and Burt (1937) reached the same conclusion from experimental evidence and case histories, interest in the matter disappeared. Therefore in the many books and articles on handedness published during this period (e.g., Beeley, 1919; Blau, 1946; Cuff, 1928; Jackson, 1905; Parson, 1924; Schiller, 1936; Selzer, 1933; Smith, 1917; Wile, 1934), side-of-hold was mentioned only as a repudiated explanation of handedness rather than as something worth studying in its own right. A notable exception was the child psychologist Gertrude Hildreth (1949), who called for "a thorough study of infant handedness and maternal postures" (p. 257). In humans, that study remains to be done. The chimpanzee and monkey studies (Hopkins, 1999; Hopkins et al., 1993; Zhao et al., 2008) are a start in this direction.

In rediscovering the left bias, Salk's (1960) real contribution, therefore, was to show that it was not a simple product of the holder's handedness, and that something else must be at work. Although his heartbeat explanation has been questioned, it had the virtue of showing how the left hold might serve the infant in ways beyond freeing the holder's right hand for acts of infant care. Previously, only Kenealy (1920) and the rabbis of ancient times addressed this possibility, but Salk proposed benefits for both parties and, to that extent, showed how side-of-hold could be a means for studying the mother–infant bond.

As I have noted, there is no reason to suppose that Salk knew of the long history of opinion and observation about this phenomenon. Neither, it seems, did most of his own predecessors. Not only Salk's reports, then, but those coming before look like instances of "multiples"—and thus as demonstrations of what historians and sociologists of science call "the inevitability of scientific discovery" (Ihde, 1948). Given the enduring interest in the search for the origins of handedness, it was perhaps inevitable that so many came to focus on something so "simple" as the side on which the infant is held. It is only because the bias is less simple than it looks that it has drawn and sustained the attention of a new scientific generation.

ACKNOWLEDGEMENTS

I am grateful to the many people who have supported my work on this article. Librarians at the Michigan State University (MSU) Library and other institutions, especially the Regenstein Library of the University of Chicago and the Newberry Library, Chicago, helped me find original source material from their collections. Victoria Manning, a British historian of nursing and midwifery, and Louise Selanders and Rachel Schiffman (College of Nursing, MSU), provided information on current practices in nurse-training. Chris McManus (University College, London) brought the photograph in Figure 24 to my attention. Jason Almerigi, Rodrigo Cárdenas, Elizabeth Kirsch, Pamela Woodhouse (MSU), and Harry Whitaker (Northern Michigan University) made thoughtful comments and gave encouragement along the way. The majority of images reproduced in this article are in the public domain. The rest are used courtesy of the copyright owners, except in two cases where, despite every effort, the owner could not be found. For their help in identifying the images and/or arranging for permission for their use, I thank Christopher Coe, Director, Harlow Primate Laboratory, University of Wisconsin-Madison (UW-Madison); Robert Dodsworth, Director of the Photo Laboratory, Primate Research Center photographic services, 1969–1993 (UW-Madison); Rachael Cross, Picture Researcher, The Wellcome Trust, London; Dennis Daily, Special Collections, Pikes Peak Library District, Pikes Peak, Colorado; Mary Hannigan, Annals of the New York Academy of Sciences; Ann Brownell Sloane, The Institute for Intercultural Studies, Inc., New York; Matthew Westerby, The Image Library of The Metropolitan Museum of Art, New York; Mary Whelan, Globe Photos, Inc., New York; and Victor LaCerva, Department of Paediatrics, University of New Mexico. I also thank Amy Blair, Reference Librarian, MSU Library, for information pertaining to copyright and public domain.

This article is dedicated to my students, past and present, and in grateful memory of three of my teachers: John C. Wright, my advisor at the Institute of Child Development, University of Minnesota; Harold W. Stevenson, the Institute Director; and Harriet L. Rheingold, for whom I worked as a summer research assistant at the National Institutes of Health following my first year of graduate study.

REFERENCES

Abt, A.F. (Ed.). (1965). *Abt-Garrison history of paediatrics.* [Reprinted from *Paediatrics* by various authors, Vol. 1, with new chapters on the history of paediatrics in recent times by A.F. Abt.] Philadelphia & London: W.B. Saunders Company.

Abel-Smith, B. (1975). *A history of the nursing profession.* London: Heinemann. [First published, 1960.]

Alley, T. R., & Kolker, J. I. (1988). Psychological gender, hand preferences, and sex differences in book-carrying styles. *Perceptual and Motor Skills, 66*, 815–822.

Almerigi, J.B., Carbary, T., & Harris, L.J. (2002). Most adults show opposite-side biases in the imagined holding of infants and objects. *Brain and Cognition, 48*, 258–263.

Anderson, V. E., & McDonald, P. M. (1979). *The sinister infant: Unexpected laterality at three to eight weeks.* Paper presentation, Canadian Psychological Association, Quebec City, Quebec, Canada.

Andry, N. [Andry de Bois-Regard] (1743). *Orthopaedia: Or, The Art of Correcting and Preventing Deformities in Children: By such Means as may be easily put in practice by Parents themselves, and all such as are employed in Educating Children.* [Translated from the French. 2 volumes. London: Printed for A. Miller. First published as L'Orthopédie ou *L'Art de Prevenir et de Corriger dans les Enfans, les Difformités du Corps. Le Tout Par Des Moyens à la Portée des*

Pères & des Mères, & de toutes les personnes qui ont des Énfans à Élever. Paris: La Veuve Alix; Lambert & Durand; Au Imprimerie Lienhart, 1741.]

Anon. (1810). Anatomy. In *Encyclopedia Brittanica, or A dictionary of arts, sciences, and miscellaneous literature* (4th ed., 20 vols). Edinburgh: A. Bell & C. Macfarquhar.

Anon. (1857). [Quoted p. 5050 in Nutting, M. A., & Dock, L. L. (1907). *A history of nursing: The evolution of nursing systems from the earliest times to the foundation of the first English and American training schools for nurses* (in 2 volumes). New York & London: G. P. Putnam's Sons.]

Aristotle. (1912a). *De Animalium Incessu.* [Translated, with notes and introduction, by A. S. L. Farquharson.] In J. A. Smith & W. D. Ross (Eds.), *The works of Aristotle* (Vol. 5). Oxford, UK: Clarendon Press.

Aristotle. (1912b). *De Partibus Animalium.* [Translated, with notes and introduction, by W. Ogle.] In J. A. Smith & W. D. Ross (Eds.), *The works of Aristotle* (Vol. 5). Oxford, UK: Clarendon Press.]

Aristotle. (1910). *Historia Animalium.* [Translated by D'Arcy Wentworth Thompson.] In *The works of Aristotle* (Vol. 4). Oxford, UK: Clarendon Press.

Armstrong, G. A. (1777). *An Account of the Diseases Most Incident to Children, From Their Birth to the Age of Puberty; With a Successful Method of Treating Them. To Which Is Added, An Essay on Nursing. Also A General Account of the Dispensary for the Infant Poor, From Its First Institution in 1769 to the Present Time.* London: Printed for T. Cadell in The Strand.

Auvard, A., & Pingat, H. (1889). *Hygiène Infantile Ancienne et Moderne.* Paris: G. Rongier & Co.

Baldwin, J. M. (1890). Origin of right or left handedness. *Science, 16*, 247–248.

Baldwin, J. M. (1894). The origin of right-handedness. *Popular Science Monthly, 44*, 606–615.

Ballin, H. (1896). Symmetry in education. *The Child-Study Monthly, 2*, 306–309.

Bateson, G., & Mead, M. (1942). *Balinese character: A photographic analysis.* New York: Special Publications of the New York Academy of Sciences, Vol II.

Beeley, A. L. (1919). Left-handedness. *American Journal of Physical Anthropology, 2*, 389–400.

Bellis, M. (2004). *The history of baby carriages.* Retrieved 20 August 2004, from http://inventors.about.com/library/inventors/blbabycarriage.htm

Benda, B. J., Riley, P. O., & Krebs, D. E. (1994). Biomechanical relationship between center of gravity and center of pressure during standing. *IEEE Transactions on Rehabilitation Engineering, 2*, 3–10.

Biancuzzo, M. (1999). *Breastfeeding the newborn: Clinical strategies for nurses.* St. Louis, MO: Mosby.

Blau, A. (1946). *The master hand: A study of the origin and meaning of right and left sidedness and its relation to personality and language.* (Research Monograph No. 5). New York: American Orthopsychiatric Association, Inc.

Blümner, H. (1895). *The home life of the Ancient Greeks.* [Translated from the German by Alice Zimmern. New and revised edition.] London, Paris, & Melbourne: Cassell & Company, Ltd.

Bogren, L. Y. (1985). The couvade syndrome and side preference in child holding. *Acta Psychiatrica Scandinavica, 71*, 311–314.

Bourne, V. J., & Todd, B. K. (2004). When left means right: An explanation of the left cradling bias in terms of right hemisphere specialization. *European Journal of Neuroscience, 12*, 731–741.

Brennan, B., & Heilman, J.R. (1977). *The complete book of midwifery.* New York: Dutton.

Bresson, F., Maury, L., Pieraut-le Bonniec, G., & de Schonen, S. (1977). Organization and lateralisation of reaching in infants: An instance of asymmetric functions in hands collaboration. *Neuropsychologia, 15*, 311–320.

Broca, P. (1865). Sur le siège de la faculté du langage articulé. *Bulletins de la Société d'Anthropologie de Paris, 6*, 377–393.

Brown, A. K. (2004). *The golden age of carriages.* Retrieved 20 August 2004, from www.victoriana.com/lady/buggy.html

Browne, Thomas (1646). *Pseudodoxia Epidemica, or, Enquiries into Very Many Received Tenents, and Commonly Preserved Truths*. London, printed by T. H. for Edward Dod.

Brüser, E. (1981). Child transport in Sri Lanka. *Current Anthropology, 22*, 288–290.

Buchanan, A. (1862a). Mechanical theory of the predominance of the right hand over the left; or, more generally, of the limbs of the right side over those of the left side of the body. *Proceedings of the Philosophical Society of Glasgow, 5*, 142–167.

Buchanan, A. (1862b). *Mechanical theory of the predominance of the right hand over the left; or, more generally, of the limbs of the right side over those of the left side of the body*. Glasgow: Bell & Bain.

Burt, C. (1937). *The backward child*. New York: Appleton-Century.

Cárdenas, R. A., Almerigi, J. B., Puts, D. A., & Harris, L. J. (2007). *Is the preference for holding infants on the left a female adaptation?* Poster presentation, Human Behavior & Evolution Society, College of William and Mary, Williamsburg, Virginia, May 30 – June 3.

Carlson, D. F., & Harris, L. J. (1985). Development of the infant's hand preference for visually-directed reaching: Preliminary report of a longitudinal study. *Infant Mental Health Journal, 6*, 158–174.

Carmichael, S. (2007). *Infant carrying apparatus*. Retrieved 19 July 2007, from http://www/google.com/patents?hl=en&lr=&vid=USPAT4717056&id=zdAtAAAAEBAJ

Chiron, C., Jambique, I., Nabbout, R., Lounes, R., Syrota, A., & Dulac, O. (1997). The right brain hemisphere is dominant in human infants. *Brain, 120*, 1057–1065.

Clutton-Brock, T. H. (1991). *The evolution of parental care*. Princeton: Princeton University Press.

Coghill, R. C., Gilron, I., & Iadarola, M. J. (2001). Hemispheric lateralisation of somatosensory processing. *The Journal of Neurophysiology, 85*(6), 2602–2612.

Comte, J. A. (1828). Recherches anatomico-physiologique, relatives à la prédominance du bras droit sur le bras gauche. *Journal de Physiologie Expérimentale et Pathologie, 8*, 41–80.

Corballis, M. C., & Morgan, M. J. (1978). On the biological basis of human laterality: I. Evidence for a maturational left–right gradient. *Behavioral and Brain Sciences, 1*, 261–269.

Corkin, S. (1978). The role of different cerebral structures in somesthetic perception. In E. C. Carterette & M. P. Friedman (Eds.), *Handbook of perception* (Vol. 6, pp. 105–155). New York: Academic Press.

Cosmovici, C. (1889). Comment on devient gaucher [letter to the editor]. *Revue Scientifique, 44*(November 2), 572.

Crews, W. D., Harrison, D. W., Rhodes, R. D., & Demaree, H. A. (1995). Hand fatigue symmetry in the motor performances of women with depressed mood. *Neuropsychiatry, Neuropsychology, and Behavioral Neurology, 8*, 277–281.

Cuff, N. (1928). The interpretation of handedness. *Journal of Experimental Psychology, 11*, 27–39.

Cushing, F. H. (1892). Manual concepts: A study of the influence of hand-usage on culture-growth. *The American Anthropologist, 5*, 289–317.

Dagenbach, D., Harris, L. J., & Fitzgerald, H. E. (1988). A longitudinal study of lateral biases in parents' cradling and holding of infants. *Infant Mental Health Journal, 9*, 218–234.

Damerose, E., & Vauclair, J. (2002). Posture and laterality in human and non-human primates: Asymmetries in maternal handling and the infant's early motor asymmetries. In L. J. Rogers & M. Andrews (Eds.), *Comparative vertebrate lateralisation* (pp. 306–362). Cambridge, UK: Cambridge University Press.

Danneels, L. A., Vanderstraeten, G. G., Cambier, D. C., Witvrouw, E. E., Stevens, V. K., & De Cuyper, H. J. (2001). A functional subdivision of hip, abdominal, and back muscles during asymmetric lifting. *Spine, 26*, E114–E121.

Dearborn, G. V. N. (1910). *Moto-sensory development*. Baltimore, MD: Warick & York.

de Château, P. (1983). Left-side preference for holding and carrying newborn infants: Parental holding and carrying during the first week of life. *Journal of Nervous and Mental Disease, 171*, 241–245.

de Château, P. (1991). Clinical application of asymmetrical behavioral communication in parent-infant interaction. In H. E. Fitzgerald, B. M. Lester, & M. W. Yogman (Eds.), *Theory and research in behavioral paediatrics* (Vol. 5, pp. 185–208). New York: Plenum.

de Vallambert, S. (1565). *Cinq Livres de la Maniere de Nourrir et Gouverner des Enfans des Leur Naissance.* Poictiers [Poitiers]: de Marnesz & Bouchetz.

Dewees, W. P. (1826). *A treatise on the physical and medical treatment of children* (2nd ed., with corrections). Philadelphia: H.C. Carey & I. Lea,

Dienske, H., Hopkins, B., & Reid, A.K. (1995). Lateralisation of infant holding in chimpanzees: New data do not confirm previous findings. *Behaviour, 132*, 801–809.

Domhoff, G. W. (1969). But why did they sit on the king's right in the first place? *Psychoanalytic Review, 56*, 586–596.

Donnison, J. (1988). *Midwives and medical men: A history of the struggle for the control of childbirth.* London: Historical Publications.

Donnot, J., & Vauclair, J. (2005). Biais de latéralité dans la façon de porter un très jeune enfant: Une revue de la question. *Neuropsychiatrie de l'Enfance et de l'Adolescence, 53*, 413–425.

Donnot, J., & Vauclair, J. (2007). Infant holding preferences in maternity hospitals: Testing the hypothesis of the lateralised perception of emotions. *Developmental Neuropsychology, 32*, 881–890.

Duggar, B. C. (1962). The center of gravity of the human body. *Human Factors, 4*, 131–148.

Erber, N. L., Almerigi, J. B., Carbary, T. J., & Harris, L. J. (2002). The contribution of postural bias to lateral preferences for holding human infants. *Brain and Cognition, 48*, 352–356.

Fagot, J., Lacreuse, A., & Vauclair, J. (1997). Role of sensory and post-sensory factors on hemispheric asymmetries in tactual perception. In S. Christman (Ed.), *Cerebral asymmetries in sensory and perceptual processing* (pp. 469–494). Amsterdam: Elsevier Science BV.

Finger, S. (1975). Child-holding patterns in Western art. *Child Development, 46*, 267–271.

Flusser, D. (1980). *Sefer Yosifon: yotse la-or-sadur u-mugah 'al-pi kitvé yad bi-levayat mavo, bi'urim ve hilufé girsa' ot [The Josippon* (Josephus Gorionides); edited with an introduction, commentary, and notes by David Flusser]. Jerusalem: Bialik Institute.

Forbes, T. R. (1959). The prediction of sex: Folklore and science. *Proceedings of the American Philosophical Society, 103*, 537–544.

Fritsch, V. (1968). *Left and right in science and life.* London: Barrie & Rockliff.

Galin, D., Diamond, R., & Braff, D. (1977). Lateralisation of conversion symptoms: More frequent on the left. *American Journal of Psychiatry, 134*, 578–580.

Galton, F. (1874). *English men of science: Their nature and nurture.* London: Macmillan & Co.

Gard, S. A., Miff, S. C., & Kuo, A. D. (2004). Comparison of kinematic and kinetic methods for computing the vertical motion of the body center of mass during walking. *Human Movement Science, 22*, 597–610.

Gesell, A. (1925). *The mental growth of the pre-school child: A psychological outline of normal development from birth to the sixth year, including a system of development diagnosis.* New York: The Macmillan Company.

Gesell, A. (1934). *An atlas of infant behavior: A systematic delineation of the forms and early growth of human behavior patterns* [two volumes illustrated with 3200 action photographs. Volume 2: Naturalistic series]. New Haven, CT: Yale University Press.

Gill, J. K. (1933). *Gill's dictionary of the Chinook jargon, with examples of use in conversation and notes upon tribes and tongues* (17th ed). Portland, OR: J. K. Gill Company.

Girdwood, G. P. (1908). Thoughts and facts on right and left handedness in an attempt to explain why the majority of men are righthanded. *Transactions of the Royal Society of Canada, 2*, 186–187.

Godfrey, J. (1747). *A Treatise Upon the Useful Science of Defence, Connecting the Small and Back-Sword, and Shewing the Affinity Between Them.* London: T. Gardner.

Gonzalez, A. Q., & Koestner, R. (2005). Parental preference for sex of newborn as reflected in positive affect in birth announcements. *Sex Roles*, *52*, 407–411.

Grimshaw, G. M., & Bryden, M. P. (1994). *Are there meaningful handedness subtypes?* Poster presentation, International Neuropsychological Society, Cincinnati, OH, 4 February. [Abstract in *Journal of the International Neuropsychological Society*, 1995, *1*, 367.]

Guillemeau, J. (1612). *Child-Birth or, The Happy Delivery of Women* [English translation (uncredited) of the original French text.] London: A. Hatfield.

Gupta, M. D. (1987). Selective discrimination against female children in rural Punjab, India. *Population and Development Review*, *13*, 77–100.

Gupta, M. D., Zhenghua, J., Bohua, L., Zhenming, X., Chung, W., & Hwa-Ok, B. (2002). *Why is son preference so persistent in East and South Asia? A cross-country study of China, India and the Republic of Korea.* Policy Research Working Paper 2942 (December, 34 pp.). The World Bank Development Research Group, Public Services and Rural Development,

H. M. (1889). Sur la gaucherie [letter to the editor]. *Revue Scientifique*, *44*, 764.

Hall, G. S., & Hartwell, E. M. (1884). Research and discussion, bilateral asymmetry of function. *Mind*, *9*, 93–109.

Hank, K., & Kohler, H-P. (2000). Gender preferences for children in Europe: Empirical results from 17 FFS countries. [*Demographic Research*, *2*, Article 1, 21 pages. Max Planck Institute for Demographic Research.] Retrieved 4 March 2008, from http://www.demographic-research.org/Volumes/Vo.2/1/

Harris, L. J. (1989). Hand preference in gestures and signs in the deaf and hearing: Some notes on early evidence and theory. *Brain and Cognition*, *10*, 189–219.

Harris, L. J. (1991). The human infant in studies of lateralisation of function. A historical perspective. In H. E. Fitzgerald, B. M. Lester, & M. W. Yogman (Eds.), *Theory and research in behavioral paediatrics* (Vol. 5, pp. 129–154). New York: Plenum.

Harris, L. J. (2003). What to do about your child's handedness? Advice from five eighteenth-century authors, and some questions for today. *Laterality*, *8*, 99–120.

Harris, L. J. (2007). Babes in arms: Studies in laterality of function. In H. Cohen & B. Stemmer (Eds.), *Consciousness and cognition: Fragments of mind and brain* (pp. 83–113). New York: Academic Press.

Harris, L. J. (2010a). In fencing, what gives left-handers the edge? Views from the present and the distant past. *Laterality*, *15*, 15–55.

Harris, L. J. (2010b). On teaching infants "the right use of their hands": Advice and reassurance from Mary Palmer Tyler's *The Maternal Physician* (1811). *Laterality*, *15*, 4–14.

Harris, L. J., Almerigi, J. B., Carbary, T., & Fogel, T. (2001). Left side infant-holding: A test of the hemispheric arousal-attentional hypothesis. *Brain and Cognition*, *46*, 159–165.

Harris, L. J., Almerigi, J. B., & Kirsch, E. A. (2000). Side-preference in adults for holding infants: Contributions of sex and handedness in a test of imagination. *Brain and Cognition*, *43*, 246–252.

Harris, L. J., Jentoft, C., & Almerigi, J. B. (2002). *Do biases against left-hand use affect side preferences for holding infants? Evidence from photographs in Bateson and Mead's (1942) and Mead and McGregor's (1951) studies of the people of Bajoeng Gedé, Bali.* Poster presentation, International Society for the Study of Behavioural Development, Ottawa, Ontario, Canada, August 2–6.

Harris, L. J., Spradlin, M. P. Jr., & Almerigi, J. B. (2007). Mothers' and fathers' lateral biases for holding their newborn infants: A study of images from the World Wide Web. *Laterality*, *12*(1), 64–86.

Hatta, T., & Koike, M. (1991). Left-hand preference in frightened mother monkeys in taking up their babies. *Neuropsychologia*, *29*, 207–209.

Helander, M. G., & Zhang, L. (1997). Field studies of comfort and discomfort in sitting. *Ergonomics*, *40*, 895–915.

Hertz, R. (1909). The pre-eminence of the right hand: A study in religious polarity. In R. Needham (Ed.), *Right and left: Essays on dual symbolic classification* (pp. 3–31). Chicago and London: The University of Chicago Press, 1973. [Translation by R. Needham of "La prééminence de la main droite: étude sur la polarité religieuse. First published in *Revue Philosophique*, 1909, *68*, 553–580.]

Hildreth, G. (1949). The development and training of hand dominance: III. Origins of handedness and lateral dominance. *The Journal of Genetic Psychology*, *75*, 255–275.

Hopkins, W. D. (1999). Heritability of hand preferences in chimpanzees (*Pan troglodytes*): Evidence from a partial interspecies cross-fostering study. *Journal of Comparative Psychology*, *113*, 307–313.

Hopkins, W. D., Bard, K. A., Jones, A., & Bales, S. L. (1993). Chimpanzee hand preference in throwing and infant cradling: Implications for the origin of human handedness. *Current Anthropology*, *34*, 786–790.

Hopkins, W. D., & de Waal, F. B. M. (1995). Behavioral laterality in captive bonobos (*Pan paniscus*): Replication and extension. *International Journal of Primatology*, *16*, 261–276.

Hughes, C. H. (1890). Note on the conundrum why we are right-handed. *Western Medical Reporter*, *12*, 147.

Iacoboni, M., Woods, R. P., Brass, M., Bekkering, H., Mazziotta, J. C., & Rizzolatti, G. (1999). Cortical mechanisms of human imitation. *Science*, *286*, 2526–2528.

Ihde, A. (1948). The inevitability of scientific discovery. *The Scientific Monthly*, *67*, 427–429.

Ing, R., Ho, J. H. C., & Petrakis, N. L. (1977a). Unilateral breast-feeding and breast cancer. *The Lancet*, July 16, 124–127.

Ing, R., Ho, J. H. C., & Petrakis, N. L. (1977b). Unilateral suckling and breast cancer. Reply to MacMahon and Trichopoulos. *The Lancet*, September 24, 656–657.

Ingalls, N. W. (1928). On righthandedness. *The Scientific Monthly*, *27*, 307–321.

J. H. (1889). La gaucherie acquise [letter to the editor]. *Revue Scientifique*, *44*, November 30, 701.

J. S. (1881). Babies and science. *The Cornhill Magazine*, *63*, 539–554.

Jackson, J. (1905). *Ambidexterity or two-handedness and two-brainedness.* London: Kegan Paul, Trench, Trubner & Co.

Kang, Y. (1992). *The factor structure of human handedness: A normative study of American college students.* PhD dissertation, Department of Psychology, Michigan State University.

Kaplan-Solms, K. L., & Saling, M. (1988). Lateral asymmetry and tactile sensitivity. *Perceptual and Motor Skills*, *67*, 55–62.

Kenealy, A. (1920). *Feminism and sex-extinction.* London: T. Fisher Unwin, Ltd.

Kenner, C., Amlung, S. R., & Flandermeyer, A. A. (1998). *Protocols in neonatal nursing.* Philadelphia: Saunders.

Kirkpatrick, T. P. C. (1913). *The book of the Rotunda Hospital: An illustrated history of the Dublin Lying-In Hospital from its foundation in 1745 to the present time* (Edited by H. Jellett). London: Adelard & Son, Bartholomew Press.

Klaus, M. H., & Kennell, J. H. (1970). Mothers separated from their newborn infants. *Paediatric Clinics of North America*, *17*, 1015–1037.

Klaus, M. H., & Kennell, J. H. (1982). *Parent–infant bonding*. St. Louis, MO: C. V. Mosby.

Klein, A. E. (1932). *Child life in Greek art*. New York: Columbia University Press.

Klein, M. (1998). *A time to be born: Customs and folklore of Jewish birth.* Philadelphia, PA: Jewish Publication Society.

Kraemer, S. (2008). The fragile male. *British Medical Journal*, *321*, 1609–1612.

LaCerva, V. (1981). *Breastfeeding: A manual for health professionals.* Garden City, NY: Medical Examination Publ. Co.

Lederer, R. K. (1939). An exploratory investigation of handed status in the first two years of life. *Iowa Studies in Child Welfare: Studies in Infant Behavior*, *16*(2), 9–103.

Lin, M. R., Tsauo, J. Y., & Wang, J. D. (1996). Determinants of economic cost related to low back pain among nurses at a university hospital. *International Journal of Occupational and Environmental Health*, *2*(4), 257–263.

Lloyd, G. (1973). Right and left in Greek philosophy. In R. Needham (Ed.), *Right and left: Essays on dual symbolic classification* (pp. 167–186). Chicago & London: The University of Chicago Press.

Lockard, J. S., Daley, P. C., & Gunderson, V. (1979). Maternal and paternal differences in infant carry: U.S. and African data. *The American Naturalist*, *113*, 235–246.

Lomax, E. M. R. (1996). *Small and special: The development of hospitals for children in Victorian Britain* (*Medical History*, Supplement No. 16). London: Wellcome Institute for the History of Medicine.

Long, D. A. (1994). Hand differences and reported intensity of nociceptive stimuli. *Perceptual and Motor Skills*, *79*, 411–417.

Lonsdorf, E. V., & Hopkins, W. D. (2005). Wild chimpanzees show population-level handedness for tool use. *Proceedings of the National Academy of Sciences*, *102*, 12634–12638.

Lydon, F. F. (1907). *Ambidextrous and free-arm blackboard drawing and design* (2nd ed.). London: George Philip & Son, Ltd. [First published 1900.]

MacPhail, S. R. (1891–1894). Left-handedness. *Caledonian Medical Journal, 1 (New Series)*, 54–59.

Magendie, F. (1827). Notes (trans. by G. Hayward) on X. Bichat's *Physiological Researches Upon Life and Death* [trans. by F. Gold of 4th ed. of *Recherches Physiologique sur la Vie et la Mort*]. Boston: Richardson & Lord. [Original French publication: Paris: Gabou, Bechet Jeuve, 1822.]

Manning, J. T. (1991). Sex differences in left-side infant holding: Results from "family album" photographs. *Ethology and Sociobiology*, *12*, 337–343.

Manning, J. T., & Chamberlain, A. T. (1990). The left-side cradling preference in great apes. *Animal Behaviour*, *39*, 1224–1227.

Manning, J. T., Heaton, R., & Chamberlain, A. T. (1994). Left-side cradling: Similarities and differences between apes and humans. *Journal of Human Evolution*, *26*, 77–83.

Mauriceau, F. (1710). *The Diseases of Women With Child, and in Child-Bed* (4th ed.). London: Printed for A. Bell. [Reprinted in the series, *Marriage, sex, and the family in England, 1660–1800*. New York & London, Inc., 1985. Translated from the French, *Traité des Maladies des Femmes Grosses et Accouchées*. Paris: L'Auteur, 1668.]

McGrew, W. C., & Marchant, L. F. (1997). On the other hand: Current issues in and meta-analysis of the behavioral laterality of hand function in nonhuman primates. *Yearbook of Physical Anthropology*, *40*, 201–232.

McManus, I. C. (2006). The modern mythology of the left-handedness of Alexander the Great. *Laterality*, *11*, 566–572.

Mead, M. (1942). Balinese character. In G. Bateson & M. Mead (Eds.), *Balinese character: A photographic analysis* (pp. 1–48). New York: Special Publications of the New York Academy of Sciences, Vol. II.

Mead, M., & Macgregor, F. C. (1951). *Growth and culture: A photographic study of Balinese childhood*. New York: G. P. Putnam's Sons.

Merton, R. K. (1957). Priorities in scientific discovery: A chapter in the sociology of science. *American Sociological Review*, *22*, 635–659.

Merton, R. K. (1961). Singletons and multiples in scientific discovery: A chapter in the sociology of science. *Proceedings of the American Philosophical Society*, *105*, 470–486.

Meyer, M. (1911). *The fundamental laws of human behavior*. Boston: Richard G. Badger.

Meyer, M. (1913). Left-handedness and right-handedness in infancy. *Psychological Bulletin*, *10*, 52–53.

Michel, G. F., Sheu, C-F., & Brumley, M. R. (2002). Evidence of a right-shift factor affecting infant hand-use preferences from 7 to 11 months of age as revealed by latent class analysis. *Developmental Psychobiology, 40*, 1–13.

Miller, J. (1977). Delaware anatomy: With linguistic, social, and medical aspects. *Anthropological Linguistics, 19*, 144–166.

Miller, J. (1980). The matter of the (thoughtful) heart: Centrality, focality, or overlap. *Journal of Anthropological Research, 36*, 338–342.

Miller, J. M., & Stark, M. A. (2007). *Health care professionals' perceptions of right-sided positioning as a complementary therapy for postoperative nausea and vomiting*. The University of Arizona College of Nursing. Retrieved 31 July 2007, from http://juns.nursing.arizona.edu/articles/Fall%202004/miller_stark.htm

Min, S. J., & Lee, B. O. (1997). Laterality in somatization. *Psychosomatic Medicine, 59*, 236–240.

Mollon, J. D. (1978). Weber on sensory asymmetry. In M. Kinsbourne (Ed.), *Asymmetrical function of the brain* (pp. 318–325). London: Cambridge University Press. [Passages translated from E. Weber, *De Pulsu, Resorptione, Auditu et Tactu*. Leipzig: C. F. D. Koehlerk, first Latin publication 1834.]

Moore, M. L. (1972). *The newborn and the nurse (Saunders Monographs in Clinical Nursing, 3)*. Philadelphia: W. B. Saunders Company.

Moore, M. L. (1981). *Newborn family and nurse* [with a contribution by K. G. Galloway]. Philadelphia: W. B. Saunders Company.

Myers, C. S. (1908). Some observations on the development of the colour sense. *British Journal of Psychology, 2*, 353–363.

Nakamichi, M. (1996). The left-side holding preference is not universal: Evidence from field observations in Madagascar. *Ethology and Sociobiology, 17*, 173–179.

Needham, R. (Ed.). (1973). *Right and left: Essays on dual symbolic classification*. Chicago: The University of Chicago Press.

Nelson, J. (1756). *An Essay on the Government of Children*. [Facsimile reprint in the series, *Marriage, sex, and the family in England, 1660–1800*. New York & London, Inc., 1985. Originally published: London: Printed for R. & J. Dodsley.]

Nishida, T. (1993). Left nipple suckling preference in wild chimpanzees. *Ethology and Sociobiology, 14*, 45–52.

Nutting, M. A., & Dock, L. L. (1907). *A history of nursing: The evolution of nursing systems from the earliest times to the foundation of the first English and American training schools for nurses* (2 vols.). New York & London: G. P. Putnam's Sons.

Ogle, W. (1871). On dextral pre-eminence. *Medical-Chirurgical Transactions (Transactions of the Royal Medical and Chirurgical Society of London), 54*, 279–301.

Ottino, A. (2000). *The universe within: A Balinese village through its ritual practices*. Paris: Éditions Karthala.

Paget, J. (1914). *Hospital*. June, 6, 276.

Parson, B. S. (1924). *Lefthandedness: A new interpretation*. New York: The Macmillan Company.

Pawlowski, B., & Grabarczyk, M. (2003). Center of body mass and the evolution of female body shape. *American Journal of Human Biology, 15*(2), 144–150.

Peters, M. (1996). Hand preference and performance in left-handers. In D. Elliott & R. Roy (Eds.), *Manual asymmetries in motor performance* (pp. 123–142). Boca Raton, FL: CRF Press.

Peters, M., & Servos, P. (1989). Performance of subgroups of left-handers and right-handers. *Canadian Journal of Psychology, 43*, 341–358.

Plato (1937). *The Laws*. In B. Jowett, trans., *The dialogues of Plato* (Vol. 2). New York: Random House. [First published, 1892.]

Pooler, W. S. (1991). Sex of child preferences among college students. *Sex Roles, 25*, 569–576.

Previc, F. H. (1991). A general theory concerning the prenatal origins of cerebral lateralisation in humans. *Psychological Review, 98*, 299–334.

Pye-Smith, P. H. (1871). Left-handedness. *Guy's Hospital Reports (34e Series)*, *16*, 141–146.
Quintilian [Quintilianus, M. F.]. (1936). *The Institutio Oratoria of Quintilian* (with an English translation by H. E. Butler, Vol. IV). Cambridge, MA: Harvard University Press [Originally published 1922.]
Read, M. L. (1916). *The mothercraft manual*. Boston: Little, Brown, & Company.
Reade, C. (1878). "The coming man." Letters to the editor of *Harper's Weekly*: Jan. 19, 50–51; Jan. 26, 74; Feb. 2, 94–95; March 2, 174–175; March 23, 234–235; May 18, 394–395.
Rheingold, H. L., & Keene, G. C. (1965). Transport of the human young. In B. M. Foss (Ed.), *Determinants of infant behavior* (Vol. 3, pp. 87–110). London: Bethner.
Roopnarine, J. L., Talukder, E., Jain, D., Joshi, P., & Srivastava, P. (1990). Characteristics of holding, patterns of play, and social behaviors between parents and infants in New Delhi, India. *Developmental Psychology*, *26*, 667–673.
Rousseau, J-J. (1762/1962). *Émile, ou, de l'Éducation*. Paris: Éditions Garniers Frères. [First published 1762.]
Sadler, L. J. (1925). *How to feed the baby*. Chicago: A. C. McClurg & Co.
Sadler, W. J., & Sadler, L. J. (1919). *The mother and her child*. Chicago: A. C. McClurg & Co.
Sainburg, R. L. (2002). Evidence for a dynamic-dominance hypothesis of handedness. *Experimental Brain Research*, *142*, 241–258.
Sainburg, R. L., Ghez, C., & Kalalanis, D. (1999). Intersegmental dynamics are controlled by sequential anticipatory, error correction, and postural mechanisms. *Journal of Neurophysiology*, *81*, 1040–1056.
Saint-Marthe, Scévole de (1584/1797). *Paedotrophia, or, The art of Nursing and Rearing Children: A Poem, in Three Books*. [Translation from the Latin, *Paedotrophiae libri tres*, with medical notes; with the life of the author, from the French of Michael and Jean-Pierre Niceron, by H. W. Tytler.] London: John Nichols. [First Latin publication 1584.]
Saling, M., & Cooke, W. L. (1984). Cradling and transport of infants by South African mothers: A cross-cultural study. *Current Anthropology*, *25*, 333–335.
Saling, M., & Tyson, G. (1981). Lateral cradling preferences in nulliparous females. *Journal of Genetic Psychology*, *139*, 309–310.
Salk, L. (1960). The effects of the normal heartbeat sound on the behavior of the newborn infant: Implications for mental health. *World Mental Health*, *12*, 168–175.
Salk, L. (1961). The importance of the heartbeat rhythm to human nature: Theoretical, clinical, and experimental observations. In *Proceedings of the Third World Congress of Psychiatry* (pp. 740–746). Toronto: University of Toronto Press.
Salk, L. (1970). The critical nature of the post-partum period in the human for the establishment of the mother–infant bond: A controlled study. *Diseases of the Nervous System*, *31*, 110–116.
Salk, L. (1973). The role of the heartbeat in the relations between mother and infant. *Scientific American*, *228*, 24–29.
Sarup, G. (1978). Historical antecedents of psychology: The recurrent issue of old wine in new bottles. *American Psychologist*, *33*, 478–485.
Schiller, A. (1936). Theories of handedness. *Journal of Applied Psychology*, *19*, 694–703; *20*, 77–92.
Schmitt, V., Melchisedech, S., Hammerschmidt, K., & Fischer, J. (2008). Hand preferences in Barbary macaques (*Macaca sylvanus*). *Laterality*, *13*, 143–157.
Sebeok, T. A., & Umiker-Sebeok, D. J. (1978). *Aboriginal sign languages of the Americans and Australians. The Americas and Australia, vol. 2*. New York: Plenum Press.
Selzer, C. A. (1933). *Lateral dominance and visual fusion: Their application to difficulties in reading, writing, spelling, and speech. Harvard monographs in education*, No. 12. Cambridge, MA: Harvard University Press.
Shakespeare, W. (1977). *As you like it*. New York: Modern Language Association of America.

Sigerson, G. (1884). Considerations of the structural and acquisitional elements in dextral pre-eminence, with conclusions as to the ambidexterity of primeval man. *Proceedings of the Royal Irish Academy, Dublin, 4* (Series 2 Science), 38–50.

Smith, L. C. (1917). Brief survey of right- and left-handedness. *Pedagogical Seminary, 24*, 19–35.

Soranus (1956). *Soranus' Gynecology*, Book II. [Translated with an introduction by Owsei Temkin.] Baltimore, MD: The Johns Hopkins University Press.

Sperber, Z., & Weiland, H. (1973). Anxiety as a determinant of parent–infant contact patterns. *Psychosomatic Medicine, 35*, 472–483.

Steenhuis, R. E., & Bryden, M. P. (1989). Different dimensions of hand preference that relate to skilled and unskilled activities. *Cortex, 25*, 289–304.

Still, G. F. (1965). *The history of paediatrics: The progress of the study of the diseases of children up to the end of the XVIIIth century.* London: Dawsons of Pall Mall. [First published by the Oxford University Press, 1931.]

Stone, J., Sharpe, M., Carson, A., Lewis, S. C., Goldbeck, R., & Warlow, C. P. (2002). Are functional motor and sensory symptoms really more frequent on the left? A systematic review. *Journal of Neurology, Neurosurgery, and Psychiatry, 73*, 578–581.

Stone, J., Smyth, R., Carson, A., Warlow, C., & Sharpe, M. (2006). La belle indifférence in conversion symptoms and hysteria. *British Journal of Psychiatry, 188*, 204–209.

Sussman, G. D. (1982). *Selling mothers' milk: The wet-nursing business in France, 1715–1914.* Urbana, IL: University of Illinois Press.

Suter, S. E., Huggenberger, H. J., & Schächinger, H. (2007). Cold pressor stress reduces left cradling preference in nulliparous human females. *Stress: The International Journal on the Biology of Stress, 10*(#1), 45–51.

Sweet, B. R. (1982). *Mayes' midwifery: A textbook for midwives.* London: Ballière Tindall.

Tanaka, I. (1989). Change of nipple preference between successive offspring in Japanese macaques. *American Journal of Primatology, 18*, 321–325.

Tcherkézoff, S. (1987). *Dual classification reconsidered.* London/Paris: Cambridge University Press/ Editions de la Maison des Sciences de L'Homme.

Thoms, H. (1960). *Our obstetrical heritage: The story of safe childbirth.* Springfield, IL: Charles C. Thomas.

Tomaszycki, M., Cline, C., Griffin, B., Maestripieri, D., & Hopkins, W. D. (1998). Maternal cradling and infant nipple preference in rhesus monkeys (*Macaca mulatta*). *Developmental Psychobiology, 32*, 305–312.

Trevathan, W. R. (1982). Maternal lateral preference at first contact with her newborn infant. *Birth, 9*, 85–89.

Troussseau, A. (1868). *Lectures on clinical medicine.* London: New Sydenham Society.

Turnbull, O. H., & Lucas, M. D. (2000). Tell me, where is [this] fancy bred?" The cardiac and cerebral accounts of the lateral cradling bias. In M. K. Mandal, B. Bulman-Fleming, & G. Tiwari (Eds.), *Side bias: A neuropsychological perspective* (pp. 267–287). The Netherlands: Kluwer Academic Publishers.

Vallortigara, G., & Rogers, L. J. (2005). Survival with an asymmetrical brain: Advantages and disadvantages of cerebral lateralisation. *Behavioral and Brain Sciences, 28*, 575–589.

Van der Meer, A., & Husby, T. (2006). Handedness as a major determinant of functional cradling bias. *Laterality, 11*, 263–276.

VRoma. (2008). *The VRoma Project.* Project Co-Directors: Barbara F. McManus & Suzanne Bonefas. Web Design: Barbara F. McManus & Daniel Jung. Retrieved 8 May 2008, from http://www.vroma.org/

Wall-Scheffler, C. M., Geiger, K., & Steudel-Numbers, K. L. (2007). Infant-carrying: the role of increased locomotory costs in early tool development. *American Journal of Physical Anthropology, 133*, 841–846.

Watson, J. B. (1924). *Behaviorism*. New York: The People's Institute Publishing Co., Inc.

Watson, J. B., & Watson, R. R. (1921). Studies in infant psychology. *The Scientific Monthly, 13*, 493–515.

Weatherill, R. P., Almerigi, J. B., Levendosky, A. A., Bogat, G. A., von Eye, A., & Harris, L. J. (2004). Is maternal depression related to side of infant holding? *International Journal of Behavioral Development, 28*, 421–427.

Webster, T., & Parkes, [Mrs.] W. (1848). *Encyclopedia of domestic economy*. New York: Harper & Brothers.

Weinstein, S. (1968). Intensive and extensive aspects of tactile sensitivity as a function of body part, sex, and laterality. In D. R. Kinshalo (Ed.), *The skin senses* (pp. 195–218). Springfield, IL: Charles C. Thomas.

Weisberg, Y. D. (1986). *Sefer Otzar Ha-Brit, Vol. 1*. Jerusalem: Makhon Torat Ha-Brit.

Wertz, R. W., & Wertz, D. C. (1989). *Lying-in: A history of childbirth in America* (expanded ed.). New Haven, CT: Yale University Press. [Originally published 1977, Free Press.]

Wieschhoff, H. A. (1973). Concepts of right and left in African cultures. In R. Needham (Ed.), *Right and left: Essays on dual symbolic classification* (pp. 59–73). Chicago & London: The University of Chicago Press. [Reprinted from the *Journal of the American Oriental Society*, 1938, *58*, 202–217.]

Wile, I. S. (1934). *Handedness right and left*. Boston: Lothrop, Lee & Shepard Company.

Wilson, D. (1891). *The right hand: Left-handedness*. New York: Macmillan.

Wilson, L. L. (1924). *The Roman toga*. Baltimore, MD: The Johns Hopkins University Press.

Witkowski, G-J. (1890). *Les Accouchements a la Cour*. Paris: G. Steinheil.

Wolff, B. B., & Jarvik, M. E. (1964). Relationship between superficial and deep somatic thresholds of pain with a note on handedness. *American Journal of Psychology, 77*, 589–599.

Woodham-Smith, C. B. F. (1951). *Florence Nightingale, 1820–1910*. New York: McGraw-Hill.

Woolley, H. T. (1910). The development of right-handedness in a normal infant. *Psychological Review, 17*, 37–41.

Wong, D. L., & Perry, S. E. (1998). *Maternal child nursing care*. St. Louis, MO: Mosby.

Wren, C. (n.d.). *Notes on Thomas Browne (1646), Pseudodoxia Epidemica, or, Enquiries into Very Many Received Tenents, and Commonly Preserved Truths*. [Transcribed and reprinted by S. Wilkin (1852) in *The Works of Sir Thomas Browne* (revised version of 1836 ed.). London: Henry Bohn. Note 4, p. 18, from Chapter V, "Of the right and left Hand"; posted by James Eason.] Retrieved 18 July 2007, from http://penelope.uchicago.edu/pseudodoxia/pseudo45.html

Wurtz, F. (1656). *The Children's Book*. English translation from the German of a treatise written in 1563 and appended as pp. 339–366 to the author's *An Experimental Treatise of Surgerie, in Four Parts*. London: Gartrude Dawson.

Wyeth, J. A. (1880). The anatomical reasons for dextral preference in man. *Annals of the Anatomical and Surgical Society, 2*, 121–132.

Young, G., Segalowitz, S. J., Misek. P., Alp, I. E., & Boulet, R. (1983). Is early reaching left-handed? Review of manual specialization research. In G. Young, C. Corter, S. J. Segalowitz, & S. E. Trehub (Eds.), *Manual specialization and the developing brain* (pp. 13–32). New York: Academic Press.

Zhao, D., Gao, X., Li, B., & Watanabe, K. (2008). First wild evidence of neonate nipple preference and maternal cradling laterality in Old World monkeys: A preliminary study from *Rhinopithecus roxellana*. *Behavioural Processes, 77*, 364–368.

LATERALITY, 2010, 15 (1/2), 136–165

Science in the Making: Right Hand, Left Hand. I: A BBC television programme broadcast in 1953

I. C. McManus, Richard Rawles, James Moore, and Matthew Freegard

University College London, UK

In August 1953, the BBC broadcast a television science programme entitled *Science in the Making: Right Hand, Left Hand.* The programme was broadcast live, being presented by Dr Jacob Bronowski in collaboration with Dr Kenneth Smith, and produced by George Noordhof. It not only presented a popular account of current ideas about right- and left-handedness, by using a group of celebrities (and a chimpanzee) in the studio, but also asked viewers to complete a brief questionnaire on handedness, which was printed in the *Radio Times.* Recently 6,336 of the returned questionnaires, which were said to have been analysed by Sir Cyril Burt and a colleague, were found in the archive of the Psychology Department of University College London. The present paper describes what we have discovered about the programme from various sources, including the producer and the son of Dr Kenneth Smith, and also presents basic descriptions of the postcards and the response to the programme. In two subsequent papers we will describe our analysis of the data from the postcards, which represents an unusual, large-scale survey of handedness in the mid-twentieth century.

The present study was prompted by the discovery, in the summer of 2002, of two medium-sized cardboard boxes crammed with about 6,000 postcards dating from August 1953. The discovery was made by one of us (RR), in the archive of UCL Department of Psychology. The story will be told chronologically at first, in order to describe how the history of these cards was uncovered, and then, after a brief analysis of some statistical aspects of the cards, the remainder of this paper will be devoted to a discussion of the programme, its participants, its context, and the survey that was carried out as a part of the programme. Two subsequent papers will analyse in more detail the data contained on the cards, looking separately at the two

Address correspondence to: I. C. McManus, UCL Department of Psychology, University College London, Gower Street, London WC1E 6BT, UK. E-mail: i.mcmanus@ucl.ac.uk

We are extremely grateful to Dr Michael Apter, Mrs Vera Smith, and Mr George Noordhof for giving of their time and their memories in the writing of this paper.

DOI: 10.1080/13576500802559803

questions of the incidence of handedness, and the role of directional scanning in the duck–rabbit illusion.

SCIENCE IN THE MAKING: RIGHT HAND, LEFT HAND

The postcards contained in the boxes were mostly of a very standard format, typified by that shown in Figure 1. Postmarked mostly towards the end of August 1953 (see also Figure 7, below), the postcards were addressed to

a Recto

b Verso

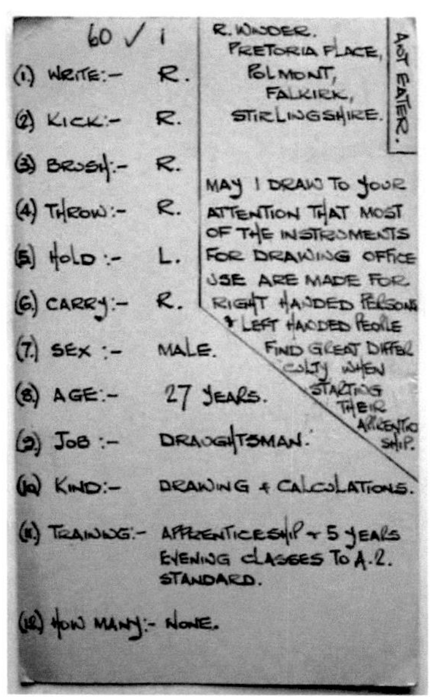

Figure 1. Typical postcard contained in the boxes in the archive: (a) recto and (b) verso.

"Right Hand, Left Hand, BBC Television Service, Alexandra Palace, London N.22". On the verso the cards showed a list of answers to what were clearly 12 questions, indicated synoptically by phrases such as "Write", "Kick", "Brush", etc., which were obviously to do with handedness. A few other statements were to do with age, sex, and other demographic features. On many cards, at right angles to the main line of writing, was the name of an animal (such as "Ant eater" in Figure 1b). Some cards also contained other comments as in Figure 1b. In a separate hand, written in red biro, were what seemed to be codes, such as "60 ✓ 1" in Figure 1b.

Sorting through the boxes eventually revealed a few cards, such as that in Figure 2, on which had been pasted an extract from the *Radio Times*, the weekly magazine in which the BBC listed (and continues to list) details of upcoming radio and television programmes. This contained the full text

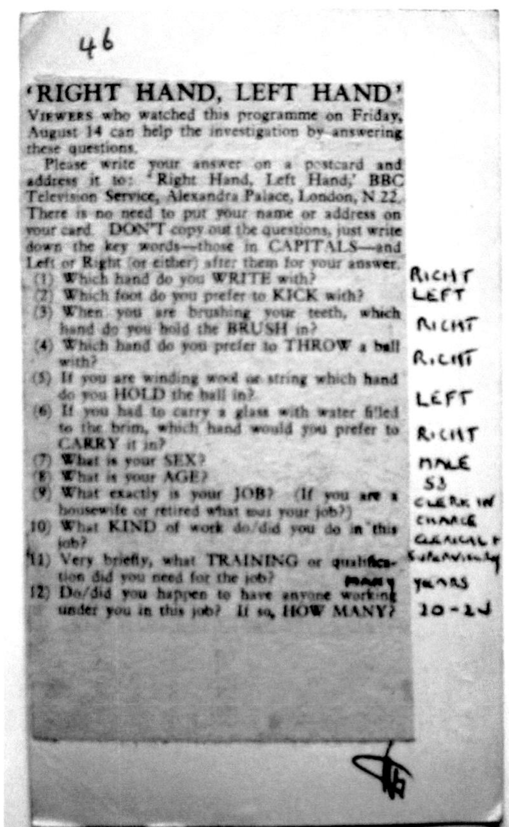

'RIGHT HAND, LEFT HAND'

VIEWERS who watched this programme on Friday, August 14 can help the investigation by answering these questions.

Please write your answer on a postcard and address it to: 'Right Hand, Left Hand,' BBC Television Service, Alexandra Palace, London, N.22. There is no need to put your name or address on your card. DON'T copy out the questions, just write down the key words—those in CAPITALS—and Left or Right (or either) after them for your answer.

(1) Which hand do you WRITE with?
(2) Which foot do you prefer to KICK with?
(3) When you are brushing your teeth, which hand do you hold the BRUSH in?
(4) Which hand do you prefer to THROW a ball with?
(5) If you are winding wool or string which hand do you HOLD the ball in?
(6) If you had to carry a glass with water filled to the brim, which hand would you prefer to CARRY it in?
(7) What is your SEX?
(8) What is your AGE?
(9) What exactly is your JOB? (If you are a housewife or retired what was your job?)
(10) What KIND of work do/did you do in this job?
(11) Very briefly, what TRAINING or qualification did you need for the job?
(12) Do/did you happen to have anyone working under you in this job? If so, HOW MANY?

Figure 2. A postcard on which the respondent has pasted an extract from the *Radio Times*.

of most of the questions that had been asked, along with instructions on how to provide answers. The *Radio Times* is available in the British Library, and it was straightforward to find that on Friday 14 August 1953, at 9.45 pm, immediately after "International Speedway racing, Scotland vs England", and just before "News (sound only)" and the Close Down (during which the National Anthem would have been played), was broadcast a half-hour programme called "Science in the Making: Right Hand, Left Hand",[1] hereafter *RHLH*, presented by Dr Jacob Bronowski. An announcement of the programme was made in the *Radio Times* dated 7 August (p. 36):

> Dr. Kenneth Smith shows that left handedness is not limited to writing, and demonstrates by means of experiments with well-known personalities that most right-handed people are left-handed in some ways.
>
> Vewers are asked to perform certain simple tests and invited to submit the results in writing to. 'Right hand, Left hand'. BBC Television Service, Alexandra Palace, London N.22. Produced by George Noordhof.

The questionnaire itself was included in the issue dated 14 August: "Viewers who watched this programme on Friday August 14 can help the investigation by answering these questions".

THE PROGRAMME

The BBC's Written Archives Centre in Reading, UK, had no photographs or other visual records of the programme,[2] but could provide both the scripts and transcripts[3] ("transcribed by a Telediphone recording"), not only for *RHLH*, but also for the remaining six programmes in the series. The next five programmes, broadcast over the next 8 months, were entitled "The Common Cold" (Monday 12 October 1953), "Twin Sister, Twin Brother" (Monday 9 November 1953), "Like Father Like Son" (Wednesday 27 January 1954), "The Sense of Sight" (Wednesday 24 February, 1954), and "The Living Memory" (Friday 16 April, 1954). The seventh and final programme, on Monday 14 June 1954, contained a summary of viewers' responses to three of the programmes, on visual acuity, on twins, and on asthma, but did not mention again the question of handedness. All the programmes in the series were presented by Dr Jacob Bronowski, and

---

[1] The *Radio Times* questionnaire referred to the programme as "RIGHT HAND, LEFT HAND", whereas the script refers to it as "Right hand left hand" on its title page.

[2] Only important programmes were "kinescoped", in which a 16-mm film camera was put in front of a television monitor, video-tapes not then being available (GHN).

[3] The transcript of *RHLH* is dated "14th June 1954", which presumably is the date of transcription.

produced by George Noordhof. Dr Kenneth Smith took part only in the first programme of the series, where Bronowski introduced him and the programme by saying, "let me introduce an expert to tell us what we do know about right hand – left hand – Dr. Kenneth Smith".[4]

The programme itself contained many of the devices and tricks that are still popular in television science programmes, including a series of celebrities who tried out various tasks with their right and left hands, and whose eyedness and hand-clasping were also assessed; there was film of Dennis Compton, a cricketer who bowled left-handed and batted right-handed, bowling to the Australian Neil Harvey, who batted left-handed but bowled right-handed; there was Charlie Chaplin in *Limelight* playing the violin left-handed; there was a brief discussion of mirror-writing; and finally there was a chimpanzee in the studio who ate a banana with both hands to make the point that "man is the only animal to have a marked preference for one side". The programme was broadcast live, and there was seemingly no film or photographic record of it.

An unusual feature of the programme, as Bronowski announced at the beginning and as its series title implied, was that "viewers will be asked to submit certain details about themselves and help scientists in their investigations". Near the end of the programme, Bronowski says in the transcript:

> Now for many years now famous experts in this subject have been anxious to collect large numbers of answers and questions on this [topic]. We consulted a most distinguished authority, Sir Cyril Burt, and he drew up some questions which have never in the past been answered by many people. We hope to get answers from – oh – thousands of people – from you. The questions are on page 15, bottom right-hand corner of the Radio Times but next week's Radio Times, the one that came today and starts with Sunday's programmes.

The transcript then takes a slight detour, Bronowski saying that before he describes how to answer the questions, "I'd like to show you a picture, a puzzle picture. Here is a picture that has something to do with left-handedness and right-handedness. Will you look at it carefully?" The picture is a version of Jastrow's famous duck–rabbit illusion, and the details of precisely what was asked, and how the answers were to be recorded, will be left until later when the data themselves are analysed. For reasons that are not clear, viewers were asked to write their response to the duck–rabbit figure at a right-angle to the main answers, in a way that was presumably demonstrated on the television screen, and can be seen in Figure 1.

---

[4] Quotations in general are from the transcript.

The programme finished with Bronowski saying:

> ... the next programme in this series will run on Oct 12th, and by that time I hope that Sir Cyril Burt's team will have analysed your answers sufficiently for me to be able to give you some information about it. I'll also be able to tell you why the puzzle picture is connected with rightness and leftness, so let me say goodnight to you, and show you the puzzle picture for a last time – WHAT IS IT?"

The second programme in the series on October 12, entitled "The common cold", and featuring Dr C. H. Andrewes, of the National Institute for Medical Research, mentioned at the end the analysis of the postcards from the previous programme concerning handedness. First, Bronowski talked about the duck–rabbit illusion, discussion of which will be deferred until later. The transcript then continued:

> The information came from all over Great Britain and far beyond it, we had over 8,000 postcards, rather more than half by women, rather less by men – this has nothing to do with the figures I quoted earlier. The great majority came from London, Yorkshire was next, and Lancashire immediately afterwards. Our most distant postcard came from Norway. And I may say that postcards are still coming, there is a postcard that arrived only today. The larger number – a disproportionately high number of cards came from left-handed people, and many of them, like the envelope I'll show you now, were in mirror writing. And one is addressed to our producer George Noordhof, and I can only suppose that the Post Office supplied mirrors to its postmen for the purpose of its delivery.
>
> We were particularly interested, as you will recall, with how left-handedness in writing goes with left-handedness in sewing or left-handedness in kicking, and the like. Now there we found something which really is rather interesting about educational policy in the past. That if you analyse the replies by age groups then you found that people who've been to school, oh, about, 40 years ago, had on the whole been bullied out of being left-handed. That is, we had many left-handed throwers or left-handed kickers who were right-handed writers. But as we come down the age scale to modern times we found this less and less, until in the present generation of schoolchildren we found that almost no left-handed throwers were right-handed writers. I'm afraid that Dr Smith wouldn't care for this very much, but those are the facts.
>
> I'm only giving you a kind of stop press report on this, because there has been far too large a response for me or anyone to be able to do a complete analysis. The analysis has been done by the Department of Psychology of the University College of London, under the direction of Sir Cyril Burt. And he asks me to thank viewers for giving him an amount of information which is, oh, many tens of times larger than it's ever been obtained on this topic before. I hope that you will make Dr Andrews this evening feel equally obliged to you. Goodnight.

None of the ensuing programmes gave any further information about the survey of handedness, and as far as we can tell none of the data have ever been published in any form.

THE PARTICIPANTS IN THE PROGRAMME

The programme transcript has on its opening page:

PRODUCED BY: G E O R G E N O O R D H O F

Those taking part:

Dr J. Bronowski
Dr K. Smith
Helen Cordet
Philip Harben
Elizabeth Allan
Mervyn Levy
Brenda Bruce
Eamonn Andrews
Chimpanzee

Among the celebrities were Helen (properly, Hélène) Cordet (1924–1996), who was just finishing a run of presenting a Saturday evening cabaret show entitled *Café Continental*; Philip Harben (1906–1970) the first TV chef on the BBC; Elizabeth Allan (1908–1990), a film actress who achieved stardom on BBC TV's *What's my Line?*; Mervyn Levy (1915–1996), an artist whose portraits of Dylan Thomas are in the National Portrait Gallery, London, who subsequently became a friend of Kenneth Smith, and whose portrait of Smith is owned by his family; Brenda Bruce (1918–1996), a television and film actress; and Eamonn Andrews (1922–1987), the television presenter who at the time of the programme was on *What's my Line?* and subsequently found lasting fame with *This is Your Life*.

The identity of the chimpanzee is not known, but a newspaper clipping of unknown provenance said that "George Cansdale would be taking part". Cansdale (1909–1993) was the Superintendent of the London Zoo, who had been working with animals on television since 1948. Another newspaper clipping commented, "But it was hardly tactful to introduce a chimpanzee after the fuss over J. Fred Muggs", a reference to a chimpanzee who from 1953 to 1957 was the mascot of the American NBC's *Today Show*. The "fuss" probably refers to a controversy over whether the chimpanzee trivialised the *Today Show*, a story that eventually resulted in a comment in 1955 in the

Soviet newspaper *Izvestiia* that "Muggs is necessary in order that the average American should not look into reports on rising taxes, and decreasing pay, but rather laugh at the funny mug of a chimpanzee".[5]

One of the participants, Dr Jacob Bronowski, and also one of the collaborators in the programme mentioned several times in the script, Professor Sir Cyril Burt, are well known, and biographical information is readily available.

Dr Jacob Bronowski (1908–1974)

A distinguished scientific broadcaster, who studied maths at Cambridge, and was subsequently lecturer in mathematics at University College Hull (Sheets-Pyenson, 2004). During the war he carried out operations research, including studying the effects of the atomic bomb at Nagasaki. After the war he worked for the National Coal Board, but was also gaining a reputation as a broadcaster, particularly on television programmes such as *The Brains Trust*, where he was particularly successful because of his wide range of interests, his first two books, published in 1939 and 1944, being on poetry and on William Blake. He subsequently published extensively on science and values, and the two cultures. His best-known achievement in television was his 13-part series, broadcast in 1973, *The Ascent of Man*. Figure 3 shows Bronowski in action in a programme from the early 1960s, in which he was describing the Platonic solids (Bronowski, 1964, p. 105). He had first appeared on television in 1951, and in 1953 wrote a letter to George Noordhof, the producer of *Science in the Making*, summarising his approach to presenting science on television:[6] "I like the logical unfolding of a scientific idea. I do not care for programmes which work by the accumulation of points. I find it easiest to explain a scientific idea by presenting its evolution, because I want to explain its inner logic." At the time of *RHLH*, Bronowski was working at the National Coal Board's Central Research Establishment at Stoke Orchard, Cheltenham, of which he had been director since 1950.

Sir Cyril Burt (1883–1971)

An important but controversial figure in the history of British psychology (Mazumdar, 2004). As an educational psychologist he was extremely influential, contributing extensively to the work of the Board of Education. In 1932 he was appointed Professor of Psychology at University College

[5] en.wikipedia.org/wiki/J._Fred_Muggs
[6] atschool.eduweb.co.uk/stevemoss/bron/noordhoff.htm

Figure 3. Dr Jacob Bronowski in a television programme from the early 1960s.

London, succeeding Charles E. Spearman, and he remained there until his retirement in September 1950. His retirement was not a relaxing one, not least because of financial problems which meant that even until his last days he was carrying out large amounts of routine work, such as marking of exam papers and theses. Relatively soon after his retirement his ideas were also becoming controversial in the media, particularly because of his emphasis on eugenics. He died in 1971 and controversy re-erupted in 1976 when, in the London *Sunday Times*, he was accused of fraud. The existence of several of his research assistants was questioned and the suggestion made that many of his data on separated identical twins were fabricated. The controversy has continued since then with a series of books on the topic, taking many different positions (Hearnshaw, 1979; Joynson, 1989; Fletcher, 1991; Mackintosh, 1995). Burt was a frequent contributor to BBC Radio—as for instance in the talks published in 1933 under the title *How the Mind Works* (Burt, 1933), to which Burt both edited and contributed. However his last radio talks were in 1950, and although the BBC had regarded him as a good broadcaster these last talks did not go down well, the BBC thinking that they "seemed dated" (Hearnshaw, 1979, p. 189), and Burt putting the problem down to problems with his hearing, "which prevents me from knowing quite what my voice is doing". It is hardly surprising, therefore, that Burt was not a studio participant for *Right Hand, Left Hand*. Burt's involvement with the programme was relatively late, his diary for 1953 including the entries:[7]

July 27	Heavy showers p. m. to Valentine Letter to Noordhof (TV)
July 31	Noordhof calls about television (Right Hand and Left Hand)
August 14	Climbed to quarry and back via Graham Rd TV (Right Hand Left Hand)

Although in general Burt had a tendency to record even relatively trivial events in his diary (as for instance on March 28 1956, when he wrote, "Cold out. Liby. returning theol. books. Logistic curve. Roes on toast"), the diary for 1953 is relatively sparse, the last entry being on September 4 ("Dullish"), with no entries before March 31, and none for May or June. Therefore, that Burt does mention the programme is of some interest. Although at first sight it may seem surprising that there is no mention of analysing data from the programme, it must be said that, despite Burt being on holiday from 17 July to 28 August, staying with his sister Marion in Malvern, he spoke by telephone with Charlotte Banks on 19, 23, and 25 August, and he met with her after his return to London on 29, 30, and 31 August (her birthday). It is therefore more than possible that the *RHLH* data were spoken about on some of those occasions. The idea of analysing large-scale data collected from the mass media was not novel for Burt, for in 1933 he had carried out a mass media study of experimental aesthetics (Burt, 1933), based on the paired comparison tests devised by Margaret Bulley (1925, 1933). Nine pairs of pictures were printed in *The Listener*, the BBC magazine, the pictures were then discussed in a radio programme, and listeners were asked to send in their responses on a postcard—about 6,000 people apparently did so.

The other two main participants in the programme, Mr George Noordhof and Dr Kenneth Smith, were more problematic to trace.

[7] These excerpts are taken from a typed transcript of the diaries (which are lodged in the University of Liverpool Archives [D191/1-5]). It was made by Charlotte Banks after Burt's death, and subsequently John and Margaret Bate kindly presented it to Richard Rawles in May 2006.

Mr George Noordhof (b. 1922)

George Noordhof was the last of the main participants to be found. A few sparse details about him had been gleaned from the Internet. Noordhof was a student in Cambridge in 1949, where he was a member of the Footlights Company, and was also its property master. In 1953–1954 he produced *Science in the Making* for BBC TV, and he also produced a programme called *Science News*, which Arthur Dungate said "must have been one of the first science programmes on television".[8] Much later, from 1987 to 1988, he was Head of Media Services at Brunel University, where he acted as an educationalist and producer of educational television, and in 1988 he also wrote the introduction to a book on audiovisual communication (McPherson & Timms, 1988).

Eventually, in August 2005, we managed to find Mr Noordhof, who was living in London, aged 83, with an excellent memory of the events surrounding *Science in the Making.*[9]

George H. Noordhof was born in Haarlem in the Netherlands in 1922, and at the age of 9 came to live in London, where he attended a school in Golders Green. He studied metallurgy at Imperial College from 1940 to 1943, and then, being fluent in English, Dutch, and German, went to Holland and Germany as a military liaison officer. After the war, in October 1945, he went up to Cambridge and started but never completed a PhD on corrosion. A year spent in industry gave him experience of making presentations to varied audiences, and he joined the BBC in 1951, where he was the first science producer for "Television Talks", as the department was then known. The head of department was Mary Adams (1898–1984) who had worked in television from 1930,[10] was herself a Cambridge science graduate in biology, and had also started but not completed a PhD. His immediate superior was Andrew Miller-Jones (1910–1994), perhaps best known for creating the BBC television news magazine programme *Panorama* in 1953. Among the programmes that Noordhof produced before *Science in the Making* were *Inventor's Club*, *Science Review*, and *Looking at Animals.* Subsequently he produced many programmes for television, including at

---

[8] www.bbctv-ap.co.uk/marriage.htm

[9] George Noordhof was interviewed by telephone on 8 August 2005, and in more detail on 4 October 2005, for the BBC Radio 4 programme, *6000 postcards*, broadcast 6 January 2006 – see http://www.bbc.co.uk/radio4/factual/pip/89q7m/ (recording available from http://www.talking-book-store.com/list.aspx?catID'87). Much of what follows immediately is a result of those interviews. Comments elsewhere are indicated by the initials GHN. We are very grateful to him for his help and enthusiastic collaboration in carrying out this research.

[10] mymovies.imdb.com/name/nm0011196/; www.televisionheaven.co.uk/history3.htm; www.museum.tv/archives/etv/W/htmlW/watchwithmo/watchwithmo.htm

least one other, in collaboration with Donald Broadbent in about 1964, from which adequate data were also collected for scientific analysis (Broadbent & Gregory, 1965).

Dr Kenneth Smith (1910–1999)

The fourth major participant in *RHLH* was particularly problematic to identify, especially before George Noordhof had been traced. All that was known from the script was the name, "Dr Kenneth Smith". An initial false trail led to Dr Kenneth (Manley) Smith (1892–1981) who wrote a series of textbooks, as well as popular science books for Penguin, including his *Beyond the Microscope* of 1943 (revised edition 1957). However he restricted himself to writing on virology and related subjects.

A search through *Psyclit*, *Medline*, and similar databases found no papers on handedness by an author named Smith, and for nearly a year the trail ran cold. Finally, in October 2003, a Google search on "Kenneth Smith Bronowski left-handedness" found an obituary notice in the Royal College of Psychiatrists' *Bulletin* (Early, 2000), written by Dr D. F. Early, for Dr Kenneth Carl Pfeiffer Smith (1910–1999), a psychiatrist who had been Medical Director of Wiltshire Child Guidance Services and in which it was commented most crucially, but not entirely accurately, that:

> In the late 1950s he researched and presented a programme on left-handedness produced by Dr Jacob Bronowski, one of the first TV programmes to deal seriously from a psychological view point, with a topic of everyday interest.

Obituaries of Smith were also published in *The Independent* (London) on 5 November 1999, *The Guardian* (London) on 9 November 1999, and the *British Medical Journal* on 11 December 1999, of which only the latter, also written by Early, mentioned handedness (but not Bronowski). Subsequently, after making contact with Dr Early's wife (Dr Early being unable to help because of illness), we were put in touch with Dr Smith's widow Vera, a painter and ceramicist, and also with Dr Smith's son, the distinguished psychologist Dr Michael J. Apter,[11] who is now known by his mother's maiden name. Apter has published extensively on "reversal theory", an

[11] Professor Apter was interviewed at length on 19 December 2003 by ICM, and a somewhat shorter discussion was also held on the same day with Kenneth Smith's widow, Vera. Much of the material in this section comes from those interviews, and from press cuttings and other memorabilia in the possession of the Smith family. Comments elsewhere referring to the interviews are indicated as MJA.

approach to psychology that was initiated in collaboration with his father, whose clinical observations had engendered the theory, and Apter's 2001 overview of the theory is dedicated to Kenneth Smith (Apter, 2001).

Kenneth Smith (Figure 4) was born in Bristol in 1910, and spent most of his life in the area. He qualified in medicine from the University of Bristol in 1937, went into the RAF on a short-service commission, and attained the rank of Squadron Leader. Always interested in show business, in the RAF he met a number of famous artists while presenting a national radio programme, "Aircraftsman Smith Entertains". After demobilisation he returned to medicine, specialising in psychiatry initially before entering general practice, and finally becoming director of the Wiltshire Child Guidance Service. While practising he continued his interests in show business and sport (and for many years was medical officer to Bristol Rugby Club and Gloucestershire County Cricket Club), as well as gaining extensive knowledge of antiques, particularly art nouveau and art deco. A large man in every sense, with a big personality, who was a good pianist, singer, compère and raconteur, he loved being in and around the entertainment industry, and he had many long-lasting friendships, with Leslie Howard and Paul Robeson among others. The interest in entertainment passed in part to

Figure 4. Dr Kenneth Smith, drawn in 1953 by Mervyn Levy, whom Smith met while taking part in *Right Hand, Left Hand*. Pencil on paper, slightly foxed; the picture is in the possession of Dr Smith's family.

his sons, the younger of whom, Paul, is a producer for BBC TV. The older son, Michael, though now a psychologist, had at one time appeared on student television.

Kenneth Smith's interest in left-handedness came about through his clinical work, since so many children seemed to be left-handed or ambidextrous. He never published any formal research on the topic (nor indeed on anything else), but had a life-long interest in the topic, seeing it as "an awkward way of interacting with the world". He was not left-handed himself, and neither was there a history of left-handedness in the family. He had at some time sent data on handedness to Malcolm Piercy and Oliver Zangwill in Cambridge (and he had a copy of Zangwill's 1960 monograph), but had been disappointed that nothing had come from that initiative.

RHLH was apparently Smith's first television appearance, but subsequently he appeared on a number of other programmes in the 1950s, including an ITV programme entitled *Crossroads*,[12] which was broadcast on 29 September 1955 in the very first week of ITV's broadcasting. It was a panel discussion chaired by Leslie Mitchell (1905–1985),[13] subsequently Head of Discussion Features, and the co-panellists with Smith were the actress Lesley Osmond,[14] and the future MP Jeremy Thorpe[15] (see Figure 4 and Figure 5, which give a good idea of how Smith would have looked at the time of recording *RHLH*). The programme had a very psychological approach, taking a participant at a critical moment, a crossroads in their lives, discussing what options might have been available to them, and then finding out from the participant what they had actually done.

It is not clear how Kenneth Smith became involved in *RHLH*, although it is possible that he had previously done a radio programme on the topic – "and he was the local psychological expert". George Noordhof was also very clear that Smith was "a television natural", relaxed, unstuffy, humorous, and with a good presence. Smith did not know Bronowski (and indeed he apparently only met Bronowski on the day of the programme [MJA], and "regarded [Bronowski] as a bit of a charlatan"). Smith did know Burt a little, as perhaps would anyone who worked in child guidance, given the prominence of books by Burt, including the two parts of *The sub-normal*

[12] Not to be confused with the subsequent soap opera of the same name which was broadcast from 1964 to 1988.

[13] http://www.doramusic.com/LeslieMitchell.htm

[14] We have been unable to find much in the way of biographical details, except that she was born in 1921 and died in 1987. Between 1942 and 1951 she appeared in a series of films (www.imdb.com), with IMDb describing *Death is a number* (1951) as "A good contender for possibly the worst British feature film of all time."

[15] Jeremy Thorpe (b. 1929), who from 1954 worked as both a barrister and a TV presenter, was subsequently an MP and leader of the Liberal Party. His career collapsed in scandal in 1976 (en.wikipedia.org/wiki/Jeremy_Thorpe).

Figure 5. A studio photograph taken on the set of the ITV programme *Crossroads*, probably of the edition broadcast on 10 November 1955. The woman on the left is a member of the public who is the "story-teller", describing a crucial moment in her life. The other individuals from left to right are: Leslie Mitchell, the chairman; Lesley Osmond, an actress; an unidentified woman; Dr Kenneth Smith, with pipe in hand; and Jeremy Thorpe, then a barrister and TV presenter.

school child—volume 1 being *The Young Delinquent* (Burt, 1925), first published in 1925, with its fourth edition in 1944 (reprinted 1969) and volume 2 being *The Backward Child*, first published in 1937 and by 1961 in its fifth edition (reprinted 1969), with a 90-page chapter on "Left-handedness" (Burt, 1961).[16] As far as Smith's other reading is concerned, he certainly owned a copy of Blau's *The Master Hand* (1946), as well as Woodworth's *Experimental Psychology* (1938).

MAKING THE PROGRAMME

Kenneth Smith's contract with the BBC stipulated that he would be paid £31.10.0d plus expenses, and said there would be rehearsals at 6.00 pm on 13 August and 3.00 pm on 14 August, although Smith only attended the rehearsal on the 14th. The programme itself was broadcast at 9.45 pm on 14

[16] Although *The Backward Child* went into five editions, a comparison of the 1st and 5th editions shows very few changes, apart from the addition on the title page of Burt's knighthood and a collection of honorary degrees. The pagination of the 1st edition is identical to that of the 5th edition for all six chapters (and in particular, Chapter X on left-handedness is from pp. 270–359). The only major change in pagination is that the last Appendix, III, "Statistical criteria", runs from pp. 658–674 in the first edition, and pp. 658–684 in the fifth edition. Likewise the tables and figures are identical. We can find no differences of any sort in the chapter on left-handedness. Certainly there is little evidence for Burt's comment in the Preface to the 5th edition of him taking the opportunity "to incorporate the results of recent research ...".

August, at the Lime Grove Studios in Hammersmith, West London,[17] from Studio D which had been the first to go live in 1950.[18] Michael Apter, then aged 14, and his mother were present in the studio at the recording. The younger son Paul, aged 10, stayed at home and, as the family didn't have a television, watched the programme at a neighbour's. He remembers standing in the garden moving the aerial around as those inside shouted whether the picture was better or worse. Michael Apter remembers the studio as very hot because of the lights, and rehearsals went on all day. "A little before the programme went out my father said I can't go on, I need a breath – get some air." And so he walked up and down the street for half an hour with Michael and his mother. When they got back "there was absolute panic in the studio". However Smith "was not panicking – [he] already had some understanding of reversal theory – need[ed] to reverse at some point".

Michael remembers his father talking to the family during the rehearsals, but also recalls that none of the other participants, including Bronowski, talked to the family, with the sole exception of Eamonn Andrews, and "My mother fell in love with him on the spot."

As with much early live television there were technical problems, such as Smith being unable to see any of the films that were being transmitted, since they were broadcast from Alexandra Palace and could only be seen on a single monitor. The movements were acted out by a technician, and those in the studio had to guess what was happening.

RESPONSES TO THE PROGRAMME

The programme was reviewed in *The Listener* on 20 August 1953, by Reginald Pound, the "Critic on the hearth" (p. 314). The review was not especially good, and in particular did not like the use of celebrities:

> A more discerning instinct would have rejected the celebrity notion as hackneyed ... The theme was curiously muddled, and because of it was made at times to seem embarrassingly trivial. I think it would have been better to leave the doctor to make his points in his own engagingly homespun fashion, with the aid of the cartoons. Fine as are Bronowski's expository powers, they were clouded on this occasion by his oozing suavity.

We are aware of only one other brief review, in an unidentified newspaper, which commented that "it is possible to be instructive without boring". We have also searched the full-text *Times Digital Archive,* which apparently

[17] en.wikipedia.org/wiki/Lime_Grove_Studios

[18] For pictures see www.bbctv-ap.co.uk/lgdem01.htm and www.bbctv-ap.co.uk/lgdem05.htm

contains no mention of the programme. The Apter family does have a few press cuttings, from unidentified newspapers, one of which is entitled "Tele-talk", and contains some comments by George Noordhof:

> Although these are basically serious science programmes, I want them to be fun. . . . At the same time I hope that, with the co-operation of viewers, we shall be able to make a valuable contribution to scientific knowledge.

The force of the piece might have been a little greater if the author had not also commented, entirely wrongly as it turned out, that "The second programme – in the autumn – on *Humour*, will endeavour to find out the kind of jokes that make people laugh most".

An undated piece in the London *Daily Mail*, entitled "Viewers will aid science", fairly accurately described three of the questions that would be used in the questionnaire, but was also under the impression that the second programme in the series would be on humour.

METHOD

A preliminary sort of the postcards was carried out by ICM, RR, JM, and MF, and the cards were organised by age, sex, and handedness (see Figure 6). The postcards in the archive were numbered using an automatic numbering stamp, and as many details as possible entered into the computer by JM and MF, as part of their final-year undergraduate projects for the BSc degree. JM and MF were equally and jointly responsible for data entry, although JM's

Figure 6. One of the authors (RR) sorting the postcards by age, sex, and handedness. These cards, from female right-handers, are grouped by decade of age, and literally form a histogram.

project primarily concerned the incidence of handedness, whereas MF's concerned the duck–rabbit illusion.

RESULTS

Only basic descriptive statistics will be presented here, more detailed analyses being reserved for the subsequent two papers.

Altogether 6,336 postcards were found in the archive, of which 213 contained information from multiple individuals, almost always members of the same family, and therefore details of 6,549 individuals were known. Not all information was available for all individuals.

Date of posting

Figure 7 shows the distribution of date of posting in our set of postcards. The programme was broadcast late on Friday 14 August (which we have described as day 0), and most postcards were postmarked Saturday 15th (+1), there was then a slight dip for Sunday 16th (+2) (and in 1953 there were Sunday postal collections throughout the UK), and the numbers then rose again on Monday 17th (+3). The number of cards returned is almost

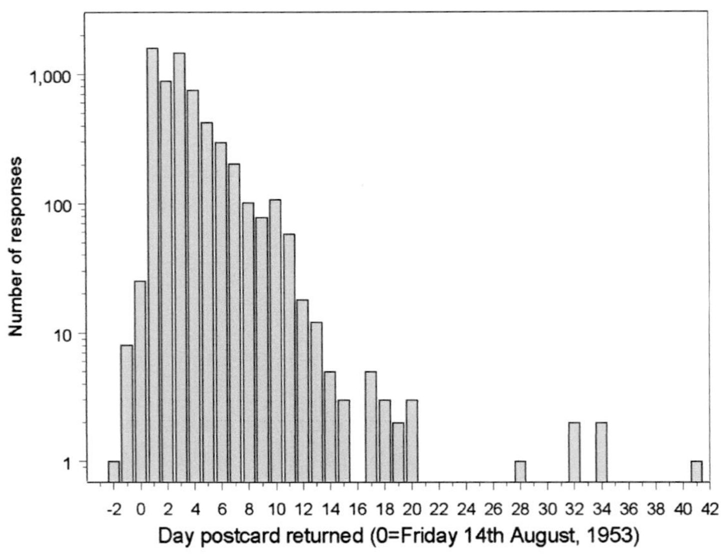

Figure 7. Date of response. Day 0 is the day of broadcast of the programme. Note that the vertical axis is logarithmic.

linear when plotted on a logarithmic scale, as in Figure 7, indicating that to a first approximation the number of returns declines exponentially. A few postcards are dated on or before 14 August (0, –1, or –2), and from comments made on some postcards these are probably from people who answered the *Radio Times* questionnaire before watching the programme (and, interestingly, some postcards indicated that they were returned by people who did not have a television, but were still interested in the topic). The last postcard in our collection is dated 24 September (day 41).

Age and sex

The respondents ranged in age from 5 to 89 (mean 35.8; SD 14.8; median 33; quartiles 25 and 44; 5th percentile 15; 95th percentile 65). A total of 3,014 respondents were male (46.0%), 3,534 were female (56.0%), and one did not give their sex.

The handedness questions

The details of these will be left to a succeeding paper. Suffice it here to say that 5,444 (83.1%) individuals said that they used the right hand for writing; 64 (1.0%) said that they used the right hand for writing but added a comment that they had at one time used the left hand for writing; 107 (1.6%) said they used either hand for writing; and 934 (14.3%) used the left hand for writing. Altogether, therefore, 1,105 (16.9%) of individuals did, had, or could use the left hand for writing. That proportion is higher than most current estimates of the rate of left-handedness, and suggests a response bias—a conclusion that will be analysed in more detail in a succeeding paper. Table 1 shows the responses to each of the handedness questions.

The duck–rabbit question

All analysis of this will be deferred until the succeeding paper. However it is of interest to note here that only 3,701 (56.5%) of the 6,549 respondents answered the question about the mystery animal, with 2,268 (61.3%) saying it was a duck (or duck-like), 911 (24.6%) saying it was a rabbit or rabbit-like, and 522 (14.1%) mentioning both duck-like and rabbit-like answers. The high proportion of non-responders to this question probably reflects the fact that, first, the question was not on the *Radio Times* questionnaire, and second, some respondents did not watch the television programme but only replied to the questionnaire that they had seen printed in the *Radio Times*.

TABLE 1
The questions and some answers

		Right	*Either*	*Left*	*Total*
(1)	Which hand do you WRITE with?	5444 (83.1%)	107 (1.6%)	998+ (15.2%)	6549
(2)	Which foot do you prefer to KICK with?	4559 (69.6%)	490 (7.5%)	1499 (22.9%)	6548
(3)	When you are brushing your teeth, which hand you hold the BRUSH in?	4827 (73.7%)	250 (3.8%)	1470 (22.4%)	6547
(4)	Which hand do you prefer to THROW a ball with?	4916 (75.1%)	151 (2.3%)	1476 (22.6%)	6543
(5)	If you are winding wool or string which hand do you HOLD the ball in?	1792 (27.4%)	321 (4.9%)	4427 (67.7%)	6540
(6)	If you had to carry a glass with water filled to the brim, which hand would you prefer to CARRY it in?	4103 (62.7%)	883 (13.5%)	1555 (23.8%)	6541
(7)	What is your SEX?				
(8)	What is your AGE?				
(9)	What exactly is your JOB? (If you are a housewife or retired what *was* your job?				
(10)	What KIND of work do/did you do in this job?				
(11)	Very briefly, what TRAINING or qualification did you need for the job?				
(12)	Do/did you happen to have anyone working under you in this job? If so, HOW MANY?				

The 12 questions included in the *Radio Times*, and the proportion of respondents answering Right, Either, or Left to the six handedness questions. The words in capitals are the terms that respondents were asked to use when describing the questions.

+ Includes 64 who indicated that they currently used their right hand but had used their left hand in the past.

DISCUSSION

Right Hand, Left Hand, the first of seven episodes of *Science in the Making*, was an important early achievement of Dr Jacob Bronowski,[19] and helped to consolidate his position as a television personality and scientific presenter. Bronowski's philosophy of making science accessible took several forms. In *RHLH* he allowed programme contributors to carry out model experiments for demonstrating principles, and subsequently, by allowing viewers to partake in the process of data collection itself, he demonstrated the ways by which science makes progress. Later, in *The Ascent of Man*, he was most

[19] *Science in the making* was not Bronowski's first television programme on science, his debut being "in a programme which he guided himself" in 1951 (http://atschool.eduweb.co.uk/stevemoss/bron/noordhoff.htm). He is also likely to have taken part in Noordhof's earlier series, *Science News*.

clearly to demonstrate his belief that "the other possible method is to trace the evolution of a scientific idea".

The title of the programme

It was not coincidence that the topic of handedness was chosen for the first programme in the series for, as Noordhof said, it was something on which everyone has made observations. Everyone is clear about their own handedness, most people are aware that a sizeable minority of the human population is left-handed, and many, not least left-handers themselves, have wondered why. It is therefore a perfect topic with which to engage studio participants and viewers, particularly as Bronowski, "really didn't want to talk about theories [but] generally wanted to make it easy [for people] to note things that were peculiar [about the world]" (GHN).

The title was also guaranteed to attract attention. A few years earlier, in 1945, Sir Osbert Sitwell had published the first volume of his autobiography, the five volumes together going under the collective title of *Left Hand, Right Hand!*[20] For the time it was a major publishing sensation,[21] selling over 141,500 copies by 1948 (Ziegler, 1999), and therefore was well known among the book-reading classes who also were likely to watch serious television programmes on science. The title of the programme was Noordhof's, who also created the other titles in the series [GHN]. The near universal knowledge about Sitwell is shown by the fact that Kenneth Smith apparently had his book, despite the fact that he "didn't read much fiction or biography" (MJA).

The analysis of the questionnaire

The questionnaire included in the *Radio Times* was returned, according to the comment in the programme itself, by 8000 individuals. Perhaps the most intriguing and most disappointing of the outcomes of the programme was how little was done with the data (and Noordhof was shocked, in 2005, to find that little had been done with the data in comparison, say, with the data

[20] The exclamation mark is a part of Sitwell's title. One of us (ICM) has also published a book entitled *Right Hand, Left Hand* (McManus, 2002). That title was a direct modification of Sitwell's title, but at the time of writing the author was completely unaware of the BBC programme of the same title, and indeed would have referred to it if he had been so aware.

[21] The impact can be assessed from the fact that John Lennon, for his first book, published in 1964 as *In his own write*, had apparently considered adapting Sitwell's title as *Left Hand, Left Hand* (see e.g., www.kirjasto.sci.fi/lennon.htm).

Figure 8. Dr Charlotte Banks, who collaborated with Sir Cyril Burt (original in Department of Psychology Archive, University College London; date unknown).

from the twin programme[22]). Bronowski refers rather grandly to Sir Cyril Burt "and his team", but it seems unlikely that there was much of a team for, as Hearnshaw (1979, p. 245) said, "After his retirement [Burt] had few, if any, co-workers, apart from Charlotte Banks, who assisted him with a small number of articles." The only person who can be identified with any certainty is Dr Charlotte Banks (Figure 8), a lecturer in psychology at University College London from about 1950 to the 1970s, who published research papers with Burt (Banks & Burt, 1953, 1954; Burt & Banks, 1947), edited a *Festschrift* for him (Banks & Broadhurst, 1966), and later published her reminiscences of Burt (Banks, 1983). The marks in red biro on the cards are in her handwriting, and occasional cards also carry the tell-tale signs of burns from a cigarette left on a card—Banks was an inveterate smoker. All but about 2% of the cards have red ticks upon them, and therefore almost all of those that we had processed had also been processed by Banks. There is, however, no record of Banks ever publishing any research on handedness. Some processing of the data was clearly carried

[22] Professor James Shields (1918–1978) had collaborated in the programme on twins, and the data collected in the audience survey, in particular on pairs of twins separated early in life, contributed to his subsequent book on the subject (Shields, 1962).

out, demonstrated by the comments at the end of the second TV programme, although these say relatively little. The first (numerical) code written on the cards seems to refer to the place of origin, and the third (numerical) code indicates whether the mystery picture was seen as a duck (1), a rabbit (2), or a mixed answer (3). Place of origin and duck/rabbit were each referred to in the second programme. What the tick indicated is not at all clear. Altogether 61.7% of cards had a tick on them, but we could find no correlation with any other aspect of the data that we had coded.

The questions on the questionnaire

In the programme Bronowski is explicit that the handedness questionnaire was written by Burt: "We consulted a most distinguished authority, Sir Cyril Burt, and he drew up some questions which have never in the past been answered by many people." The questions on the questionnaire are also interesting, not least because the specific set of questions is unusual, and does not seem to have been used before in this form. The idea of a questionnaire for assessing handedness was not new even in 1953. Humphrey (1951), who presented results of a 20-item questionnaire, said that it was based on Hull (1936), and that "Numerous questionnaires on handedness and laterality have been prepared by previous investigators...". It is unlikely that Burt would have been unaware of Humphrey's paper, since it was published in the *British Journal of Educational Psychology*, of which Burt was a member of the Editorial Board. However, of the six questions used in the BBC survey, only three—Writing hand, Throwing hand, and Hand to use a toothbrush—are included among Humphrey's 20 items. The inclusion of the foot for kicking, the hand for holding a ball of wool or string while winding, and the hand for carrying a glass of water full to the brim, suggest that Humphrey's paper had little influence on the BBC questionnaire.

Burt himself, in *The Backward Child*, does say, "For group inquiries a questionnaire on the following lines will pick out about 90 per cent. of those with left-handed tendencies" (1961, p. 279), and there then follows a list of 10 tasks. However only four of them are in the BBC questionnaire, three being the same as those in the Humphrey questionnaire (Write, Throw, Brush), and the fourth being the somewhat unusual item "to carry a cup of water or lift a glass in drinking"; the wording is not, however, as specific as that used in the BBC question. Holding a ball of wall and kicking are not mentioned by Burt (and indeed Burt does not seem to mention foot preference at any point). Burt does suggest that a 3-point answering scale should be used ("The words 'left', 'right', 'either hand' are printed as alternative answers against each question"). Although the BBC questionnaire does allow three responses—"Left or Right (or either)"—the parentheses and the lower-case for "either" suggest that it is hoped few people would use it (as indeed was the case). In the transcript, Bronowski explains how to fill in the questionnaire, and does at least mention the possibility of replying "either", saying:

> ... pick out the first question which says: 'Which hand do you write with?". Just write the word 'WRITE'[23] there, and put R for right. Which foot do you kick with? Write the word in capitals – KICK – oh let's say that I kick with either foot. Which hand do you brush your teeth with? Just pick out the word BRUSH and white – right hand, and so on down the card ...

Although the use of a 3-point scale might seem to reflect Burt's influence, Humphrey also used a 3-point scale in his study.

Perhaps the most unusual feature of the questionnaire is the question asking "If you are winding wool or string which hand do you hold the BALL in?". A strong right-hander would typically hold the string in their right hand, and hence the ball in their *left* hand, so that most people would be expected to answer "left" (as was indeed the case). Such reversed items are common nowadays in handedness questionnaires, but were not used either in Humphrey's questionnaire or in the set of 10 questions that Burt described. Why it was included in the BBC questionnaire is not at all clear.

When asked about Burt's contribution to the questionnaire, Noordhof suggested that "what Bruno [Bronowski] said [about Burt's contribution] in the programme was one thing – but I don't think he was greatly enamoured by the connection with Cyril Burt" (GHN). Burt had apparently not got on well with Noordhof, in part following on from Burt having a number of other bad incidents involving the media, and he was very caustic to Noordhof and the others. The only one who got on well with the *RHLH* team was Charlotte Banks, described as "a jolly hockey-sticks sort of woman" (GHN).

Six of the questions do not ask about handedness. Two, on sex and age, are standard for almost any survey and are uninteresting. The remaining questions are less obvious, and are concerned with the person's job. "What exactly is your JOB?" and "What KIND of work do/did you do in this job?" are somewhat overlapping, but nevertheless fairly useful in any survey, as perhaps also is the question on qualifications, which effectively is about educational level: "Very briefly, what TRAINING or qualifications did you need for the job?" The final question, though, is unusual: "Do/did you happen to have anyone working under you for this job? If so, how MANY?" Even ignoring what is now the rather strange usage of "happen", with its

[23] The transcript actually says "the word 'Right'", but it is an easy error to make, and few of us are entirely innocent of it.

modern implication that this somehow occurred absent-mindedly or by chance, the purpose of the question is obscure. At the time of the survey there was undoubtedly literature showing a sex and probably an age/cohort difference in the rate of left-handedness, described among others by Burt (1961), but we are unaware of any work on handedness and social class, job type, educational level, or responsibility for others in employment. In reality the answers to the questions do not seem to have been analysed—and it is not surprising, to anyone used to analysing questionnaires, that the answers are in fact pretty well unanalysable (and we did not even attempt to code them in our re-analysis). Although the questions themselves are quite interesting and, as Noordhof emphasised to us, he was keen to have them included as they were there to show the breadth of the social background of the respondents, in reality little systematic work could be done with them.

On balance it is not at all clear where several aspects of the BBC questionnaire came from. Although Bronowski clearly attributes it to Burt, there are sufficient discrepancies from Burt's own published thoughts to make it possible that he did not actually write the questions, and that may be reinforced by the fact that subsequently he seems never to have published anything on them, not even in subsequent editions of *The Backward Child*, where it seems highly surprising that he does not comment on such a large survey. The questionnaire may have been put together on an ad hoc basis by diverse hands, several perhaps unskilled at questionnaire construction (and that is supported by the inclusion of the near unanalysable question on employment, training, and job responsibilities). However the questions on employment do suggest that the author must have had some prior research questions, but precisely who that author was, and what the questions were, are very unclear. Certainly the data obtained on those questions still remains unanalysable in any straightforward quantitative way, at least by us. However, a more qualitative analysis might reveal something of historico-sociological interest.

The number of responses

To recapitulate, we found 6,336 postcards in the archive, of which 213 contained information from multiple individuals, almost always members of the same family. Therefore the handedness of a total of 6,549 individuals was known. In the second programme however, Bronowski comments that "we had over 8,000 postcards, rather more than half by women, rather less by men". Our total of 6,336 is therefore somewhat less than that reported, although we also found a small excess of women (54.0%). Bronowski also comments that, "Our most distant postcard came from Norway. And I may say that postcards are still coming, there is a postcard that arrived only today." However, we did not find a card from Norway among our collection.

Although Bronowski comments in the second programme, on 12 October, "that postcards are still coming, there is a postcard that arrived only today", our analysis of the date of posting of the cards in our collection suggests that there are unlikely to be many late arrivals (and certainly there are none in our collection). Interviews with Noordhof also made it clear that Bronowski and the rest of the team saw few, if any, of the returned questionnaires (and anyway, would have been busy working on the next programme when the replies were arriving).

An important question concerns whether our collection of 6,336 cards is in fact the entire collection, or whether there were actually "over 8,000" and another 1,700 or more have been lost or are lurking elsewhere. When the postcards were found, in their two cardboard boxes, they were not obviously organised in any chronological or other order, with no rubber bands or other method of classifying them. The negative exponential rate of responding after the programme in our set of cards suggests they are probably at the least a random sub-set of the entire data, if the true number is indeed larger than 6,336. More likely, we suspect, is that the data had never been completely analysed for the programme, and that Bronowski's figure is at best a guesstimate and perhaps an optimistic one at that. In a revealing comment on Bronowski's attitude to the absence of precise numbers during broadcasting, Michael Apter recalled how, during the rehearsals, his father had talked to him and his mother about how Bronowski wanted Smith to say what percentage of the population was left-handed. Smith had said, "We can't say that because we're not sure," to which Bronowski had apparently replied, "You say, 'Ooooh ... there are about ten per cent' ... that's what I do when I'm not sure."

The response rate

Calculating a response rate for the questionnaire is not straightforward because although the numerator is known, the denominator is very unclear. The *Radio Times*, in which the questionnaire was printed, at one time had the largest circulation of any magazine in the UK, selling about eight million copies a week.[24] However most of the readers would have been primarily interested in the radio rather than the television schedule. The number of television sets in the UK was very low when television broadcasting restarted after the Second World War, there being only 15,000 households watching in 1946, a figure that had risen to 90,000 by 1949 (Dunn, 2003). For most of the

[24] www.offthetelly.co.uk/features/rt1.htm

public the turning point for BBC television was the Coronation, on 2 June 1953, which was watched by about 20 million people in the UK, often on television sets erected in church halls or with a dozen or 20 people sitting in a living room. The percentage of homes with a television licence rose from 0.1% in 1947, to 48.1% in 1957, and 88.1% in 1967[25], with about 12% of households having a licence in 1953 (Macmillan & Smith, 2001). If the UK population was about 52 million, and making some adjustment for the old and the young who would not watch television, then perhaps 5 million people had regular access to TV in their homes. Of these, only a small percentage were likely to watch a science programme, particularly one broadcast after speedway racing. However, it was a Friday evening, presumably a good spot. If 1% of those with a television watched the programme, then that would have meant about 50,000 viewers. Not all of those would have had the *Radio Times* to hand (although probably most would have, given its penetration of the market), and not all would have wanted to take part. The 6,336 respondents are perhaps 12% or so of the total viewers, although it is accepted that the figure is a very broad estimate, and the true rate could be much lower than that—it is unlikely to be much higher. Certainly the response rate leaves room for response bias to occur and, as has already been seen, there is a clear excess of left-handers among the respondents (and that will be discussed in detail in a subsequent paper).

The script

Michael Apter commented that his father, Kenneth Smith, was unlikely to have written any of the script as such, "as he practically never wrote anything. But he obviously had an input" [MJA]. That was supported by George Noordhof who described how the basic writing of the script was done by Noordhof himself, "although Kenneth gave us a number of for-instances ... and Kenneth was [used] as a sounding board" [GHN]. Noordhof also described taking the script to Bronowski at his home in Cheltenham (Bronowski's "day-job" still being with the National Coal Board laboratories, which were based there): "used to visit him, stay over, ... and we'd talk about things. [Then we would] have the basic structure." Noordhof also described how "Bruno [Bronowski] was a marvellous presenter – he made his own thing of it, based on the script we gave him", a comment that is supported by a detailed comparison of the script and the transcript. It seems unlikely that Cyril Burt was involved

[25] www.iser.essex.au.uk/pubs/workpaps/pdf/1990–03.pdf

directly in the writing of the script of *RHLH*, and Noordhof did comment on how Burt "in some peculiar way, was rather difficult to me", being "rather caustic", and "annoyed by people of the likes of me [i.e., from the media]". Certainly some of the comments in the programme do not look as if they could have come from Burt. For instance, Bronowski's comment in the second programme about "people who've been to school, oh, about, 40 years ago, had on the whole been *bullied* out of being left-handed" (our emphasis) hardly fits with Burt's own view, expressed even in the final 1969 edition of *The Backward Child* that "in general ... parents and teachers will in the long run earn the gratitude of the child if they do all they can to make him right-handed from the very start" (p. 323).[26] The words given to Smith in the programme script are a little more liberal:

> One piece of advice – begin at the earliest possible moment before the age of six, if your child is left-handed, try to help it to be right handed. It is in many ways more convenient to be right handed in a right handed world, but do not force [the child] to be right-handed. Give the child the opportunity to be right handed.

In the programme itself, though, the transcript finds an even less forceful Smith actually saying:

> Well, the advice I would give is from the earliest possible days to give right-handedness the first chance, for toys, spoons, in the position where they are more convenient for the right hand. But I must issue a warning as well; be patient, be gentle. Don't fuss, don't be insistent, and don't be obvious.

The implication is that Smith himself had not written the precise words in the script, and that being, like Bronowski, a seasoned and experienced performer, he was willing to improvise around the text. Likewise, in those words of Smith's one can also hear the practised words of an experienced clinician used to advising in the clinic. None of that, however, is compatible with Burt.

[26] This comment of Burt's is, however, at odds even with some other of Burt's own statements in *The Backward Child*, where he discusses how "in the more advanced of our modern infants' schools, greater freedom is nowadays allowed for the natural inclinations of each child" (p. 289). Whether that is beneficial or not cannot, he says, be known until more is understood about left-handedness: "Only when we have solved these problems can we say whether a right-hand training for the left-hander is feasible and wise, or whether it will be attended by unsuspected risk and perhaps by insuperable difficulties" (p. 290).

CONCLUSIONS

The programme *Right Hand, Left Hand* is an interesting example of a very modern approach to television broadcasting, with the use of celebrities in a studio carrying out a range of tasks, and viewers sending in data by means of postcards. Large-scale surveys of handedness are relatively rare in the middle decades of the twentieth century, and *Right Hand, Left Hand* potentially offers an unusual and useful source of data. Two subsequent papers will look at the data in more detail.

REFERENCES

Apter, M. J. (2001). *Motivational styles in everyday life: A guide to reversal theory.* Washington, DC: American Psychological Association.

Banks, C. (1983). Professor Sir Cyril Burt: Selected reminiscences. *AEP (Association of Educational Psychologists) Journal, 6*, 21–42.

Banks, C., & Broadhurst, P. L. (1966). *Stephanos: Studies in psychology presented to Cyril Burt.* Oxford, UK: Barnes & Noble.

Banks, C., & Burt, C. (1953). Statistical analysis in educational psychology. In C. A. Mace & P. E. Vernon (Eds.), *Current trends in British psychology* (pp. 152–171). London: Methuen.

Banks, C., & Burt, C. (1954). The reduced correlation matrix. *British Journal of Statistical Psychology, 7*, 107–111.

Blau, A. (1946). *The master hand: A study of the origin and meaning of right and left sidedness and its relation to personality and language.* New York: American Orthopsychiatric Association.

Broadbent, D. E., & Gregory, M. (1965). Some confirmatory results on age differences in memory for simultaneous stimulation. *British Journal of Psychology, 56*, 77–80.

Bronowski, J. (1964). *Insight.* London: Macdonald.

Bronowski, J. (1973). *The ascent of man.* London: British Broadcasting Corporation.

Bulley, M. H. (1925). *Art and counterfeit.* London: Methuen.

Bulley, M. H. (1933). *Have you good taste? A guide to the appreciation of the lesser arts.* London: Methuen.

Burt, C. (1933). A test in aesthetics. In M. H. Bulley (Ed.), *Have you good taste?* (pp. 44–52). London: Methuen.

Burt, C. (1961). *The backward child* (5th ed.). London: University of London Press.

Burt, C. (1933). *How the mind works.* London: Allen & Unwin.

Burt, C., & Banks, C. (1947). A factor analysis of body measurements for British adult males. *Annals of Eugenics (Cambridge), 13*, 238–256.

Burt, C. L. (1925). *The young delinquent.* London: University of London Press.

Dunn, K. (2003). *Do not adjust your set.* London: John Murray.

Early, D. F. (2000). Kenneth Carl Pfeiffer Smith. *Psychiatric Bulletin, 24*, 158.

Fletcher, R. (1991). *Science, ideology, and the media: The Cyril Burt scandal.* London: Transaction.

Hearnshaw, L. S. (1979). *Cyril Burt, psychologist.* London: Hodder & Stoughton.

Hull, C. J. (1936). A study of laterality test items. *Journal of Experimental Education, 4*, 287–290.

Humphrey, M. E. (1951). Consistency of hand usage: A preliminary inquiry. *British Journal of Educational Psychology, 21*, 214–225.

Joynson, R. B. (1989). *The Burt affair.* London: Routledge.

Mackintosh, N. J. (1995). *Cyril Burt: Fraud or framed?* Oxford, UK: Oxford University Press.

Macmillan, P., & Smith, I. (2001). Explaining post-war cinema attendance in Great Britain. *Journal of Cultural Economics, 25*, 91–108.

Mazumdar, P. M. H. (2004). Burt, Sir Cyril Lodowic (1883–1971). In *Oxford dictionary of national biography.* [http://www.oxforddnb.com/view/article/30880, accessed 5 Aug 2005.]. Oxford, UK: Oxford University Press.

McManus, I. C. (2002). *Right hand, left hand: The origins of asymmetry in brains, bodies, atoms and cultures.* London/Cambridge, MA: Weidenfeld & Nicolson/Harvard University Press.

McPherson, A., & Timms, H. (1988). *Audiovisual handbook: How to communicate ideas with the aid of sound and pictures.* London: Pelham.

Sheets-Pyenson, S. (2004). Bronowski, Jacob (1908–1974). In *Oxford dictionary of national biography.* [http://www.oxforddnb.com/view/article/30859, accessed 5 Aug 2005.]. Oxford, UK: Oxford University Press.

Shields, J. (1962). *Monozygotic twins brought up apart and brought up together: An investigation into the genetic and environmental causes of variation in personality.* Oxford, UK: Oxford University Press.

Woodworth, R. S. (1938). *Experimental psychology.* New York: Henry Holt.

Zangwill, O. L. (1960). *Cerebral dominance and its relation to psychological function.* Edinburgh, UK: Oliver & Boyd.

Ziegler, P. (1999). *Osbert Sitwell: A biography.* London: Pimlico.

LATERALITY, 2010, 15 (1/2), 166–185

Science in the Making: Right Hand, Left Hand. II: The duck–rabbit figure

I. C. McManus, Matthew Freegard, James Moore, and Richard Rawles

University College London, UK

The BBC television programme *Right Hand, Left Hand*, broadcast in August 1953, showed a version of the duck–rabbit figure and asked viewers to say what they could see in the "puzzle picture". Nearly 4,000 viewers described the image, and the answers to those questions have recently been found and analysed. The programme probably used the same version of the figure as appeared in Wittgenstein's *Philosophical Investigations*, which had been published a month or two previously. Although Dr Jacob Bronowski, the presenter of the programme, had suspected that left- and right-handers might differ in their perception of the figure, since they might scan it from different sides, in fact there is no relationship in the data between six measures of lateralisation and a propensity for seeing a duck or a rabbit. However the large data set does show separate effects of both age and sex on viewing the figure, female and older viewers being more likely to report seeing a rabbit (although a clear majority of viewers reported seeing a duck). There was also a very significant tendency for female viewers to use more typical descriptions of the duck, whereas males used a wider variety of types.

Keywords: Ambiguous figures; Duck–rabbit figure; Handedness; Lateralisation; Scanning.

An unusual feature of the 1953 BBC television programme *Science in the Making: Right Hand, Left Hand*, which was described in detail in our previous paper (McManus et al., 2010 this issue), was the inclusion, at the end, of a version of the duck–rabbit figure.

The duck–rabbit figure is now one of the most famous of visual phenomena, appearing in a host of introductory psychology textbooks,

Address correspondence to: I. C. McManus, UCL Department of Psychology, University College London, Gower Street, London WC1E 6BT, UK. E-mail: i.mcmanus@ucl.ac.uk

We are very grateful to Professor Lisa Jardine, Mrs Rita Bronowski, Mr George Noordhof, Professor Elizabeth Valentine, Professor Peter Geach, Professor Ray Monk, and Professor Michael Apter for their help in preparing this paper, and to Mike Nicholls and Peter Brugger for comments on an earlier version of this paper.

DOI: 10.1080/13576500802564266

the earliest of which we are aware being Yerkes (1911, p. 271). It also occurs in many other situations where popular science is being presented, such as introductory and expository books—e.g., Jonathan Miller's *Darwin for Beginners* (1986, p. 8)—as well as in Christmas crackers and cereal packets (ICM, the first author, even has a pack of playing cards from the 1980s advertising Kellogg's "Raisin Splitz", each card of which has a different visual phenomenon, with the Queen of Hearts being the duck–rabbit figure). Recently, at an interdisciplinary conference, the psychologist Stephen Kosslyn wished to explain psychological testing to the Dalai Lama, and chose the duck–rabbit figure for the demonstration (Barinaga, 2003). A history of the duck–rabbit figure by John F. Kihlstrom can be found on the Internet (Kihlstrom, 2005). Although often referred to as an illusion, as Kihlstrom points out the duck–rabbit figure is actually an ambiguous, reversible, or bi-stable figure.

The duck–rabbit figure first appeared in the bottom right-hand corner of a page of the humorous German magazine *Fliegende Blätter*[1] on 23 October 1892 (p. 147), without any attribution (Figure 1a) (Kihlstrom, 2005).[2] It was captioned "*Welche Thiere gleichen einander am meisten?*" (Which animals are most like each other?"), and underneath it said "*Kaninchen und Ente*" (rabbit and duck). A month or so later the figure appeared in *Harper's Weekly* (19 November 1892, p. 1114), where it had become slightly more horizontal (Figure 1b). Seven years later the figure was used by the psychologist Joseph Jastrow (Blumenthal, 1991), who describes "the ingenious conceit of the duck–rabbit". The figure was once again somewhat redrawn and was now almost completely horizontal (see Figure 1c), first in an article in a popular science magazine (Jastrow, 1899), and then in a book (Jastrow, 1900). As Jastrow (1899, p. 292) points out:

> When it is a rabbit, the face looks to the right and a pair of ears are conspicuous behind; when it is a duck, the face looks to the left and the ears have been changed into the bill. Most observers find it difficult to hold either interpretation steadily, the fluctuations being frequent, and coming as a surprise.

---

[1] Gombrich (1960) refers to *Die Fliegenden Blätter* whereas Kihlstrom refers to *Fliegende Blätter*; both are correct usage. The actual title page of the journal says "FLIEGENDE BLÄTTER" (see http://www.libraries.uc.edu/libraries/arb/ger_americana/exhibits/pages/fliegende%20blatter.html) or subsequently, "Fliegende Blätter" (see http://shots.oxo.li/flyers/fliegende_blatter/pages/Dscf0442.htm). However *Die Fliegende Blätter* is incorrect usage, although it is found, for instance, at psychclassics.yorku.ca/Freud/Dreams/dreams6d.htm

[2] The duck–rabbit figure is not the only contribution of *Fliegende Blätter* to the classic literature of psychology. Sigmund Freud also quotes a joke from it in *The interpretation of dreams*, originally published in 1900 (Freud, 1976, p. 598): the magazine's advice on how to catch lions was "Take a desert and put it through a sieve and the lions will be left over."

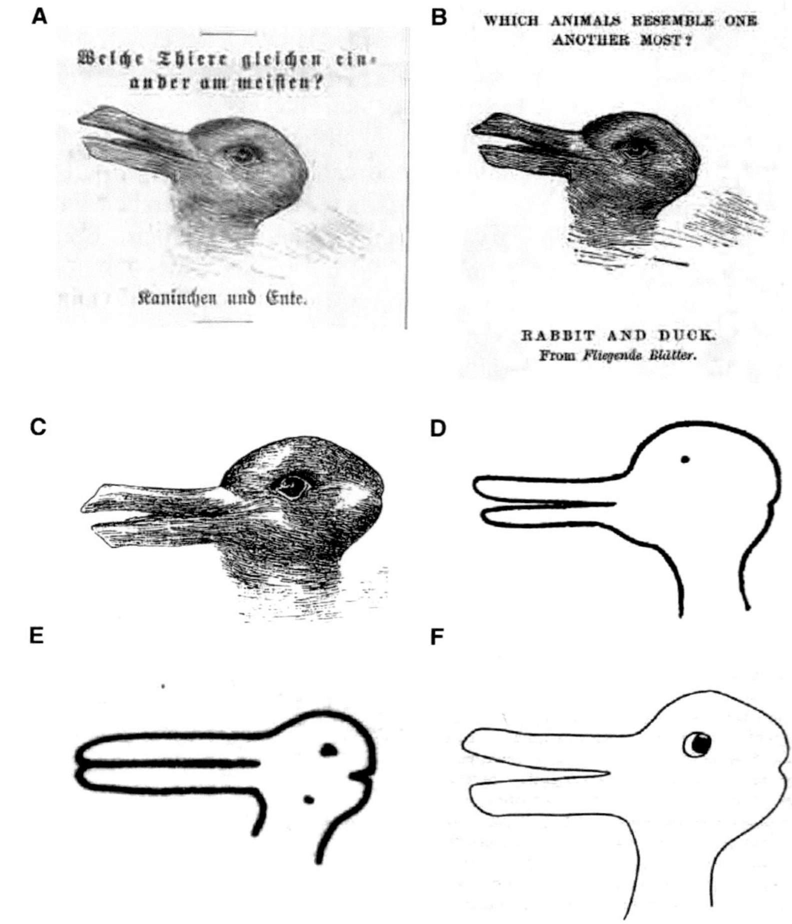

Figure 1. Drawings of the duck–rabbit figure. (a) The original drawing in the 1892 *Die Fliegenden Blätter*. (b) The version in *Harper's Magazine* of 1892. (c) The version used by Jastrow in 1900. (d) Wittgenstein's version in the *Philosophical Investigations* of 1953. (e) Geach's drawing of the duck–rabbit figure from his notes for Wittgenstein's 1946–47 lectures, for which the entire image is only 10 mm in width, and it is assumed that the tiny lower dot is an error occurring during printing. (f) The version shown in Monk's biography of Wittgenstein and said to be that used in the 1947 lectures.

The duck–rabbit figure has been much reproduced in psychology textbooks, often being redrawn in a host of ways (see for example the 12 different versions given by Brugger, 1999). Despite being relatively well

TABLE 1
Perception of the duck–rabbit figure in relation to sex

	Males	*Females*	*Total*
Duck	1175 (66.0%	1093 (56.9%)	2268 (61.3%)
Duck&Rabbit	242 (13.6%)	280 (14.6%)	522 (14.1%)
Rabbit	362 (20.3%)	549 (28.6%)	911 (24.6%)
Total	1779 (48.1%)	1922 (51.9%)	3701

known,[3] the figure has not been used in many research papers: a search through the *PsycINFO* database in January 2006 found only 17 mentions of the figure, the first by Porter (1938), and the next, by two Georgians, occurring only in the early 1970s (Chkhartishvili, 1971; Kechkhuashvili, 1972). In contrast Jastrow's 1899 and 1900 works have been cited 54 times since 1980 (*ISI Web of Knowledge*, Jan 2006). There are also passing mentions of the figure in earlier literature, without any source citation, as in the paper by Wever (1927).

Outside psychology, the two most well-known appearances of the duck–rabbit figure are in Wittgenstein's *Philosophical Investigations* (1953), and Sir Ernst Gombrich's *Art and Illusion* (1960)—see Lycan (1971) for a discussion of their intellectual similarities, although there is no mention of the specific figure itself. Gombrich uses a version of the duck–rabbit figure that, from the angle and the white blobs on the rabbit's nose, appears to be from Jastrow (1900), although the text refers to "the humorous weekly *Die Fliegenden Blätter*" and the endnote cites Wittgenstein's *Philosophical Investigations.* However the version used by Wittgenstein himself, which is shown in Figure 1d, is a simple line drawing, despite Wittgenstein also citing Jastrow (1899) as the source.[4] It is clearly identical to version 2 in Brugger's Table 1, where it is cited as coming from Rentschler, Caelli, and Maffei (1988), but those authors merely refer to "Jastrow's duck–rabbit". Wittgenstein first used the duck–rabbit figure in his lectures in 1947, for which Geach in his lecture

[3] As an example, in 1931 the final examination paper in Psychology at University College London contained the question, "Explain how it happens that the same drawing may at one time look like the head of a duck and at another time like that of rabbit." (E. Valentine, personal communication). The question was probably set by J. C. Flügel (who was one of the two examiners), particularly as Flügel had earlier published a paper on reversible perspective illusions (Flügel, 1913).

[4] "I shall call the following figure, derived from Jastrow, the duck-rabbit"; "*Die folgende Figur, welche ich aus Jastrow entnommen habe, wird in meinem Bermerkungen der H-E-kopf heiβen*" (Wittgenstein, 2001, pp. 165 & 165[e]). In a footnote Wittgenstein simply references "Fact and Fable in Pyschology", with no date, publisher, or page number. Apparently Wittgenstein corresponded with Köhler to ascertain the source of the duck–rabbit figure (Geach, personal communication, 20 March 2006).

notes has a figure that is different from the one used by Wittgenstein himself (Geach, Shah, & Jackson, 1988; see Figure 1e), and which differs yet again from the figure describing the 1947 lectures in Monk's biography (Monk, 1990), shown in Figure 1f, which Monk has said was "based on Wittgenstein's [i.e. Figure 1d]... with 'improvements' by the design & production team at Jonathan Cape".[5] Correspondence with Professor P. T. Geach[6] tells us that Wittgenstein drew the duck–rabbit figure himself, in his manuscripts, and this is the one shown in Figure 1d;[7] that experience probably underlies the comment made in a question Wittgenstein asks in a lecture in 1947 when he says, "What else happens besides the verbal description? For one thing we *copy* differently. And so: if you copy the duck/rabbit drawing and try to get the duck's expression right, you can't go on to see it as a rabbit" (Geach et al., 1988, p. 109, emphasis in original). Some further questions may be answerable if the final typescript for Part II of the *Philosophical Investigations* were available, but regrettably it has been lost, and the preliminary studies for Part II do not seem to contain any duck–rabbit figures (Wittgenstein, 1982).

Jacob Bronowski first refers to the duck–rabbit figure towards the end of *Right Hand, Left Hand*, although of course at that stage he does not refer to it by that name. He has started to explain to viewers how to complete their postcards in response to the questionnaire printed in the *Radio Times*, when he comments, as recorded in the transcript:

> I want to show you how to answer the questions in a moment, but before I do so, I'd like to show you a picture, a puzzle picture. Here is a picture which has something to do with left-handedness and right-handedness. Will you look at it carefully?
> This is plainly the picture of a living being, and I want you to write on the postcard, in the first place, what you think it is. I propose to say that it's an ant-eater and that I write here. Then turn your postcard this way up; look at the *Radio Times*; pick out the first question which says, 'Which hand do you write with?'. Just write the word 'WRITE'[8] there, and put R for right. [etc].

After explaining the questionnaire, Bronowski says that the next programme will be on 12 October,

> and by that time I hope that Sir Cyril Burt's team will have analysed your answers sufficiently for me to be able to give you some information about it. I'll also be

[5] E-mail from Ray Monk, 23 January 2006.

[6] Personal communication to ICM, dated 20 March 2006.

[7] In an e-mail to ICM, Professor Monk commented, "I think it's quite likely that W drew it himself" (25 January 2006).

[8] As mentioned in the previous paper, the transcript actually says "the word 'Right'".

> able to tell you why the puzzle picture is connected with rightness and leftness, so let me say goodnight to you, and show you the puzzle picture for a last time – WHAT IS IT?[9]

The script is somewhat different from the transcript. This is what Bronowski was meant to say:

> Just before I tell you how to fill it in, let me show you a picture. I would like you to look at it very closely. What is it. While to some people it is duck to others it is a rabbit. Actually children do make mistakes, for example for NO they say may read ON and for ON they may read NO. Some children may make mistakes between D and B for that reason, and if that does not explain 'Mind your ps and qs' I do not know what does. Depends on the way you look at the picture, from right to left, or from left to right. Write what you think this is on the top right hand corner of your card.

Fortunately, Bronowski avoided the error of talking about ducks and rabbits, and of mentioning right–left or left–right scanning, although he did introduce, if one may call it such, the red herring of the anteater.

At the end of the second programme on 12 October, Bronowski comments on the handedness questionnaire. He starts, however, by saying:

> With that I want to leave the subject of the cold and remind you of the picture that you saw two months ago on August 14th. Do you recall this picture? Yes, it's the puzzle picture which goes with, not exactly left-handedness or right-handedness, but with the fact that it looks different according to whether your eyes are in the habit of travelling from left to right or right to left; you see, if you look at the left side first and sweep to the right then the thing looks like a bird, because you meet the beak first, but if you're a person who tends to look from right to left, why then it looks like a rabbit because you meet the, as it were, the front of the face first and the ears last. I would really like to have seen this trick tried out in one of those countries which reads from right to left. However, I can tell you this about our replies, and we got an enormous number of replies. They showed that this is in no way connected with left-handedness and right-handedness, but an extraordinary thing. It's usual to find that children see this rather indifferently, and that adults are predominantly people who see it as a bird of some kind. But on this occasion we did not find that. A majority of women in fact saw it as a rabbit. I have no idea what this means and neither has anybody else. I tell it to you as one of those facts which have struck us out of the blue from the information that you've sent.

To our knowledge, no further analyses of the data were ever published. Neither are we aware of the origin of the comments about "children see this

---

[9] Capitals in original transcript.

rather indifferently" and "adults are predominantly people who see it as a bird of some kind". The only research paper in the literature before 1953 that mentions the figure is that of Porter (1938), and he does not seem to mention differences between children and adults. Jastrow's version of the duck–rabbit figure is shown on p. 134 of Blau's *The Master Hand* (1946),[10] and Blau describes how "the right or left direction of viewing can each result in an entirely different picture: a duck when viewed from the left, a rabbit from the right". It should also be mentioned that Blau cites Orton's influential views on the role of directional scanning in reading (Orton, 1937). Kenneth Smith owned a copy of Blau's book, now in the possession of Michael Apter, but it seems unlikely that the inclusion of the duck–rabbit figure in the programme was derived from Blau since (a) it was clearly Bronowski's idea to include the figure, (b) Bronowski and Smith did not meet until the day of transmission, (c) the script, which was prepared earlier and without Smith's direct involvement, clearly contains a discussion of the figure, and finally (d) Blau does not mention either sex differences or children having difficulty seeing the figure (although he does later talk about a minority of children having reading difficulties because of failure of directional scanning). Although there is no evidence that Bronowski, Smith, or Burt was aware of it—given Bronowski's comment that "I would really like to have seen this trick tried out in one of those countries which reads from right to left"—it is of interest that only the previous year, in 1952, two papers had been published showing that the tendency to draw profile faces facing to the left is essentially similar in countries writing from left to right and right to left (Jensen, 1952a,b).

A problem for interpreting the duck–rabbit data from *Right Hand, Left Hand* is that there is no visual material from the original programme. Discussions with George Noordhof, the producer of the programme,[11] suggest that the duck–rabbit figure was introduced into the programme late in the production process, by Jacob Bronowski himself:

> I wasn't in agreement with it [i.e., using the duck–rabbit figure] ... I didn't feel that it linked [but] ... Bruno wanted to show it. ... Bruno was to a certain extent interested in optical illusions ...

Bronowski had a longstanding interest in the work of Wittgenstein, and refers to both early and late Wittgenstein in his writings (Bronowski, 1956). Bronowski was an undergraduate and then a postgraduate in Cambridge

---

[10] Interestingly the bill of the duck in this version is tilted downwards at an angle of about 10 degrees, compared with the horizontal bill in Jastrow, and the upward bills in the *Fliegende Blätter* and *Harper's* versions.

[11] Interview with ICM, 4 October 2005.

from 1927 to 1934, and therefore overlapped with Wittgenstein's second stay in Cambridge, from 1929 until 1941, and it is probable that Bronowski became aware of him then. It also seemed likely to us that Bronowski's interest meant that he would have acquired the *Philosophical Investigations* soon after it was published. The exact date of publication of the book is not entirely clear, but the book was listed under "Books received" in the *British Journal for the Philosophy of Science* issue of August 1953, and in *Mind* in the issue of October 1953 (both journals publishing quarterly), as well as in the 13 August issue of the *Journal of Philosophy*, which was published fortnightly, and it was reviewed in the *Times Literary Supplement* on 28 August. Given the inevitable delays in journal publishing it seems likely that the book would have been available in June or July, when Bronowski could have read it, relatively soon before the details of the programme were finalised, but perhaps after the copy for the *Radio Times* questionnaire had been sent to press, requiring the item to be added on specially at the time of the broadcast. Professor Lisa Jardine, Bronowski's daughter who was 8 at the time the programme was broadcast, tells us (e-mail to ICM, 13 Jan 2006)[12] that she remembers her father talking about the *Philosophical Investigations*, adding:

> I remember lots about my father trying out the duck/rabbit illusion on myself and my sister, and therefore recognised the Wittgenstein pic[ture] as the one he used. I am pretty sure you are right about his seeing the image and deciding to use it.

It is perhaps worth noting that Bronowski was intrigued by the left-handedness of his daughter Lisa, who was strongly left-handed, and the only known left-hander in the family.

Subsequent investigations have revealed that Bronowski owned a first edition of the *Philosophical Investigations*, which was signed inside "J Bronowski" with "1953" written beneath,[13] and that, as Mrs Bronowski commented to Professor Jardine: "... if you look at the volume end on (i.e., at the pages), two places in the book are darkened by use, and the book tends to fall open there. One of these is at the duck/rabbit picture."

On balance it seems therefore that we are justified in assuming that the Wittgenstein version of the duck–rabbit figure was the one broadcast on

[12] In ICM's e-mail to Jardine he had referred to the duck–rabbit illusion, and therefore Jardine replied using the same terminology.

[13] E-mails from Mrs Rita Bronowski, 16 January 2006, and Lisa Jardine, 16–17 January 2006. Bronwoski's version of the *Philosophical Investigations* was unannotated except for occasional changes in the English version (the book was printed with Wittgenstein's original German on the left-hand page and the English translation on the right). Bronowski, although born in Poland, first went to school in Germany (Bronowski, 1985).

Right Hand, Left Hand, and it was in all likelihood also the version that Bronowski showed to his daughters, probably in the days before the programme was broadcast.

Bronowski's interest in the duck–rabbit figure in relation to lateralisation clearly derives, as he says in the follow-up programme of 12 October 1953 (quoted earlier), from the possibility that the direction of visual scanning from right to left or left to right influences the perception of the figure. This idea is also related to the comment that Wittgenstein himself makes in para. 212, where he says, in an idea that anticipates the scanpath hypothesis of Noton and Stark (1971):

> Imagine a physiological explanation of the experience. Let it be this: When we look at the figure, our eyes scan it repeatedly, always following a particular path. The path corresponds to a particular pattern of oscillation of the eyeballs in the act of looking. It is possible to jump from one such pattern to another and for the two to alternate.

Wittgenstein's earlier comments from 1949, on which para. 212 is based, then continue, "hence I cannot see the duck–rabbit as the picture of the head of a rabbit superimposed on the head of duck . . ." (Wittgenstein, 1982, para. 777, p. 99e).

Bronowski's subsequent comments say that the results "showed that [the duck–rabbit phenomenon] is in no way connected with left-handedness and right-handedness", although no data were ever presented to that effect. Here we will analyse the data formally, and also investigate some other aspects of the ambiguity of the duck–rabbit figure, as revealed by the responses sent on postcards by the viewers of *Right Hand, Left Hand*, broad details of which have been provided in the previous paper (McManus et al., 2010 this issue).

METHOD

Analysis was undertaken of postcards returned by the viewers of *Right Hand, Left Hand*, which was broadcast on BBC television on Friday 14 August 1953. Viewers answered 12 questions printed in a questionnaire in that week's *Radio Times*, and in addition the presenter asked viewers to write their description of the "puzzle picture", as in the transcript presented earlier. Data from the postcards were entered into a computer, with conventional statistical analyses carried out using SPSS 11.5. See the previous paper for further details of the sample etc. (McManus et al., 2010 this issue).

RESULTS

Although 6,336 postcards were found in the archive, some contained information on multiple individuals, so that data were available for 6,549 people; however not all information was available for all individuals. In particular, the answer to the question about the "puzzle picture" was provided by only 3,957 individuals. The lack of answers from the remaining 2,592 respondents probably reflects the fact that some did not see the puzzle picture, or did not see or understand Bronowski's instructions. In addition we also know from comments on the cards that some respondents had not seen the television programme, but had still returned the questionnaire from the *Radio Times* out of interest. Of the 3,957 individuals describing the duck–rabbit figure, 3,292 (83.2%) had written a single description, 642 (16%) had written two descriptions, and 23 (0.6%) had written three descriptions.

Descriptions were coded numerically, with each novel description being given a unique code number. Descriptions were often extremely varied, with answers transcribed into the computer as written (e.g., "duck-billed platypus", "umbrella handle", "rabbit drawn by left-handed person", "pipe and tobacco pouch arranged to look like a bird's head", or "shadow of clenched left hand holding a pencil"). A total of 114 answers suggested, as Bronowski had prompted, that the picture was an anteater.

For the first analysis of the data, all answers were coded as "duck-like" (e.g., any bird), "rabbit-like" (e.g., rabbits, hares, etc.) or "other". Of 4,641 responses, 2,870 (72.6%) were duck-like, 1,467 (37.1%) were rabbit-like, and 304 (7.7%) were coded as other. Individuals who gave only duck-like responses were classified as "Duck", those giving only rabbit-like responses were coded as "Rabbit", those giving both a duck-like and a rabbit-like response were coded as "Duck&Rabbit", and those giving only "other" responses were coded as missing. Altogether 3,701 respondents gave a non-missing answer, of whom 2,268 (61.3%) were classified as "Duck", 911 (24.6%) as "Rabbit", and 522 (14.1%) as "Duck &Rabbit". A total of 256 individuals did not give any answer recognisable as a duck or a rabbit (including those who answered "anteater"). We will analyse these categories in relation to the background variables of sex, age group, and handedness.

Sex

Table 1 shows the sex of respondents in relation to their classification. A majority of both men and women saw the figure as a duck, although men were somewhat more likely to report the figure as a duck ($\chi^2 = 38.65$,

2 *df*, $p < .001$). Slightly more women than men reported both duck and rabbit.

Age

Table 2 shows the reports of participants in relation to age, which was grouped by decades. Only seven children under the age of 10 had responded (five of whom had seen the figure as a duck), and they were grouped with those aged 10 to 19. Likewise, those aged 60 or over were grouped together. There is a highly significant difference between age groups ($\chi^2 = 69.70$, 10 *df*, $p < .001$). A multiple regression of response (with Duck coded as 1, Duck&Rabbit as 2, and Rabbit as 3) on age and sex found a significant (linear) effect of age (beta = .103), $t(3684) = 6.33$, $p < .001$, and of sex (beta = .109), $t(3684) = 6.69$, $p < .001$), but no interaction of sex with age, $t(3683) = -0.609$, $p = .543$. As can be seen in Table 2, the proportion of Rabbit responses increases with age, while the proportion of Duck responses decreases with age, and the multiple regression suggests that this process occurs in a similar way in males and females.

Lateralisation

Respondents were asked six questions about their handedness and lateralisation, with responses being coded as Right, Left, or Mixed/Both. Table 3 shows the association between responses to the duck–rabbit figure and lateralisation. Writing hand did not show a significant association with response ($\chi^2 = 8.21$, 4 *df*, $p = .084$; linear-by-linear association, $\chi^2 = 1.37$, 1 *df*, $p = .242$), neither did holding a brush ($\chi^2 = 5.63$, 4 *df*, $p = .228$; linear-by-linear association, $\chi^2 = 0.152$, 1 *df*, $p = .697$), throwing a ball ($\chi^2 = 4.93$, 4 *df*, $p = .295$; linear-by-linear association, $\chi^2 = 0.138$, 1 *df*, $p = .710$), or

TABLE 2
Perception of the duck–rabbit figure in relation to age

Age group	*Duck*	*Duck&Rabbit*	*Rabbit*	*Total*
0–19	302 (68.6%)	45 (10.2%)	93 (21.1%)	440
20–29	671 (67.4%)	118 (11.9%)	206 (20.7%)	995
30–39	740 (60.8%)	185 (15.2%)	292 (24.0%)	1217
40–49	327 (50.5%)	120 (18.5%)	200 (30.9%)	647
50–59	137 (56.1%)	40 (16.4%)	67 (27.5%)	244
60+	83 (57.6%)	13 (9.0%)	48 (33.3%)	144
Total	2660 (61.3%)	521 (14.1%)	906 (24.6%)	3687

TABLE 3
Perception of the duck–rabbit figure in relation to lateralisation

		Duck	*Duck&Rabbit*	*Rabbit*	*Total*
Which hand do you WRITE with?	Right	1916 (60.8%)	454 (14.4%)	779 (24.7%)	3149
	Mixed/Both	21 (48.8%)	10 (23.3%)	12 (27.9%)	43
	Left+	331 (65.0%)	58 (11.4%)	120 (23.6%)	509
Which foot do you prefer to KICK with?	Right	1674 (61.9%)	382 (14.1%)	649 (24.0%)	2705
	Mixed/Both	136 (51.1%)	52 (19.5%)	78 (29.3%)	266
	Left	458 (62.7%)	88 (12.1%)	184 (25.2%)	730
When you are brushing your teeth, which hand do you hold the BRUSH in?	Right	1743 (60.8%)	424 (14.8%)	701 (24.4%)	2868
	Mixed/Both	79 (62.7%)	17 (13.5%)	30 (23.8%)	126
	Left	445 (63.1%)	80 (11.3%)	180 (25.5%)	705
Which hand do you prefer to THROW a ball with?	Right	1789 (61.2%)	425 (14.5%)	707 (24.2%)	2921
	Mixed/Both	44 (55.0%)	13 (16.3%)	23 (28.8%)	80
	Left	433 (62.1%)	83 (11.9%)	181 (26.0%)	697
If you are winding wool or string, which hand do you HOLD the ball in?	Right	608 (62.7%)	123 (12.7%)	238 (24.6%)	969
	Mixed/Both	102 (59.3%)	32 (18.6%)	38 (22.1%)	172
	Left	1554 (60.8%)	367 (14.4%)	633 (24.8%)	2554
If you had to carry a glass with water filled to the brim, which hand would you prefer to CARRY it in?	Right	1480 (61.3%)	345 (14.3%)	589 (24.4%)	2414
	Mixed/Both	321 (63.8%)	81 (16.1%)	101 (20.1%)	503
	Left	472 (59.4%)	96 (12.3%)	220 (28.3%)	778

+Includes 64 who indicated that they currently used their right hand but had used their left hand in the past.

winding a ball of string ($\chi^2 = 4.96$, 4 *df*, $p = 0.505$; linear-by-linear association, $\chi^2 = 0.444$, 1 *df*, $p = 0.505$). Kicking a ball did show a significant association ($\chi^2 = 15.58$, 4 *df*, $p = .004$; linear-by-linear association, $\chi^2 = 0.418$, 1 *df*, $p = .518$), with mix/both footers being more likely to answer Rabbit or Duck&Rabbit. Carrying a glass of water also showed an association with response ($\chi^2 = 12.67$, 4 *df*, $p = .013$; linear-by-linear association, $\chi^2 = 1.40$, 1 *df*, $p = .238$), with mixed/both responders less likely to answer Rabbit. Since lateralisation correlates with age ($r = -.241$, $p < .001$), older respondents being less likely to be left-handed, the effects of lateralisation on duck–rabbit response were assessed by multiple regression, with duck–rabbit response as the dependent variable, and first taking age and sex into account. None of the six measures of lateralisation showed a significant prediction of duck–rabbit response, with the lowest of the *p* values only being .180.

TABLE 4
Typicality scores of respondents with Duck, Duck&Rabbit, and Rabbit responses

	Duck	*Duck&Rabbit*	*Rabbit*	*Total*
Mean($\log_{10}$(tokens))	2.011	2.497	2.905	2.300
SD($\log_{10}$(tokens))	.924	.657	.502	.890
N	2268	522	911	3701

Typicality of particular duck-like and rabbit-like responses

Thus far the analysis has concentrated on responses grouped in the traditional way as duck, rabbit, or both. However the method of data collection meant that there was a wide range of answers actually given. This was particularly striking for the duck-like responses, which included far more specific ornithological identifications, including, for instance, "sea-gull", "gannet", "cormorant", "pelican", "puffin", "oystercatcher", "heron", "snipe", "emu", "dodo", "kiwi", "dunlin", "flamingo", etc. We therefore wished to look at the variation in responses, and assess the factors affecting it.

A typicality index was calculated by first grouping together all responses that seemed to be directly equivalent (taking account of spelling errors, equivalences such as "duck" and "duck's head", etc.). A total of 274 different response types were found. The number of tokens of each type was then calculated. The 10 most-used types had frequencies of 1266 ("Rabbit"), 818 ("Duck"), 605 ("Bird"), 173 ("Seagull"), 170 ("Hare"), 164 ("Bird's head), 129 ("Long/large billed/beaked bird"), 114 ("Anteater"), 94 ("Emu"), and 67 ("Duck-billed platypus"), with 171 types occurring only once, so that the median token frequency was 1, whereas the mean was 16.95 and the standard deviation was 99.54. Since the distribution is extremely skewed, and similar to a Zipf distribution, the logarithm to the base 10 of the token frequency was used as a measure of how often a particular type occurred. In passing it should be noted that $\log_{10}$(tokens) correlates 0.963 with normal scores calculated on the token frequencies score using the procedure in the SPSS RANK program

A typicality index was calculated for each respondent as $\log_{10}$(tokens), which for respondents giving two or three answers was the more unusual (i.e., lower) of the scores. Respondents with Duck responses had lower typicality scores than those with Duck&Rabbit responses, who in turn had lower typicality responses than those with Rabbit responses (see Table 4). One-way ANOVA confirmed the differences, $F(2, 3698) = 420.4$, $p < .001$, with all sub-groups being different from one another on a Scheffe post-hoc comparison. Examination of the data showed that although in particular there were many different ornithological terms used for the duck, there were few alternatives for the rabbit, these being restricted to terms such as "hare", "shadow rabbit", "walking stick in shape of rabbit's head", "frightened long-eared rabbit", and "rabbit head upside down". The remainder of this analysis is therefore restricted to respondents giving only a duck-like answer.

Influence of sex, age, and laterality on types of responses

A multiple regression was carried out in which $\log_{10}$(typicality) of a duck-like response was used as the dependent variable, and sex, age, and laterality were entered at successive stages. The effect of sex was highly significant, $t(3925) = 5.38$, $p < .001$, at the first step. Age was entered as linear and quadratic effects, which were jointly highly significant, $F(2, 3923) = 9.07$, $p < .001$. At the next two steps the linear age × sex and the quadratic age × sex interactions were added, although neither was significant, $t = -1.690$ and .187 respectively. Finally each of the six laterality measures was entered, and none achieved significance. Figure 2 shows the joint effects of sex and age on the typicality of the duck-like responses, and it is clear that at all ages women have more typical answers than do men, with younger and older respondents having less typical responses than those in the middle of the age range.

DISCUSSION

Although the duck–rabbit figure is a popular feature in many introductory psychology (and philosophy) courses, there is a surprisingly small amount of serious research into it, and most that has been done uses relatively small sample sizes. The present study, with its large sample size and its population with a wide range of ages, is therefore unusual in its own right. It is also unusual for having been carried out over 50 years ago and only now being analysed.

The duck–rabbit was clearly incorporated into the BBC television programme *Right Hand, Left Hand* at the last moment, primarily because the polymathic presenter, Dr Jacob Bronowski, had an interest in philosophy, and had just read Wittgenstein's newly published *Philosophical Investigations.* Wittgenstein had himself talked about the possibility of scan patterns having a role to play, and Bronowski decided to test that hypothesis, albeit indirectly, by comparing the responses of right- and left-handers to the duck–rabbit figure.

The duck–rabbit figure was presented at the end of the programme as a "puzzle picture", and nearly 4,000 people described what they thought they had seen. Although well known now, it is likely that the figure was much less in the public eye in 1953, and certainly many of the respondents answered

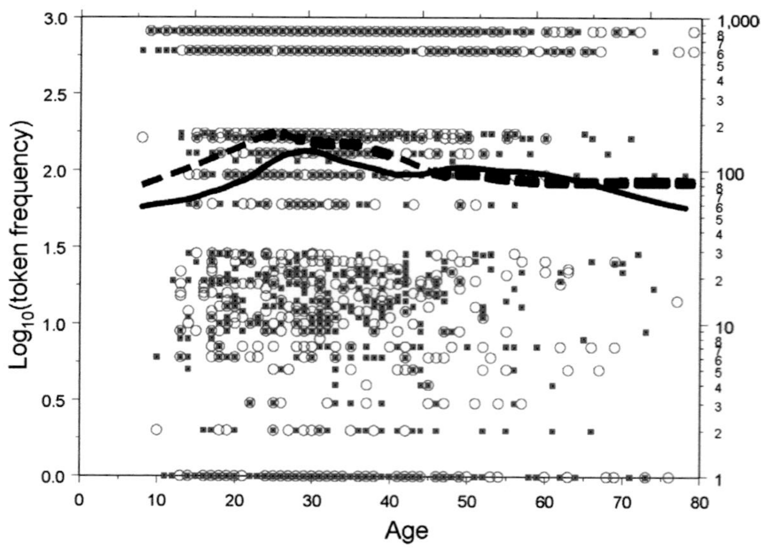

Figure 2. Typicality of response of individuals who gave duck-like responses in relation to age. Left-hand axis shows $\log_{10}$(typicality), and right-hand axis (on a logarithmic scale). Males are shown as small, solid square points and a solid black line, and females as open circles and a pale grey line. Fitted lines are loess curves (locally weighted least square lines, which are in effect a non-parameteric form of regression).

with terms other than "duck *and* rabbit". Bronowski speculated in the second programme in the series that the duck–rabbit figure "looks different according to whether your eyes are in the habit of travelling from left to right or right to left". Although there has been little research on the topic since, there are at least hints that some people have a characteristic pattern of eye movements (Zangemeister, Sherman, & Stark, 1995), and that lateral saccadic eye-movements may differ to some extent in right- and left-handers (Hutton & Palet, 1986). There is also a suggestion that eye-movements are related to the spontaneous reversals of the Necker Cube, another well-known ambiguous figure (Ellis & Stark, 1978).

Bronowski had no direct measure of eye movements; instead he assumed that right- and left-handers differed in the direction of scanning patterns, and there is some evidence to suggest that might be the case, at least in part. Right- and left-handers differ, at least in a statistical basis, in the direction in which they draw profiles (Albers & Suchenwirth, 1979; De Agostini & Chokron, 2002; Hammer & Kaplan, 1964; Mäki, 1928; Scheirs, 1990), or circles (Van Sommers, 1984), and they also show different directions of spontaneous rotation (Ruisel, 1973; Bracha, Seitz, Otemaa, & Glick, 1987), although there are large individual differences, and of course motor asymmetries related to handedness may not reflect perceptual asymmetries. However, it is feasible that right and left-handers might have shown differences in their perception of the duck–rabbit figure. But as Bronowski admits in the second programme, there is no evidence of any effect of handedness at all.

What is not at all clear about the programmes and the analysis is the extent to which the postcards were analysed in 1953. The cards do contain a few marks in red pen, which are thought to have been made by Charlotte Banks, the research assistant to Professor Cyril Burt, who was charged with analysing the data. One set of numbers, which consists entirely of 1s, 2s, and 3s, corresponds almost exactly to our classification of duck-like, rabbit-like, and mixed duck and rabbit responses, and are present on 3,617 cards, suggesting that Banks had been through the entire set of cards coding the responses. However, whether a formal cross-tabulation by sex and handedness had been carried out is less clear. In particular, Bronowski comments in the second programme that "A majority of women in fact saw it as a rabbit". As has already been seen in Table 1, the majority of women in fact saw the figure as a duck, although there was a statistically higher proportion of women who answered "rabbit" (and in passing it is worth noting that the present large sample size allows the effect to be found, even though Brugger's smaller 1999 study suggests there is no sex difference). The comment about children is also confusing, but it is clear in the current data that even if there is a slightly higher proportion of younger people who see the figure as a duck, there is no evidence of younger respondents not seeing the duck and/or the rabbit in the figure. It is possible that Banks presented subtle statistical differences to Bronowski, and that these subtleties got lost and resulted in an erroneous result being presented. If so, it is surprising that Banks never published the result of what must have been a tedious analysis without computer assistance. More likely is that Banks classified the cards into three response groups, but that there was not then time to carry out the cross-classification: a sample, perhaps non-randomly chosen, was analysed, and it gave an erroneous result.

What is undoubtedly a robust result is that there is no association with direction of lateralisation in these data, as Bronowski said. In some ways that is surprising, and it is reassuring to be able to put the result securely into the scientific literature. Whether Bronowski had robust evidence for his conclusions at the time is another matter, but he was undoubtedly correct.

A striking feature of the present data is the predominance of duck responses—nearly two and a half times as many as rabbit responses. That result is consistent with the findings of Brugger (1999) who found the Wittgenstein figure to be one of the most duck-like of the figures. Even small differences in contour, in the position of the eye, and in the inclination of the beak/ears seem to influence the dominance of perception of duck or rabbit, and it is clear that the Wittgenstein figure is very biased towards the duck. Analysing the reasons for that are not easy given the present data, but one possibility is that most individuals, regardless of handedness, tend to scan from left to right (see, for instance, Ebersbach et al., 1996, who suggest that initial visual exploration usually begins on the left). That may of course be secondary in part to reading direction (Chokron, Bartolomeo, Perenin, Helft, & Imbert, 1998; Dobel, Diesendruck, & Bölte, 2007; Fagard & Dahmen, 2003), or perhaps to a bias in perception of forward-facing motion (which has been suggested to relate to perception of the duck–rabbit figure; see McBeath, Morikawa, & Kaiser, 1992), but even so, as one referee pointed out to us, it should still mean that the more duck-like Wittgenstein figure should be seen more as a rabbit when laterally reversed, as in Figure 3. To our eye it does not, primarily looking like a duck either way, but that would benefit from formal testing.

Brugger (1999, p. 976) makes the interesting comment that across 12 different versions of the duck–rabbit figure, "the bird was significantly more easily identified than the rabbit", which he then goes on to speculate, as in a previous study (Brugger & Brugger, 1993), may be "an effect possibly due to the larger category size for birds compared to rabbits". The unusual nature of Bronowski's instructions, which atypically did not mention either duck or rabbit, allowed us to assess the range of answers given, and it was clear that

Figure 3. Wittgenstein's version of the duck–rabbit figure in its original orientation (top) and mirror-reversed (bottom).

while the duck can be seen as very many different types of bird, the rabbit is far more restricted, essentially being seen as a rabbit or a hare, supporting Brugger's hypothesis. The typicality of duck responses was greater in females than in males (i.e., they used a smaller range of bird names), and it was also females who were more likely to report having seen a rabbit, which is consistent with Brugger's prediction. Brugger also suggested to us, while reviewing the present study, the interesting possibility that the age effect, whereby younger viewers were more likely to see the figure as a duck, might reflect the popularity of the cartoon figure Donald Duck, which was at its zenith in the 1940s and early 1950s—an effect similar to the increased popularity of the rabbit interpretation that occurs before Easter (Brugger & Brugger, 1993).

REFERENCES

Albers, F., & Suchenwirth, R. M. (1979). Normalschrift, Spiegelschrift und Profildarstellung. *Praxis der Kinderpsychologie und Kinderpsychiatrie*, *28*, 202–204.

Barinaga, M. (2003). Buddhism and neuroscience: Studying the well-trained mind. *Science*, *302*, 44–46.

Blau, A. (1946). *The master hand: A study of the origin and meaning of right and left sidedness and its relation to personality and language.* New York: American Orthopsychiatric Association.

Blumenthal, A. L. (1991). The intrepid Joseph Jastrow. In G. A. Kimble, M. Wertheimer, & C. White (Eds.), *Portraits of pioneers in psychology* (pp. 75–87). Washington, DC: American Psychological Association.

Bracha, H. S., Seitz, D. J., Otemaa, J., & Glick, S. D. (1987). Rotational movement (circling) in normal humans: Sex difference and relationship to hand, foot and eye preference. *Brain Research*, *411*, 231–235.

Bronowski, J. (1956). *Science and human values.* New York: Messner.

Bronowski, R. (1985). Bruno: A personal view. *Leonardo*, *18*, 223–225.

Brugger, P. (1999). One hundred years of an ambiguous figure: Happy birthday, duck/rabbit! *Perceptual and Motor Skills*, *89*, 973–977.

Brugger, P., & Brugger, S. (1993). The Easter bunny in October: Is it disguised as a duck? *Perceptual and Motor Skills*, *76*, 577–578.

Chkhartishvili, S. N. (1971). The effect of need on perception and set. *Voprosy Psikhologii*, 95–105.

Chokron, S., Bartolomeo, P., Perenin, M-T., Helft, G., & Imbert, M. (1998). Scanning direction and line bisection: A study of normal subjects and unilateral neglect patients with opposite reading habits. *Cognitive Brain Research*, *7*, 173–178.

De Agostini, M., & Chokron, S. (2002). The influence of handedness on profile and line drawing directionality in children, young, and older normal adults. *Brain and Cognition*, *48*, 333–336.

Dobel, C., Diesendruck, G., & Bölte, J. (2007). How writing system and age influence spatial representations of actions. *Psychological Science*, *18*, 487–491.

Ebersbach, G., Trottenberg, T., Hättig, H., Schelosky, L., Schrag, A., & Poewe, W. (1996). Directional bias of initial visual exploration: A symptom of neglect in Parkinson's disease. *Brain*, *119*, 79–87.

Ellis, S. R., & Stark, L. (1978). Eye movements during the viewing of Necker cubes. *Perception*, *8*, 719–720.

Fagard, J., & Dahmen, R. (2003). The effects of reading–writing direction on the asymmetry of space perception and directional tendencies: A comparison between French and Tunisian children. *Laterality*, *8*, 39–52.

Flügel, J. C. (1913). The influence of attention in illusions of reversible perspective. *British Journal of Psychology*, *5*, 357–397.

Freud, S. (1976). *The interpretation of dreams*. Harmondsworth, UK: Penguin Books.

Geach, P. T., Shah, K. J., & Jackson, A. C. (1988). *Wittgenstein's lectures on philosophical psychology 1946–47*. New York: Harvester-Wheatsheaf.

Gombrich, E. H. (1960). *Art and illusion*. London: Phaidon Press.

Hammer, M., & Kaplan, A. M. (1964). Reliability of profile and front-facing directions in children's drawings. *Child Development*, *35*, 973–977.

Hutton, J. T., & Palet, J. (1986). Lateral saccadic latencies and handedness. *Neuropsychologia*, *24*, 449–451.

Jastrow, J. (1899). The mind's eye. *Popular Science Monthly*, *54*, 299–312.

Jastrow, J. (1900). *Fact and fable in psychology*. Boston: Houghton Mifflin.

Jensen, B. T. (1952a). Left–right orientation in profile drawing. *American Journal of Psychology*, *65*, 80–83.

Jensen, B. T. (1952b). Reading habits and left–right orientation in profile drawings by Japanse children. *American Journal of Psychology*, *65*, 306–307.

Kechkhuashvili, G. N. (1972). A new method for studying the structure of fixed set. *Voprosy Psikhologii*, 146–148.

Kihlstrom, J. F. (2005). *Joseph Jastrow and his duck – or is it a rabbit?* Retrived from http://ist-socrates.berkeley.edu/~ kihlstrm/JastrowDuck.htm

Lycan, W. G. (1971). Gombrich, Wittgenstein, and the duck–rabbit. *Journal of Aesthetics and Art Criticism*, *30*, 229–237.

Mäki, N. (1928). Psychologische Analysen hirnpathologischer Fälle. XII. Natürliche Bewegungs-tendenzen der rechten und der linken Hand und ihr Einfluß auf das Zeichnen und den Erkennungsvorgang. *Psychologische Forschung*, *1*, 1–19.

McBeath, M. K., Morikawa, K., & Kaiser, M. K. (1992). Perceptual bias for forward-facing motion. *Psychological Science*, *3*, 362–367.

McManus, I. C., Rawles, R., Moore, J., & Freegard, M. (2010). *Science in the making: Right hand, left hand*. I: A BBC television programme broadcast in 1953. *Laterality*, *15*, 136–165.

Miller, J. (1986). *Darwin for beginners*. London: Unwin.

Monk, R. (1990). *Ludwig Wittgenstein: The duty of genius*. London: Jonathan Cape.

Noton, D., & Stark, L. (1971). Scanpaths in saccadic eye movements while viewing and recognizing patterns. *Vision Research*, *11*, 929–942.

Orton, S. T. (1937). *Reading, writing and speech problems in children*. London: Chapman & Hall.

Porter, E. L. H. (1938). Factors in the fluctuation of fifteen ambiguous phenomena. *Psychological Record*, *2*, 231–253.

Rentschler, I., Caelli, T., & Maffei, L. (1988). Focusing in on art. In I. Rentschler, B. Herzberger, & D. Epstein (Eds.), *Beauty and the brain: Biological aspects of aesthetics* (pp. 181–216). Basel: Birkhäuser.

Ruisel, I. (1973). Body rotation as a manifestation of lateral preference. *Studia Psychologica*, *15*, 249–254.

Scheirs, J. G. (1990). Relationships between the direction of movements and handedness in children. *Neuropsychologia*, *28*, 743–748.

Van Sommers, P. (1984). *Drawing and cognition: Descriptive and experimental studies of graphic production processes*. Cambridge, UK: Cambridge University Press.

Wever, E. G. (1927). Figure and ground in the visual perception of form. *American Journal of Psychology, 38*, 194–226.

Wittgenstein, L. (1953). *Philosophical investigations.* Oxford, UK: Blackwell.

Wittgenstein, L. (1982). *Last writings on the philosophy of psychology. Volume 1: Preliminary studies for Part II of Philosophical Investigations.* (G. H. von Wright & H. Nyman, Eds.). Oxford, UK: Basil Blackwell.

Wittgenstein, L. (2001). *Philosophical Investigations: The German text, with a revised English translation.* (Third ed. Translated by G. E. M. Anscombe.). Oxford, UK: Blackwell.

Yerkes, R. M. (1911). *Introduction to psychology.* London: G. Bell.

Zangemeister, W. H., Sherman, K., & Stark, L. (1995). Evidence for a global scanpath strategy in viewing abstract compared with realistic images. *Neuropsychologia, 33*, 1009–1025.

LATERALITY, 2010, 15 (1/2), 186–208

Science in the Making: Right Hand, Left Hand. III: Estimating historical rates of left-handedness

I. C. McManus, James Moore, Matthew Freegard, and Richard Rawles

University College London, UK

The BBC television programme *Right Hand, Left Hand*, broadcast in August 1953, used a postal questionnaire to ask viewers about their handedness. Respondents were born between 1864 and 1948, and in principle therefore the study provides information on rates of left-handedness in those born in the nineteenth century, a group for which few data are otherwise available. A total of 6,549 responses were received, with an overall rate of left-handedness of 15.2%, which is substantially above that expected for a cohort born in the nineteenth and early twentieth centuries. Left-handers are likely to respond preferentially to surveys about handedness, and the extent of over-response can be estimated in modern control data obtained from a handedness website, from the 1953 BBC data, and from Crichton-Browne's 1907 survey, in which there was also a response bias. Response bias appears to have been growing, being relatively greater in the most modern studies. In the 1953 data there is also evidence that left-handers were more common among later rather than early responders, suggesting that left-handers may have been specifically recruited into the study, perhaps by other left-handers who had responded earlier. In the present study the estimated rate of bias was used to correct the nineteenth-century BBC data, which was then combined with other available data as a mixture of two constrained Weibull functions, to obtain an overall estimate of handedness rates in the nineteenth century. The best estimates are that left-handedness was at its nadir of about 3% for those born between about 1880 and 1900. Extrapolating backwards, the rate of left-handedness in the eighteenth century was probably about 10%, with the decline beginning in about 1780, and reaching around 7% in about 1830, although inevitably there are many uncertainties in those estimates. What does seem indisputable is that rates of left-handedness fell during most of the nineteenth century, only subsequently to rise in the twentieth century.

Keywords: Handedness; Rate; Historical; Nineteenth century; Response bias.

Address correspondence to: I. C. McManus, UCL Department of Psychology, University College London, Gower Street, London WC1E 6BT, UK. E-mail: i.mcmanus@ucl.ac.uk

We are extremely grateful to Dr Chuck Wysocki for providing the raw data from the Gilbert and Wysocki study.

DOI: 10.1080/13576500802565313

A major interest of the 1953 BBC television programme, *Science in the Making: Right Hand, Left Hand*, described in detail in our previous paper (McManus, Rawles, Moore, & Freegard, 2010 this issue), was analysing right- and left-handedness, and in using the medium of television to collect data on handedness from a large population sample. Here we analyse those data, looking particularly at the issues of response bias and the question of whether the data can nevertheless be informative about the historical rate of handedness, particularly for those born in the nineteenth century.

Any analysis of the historical rates of left-handedness in the twentieth century inevitably has to take as its starting point the exceptionally large study of Gilbert and Wysocki (1992), which in 1986 collected data from over 1,100,000 US men and women aged from 10 to 86 who responded to a survey published in *National Geographic* magazine. Figure 1 shows Gilbert and Wysocki's data, for men and women combined, as originally published, and plotted in terms of the year of birth of the participants. The sample size for all year points is large, and so the error bars are small. It is clear that the rate of left-handedness in these data was lowest for those born in 1900, at around 3%, and that the rate of left-handedness then rose consistently until for those born in about 1945 and onwards it reaches an asymptote at between about 11% and 12%, nearly a four-fold increase in the rate of left-handedness over half a century or so. Figure 1 also shows a Weibull curve fitted to the data (see Method and Results for details of model fitting). Not only is the fit very good, but the implication, if the only data available were

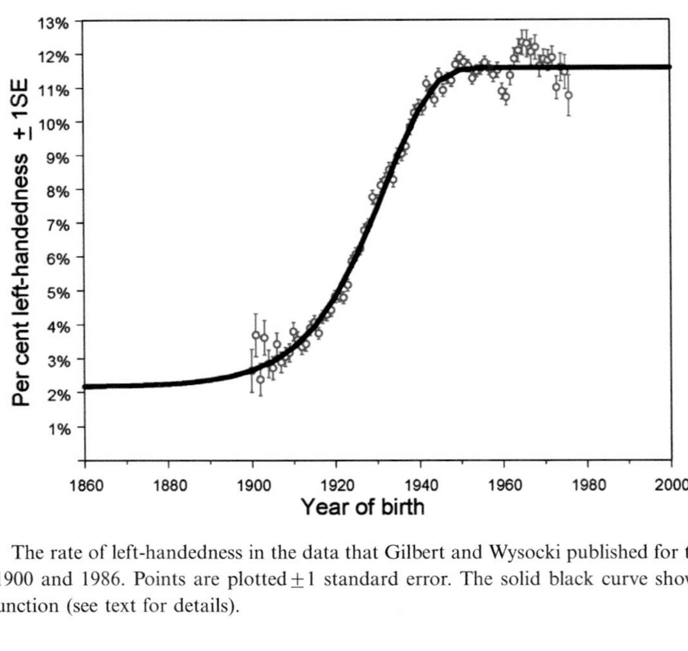

Figure 1. The rate of left-handedness in the data that Gilbert and Wysocki published for those born between 1900 and 1986. Points are plotted ±1 standard error. The solid black curve shows a fitted Weibull function (see text for details).

to be those of Gilbert and Wysocki, is that the rate of handedness in most of the nineteenth century would have been just over 2%, with the rise to modern rates of left-handedness beginning in about 1880 or 1890.

The causes of the apparently lower rate of handedness for those born earlier in the twentieth century are not clear. Some authors have suggested that the lower rate of left-handedness in the elderly reflects an earlier age of death in left-handers (Coren & Halpern, 1991; Halpern & Coren, 1988), although detailed analyses (Annett, 1993; Harris, 1993a, 1993b; Rothman, 1991), as well as prospective cohort studies (Aggleton, Kentridge, & Neave, 1993; Ellis, Ellis, Marshall, Windridge, & Jones, 1998a; Ellis, Marshall, Windridge, Jones, & Ellis, 1998b; Marks & Williamson, 1991; Wolf, D'Agostino, & Cobb, 1991), provide little support for the idea. Likewise, although in part the effect might reflect a decreasing social pressure against the use of the left hand for writing, that theory is difficult to sustain given that there is also a parallel change in the rate of left-arm waving, a behaviour that is unlikely to be subject to social pressure, and has been witnessed directly in old films, thereby removing reporting bias as an explanation (McManus & Hartigan, 2007). It has therefore to be concluded that the changing rates of left-handedness in the twentieth century were probably real, and require both exploration and explanation.

Although Gilbert and Wysocki (1992) only published data for ages from 10 to 86, the authors also stated that "Ages outside this range were not included due to relatively small (<500) sample sizes" (p. 602). However Chuck Wysocki had provided one of us (ICM) with the original raw database for the study (see McManus & Wysocki, 2005), and in the raw data were also available the handedness of a further 1950 individuals who were born before 1900, the oldest being aged 99 at the time of the study. These raw data are provided in an appendix to this paper, in the same format as Gilbert and Wysocki had originally provided as an appendix to their paper. Figure 2 shows the additional Gilbert and Wysocki data for those born in the last 13 years of the nineteenth century. Although standard errors are wide, there is a clear tendency for the points to be above the fitted Weibull curve, and a fitted curve (normal kernel, width = 15) clearly suggests that rates of left-handedness were somewhat higher for those born in the late 1880s and early 1890s. The rates of left-handedness were 7.5% for the 107 individuals born from 1887 to 1889 and 5.3% for the 376 individuals born from 1887 to 1894, compared with 3.3% for the 1467 born from 1895 to 1899, 3.2% for the 5726 born from 1900 to 1904, and 3.3% for the 16,469 born from 1905 to 1909 ($\chi^2 = 11.38$, 4 *df*, $p = .023$, linear-trend $\chi^2 = 4.11$, $p = .043$). Comparison of those born from 1887 to 1899 ($n = 483$, 5.8% left-handed) with those born from 1900 to 1909 ($n = 23{,}662$, 3.2% left-handed) showed a highly significant difference ($\chi^2 = 10.06$, 1 *df*, $p = .002$).

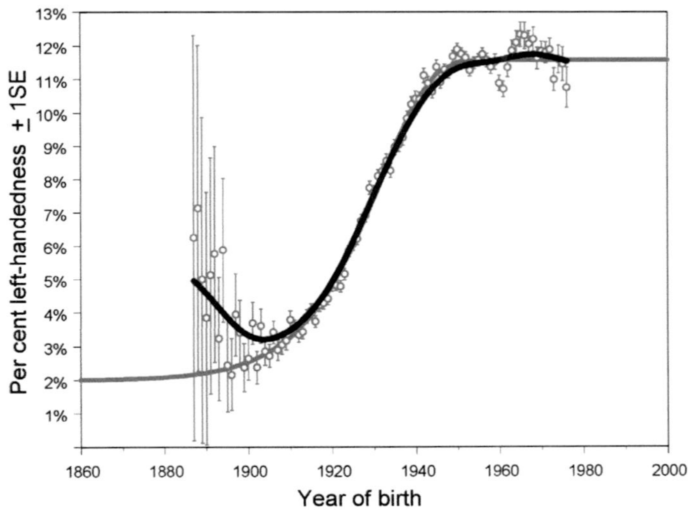

Figure 2. The same data and fitted Weibull function (shown in grey) as in Figure 1, but with the inclusion of additional data from the Gilbert and Wysocki study for those born from 1887 to 1899. The solid black line shows a fitted kernel function (normal distribution, width = 15, unweighted).

Other data on the handedness of individuals born in the nineteenth century are scarce, and it is not always clear that similar criteria have been used in determining handedness. Some studies have also been restricted only to males, and in the Gilbert and Wysocki data, and in almost all studies reported, it is generally the case that there are about five male left-handers to every four female left-handers, a meta-analysis finding the male rate to be about 27% higher than the female rate (McManus, 1991; Seddon & McManus, 1991). Here we will express historical rates in terms of the overall population, averaging both males and females, and where only males are included in a study we will present raw and also adjusted rates to take into account the typical excess of male left-handers.

The few estimates of the rate of left-handedness for those born in the nineteenth century, of which we are aware, are as follows:

1. Ogle (1871), in perhaps the first ever paper formally estimating a rate of left-handedness, reported that he had been unable to find any other reliable statistics in the literature, and therefore asked about handedness in the next 2000 patients that he saw at St George's Hospital in London. Overall, 85 (4.25%; *SE* 0.45%) were left-handed, in a sample balanced for males and females, with the rate being higher in the males (5.7%) than the females (2.8%). If the patients were adults aged 20 to 80

in 1875, then a typical year of birth might be about 1835, with a possible inaccuracy in that date of about ± 15.

2. Lombroso (1884), cited by Ludwig (1932, p. 294), found that 4.0% of 600 male workers were left-handed. Assuming a typical age of about 40, then these individuals were born in about 1840, with a confidence interval of about 10. Adjusting for sex differences there is a sex-adjusted rate of about 3.57% (*SE* 0.76%).
3. Crichton-Browne (1907), in a lecture given at the Royal Institution, described how he had asked Dr Charles Mayhew to assess the handedness of 975 male prisoners in Pentonville Prison, and found that 24 (2.46%) were left-handed (providing a sex-adjusted rate of 2.20%, with a standard error of about 0.47%). In addition 2 of the 60 prison officers were left-handed (3.33%). Assuming the prisoners were typically aged between about 20 and 50, then the typical birth year would be about 1875, with a confidence range of perhaps ± 10.
4. Stier (1911) described a very large survey, carried out in 1909, of 266,270 men in the German army, of whom 10,292 (3.87%) were left-handed, which gives a sex-adjusted rate of 3.45% with a standard error of about 0.035%. Assuming a typical conscript was aged about 19, then a good estimate of the average year of birth would be about 1890, with a confidence interval of about ± 5.
5. Ludwig (1932, p. 289) cites data from Schäfer (1911) who looked at handedness in 17,074 male and female Berlin schoolchildren, of whom overall 4.07% were left-handed, with a higher rate in males (5.15%) than females (2.98%). If these children were aged from 5 to 15 and given delays before publication, then they would probably have been born in about 1897.
6. Finally, we are also aware of the statement of Brinton (1896, p. 175) who said "Among educated Americans and Europeans of the present generation from 2 to 4% per cent are positively left-handed", although no formal statistics are provided. He was presumably referring to a cohort born perhaps 40 to 50 years earlier in, say, 1850, with a confidence range of about ± 10.

The sex-adjusted rates for these studies are plotted in Figure 3 as solid black circles at dates 1835, 1840, 1875, 1890, 1897, and 1850 respectively, and each has vertical error bars to show ± 1 standard error (and it should be noted that for Stier this is much smaller than the plotted size of the point itself). In addition, horizontal bars are provided to give some sense of the temporal uncertainty in the average date of birth of the individuals in the studies, which are at best broad estimates.

As well as the data for the nineteenth century, which we have tried to make comprehensive, Figure 3 also contains two sets of data from the

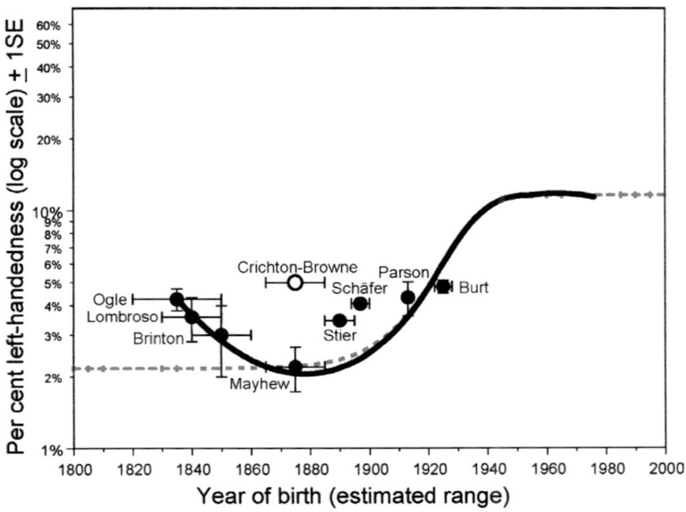

Figure 3. The rate of left-handedness in a number of studies in the literature. See text for details. Solid points indicate unbiased population estimates, whereas the single open point corresponds to the data of Crichton-Browne which probably show response bias (and can be compared with the contemporaneous data of Mayhew).

twentieth century, primarily with the intention of validating the Gilbert and Wysocki data against contemporary records.

1. Parson (1924), in 1923, examined handedness in 833 schoolchildren in New Jersey, 36 of whom (4.32%; *SE* 0.71%) were left-handed. The average age was 9.90, giving a year of birth of 1913.
2. Burt (1937) describes data from a study of 5,000 boys and girls in London schools, presumably carried out in the early 1930s, which with a typical age of 10 would mean the children on average were born in about 1925, with an uncertainty of perhaps 3 years either side. Overall 4.8% (*SE* 0.30%) were left-handed.

Figure 3 also shows as a dashed grey line the fitted Weibull function for the Gilbert and Wysocki data. Although the Mayhew data fit the line, all of the other data for those born in the nineteenth century are above the Weibull function, suggesting that handedness was not at a constant low level during that period.

A concern in any study such as that carried out in the BBC's 1953 television programme is that there will be a bias for left-handers to respond since, perhaps inevitably, they are more interested in handedness and lateralisation (although that itself may be a modern phenomenon). Cornell and McManus (1992) did find that left-handers were both more likely to respond and responded more quickly to a survey that was explicitly about handedness. Much longer ago, a similar phenomenon was also reported by Crichton-Browne (1907), who described how he had circulated a questionnaire among friends and acquaintances, of whom 40 (4.18%, $SE \pm .65\%$) out of 957 respondents said they were left-handed (and an additional 36 said they were ambidextrous). Crichton-Browne (p. 634) then comments:

> These figures, I have no doubt, place the proportion of the left-handed and ambidextrous much too high. I found that my distributors, in circulating my papers, naturally thought more of their interesting left-handed acquaintances than of the commonplace right-handed ones, and that left-handed persons, regarding themselves as unique and being generally rather proud of their eccentricity, were more ready to answer my questions than their less distinguished right-handed neighbours.

If one compares the 4.18% of left-handed respondents in Crichton-Browne's data with the sex-adjusted 2.20% in Mayhew's complete sample that Crichton-Browne also reports, then left-handers are about 4.18/2.20 = 1.90 times more likely to respond to a survey on left-handedness (odds ratio = 1.939 ×). The data for Crichton-Browne's biased sample are also shown in Figure 3, directly above the solid circle for Mayhew's data at 1875, but plotted as an open circle to indicate that the data are potentially biased. This convention of solid points for population-based estimates (or results corrected for bias) and open points for biased estimates will be used throughout this paper. Finally the solid black line in Figure 3, which after 1900 follows almost exactly the fitted Weibull function from the Gilbert and Wysocki data, is a second degree loess curve[1] fitted to all of the data (except that of Mayhew), which suggests both a minimum at about 1880 and a higher rate of left-handedness earlier in the twentieth century.

In this study we wish to describe handedness in the BBC 1953 study, and in particular the rate of left-handedness in relation to year of birth, and to assess effects of response bias by comparing the data to modern samples collected in an analogous way. By understanding response bias it is hoped that the effects can be compensated for, and hence further data added to the very limited information available on handedness of those born in the Victorian period.

[1] It should be noted that the loess curve is only a first approximation to the best-fitting line because both (a) no weighting is applied according to the size of the various data sets, and (b) it is a theory-free description of the data, unlike the Weibull function.

METHOD

Historical data

Analysis was of postcards returned by the viewers of *Right Hand, Left Hand*, which was broadcast on BBC television on Friday 14 August 1953, further details of which are provided in a previous paper (McManus et al., 2010 this issue). Viewers answered 12 questions printed in a questionnaire in that week's *Radio Times*. Data from the postcards were entered into a computer for statistical analysis, with conventional statistical analyses carried out using SPSS 11.5. See the previous paper for further details of the sample, etc. (McManus et al., 2010 this issue).

Modern control data

The website www.righthandlefthand.com, which was set up to support the book *Right Hand, Left Hand* (McManus, 2002), contained a number of questionnaires assessing aspects of handedness and lateralisation. Here we will restrict the analysis to the single question that asked: "Which hand would you use: (i) To hold a pen while writing a letter". Respondents answered on a 6-point scale: "Always use left/Usually use left/Slightly prefer left/Slightly prefer right/Usually use right/Always prefer right". The questionnaire intentionally included no response category of "Either" or "Both". Particularly relevant to the present study is the fact that individuals spontaneously chose to visit the website so that there was no possibility of ensuring the sample of participants was representative, and on the contrary it was highly likely that left-handers would be over-represented relative to the population as a whole. The data analysed here are those downloaded from the website on 29 June 2006.

Statistical analysis

A modified form of the Weibull growth curve was fitted to the various sets of data using a constrained two-parameter Weibull model. The conventional two-parameter Weibull function has two parameters, λ (lambda), the scale parameter, and k, the shape parameter, where the cumulative proportion with some characteristic, left-handedness in the present case, in relation to time, t, is:

$$p = 1 - e^{-(t/\lambda)^k} \qquad (1)$$

As t goes from $-$infinity to $+$infinity, and if k is positive, so the proportion, p, rises from 0% to 100% (whereas if k is negative then p falls from 100% to 0%). The parameter k controls the steepness of the function, and the parameter λ the time at which the proportion reaches the 50% mark. A three-parameter function, with an additional location parameter, θ, is equivalent to the two parameter function if $\theta = 0$:

$$p = 1 - e^{-((t-\theta)/\lambda)^k} \quad (2)$$

A constrained two-parameter model allows the proportion of left-handers to rise from a lower asymptote, b to an upper asymptote c, with a function:

$$p = b + (c - b)\cdot(1 - e^{-(t/\lambda)^k}) \quad (3)$$

A mixture of two constrained Weibull functions consists of two functions, in the present case a first descending function, which falls from an early, high asymptote, a, to a common lower asymptote, b, with parameters λ_d and t_d, and then rises via an (overlapping) ascending function, with parameters λ_a and t_a, to a later, high asymptote, c:

$$p = b + (a - b)\cdot(1 - e^{-(t/\lambda_d)^{k_d}}) + (c - b)\cdot(1 - e^{-(t/\lambda_a)^{k_a}}) \quad (4)$$

The sample sizes in the data were very variable, with the data of both Stier and Gilbert and Wysocki having extremely large sample Ns, with six and seven digits. In order to allow all data to be taken into account, but also so that extremely large datasets did not have an undue influence, data points were weighted by the square-root of sample size. The importance of that assumption is explored in the results section.

RESULTS

Although the main interest of this study is in the historical BBC data, it is convenient first to re-analyse the Gilbert and Wysocki data formally using Weibull functions, then to analyse the modern control data, and finally to analyse the BBC data.

Fitting Weibull models to the published Gilbert and Wysocki data

Figure 1 shows the Gilbert and Wysocki data, averaged across males and females. The sample sizes are large, and hence the standard errors are small. A constrained two-parameter Weibull model and also a constrained three-parameter Weibull model were fitted to the data (see Table 3 for fitted values, and Figure 1 for a plot of the fitted curve). The fit of the three-parameter model in terms of the weighted sum of squares was indistinguishable from that of the two-parameter model, and hence only the two-parameter model is fitted in Figure 1, and only two-parameter models are used for the remainder of the analysis.

Modern control data

By the end of June 2006, 3,463 individuals had completed the online handedness questionnaire, of whom 1,744 (50.4%) always used the right hand for writing, 184 (5.3%) usually used the right hand, 44 (1.3%) slightly preferred the right hand, 27 (0.8%) slightly preferred the left hand, 43 (1.2%) usually used the left hand, and 1,421 (41.0%) always used the left hand. Overall, therefore, 43.1% typically used the left hand for writing, a proportion much in excess of the typical 10–12% of left-handers found in modern population surveys. A total of 1,780 (51.4%) of respondents were male, and 1,683 (48.6%) female, indicating that the proportion of men and women was similar to population proportions. Altogether 43.4% of men (773/1,780) and 42.7% of women (718/1,683) were left-handed, a non-significant difference ($\chi^2 = 0.207$, 1 *df*, $p = .650$). The mean year of birth of right-handers (1971.81; $SD = 14.09$) was not significantly different from that of left-handers (1971.72; $SD = 15.01$; $t = 0.189$, 3,461 *df*, $p = .850$), and neither was there a difference in the variances ($p = .301$). Data were only available for 18 individuals born between 1900 and 1909, and for 6 born between 1910 and 1919, and these groups are therefore omitted from the graphical analysis.

Figure 4 summarises data on studies with biased responses, and also, as a visual reference and plotted in grey, the fitted Weibull function for the published Gilbert and Wysocki data and the fitted loess curve from Figure 3. The data of Crichton-Browne, which are biased, are plotted as an open circle. The modern control data are plotted as the open triangles at the top left of Figure 4.

BBC data

The primary analysis is in terms of the hand reported for writing. Of 6,549 respondents providing information on the hand used for writing, 5,444 (83.1%) reported using the right hand, 934 (14.3%) the left hand, 107 (1.6%) that they were mixed or used both, and 64 (1.0%) spontaneously reported that they used to use the left hand for writing. Although the rate of those who report having once written with their left hand increases with age, the rate of those reporting "mixed/both" shows little relation to age, suggesting that they are indeed a different subgroup, and a subgroup that is probably not related genuinely to lateralised behaviour. On that basis, and following the analysis of Peters (1998), we have therefore classified those who reported

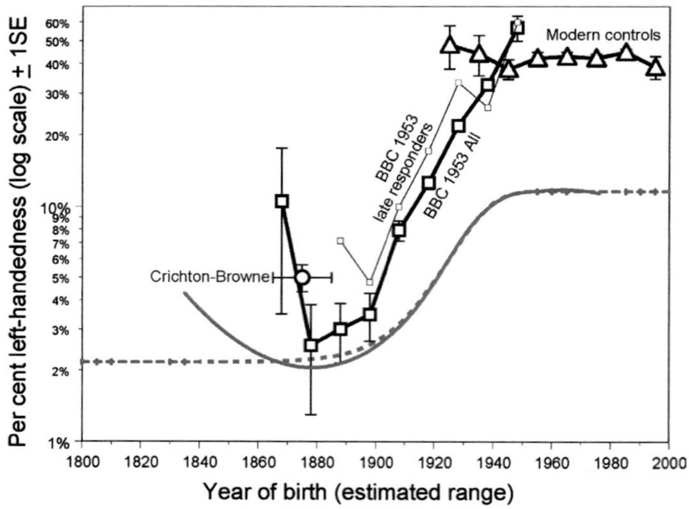

Figure 4. Open points and lines in black show the rates of left-handedness in three studies in which there is likely to be response bias on the part of left-handers. The grey lines correspond to those in Figure 3.

being "mixed" as being in the right-handed group. However the group who had previously used their left-hand for writing were included within the group of left-handers. On that basis there were 998 (15.2%) of 6,549 respondents who were left-handed. Overall the rate of left-handedness was very similar in males (459/3,014 = 15.2%) and in females (539/3,534 = 15.3%).

Handedness classified on the basis of writing hand correlated strongly with the five other measures of handedness (see Table 1), the Spearman correlations being .451, .658, .569, −.347, and .424 for kicking, brushing teeth, throwing a ball, holding a ball of wool or string, and carrying a full glass of water respectively (all $p \ll .001$). The remainder of this analysis will therefore be restricted to writing hand.

Considering left-handers as those who wrote with their left hand, or had once done so, there was a strong association with age grouped into decades (see Table 2), the overall rate of left-handedness declining strongly with age ($\chi^2 = 495.1$, 1 *df*, $p \ll .001$; linear trend, $\chi^2 = 410.2$, 1 *df*, $p \ll .001$). The large, open squares in Figure 4 show the proportion of left-handed responders in relation to decade of birth, and it can be seen that the overall rate of left-handedness becomes progressively lower in the older population. The point for those born 1864–1873 has been included for completeness, despite the N of 19 being very low, because the two left-handers, with their rate of 10.5% and its wide standard error, would give what at first appears to

TABLE 1
Relationship between writing hand and the five other laterality measures in the BBC 1953 survey

		Right	*Left*	*Total*
Which foot do you prefer to KICK with?	Right	4324 (77.9%)	235 (23.5%)	4559 (69.6%)
	Mixed/Both	416 (7.5%)	74 (7.4%)	490 (7.5%)
	Left	810 (14.6%)	689 (69.0%)	1499 (22.9%)
When you are brushing your teeth, which hand you hold the BRUSH in?	Right	4754 (85.7%)	73 (7.3%)	4827 (73.7%)
	Mixed/Both	202 (3.6%)	48 (4.8%)	250 (3.8%)
	Left	593 (10.7%)	877 (87.9%)	1470 (22.5%)
Which hand do you prefer to THROW a ball with?	Right	4737 (85.4%)	179 (18.0%)	4916 (75.1%)
	Mixed/Both	124 (2.2%)	27 (2.7%)	151 (2.3%)
	Left	688 (12.4%)	788 (79.3%)	1476 (22.6%)
If you are winding wool or string which hand do you HOLD the ball in?	Right	1152 (20.8%)	640 (64.2%)	1792 (27.4%)
	Mixed/Both	271 (4.9%)	50 (5.0%)	321 (4.9%)
	Left	4120 (74.3%)	307 (30.8%)	4427 (67.7%)
If you had to carry a glass with water filled to the brim, which hand would you prefer to CARRY it in?	Right	3911 (70.6%)	192 (19.2%)	4103 (62.7%)
	Mixed/Both	753 (13.6%)	130 (13.0%)	883 (13.5%)
	Left	879 (15.9%)	676 (67.7%)	1555 (23.8%)

be an anomalous result were it not for the point being broadly compatible with that of Crichton-Browne.

Date of posting of the questionnaire was known in most cases, and initially we expected to find that left-handers responded more quickly than right-handers, as was the case with Cornell and McManus (1992). However the converse was found: left-handers tended to respond later than right-handers (mean day of posting for right-handers = 3.31, $SD = 2.65$, $N = 5109$; left-handers mean = 3.51, $SD = 2.52$, $N = 928$; $t = -2.04$, 6035 *df*, $p = .041$). We therefore divided respondents into the early ones who replied by day seven after the programme was broadcast ($N = 5635$, 93.3%), and the 402 respondents (6.7%) who replied later. A logistic regression with writing hand as the dependent variable showed independent effects of age (B = −.581, $SE = .032$, $p < .001$) and of a late response (B = .343, $SE = .141$, $p = .015$). The small open squares in Figure 4, plotted without error bars to avoid the plot becoming too confused, show the rates of left-handers in the late responders, and in general they are higher than the data for all responders, most of whom responded early.

TABLE 2
Writing hand in relation to date of birth in the BBC 1953 data

			Responses to questionnaire					
Age group	*Years of birth*	*Mid year for plotting*	*"Right"*	*"Mixed/both"*	*"Left"*	*"Was Left"*	*"Left" + "Was left"*	*Total*
0–9	1944–1953	1948	22 (43.1%)	0 (0%)	29 (56.9%)	0 (0%)	29 (56.9%)	51
10–19	1934–1943	1938	555 (66.8%)	5 (0.6%)	270 (32.5%)	1 (.1%)	271 (32.6%)	831
20–29	1924–1933	1928	1171 (77.0%)	16 (1.1%)	325 (21.4%)	8 (0.5%)	333 (21.9%)	1520
30–39	1914–1923	1918	1580 (85.8%)	29 (1.6%)	221 (12.0%)	11 (0.6%)	232 (12.6%)	1841
40–49	1904–1913	1908	1065 (89.8%)	27 (2.3%)	75 (6.3%)	19 (1.6%)	94 (7.9%)	1186
50–59	1894–1903	1898	481 (92.7%)	20 (3.9%)	7 (1.3%	11 (2.1%)	18 (3.5%)	519
60–69	1884–1893	1888	382 (95.7%)	5 (1.3%)	5 (1.3%)	7 (1.7%)	12 (3.0%)	399
70–79	1874–1883	1878	149 (95.5%)	3 (1.9%)	0 (0%)	4 (2.6%)	4 (2.6%)	156
80+	1864–1873	1868	16 (84.2%)	1 (5.3%)	0 (0%)	2 (10.5%)	2 (10.5%)	19
Total			5421 (83.1%)	106 (1.6%)	932 (14.3%)	63 (1.0%)	995 (15.3%)	6522

Odds ratios for biased responding

Considering the modern, control sample, 42.6% of the respondents were left-handed, compared with an average value of 11.61% in the post-1950 Wysocki data, an odds ratio of 5.65 × for left-handers being more likely to respond to a questionnaire. Similar comparisons can also be made for the BBC data from the 1948, 1938, 1928, 1918, and 1908 groups, which can be compared with the appropriate Gilbert and Wysocki data, to give odds ratios of 10.44 ×, 4.43 ×, 3.77 ×, 3.21 ×, and 2.73 ×. Finally a comparison of Crichton-Browne's 1875 cohort with the Mayhew data shows an odds ratio of 1.94 × . If odds ratio is plotted against date (Figure 5), with the modern data plotted at 1970, the approximate mid-point, then there is generally a clear, almost linear relation, with the odds ratio growing with time. The value of 10.44 for the 1948 BBC data seems somewhat anomalous, but it must be remembered that this is for children aged 0–9, and since the programme was broadcast late in the evening in an era when children would normally have been in bed long before that time, it is likely to be particularly biased—hence it has been dropped from the remaining calculations.[2] The correlation of the odds ratio with date is .986 ($n = 6$, $p < .001$), and with the proportion of left-handers in the unbiased population is .936 ($n = 6$, $p <$ .001). Response bias seems therefore to have increased over the past century, perhaps as left-handedness has become both more common and of more popular interest.

The regression equation for odds ratio on date was calculated, and values then predicted for the four BBC cohorts, of 1898, 1888, 1878 and 1868, for which direct comparative data were not available, giving predicted odds ratios of 2.61 ×, 2.20 ×, 1.80 ×, and 1.39 ×, and on that basis we calculated expected values for the rate of left-handedness in an unbiased population, which were 1.36%, 1.38%, 1.44%, and 7.81% respectively. Figure 6 shows those new values as solid black diamonds, coupled with the previous data from Figure 3 shown as grey (and excluding for obvious reasons the Crichton-Browne data), along with a loess curve fitted to the entire data set, which is shown in solid black. The rate appears to have been falling from about 1840 through to 1870, when it reached a minimum over the period of about 1870 to 1890, after which it slowly began to climb again, until it reached its asymptote in about 1945–1950.

[2] The regression equation described below would predict that there should be about 4.65 × as many left-handers found compared with the general population, whereas there were actually 10.44 ×, about 2.2 × as many as expected above the normal excess of left-handers. We suspect that some parents either encouraged their left-handed children to respond or perhaps even responded on their behalf.

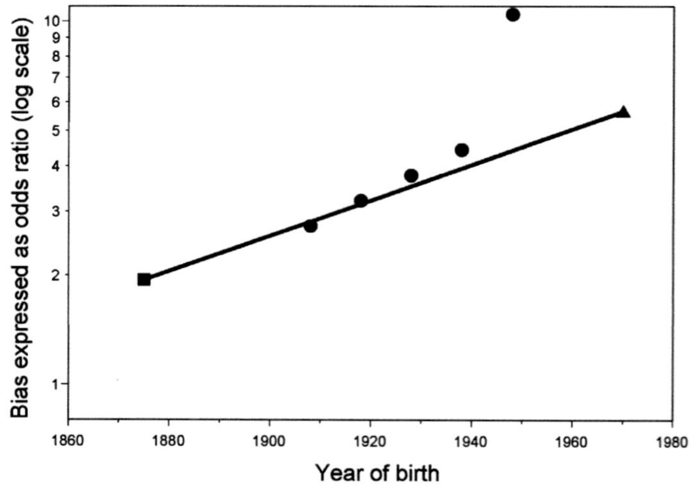

Figure 5. Bias in studies plotted as odds ratio (log scale), for the BBC data (solid circles), the Crichton-Browne and Mayhew data (solid square), and the modern control data (solid triangle). The data for the very young BBC participants have been omitted from the fitting of the least squares line.

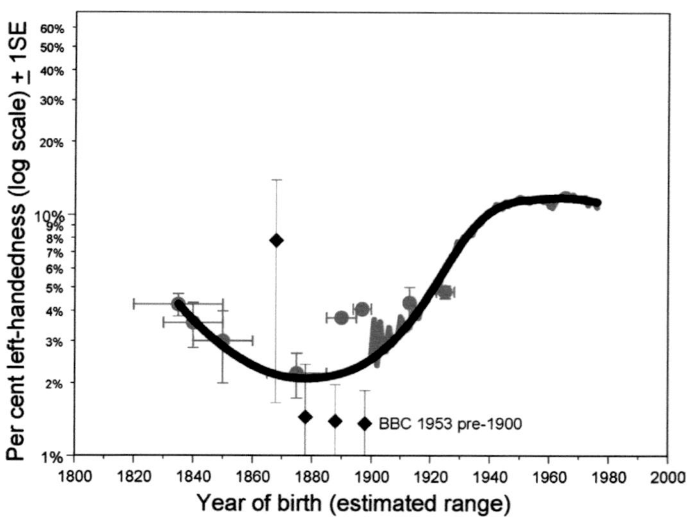

Figure 6. Grey points and lines correspond to the data plotted in Figure 3. The solid black lines are pre-1900 data from the BBC study, corrected for response bias (see text). The solid black line is a second-degree loess function fitted to all of the data points (including the Gilbert and Wysocki data, which it fits nearly perfectly).

Arm-waving data

In a previous paper we have estimated rates of left-handedness in the Victorian period using data on directly observed arm-waving in a set of early documentary films, made between about 1901 and 1906 (McManus & Hartigan, 2007). In modern populations, arm-waving is less strongly lateralised than hand-writing: about a quarter of individuals wave with their left arm. The historical data were therefore corrected for that relationship, to calculate an expected rate of left-handedness for writing. Figure 7 shows all of the data from Figure 6 in grey, and also includes, as black triangles, the calculated rate of left-handedness from the arm-waving data. In addition, the loess curve has been recalculated, and the solid black line shows the estimated rate of left-handedness taking all of the data into account.

Weibull functions fitted to the nineteenth century data

Figures 4 and 6, and 7 suggest that the rate of left-handedness might well have been falling through the nineteenth century, in contrast to the data of Figure 3 which provide strong evidence for a rising rate during the twentieth century. A constrained two-parameter Weibull function fitted the data well for the twentieth century, and therefore it also makes sense to fit a Weibull

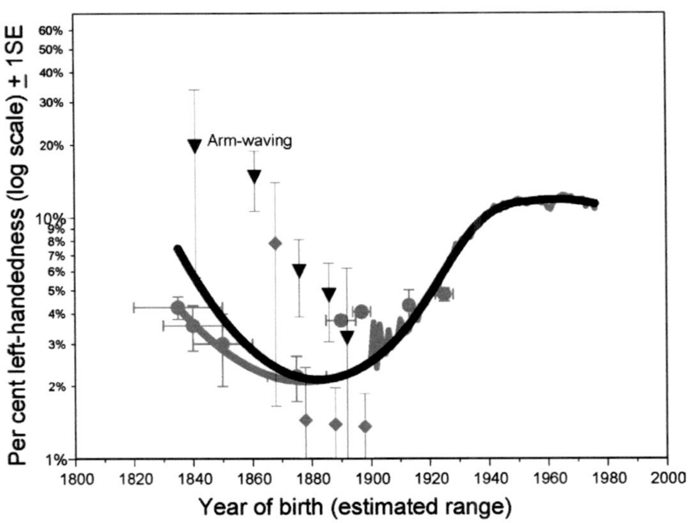

Figure 7. The grey points and lines correspond to those shown in Figure 6. The points in black are those for the arm-waving data of McManus and Hartigan, expressed as the predicted proportion of left-handers. The solid black line is a second-degree loess function fitted both to the data of Figure 6 and to the arm-waving data.

function to the nineteenth-century data. The optimal way is to fit the entire data set as a mixture of Weibull functions, a function that descends from an early high asymptote to a low asymptote, and then a second function that ascends from the common low asymptote to a later high asymptote. Table 3 summarises the various models that have been fitted. Figure 8 shows, in grey, all of the raw data that have been fitted, along with standard errors. Note also that the date range is wider than previously, and the vertical scale is also linear. The solid black line in Figure 8 shows model 3, the fitted mixture of two two-parameter Weibull functions with weighting based on the square root of the sample size. The upper asymptotes of the ascending and descending functions are allowed to be different, and the slopes of the ascending and descending functions are also allowed to be different. It can be seen that in the eighteenth century about 10.2% of the population would have been left-handed, the rate starting to decline in about 1770–1780, dropping 1% below 10.2% by 1796, reaching the midpoint of its decline in about 1818, and as the continuing, descending grey line would eventually have reached the lower asymptote of about 2.30%. However the ascending function, shown at bottom left in grey, which is very similar to the function fitted to the published Gilbert and Wysocki data, begins to increase in about 1860–1870, with a rather greater slope than the descending function, reaching the mid-point of its ascent in about 1933, and eventually by about

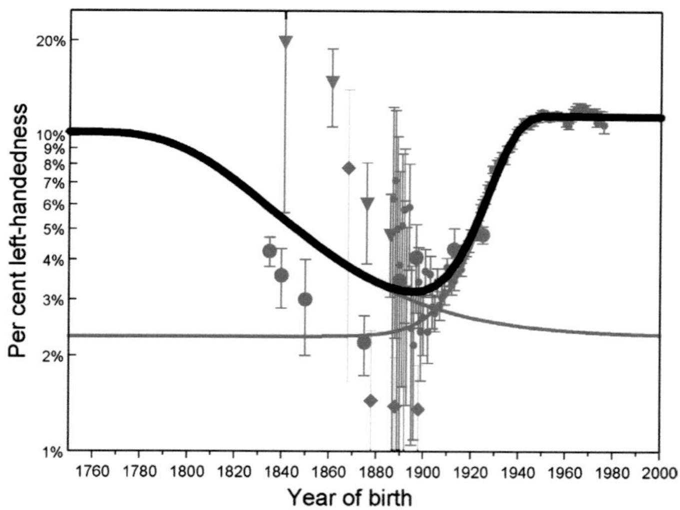

Figure 8. The grey points correspond to all of the raw data shown in the previous figures (including the pre-1900 data of Gilbert and Wysocki); however, to avoid confusion, standard errors are not shown and are very variable between studies. The solid black line is a mixture of a descending and ascending constrained Weibull functions (see text for details). The solid grey lines correspond to the two components of the mixture.

TABLE 3
Fitting of Weibull functions to the data

	Data	Model		Lower asymptote (b)	Upper asymptote(s) (a, c)	λ (λ_d, λ_a)	K (k_d, k_a)	θ	Fit
1	Gilbert and Wysocki (1900–1986)	2-parameter Weibull with range constraints	Ascending	2.17%	11.58%	1932.2	175.5	–	894.68
2	Gilbert and Wysocki (1900–1986)	3-parameter Weibull with range constraints	Ascending	2.17%	11.58%	1931.3	175.6	.844	894.68
3	All data (see Figure 8). Weighted by sqrt(*N*)	Mixture of two 2-parameter Weibulls with range constraints	Descending Ascending	2.30%	10.18% 11.40%	1818.3 1932.9	−57.50 197.12	–	4136.6
4	All data (see Figure 8). Weighted by *N*	Mixture of two 2-parameter Weibulls with range constraints	Descending Ascending	2.39%	10.17% 11.37%	1814.9 1933.1	−52.10 197.41	–	180020
5	All data (see Figure 8). No weighting	Mixture of two 2-parameter Weibulls with range constraints	Descending Ascending	0%*	9.31% 11.07%	1869.0 1932.0	−66.29 173.68	–	362.2

Fit coefficients are only comparable between models 1 and 2.
*Value constrained so that it could not be less than zero.

1945–1950 reaching the modern asymptote of 11.41%, which is a little higher than the eighteenth-century asymptote. The lowest rate of left-handedness of about 3.18% occurred in about 1896. Models 4 and 5 investigate the effect of altering the weighting, with model 4 having weighting proportional to the number of participants, and model 5 having no weighting as such (i.e., equal weighting for all points). Models 3 and 4 are extremely similar, suggesting that the precise form of the weighting is of little importance. Model 5, with equal weighting, is slightly different with a theoretical lower asymptote of zero (although since the two curves are summed, the function never actually reaches that value), and it also shows a slightly later descent during the nineteenth century. In general, though, the precise weighting used has little impact on the fitted function.

DISCUSSION

The handedness data collected by the BBC in 1953 provide a number of interesting features, which allow them to be integrated with other data sets and to provide insight both into the nature of the biased responding of left-handers in surveys, and the changing rates of left-handedness of those born in the nineteenth century, a period for which there are few directly observed data.

Left-handers are undoubtedly more likely to respond to surveys that are explicitly about handedness than are right-handers. That effect was apparent to Crichton-Browne in 1907, although his effect was relatively small. Since then, as Figure 5 shows, the effect seems to have grown, as can be seen in the modern control data derived from the website-based survey of handedness, and probably reflects a growing interest and awareness of left-handers in the nature of left-handedness (and that can also be seen in the large number of websites devoted to left-handedness—see Elias, 1998). However, the response bias does appear to be fairly systematic, and hence it is possible to correct the BBC data in order to estimate true population rates of left-handedness. Two other features are also apparent in the preferential responding of left-handers to surveys on handedness:

1. Despite most population studies finding an excess of left-handed males over left-handed females, neither in the BBC data nor in the modern control data obtained from the website is there a sex difference in the rate of left-handedness. The precise explanation of that is not clear, but the effect does seem to have been replicated and therefore is likely to be real.
2. Although Cornell and McManus (1992) found that left-handers responded more quickly to a survey that was explicitly on handedness, the BBC data found an excess of left-handers in those responding later.

> However the BBC data were still arriving several weeks after the original programme, whereas the Cornell and McManus data were only collected over a week or so. One possibility is that in the BBC survey there was a tendency for the early left-handed responders subsequently to tell other left-handers about the survey by word of mouth and encourage them also to respond (what would now be called "viral marketing"), and hence left-handers are over-represented in the later wave of respondents.

The main interest in this paper has been to try and obtain more accurate estimates of the rate of left-handedness in the nineteenth century. There seems little doubt from the published data of Gilbert and Wysocki that the rate of left-handedness rose dramatically during the twentieth century, but there is also evidence that throughout recorded history, and in prehistory, the rate of left-handedness has been relatively stable at about 10% (Bahn, 1989; Coren & Porac, 1977; de Castro, Bromage, & Jalvo, 1988; Faurie & Raymond, 2004; Fox & Frayer, 1997). The implication is therefore that at some time the rate of left-handedness must have declined, although there is no robust evidence to suggest how and when that occurred. The present study, by combining the data from the BBC study with the extended data of Gilbert and Wysocki, the few other studies of handedness in individuals born in the nineteenth century, and the data on arm-waving in early film from which handedness rates can also be estimated (McManus & Hartigan, 2007), finds the fitted Weibull mixture functions shown in Figure 8, in which the rate of left-handedness is probably at its nadir for those born between about 1880 and 1900, then begins to rise fairly quickly until it reached a plateau between about 1945 and 1950. Prior to 1900 the history is less clear, but the most parsimonious interpretation is that during the earlier eighteenth century the rate of left-handedness was broadly similar to the modern rate of about 10–11%. The rate then started to fall in the last quarter of the eighteenth century, was about 7% by 1820 or so, and eventually reached almost 3% by about 1896 (see Figure 8).

Inevitably such estimates contain many uncertainties. However, it seems undeniable that the rate of left-handedness rose three- to four-fold in the twentieth century, and given the longer-term historical data suggesting rates of around 8% to 10%, it is likely that at some time the rate must have fallen to the late Victorian values. Data from the nineteenth century are rare, but this study suggests that the rate of left-handedness was falling steadily between 1800 and 1880. The reasons for that cannot be explored here, but the potential implications for neuropsychology should be mentioned. Handedness is known to be associated with cerebral lateralisation for language, and cerebral lateralisation is thought to be associated with a number of aspects of psychopathology. If so, then an implication is that rates of psychopathology might also have changed over historical time.

REFERENCES

Aggleton, J. P., Kentridge, R. W., & Neave, N. J. (1993). Evidence for longevity differences between left handed and right handed men: An archival study of cricketers. *Journal of Epidemiology and Community Health*, *47*, 206–209.

Annett, M. (1993). The fallacy of the argument for reduced longevity in left-handers. *Perceptual and Motor Skills*, *76*, 295–298.

Bahn, P. G. (1989). Early teething troubles. *Nature*, *337*, 693.

Brinton, D. G. (1896). Left-handedness in North American Aboriginal art. *American Anthropologist*, *9*(5), 175–181.

Burt, C. (1937). *The backward child*. London: University of London Press.

Coren, S., & Halpern, D. F. (1991). Left-handedness: A marker for decreased survival fitness. *Psychological Bulletin*, *109*, 90–106.

Coren, S., & Porac, C. (1977). Fifty centuries of right-handedness: The historical record. *Science*, *198*, 631–632.

Cornell, E., & McManus, I. C. (1992). Differential survey response rates in right and left-handers. *British Journal of Psychology*, *83*, 39–43.

Crichton-Browne, J. (1907). Dexterity and the bend sinister. *Proceedings of the Royal Institution of Great Britain*, *18*, 623–652.

de Castro, J. M. B., Bromage, T. G., & Jalvo, Y. F. (1988). Buccal striations on fossil human anterior teeth: Evidence of handedness in the middle and early Upper Pleistocene. *Journal of Human Evolution*, *17*, 403–412.

Elias, L. J. (1998). Secular sinistrality: A review of popular handedness books and World Wide Web sites. *Laterality*, *3*, 193–208.

Ellis, P. J., Marshall, E., Windridge, C., Jones, S., & Ellis, S. J. (1998a). Left-handedness and premature death. *Lancet*, *351*, 1634.

Ellis, S. J., Ellis, P. J., Marshall, E., Windridge, C., & Jones, S. (1998b). Is forced dextrality an explanation for the fall in the prevalence of sinistrality with age? A study in northern England. *Journal of Epidemiology and Community Health*, *52*, 41–44.

Faurie, C., & Raymond, M. (2004). Handedness frequency over more than 10,000 years. *Proceedings of the Royal Society of London, Series B*, *271*, S43–S45.

Fox, C. L., & Frayer, D. W. (1997). Non-dietary marks in the anterior dentition of the Krapina neanderthals. *International Journal of Osteoarchaeology*, *7*, 133–149.

Gilbert, A. N., & Wysocki, C. J. (1992). Hand preference and age in the United States. *Neuropsychologia*, *30*, 601–608.

Halpern, D. F., & Coren, S. (1988). Do right-handers live longer? *Nature*, *333*, 213.

Harris, L. J. (1993a). Do left-handers die sooner than right-handers? Commentary on Coren and Halpern's (1991) "Left-handedness: A marker for decreased survival fitness". *Psychological Bulletin*, *114*, 203–234.

Harris, L. J. (1993b). Reply to Halpern and Coren. *Psychological Bulletin*, *114*, 242–247.

Lombroso, C. (1884). Sul mancinismo e destrismo tattile nei sani, nei pazzi, nei ciechi e nei sordomuti. *Archivi di Psichiatria, Neuropsichiatria, Antropologia Criminale e Medicina Legale*, *5*.

Ludwig, W. (1932). *Das Rechts-Links-Problem im Tierreich und beim Menschen*. Berlin: Verlag Julius Springer.

Marks, J. S., & Williamson, D. F. (1991). Left-handedness and life expectancy. *New England Journal of Medicine*, *325*, 1042.

McManus, I. C. (1991). The inheritance of left-handedness. In G. R. Bock & J. Marsh (Eds.), *Biological asymmetry and handedness (Ciba foundation symposium 162)* (pp. 251–281). Chichester, UK: Wiley.

McManus, I. C. (2002). *Right hand, left hand: The origins of asymmetry in brains, bodies, atoms and cultures*. London, UK/Cambridge, MA: Weidenfeld & Nicolson/Harvard University Press.

McManus, I. C., & Hartigan, A. (2007). Declining left-handedness in Victorian England seen in the films of Mitchell and Kenyon. *Current Biology*, *17*, R793–R794.

McManus, I. C., Rawles, R., Moore, J., & Freegard, M. (2010). *Science in the making: Right hand, left hand*. I: A BBC television programme broadcast in 1953. *Laterality*, *15*, 136–165.

McManus, I. C., & Wysocki, C. J. (2005). Left-handers have a lower prevalence of arthritis and ulcer. *Laterality*, *10*, 97–102.

Ogle, W. (1871). On dextral pre-eminence. *Medical-Chirurgical Transactions (Transactions of the Royal Medical and Chirurgical Society of London)*, *54*, 279–301.

Parson, B. S. (1924). *Lefthandedness: A new interpretation*. New York: Macmillan.

Peters, M. (1998). Description and validation of a flexible and broadly usable handedness questionnaire. *Laterality*, *3*, 77–96.

Rothman, K. J. (1991). Left-handedness and life expectancy. *New England Journal of Medicine*, *325*, 1041.

Schäfer, M. (1911). Die Linkshänder in den Berliner Gemeindeschulen. *Berliner klinische Wochenschrift*, *48*, 295.

Seddon, B., & McManus, I. C. (1991). *The incidence of left-handedness: A meta-analysis*. Unpublished manuscript.

Stier, E. (1911). *Untersuchungen über Linkshändigkeit und die funktionellen Differenzen der Hirnhälften. Nebst einem Anhang, "Über Linkshändigkeit in der deutschen Armee*. Jena: Gustav Fischer.

Wolf, P. A., D'Agostino, R. B., & Cobb, J. (1991). Left-handedness and life expectancy. *New England Journal of Medicine*, *325*, 1042.

APPENDIX A

Additional data on writing hand from Gilbert and Wysocki, for those born before 1900. For data for those aged 10 to 86 see Gilbert and Wysocki (1992).

		Males				Females			
Age	*Year of birth*	$L_W L_T$	$L_W R_T$	$R_W L_T$	$R_W R_T$	$L_W L_T$	$L_W R_T$	$R_W L_T$	$R_W R_T$
99	1887	0	0	0	5	1	0	1	9
98	1888	0	1	0	11	1	0	0	15
97	1889	1	0	0	12	0	0	1	6
96	1890	1	0	0	10	0	0	2	13
95	1891	0	0	3	18	2	0	1	15
94	1892	2	1	1	23	0	0	0	25
93	1893	2	1	1	51	0	0	1	37
92	1894	1	0	2	53	4	2	3	54
91	1895	1	0	0	61	2	0	1	58
90	1896	4	0	8	80	0	0	4	89
89	1897	5	1	9	118	3	1	7	109
88	1898	7	1	10	167	3	1	4	159
87	1899	3	3	8	213	4	1	10	220

LATERALITY, 2010, 15 (1/2), 209–252

The left and right hands of the eighteenth-century British musical prodigies, William Crotch and Samuel Wesley

Janet Snowman

Royal Academy of Music, London, UK

The musical prodigy William Crotch (1775–1847) used his left hand for many activities including the playing of stringed instruments, drawing and painting. Information on Crotch's handedness is available in both his own writings and watercolours, and in various portraits. This paper will use Crotch and his handedness to help illuminate how left-handedness was viewed at the end of the eighteenth century, and will also consider the handedness of another near-contemporary musical prodigy, Samuel Wesley (1766–1837). In reflecting on Crotch and Wesley, it is necessary to take account of the Enlightenment background in which they were raised, and the prevalent theories about both education and genius in general, and handedness specifically. A further aspect of great interest is that stringed instruments such as the violin, viola and cello are inherently asymmetric, with one hand bowing and the other fingering strings which are themselves arranged asymmetrically. Crotch himself, described from infancy as "self-taught", raises a number of issues about the "natural" or ergonomically "optimal" way of organising instruments, in particular the cello.

Keywords: Children; Music; Musician; Art; Artist; Handedness.

WILLIAM CROTCH AND HIS MEMOIRS

William Crotch was the first Principal of the Royal Academy of Music (founded 1822), a role held concurrently with that of Professor of Music at

---

Address correspondence to: Janet Snowman, Royal Academy of Music, Marylebone Road, London NW1 5HT, UK. E-mail: j.snowman@ram.ac.uk

Thanks to Professor Chris McManus for his encouragement; Philip Olleson, Professor of Historical Musicology, Nottingham University, for sharing his work on Susan Burney; Dr Peter Forsaith, Methodist Studies Unit, Wesley Centre, Oxford; Dr Neil Heyde, cellist of the Kreutzer Quartet and Head of Postgraduate Programmes, Royal Academy of Music, for responding to Crotch's suggestions for stringing of the cello; David Rattray, Instrument Custodian and maker, also RAM, for his help with the violin and bow held by the left-handed child; and to Norma Watt, Assistant Keeper (Fine Art), Norwich Castle Museum and Art Gallery, and the staff of the Norfolk Record Office.

DOI: 10.1080/13576500903201792

Oxford, to which he was appointed at the age of 21. On his resignation from the Academy in 1832 he set about writing his memoirs "extracted by himself and for himself from old letters &tc" (William Crotch, Memoirs, MS11244, Norfolk Record Office). A prodigious musician and artist, when a child he was regarded by the musical and scientific communities, along with Samuel Wesley a few years earlier (and the violinist Thomas Linley before him), as a candidate for the role of the "English Mozart", at a period when English musical composition was perhaps considered provincial.

Crotch's memoirs were substantially supplemented for his early years with his transcription of the major part of a document written by the poet and expert in jurisprudence, the Reverend Alexander Schomberg (1720–1792), whom he had met in June 1783 when, as a child, he had visited Oxford during one of his tours of Britain. These were undertaken from infancy with his mother Isabella, often accompanied by his older step-brother John whom, he noted, "taught me to read by placing notes before me of a piece that I could already play from memory" (MS11244, NRO, July 1781, p. 15). During his arduous journeys Crotch played the violin, harpsichord and organ and also performed on the cello. There is occasional mention of the flute (or flageolet), and a report in the *Norfolk Chronicle* of June 15, 1782 notes of his concert in Alnwick, when he played the piano forte and violin, that some of his drawings were on display during his performance which were "not deficient of merit", and that "he read to the company in a very pleasing manner". A comment in the same paper dated 30th November 1782 also supports the fact that he was "reciting". This word, in the context of musical performance, was first associated in Britain with the pianist and composer Franz Liszt, for example in London on 9th June 1840, so here the child must have been giving verbal recitations.

Schomberg's memoirs were received in 1808, and Crotch writes that "this most amiable and accomplished man, whose memory is dear to all of those who knew him, became and continued throughout his life my main patron and friend ... from this I shall now quote, omitting repetitions and a few circumstances that I am quite aware he never meant should be seen by any eye except my own" (MS11244, NRO, May 1783, p. 20). The family letters and other documents from which Crotch compiled his memoirs do not appear to have survived.

The memoir becomes a diary. Crotch's first comment relates to a document dated July 5, 1775 and the last entry is dated September 19, 1847, just over three months before he died on 29 December 1847. It is difficult to state both when he actually began recording his notes and the actual date when the change occurs to form a diary; by February 1830 he begins to enter information for specific days, including information about meteorological and tidal changes, and by 1832 there is an entry for most days. There are odd points when this also occurs, however, in the 1820s. A tabular style of recording events starts in 1839.

Figure 1 shows a portrait of Crotch composing in mid-life, with a pen in his left hand. In this lithograph, his coat buttons work the "correct" way around for a male, so the lithographic image is correct in what it conveys.

Figure 1. William Crotch MusDoc, Professor of Music at the University of Oxford. Lithograph, artist unknown. A further lithograph of Crotch drawn by W. Derby and engraved by J. Thomson, published in the *European Magazine* on November 1, 1822, the year in which he was appointed Principal of the new Royal Academy of Music, shows him seated with his body facing forward, his head turned slightly to the right and with his left arm and hand depicted, the artist not bothering to draw the right arm below the elbow. An inkwell and manuscript paper are shown alongside. [All figures can be viewed in colour in the online version of the journal.]

CHILDHOOD, ENLIGHTENMENT AND GENIUS

In *Laterality*, Lauren Harris provided a long historical context on advice for parents on attitudes towards handedness in the eighteenth century, noting that many historic writers, including Aristotle and Plato, had offered their own opinions on the subject (Harris, 2003, pp. 99–120). English doctors such as William Cadogan in his *Essay upon Nursing and the Management of Children* (1748) and John Hill (writing under the name of Juliana-Susannah Seymour) in *On the Management and Education of Children* (1754)[1] questioned the idea of swaddling, while also promoting breast-feeding and maternal care out of the hands of wet-nurses and into the arms of the child's own mother. Alongside these works on infant care, writers such as Jean-Jacques Rousseau, especially in his best-selling and influential book *Émile*, offered their own solutions to child-rearing practices. Concerns on topics such as dress, education and manners were also expressed in religious sermons by, for instance, John Wesley in his sermons written or edited for circulation, in particular his Sermon 95 *On the Education of Children,* based on Proverbs 22:6 "Train up a child in the way wherein he should go: And when he is old, he will not depart from it" (John Wesley was the uncle of Samuel Wesley. For Sermon 95, see http://new.gbgm-umc.org/umhistory/wesley/sermons/95/).

The word "Genius" was an idea of Enlightenment. It was used by the eminent critic Friedrich Grimm in a cultural newsletter about the seven-year-old Wolfgang Amadeus Mozart (1756–1791) when the child first performed in Paris in 1763. Mozart, his father Leopold and talented sister, Maria Anna (known as Nannerl, 1751–1829), who played the keyboard and composed, were on their way to London (Starobinski, July 1991). Grimm's contacts had gained the Mozart family introductions to the highest circles and the French court (Anderson, 1989, p. 43; Crowley, 1934, pp. 170–701).

> what is incredible is to see him playing by heart for an hour without interruption and then give himself up to the inspiration of his Genius and to a host of ravishing ideas which he then goes on to develop, one after another, with taste and without confusion. (Quoted in Starobinski, July 1991)

In discussing the eighteenth-century use of this word, Jean Starobinski quotes Denis Diderot's explanation of the term as "a secret, indefinable quality of the soul without which one cannot accomplish anything very great or very beautiful"—the idea of nature at work within the human imagination.

---

[1] Hill had addressed mothers in 1754, "God has given them Genius; but you, my Dear, have the Cultivation of that Gift" (p. 13); . . . "You have all the Care upon your Hands, and you will have all the Glory" (pp. 14–15).

This idea can be seen in the accompanying illustration (Figure 2) to the English writer Daines Barrington's essays on child prodigy musicians in *Miscellanies* (1781), his first-hand accounts of Mozart; Samuel Wesley and his brother Charles; Garrett Wellesley, the 1st Earl of Mornington (1735–1781), father of the Duke of Wellington; and the infant William Crotch. In this English print by Thomas Cook, a vignette showing the image of Mozart after the French print by Jean-Baptiste Delafosse brought to England for circulation by the children's father Leopold (Anderson, 1989, p. 44; the instrument is referred to as a clavecin), an accompanying verse is printed in Greek. The text is from the Homeric *Hymn to Mercury*, and relates infant genius to the young god's invention of the lyre just after his birth. It translates as "But now tell me this, resourceful son of Maia: did these marvellous accomplishments attend you from birth, or did some god or mortal give you this remarkable gift

Figure 2. Wolfgang Amadeus Mozart. Engraving by Thomas Cook, illustration for Daines Barrington's "Account of a very remarkable young musician", *Miscellanies*, published 1781. This is the first portrait of Mozart to appear in a book.

and teach you wondrous singing?" (West, 2003, p. 149) Although the child is shown at a keyboard instrument, the print is inscribed as "Compositeur et Maitre de Musique", here also associating him with the inventiveness of composition.[2]

In his *Leçons de clavecin* (1771) Diderot has the pupil ask:

> "And do you think that eventually one day I'll be able to compose? Composing is the finest skill!" To which the master replies: "And unfortunately it is the only one that cannot be taught: it is the preserve of genius ... If you have genius you will find songs ... Any music which neither paints nor speaks is bad, and you will produce it without genius ... you will swell the ranks of those I call the rag-and-bone men of music". (Quoted in Starobinski, 1991, pp. 18–21)

The idea of genius, imagination and song are also expressed in an image of William Crotch as an infant (Figure 3) in an aquatint published in 1782 by John Sanders of his painting of the child with a Muse and Pegasus (now lost, exhibited at the Royal Academy in 1781). Below the image is an engraved quotation from Joseph Warton's rapturous and passionate *Ode to Fancy* (1744)—"... Lovely Muse, Thy spirit o'er my soul diffuse, O'er all my artless songs preside" (for full text http://rpo.library.utoronto.ca/poem/2259.html). The iconography shows the female Muse with her lyre and caduceus, suggestive from the text as an image of a "noble savage", as the personification of the poetic imagination, with Pegasus, seen behind her, representing the incarnation of poetic inspiration. The imagery is explained in lines 9–13 of the poem:

> O nymph with loosely-flowing hair
> With buskin'd leg, and bosom bare
> Thy waist with myrtle-girdle bound
> Thy brows with Indian feathers crown'd
> Waving in thy snowy hand
> An all-commanding magic wand ...

Fancy (imagination) is evoked at different stages in the 148-line poem, and a banderole within the print holds the word SUADERE (to persuade, perhaps implying "to reason"). The verse suggests linking William's image with poetics as related to Enlightenment ideas of imagination, Sensibility and natural genius. In one of the most representative images of Rousseau's ideas—a child unbound, unswaddled and free of constraints, free-thinking and using his intellect and imagination to discover a new skill for himself—William is shown with bare feet, kneeling on a neo-classical stool, wearing a muslin dress. He is shown looking back at the Muse for approval as she ticks

[2] A copy of the watercolour drawing by Louis Carmontelle, from which the Delafosse print is derived, is in the collection of the British Museum.

Figure 3. William Crotch with a Muse and Pegasus. Aquatint by John Sanders junior published August 6, 1782, after a now-lost painted portrait of 1781. The lines below the image come from Joseph Wharton's *Ode to Fancy* "... Lovely Muse, Thy spirit o'er my soul diffuse, O'er all my artless songs preside". Crotch set the same text to music as an exercise for his MusDoc degree at Oxford in 1799, the full score of which was published. For this painterly print the artist has used an ink in the colour of terracotta. Terracotta chalk was associated both with Old Master drawings and was also used, in particular, by eighteenth-century British and French artists.

off his accomplishment and discoveries in the form of Handel's keyboard "Lessons"; or perhaps he is inventing his own tunes or variations to compare with those of the great Handel? While John Locke's ideas on keeping children's feet wet and cold appear strange to us (Locke, 1692, *Some Thoughts Concerning Education*, section 7), Rousseau thought going barefoot was good for the spirit, to allow creativity and genius to flower in a happy and free child (Rousseau, *Émile* (Foxley, Ed.), p. 30).

INFANCY AND HANDEDNESS

Crotch's comments on his handedness as a child support prevailing popular ideas as purveyed by Rousseau, in particular, who considered that "the only habit the child should be allowed to contract is that of having no habits; let him be carried on either arm, let him be accustomed to offer either hand, to use one or other indifferently ... prepare his way for his control of his liberty and the use of his strength by leaving his body its natural habit, by making him capable of lasting self-control, of doing all that he wills when his will is formed" (Rousseau, *Émile* (Foxley, Ed.), p. 104).

Against an entry in his memoirs for 1779, Crotch wrote:

> At this time I drew ships, soldiers, houses, fiddles and windmills with chalk on the floor ... I was however left-handed—I drew, I fenced and threw a stone with my left hand. I frequented the parades being fond of seeing soldiers and military bands. One day, perceiving that one officer's feet were not properly turned out, I ran from my mother and put it right. (MS11244, NRO, p. 9)

With regard to this last point Susan Burney, a daughter the composer and music historian Dr Charles Burney, in her unpublished diaries, recorded after a visit from William and his mother on 15 October 1779 that "nothing escapes him either that passes before his eyes or in conversation—after taking off the marching of some soldiers he turn'd his toes & knees in, & very gravely s^{d} 'but my Papa walks so'" (Susan Burney, 1779–1790, Folio 15). This visit must have followed Crotch's engagement with the soldiers and, rather than being purely of directional concern, there must have been a genuine cause for worry about his father's gait and perhaps mobility. A few years later he conveyed his concern for his own knees being exposed ... "Farewell then, jacket and trowsers, and welcome short-kneed breeches and long-skirted coats (oh no! not welcome to me—they exposed the malformation of my knees to the derision of the world. My father had the same defect but not to the same degree)" (MS11244, NRO June 2nd, 1787, p. 65. He also mentions his weak knees and ankles in 1792, p. 77, though referring to the present date).

Two separate entries for 1783 allude to his use of both hands, with predominance of the left for some activities, and Figure 4 shows his handwriting specimens which accompany the comments in the second paragraph:

> I wrote to my father from Blandford January 9th, but my hand seems to have been guided. I used to write with both hands indeed, I still make Memoranda with my left hand if my pencil happens to be in that, and about the year 1788 having cut my thumb of my right hand, I learned to write backwards with my left hand to be read in a looking glass. (MS11244, NRO December 17, 1783)

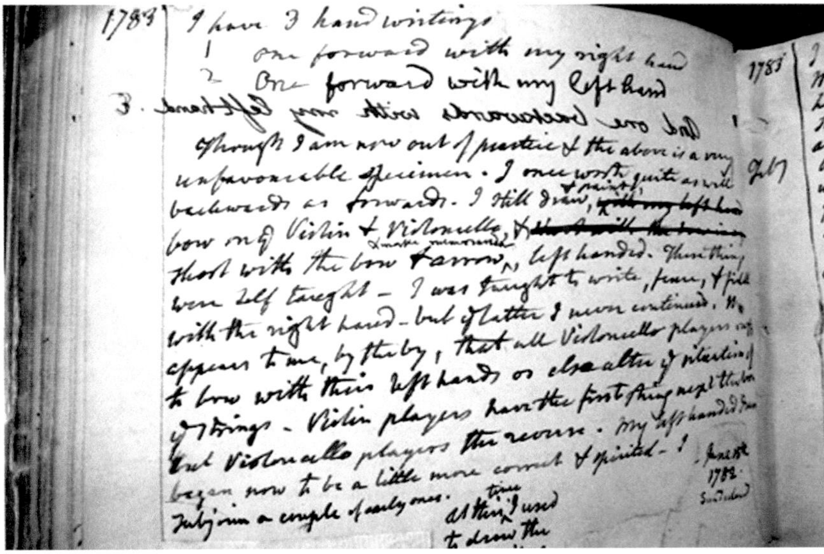
1783 I have 3 handwritings
1 One forward with my right hand
2 One forward with my left hand
Though I am now out of practice & the above is a very unfavourable specimen. I once wrote quite as well backwards as forwards. I still draw, paint, ~~with my left hand~~ bow my Violin & Violoncello & ~~shoot with the bow~~ shoot with the bow & arrow, & make memoranda left handed. These things were self taught – I was taught to write, fence, & fiddle with the right hand – but of latter I never continued. It appears to me, by the by, that all Violoncello players ought to bow with their left hands or else alter the direction of the strings – Violin players have the first string next the bow but Violoncello players the reverse. My left handed drawing began now to be a little more correct & spirited – !

Figure 4. Examples by William Crotch, when an adult, of his three styles of handwriting when younger. Norfolk Record Office MS11244.

I have three handwritings. Although I am now out of practice and the above is a very unfavourable specimen. I once wrote quite as well backwards as forwards. I still draw and paint with my left hand [the last four words crossed through], bow my violin and violoncello and ["shoot with the bow and arrow" crossed through], shoot with the bow and arrow and make memoranda left-handed. These things were self-taught. I was taught to write, fence and fiddle with the right hand. It appears to me, by the way, that all violoncello players ought to bow with the left hand or else alter the direction of the strings. Violin players have the first string next [the] bow, and violoncello players the reverse. My left-handed drawing now began to be a little more correct if spirited! (MS11244, NRO, 1783)

THE "SELF-TAUGHT" INFANT PHAENOMENON

Dr Charles Burney had taken it upon himself to examine Crotch, reporting his findings to the anatomist, obstetrician and antiquary Dr William Hunter of the Royal Society in his *Account of an Infant Musician*, read on February 18, 1779 (Ribeiro, 1991).[3]

[3] Alvar Ribeiro (p. 269) notes that "a fragment of Burney's manuscript memoirs record that on 14 February 'The Honable Daines Barrington and Dr W. Hunter came to my house to hear the paper read, which was afterwards printed in the *Philosophical Transactions*'". A letter from Burney to Hunter dated 29 July 1774, prior to Crotch's birth, refers to a shared an interest in an earlier unnamed child (p. 171).

Burney, in comparing Crotch with the equally-prodigious Samuel Wesley, nine years older, noted that, as with Mozart, Wesley had the advantage of his highly talented older brother Charles and his musical mother. "Before he was six-years-old", he recorded, "he [Samuel Wesley] arrived at such knowledge in music that his extemporary performance on keyed instruments ... was so masterly in point of invention, modulation and accuracy of execution, as to surpass in many particulars the attainments of most professors at any period of their lives ... Crotch, left to nature, has not only been without instruction, but good models of imitation, while Mozart and Westley [his spelling], on the contrary may be said to have been nursed in good music" (Burney, 1779, *Account of an Infant Musician,* p. 203).

At the same time as demonstrating his own awareness and concern for the child's general infant well-being, Burney also mentions Crotch's use of his left hand for drawing:

> ... he appears to me possessed of a general intelligence beyond his age; and he has discovered a genius and inclination for drawing, nearly as strong as for music; for whenever he is not at an instrument, he usually employs himself in sketching, with his left-hand, houses, churches, ships or animals, in his rude and wild manner, with chalk on the floor, or upon whatever other plain surface he is allowed to scrawl ... painters may, perhaps, form some judgement of his music by his drawings. (Burney, *Account*, p. 193)

He continues

> ... nor does he, as yet, seem a subject for instruction; for till his reason is sufficiently mature to comprehend and retain the precepts of a master and something like a wish for information appears, by a ready and willing obedience to his injunctions, trammels of rules would but disgust and if forced upon him, destroy the miraculous parts of his self-taught instruction ... it must not be forgotten that this child is equally delighted with drawing as with music.

Burney had a large family of his own, and his comments in the above passage, while reflecting the fashionable ideas of John Locke with regard to "reasoning", more echo Rousseau,[4] who commented:

> "Reason with children" was Locke's chief maxim ... and I hardly think it is justified by its results; those children who have been constantly reasoned with strike me as exceedingly silly. Of all man's faculties, reason, which is, so to speak, compounded of all the rest, is the last and choicest growth, and it is

[4] Burney had translated and produced Rousseau's opera *Le Devin de Village* as *The Cunning Man*, Drury Lane, 1766; and Rousseau had been a subscriber to Burney's *A General History of Music*, published in 4 vols 1776–1789. Crotch mentions his own familiarity with Rousseau's opera (1787, MS11244, p. 70, NRO).

> this you would use for the child's early training ... you begin at the wrong end, you make the end the means ... nature would have them children before they are men ... if we try to invert this order we shall produced forced fruit etc—childhood has its own ways of seeing etc ... indeed what use would reason be to him at that age. It is the curb of strength and the child does not need the curb ... (Rousseau, *Émile*, p. 315)

This idea of being "left to nature" or "self-taught", as Burney notes, again reflects Rousseau's equally-fashionable educational ideas relating to the child learning by discovering for himself, and this phrase was to accompany Crotch throughout his young life. It is of prime importance when considering his own comments and approach to his handedness and his musical performance on, and handling of, his string instruments, the cello and violin, throughout his life. The description "self-taught" is also printed on the cover of his published concerto for harpsichord or pianoforte (Figure 5), dedicated to Burney, and advertisements for his performances in Bath in 1783 (see for example *Bath Chronicle*, No. 1636, article 3b, 1783; No 741, article 3d, 1784) and Bristol in 1784 frequently refer to him as the "self-taught" musical child. Figure 6 shows a programme for a benefit concert which he gave at the Freemason's Tavern, Great Queen Street, in 1785, engaging in a duo with the eminent German violinist and orchestral leader Johann Peter Salomon, playing a work by Handel for the organ and also his own composition for the instrument.

CROTCH'S COMMENTS ON STRINGED INSTRUMENTS AND HANDEDNESS

Twice Crotch comments on the physical stringing of instruments to be played by left-handed instrumentalists (MS11244, NRO, 1783 and 1787). In considering physical performance on an instrument such as the violin, cello and viola and its acoustical construction, if adapted for a left-handed player the bass bar would have to be reversed, the bridge re-shaped and the peg holes would also require alteration to allow the instrument to be played on the right shoulder rather than the left. The stringing and bowing of each of these stringed instruments presents different challenges to a performer.

Cellist Neil Heyde of the Kreutzer Quartet (personal communication, Dr Neil Heyde, Royal Academy of Music, 2008), provides the following comments on Crotch's suggestions on the stringing of the cello for a left-handed performer:

Figure 5. Concerto for harpsichord and pianoforte, with an accompaniment for two violins and bass, published in London, 1784 and dedicated to Dr Charles Burney. Note the printed inscription, "the self taught musical child".

Crotch's proposal that cellists should play with the first (i.e., highest) string next to the bow is perhaps unsurprising for someone self-taught, and for whom handedness was clearly an issue. There are a couple of anomalies in the violin family that mean that the player's physical relationship with the larger instruments—strung in the same manner as the violin despite being held in reverse—is quite different. A spread four-note chord on the violin has the movement of the bow mirroring the natural arc of the arm as it moves from the lowest to highest string, with gravity working in tandem. The same chord played conventionally on the cello demands an "unnatural" lifting against the arc of the arm and against the pull of gravity. Stringing the instrument in reverse resolves this problem—as Crotch also did by playing the instrument strung conventionally but with the bow in the left instead of right hand. This is something that could only be addressed pedagogically at the earliest stages of learning the instrument.

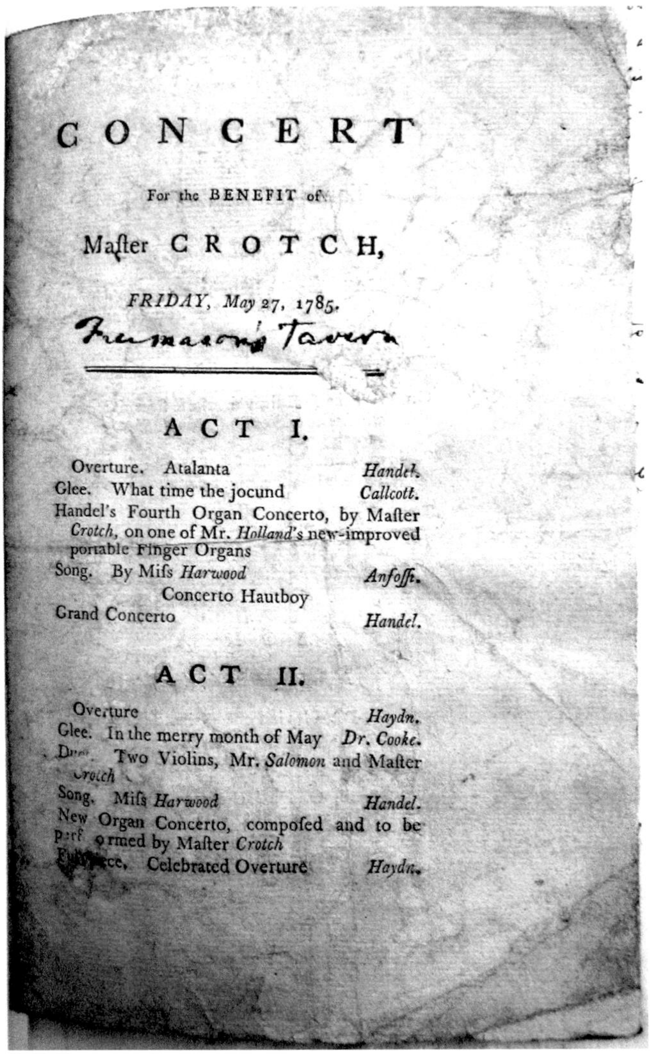

CONCERT

For the BENEFIT of

Maſter CROTCH,

FRIDAY, May 27, 1785.

Freemason's Tavern

ACT I.

Overture. Atalanta *Handel.*
Glee. What time the jocund *Callcott.*
Handel's Fourth Organ Concerto, by Maſter *Crotch*, on one of Mr. *Holland's* new-improved portable Finger Organs
Song. By Miſs *Harwood* *Anfoſſi.*
Concerto Hautboy
Grand Concerto *Handel.*

ACT II.

Overture *Haydn.*
Glee. In the merry month of May *Dr. Cooke.*
Duet. Two Violins, Mr. *Salomon* and Maſter *Crotch*
Song. Miſs *Harwood* *Handel.*
New Organ Concerto, compoſed and to be perf ormed by Maſter *Crotch*
Full piece, Celebrated Overture *Haydn.*

Figure 6. Concert programme, Freemasons Tavern, 27 May 1785. Norfolk Record Office MS11238. Johann Peter Salomon, with whom Crotch played a duo, was later responsible for bringing Haydn to England. Also noted is a performance of the child's own organ concerto.

While Crotch's proposal makes much sense from the perspective of the bow arm, it presents problems for the fingering hand. It is preferable that the highest string is nearest the hand itself, both for the fingering of melodic passages (which are often on that string alone) and for the fingering of chords, in which the shortest (little) finger is preferably reserved for the top string. Thus, while the reverse stringing assists the large motor movements of the bow arm (usually the dominant "hand") it creates problems for the smaller movements of the fingering. The violin is unusual in that the fingering hand reaches around the instrument so both it and the bow arm can approach the highest string from the same side. It is worth noting that members of the viol family, which predates the violin, were all played in the "reverse" position typical of the cello, so there were even at the beginning of the nineteenth century several hundred years of tradition that accepted the bow arm "compromise". Although the upward motion of the arm as the strings become higher is somewhat unnatural from a physiological perspective it is easily learnt and the correspondence between higher pitches and physical lifting is peculiarly effective and makes for an interesting contrast in expressive effect with the violin.

CROTCH AND HIS VIOLIN

Barrington in *Miscellanies* provides an early description of Crotch's violin playing, recording his own testing of the uncooperative infant William on 10th December 1778, this time in the presence of the 15-year-old Samuel Wesley who joined in the event, at one time testing the smaller child's ear with a cracked violin (Barrington, *Some Account of Little Crotch*, pp. 311–317). Barrington had in 1770 also reported to the Royal Society on his examination of the young Wolfgang Amadeus Mozart during the family's presence in London in 1764–1765.[5] His testing of Mozart was interrupted by the child running off to play with a cat and to trot around the room on a hobby-horse. As well as demonstrating the growing interest in scientific inquiry, Barrington's article also provides an early example of the new attitude towards children, their abilities, interests and achievements, including the concept of "childishness".

> Samuel Wesley takes little Crotch much under his protection ... the child has lately taught himself to play on the violin, which he holds as a violoncello and touches only with two of his fingers. He likewise judges most accurately of what are called extremes on the violin ... ear exquisite. I desired Master Wesley to give the treble only, and told Crotch that he could not add the bass to it; on this, the urchin sat down by Master Wesley, accompanying with the proper bass this same tune, transposed in the minor third through the whole octave ... the child both looks and is very intelligent in other matters which do not relate to music, and draws in a bold masterly way with chalk on the floor—one of the most favourite object to represent is a violin, which he forms instantaneously with a few strokes. I need scarcely mention the difficulty of reversing the two sides and S's [f-holes], which must be very obvious to penmen as well as painters. The boy likewise succeeds very well in the hasty outline of a ship.

[5] Barrington. "Account of a very remarkable young musician". Letter written to Matthew Maty, MC, Secretary of the Royal Society. *Philosophical Transactions of the Royal Society,* Vol. 60, December 1770, p. 54. XIII (written and received by the Society, November 28, 1769).

It is here though where Crotch, when later transcribing documents, seems to have confused Barrington's report, with no mention of his left hand, with Burney's—unless the family had further papers and letters available. He comments on an entry from 1778:

> This is confirmed by the Honourable Daines Barrington in his volume of *Miscellanies*, printed in 1781, in which he gives a description of my performances which he had witnessed on Dec 10 1778 and of my subsequent attempts to play the violin holding it downwards like a violoncello and bowing with my left hand. He says I stopped it very accurately in tune, making use of smaller intervals than those of equal semi-tones ... keyed instruments that I might have heard of my brother John who had been instructed on the violin by Mr Wafer. (MS11244, NRO, February 1780, p. 11)

Interestingly, as the Englishman Barrington commented on Mozart's engagement with a cat, so the German writer and philosopher Georg Lichtenberg noted the same of Crotch in his description of the English child in his *Göttingen Pocket Almanac*, relating that next to the organ and a piano, "a cat seems to afford him the most entertainment". Lichtenberg's essay is accompanied by a silhouette image of William at the keyboard (Figure 7), his enlarged head a perfect subject for the physiognomist. However the

Figure 7. Silhouette of William Crotch at three years and seven months. Reproduced in the *Gottingen Pocket Almanac,* 1780. The small publication aimed to spread the philosophy of the Enlightenment.

writer's text goes for a more cultural option: "There is almost no need of a reminder that the almost bullet-shaped form of the head is due to the hair, which the English comb down on all sides of their boys' heads and which, where it has been cut short as, for example, on the forehead, takes an inward curve which is smaller than that of the head, and this accounts for such a roundness in the shadow" (the name by which a silhouette was known).[6]

A "LEFT-HANDED" VIOLIN AND PLAYING LEFT-HANDED

Crotch records that in 1783 he was presented with a new instrument made by the London-based instrument-maker and inventor, John Joseph Merlin (1735–1803), a member of Burney's circle.

> I had a concert at Nottingham. While at this place I received a small violin made especially for me by Merlin with the strings placed contrary to the usual order that I might play it at the shoulder—thus left-handed. It was terribly well intended by somebody but very absurd as I had no chance of ever producing a good tone of what was but a degree better than a dancing master's kit. I soon learned to play it, however. (MS11244, NRO, April 7, 1783)

His comments suggest that until this time he had continued to play the violin pointing downward like a cello, as described earlier by Barrington. During his visit to nearby Leicester, he is recorded on 7 April 1783 as having played harpsichord and violin (Kroeger, 1988, pp. 449).

Merlin was described as the "ingenious mechanick", although he also described himself on a patent in 1774 as a "mathematical instrument maker"; he is known to have played the violin and is said also to have invented roller skates (Merlin catalogue, pp. 106–107). He moved in London's best musical circles and his keyboard instruments were played by those such as J.C. Bach and Burney himself. Thomas Gainsborough's portrait of the oboist Johann Christian Fischer (Royal Collection) shows the keyboard clearly marked "Joseph Merlin Londini Fecit", and his portrait of Merlin hangs at Kenwood House. Schomberg relates a later encounter in June 1785 between Merlin and the young Crotch at a soirée held at Burney's home, where they must have met for the first time:

> I knew you would be delighted with Merlin and he was not displeased with you—why you must have hit it off prodigiously together ... you remember the

[6] Georg Christoph Lichtenberg, William Crotch, das Musikalische Wunderkind in *Vermischte Schriften* Vol. 5, *Gottingen Almanac*, 1780, pp. 258–266. Typed transcription in English by Arthur Mann, (n.d.). pp. 8–19, MS11092, NRO.

> harpsichord with drums—a lady was trying it and you stood by and put your hands on one of the stops to pull it out more fully—played *Hallelujah Chorus* and none of Merlin's own magic could have produced greater astonishment. (MS11244, NRO, 1785)

Merlin also sold violins, though it is thought that some string instruments which bear his stamp are known to have been made, at least in part, by specialists, and it is suggested that he commissioned other makers to work for him. He is also said to have attempted to solve problems faced by musicians especially in relation to tuning (Merlin catalogue, p. 93). While some instruments may have been made for general sale, others, including perhaps that made for Crotch, were also produced for private patrons, and only one of his violins is known to have survived.

Reverend Schomberg wrote, having just met William in 1783:

> ... you had been in Oxford for some weeks before I could be prevailed upon to hear you—a child tinkling on the keys of a harpsichord and scraping imperfect tunes on a diminutive violin. (MS11244, NRO, p. 28)

Crotch seems to have thought about this description when transcribing this paragraph, as he has crossed through the word "violin" and replaced it with "fiddle", perhaps as a way of recalling his own feelings about the instrument and its qualities. It is not known whether this is due to Schomberg's original transcription, or Crotch's decision to edit. However; from the essence of the description, it does seem that it could at this stage have been the Merlin instrument he was playing. Schomberg noted that:

> His style of fingering [keyboard] is very singular but at present it is a style of necessity to him ... it certainly will be worthwhile without delay to teach him to bow with the right hand. (MS11244, NRO p. 22)

Crotch, a few pages on, comments against a date in 1786:

> Mahon (leader of the Cambridge Orchestra) agreeable to the hint thrown out by Dr Schomberg and endeavoured to teach me the violin with the right hand as had Mr Picktain, the leader at Bath and I think my friend Hague also—what a provoking brat I must have been. I could learn nothing—I could teach myself anything ... whenever I was taught to draw I failed; even my writing was good for nothing until I chose to imitate of my own accord a handwriting which I took a fancy to. I never conquered the difficulty of playing the violin *as required* [my italics]. I therefore abandoned the little fiddle and played any violin I'd get downwards like a violoncello, bowing with the left hand, and this I have continued ever since. (MS11244, NRO, November 1786, p. 55 (rubbed))

Figure 8 illustrates the above point and shows a later drawing of Crotch by his artist friend William Delamotte, with a subsequent comment in ink in the hand of the University of Cambridge organist Arthur Mann who at one time owned it, "playing the violin as only he knows how". It is not possible to see the stringing nor the pegs of the image. This drawing is of particular interest when considering the absence of any mention of problems with the playing of his cello when a child, and with a description of 1802 by Burney's friend, the Reverend Thomas Twining, rector of

Figure 8. William Crotch drawn by his friend, the landscape artist William Delamotte. The comments in ink on the drawing are in the hand of Arthur H. Mann (1876–1929), the University Organist at Cambridge, who collected much of the material now in the Norfolk Record Office in preparation for a book about Crotch which he never published. Norfolk Record Office MS11244.

St Mary's Colchester, also a historian and musician. Twining recorded his astonishment at hearing and seeing the adult Crotch playing the cello at a concert in Passenham, Essex.[7]

> On the Monday following, July 19th, came Dr Hague [Charles Hague] from Oxford and Dr Crotch (from Cambridge)—Dr Upton, who was to have been here, could not come ... Dr Crotch more than supplied his place, as besides his being an excellent violoncello, his accompaniment on the piano was a great treat. I have often had great enjoyment of music here, but never so great as now, particularly from our quartets, which went better than I ever bore a part in. I wished for you to have seen and heard a very extraordinary thing; a man neither proferring the instrument nor in practice, bowing with his left hand and fingering with his right on a violoncello strung as usual, playing the most difficult basses as Haydn, as well or nearly so, as any master. All so correct, so perfectly in time, and giving so exactly the effect as intended by the author. But his ear is so quick and his knowledge of composition so good that he really can play a passage by the mere guess of musical instinct. With more effect that most other players do by rule, and teaching and practice.

While Crotch continued into old age to wonder about the stringing of instruments, he continued to play his cello as he did his "upside down" violin, in a position in which he was most comfortable by choice, with normal stringing though with his left arm, and without pressure from others to change to a right-handed bowing arm nor, where the cello was concerned, reversing his strings. The use of the term "as required" in his note of November 1786, does convey frustration with external and not family pressures, and perhaps accounts for the absence of the violin and presence of the cello in the portrait of him aged ten or eleven by Sir William Beechey, mentioned below.

THE INFANT PHAENOMENON AT THE KEYBOARD

In looking at early engraved prints of Crotch as an infant, one of the most popular and perhaps the most circulated image (Figure 9) accompanied a long article in *The London Magazine*, April 1779, where the writer observed him "at the age of three years and eight months 'at Mrs Hart's, Milliner, Piccadilly, every day between 1–3 in publick". There are three states of the print, with minor alterations in hatching and colour of the paper. The one printed within the magazine is titled *The Musical Phaenomenon* and shows

[7] Thomas Twining and Richard Twining, p. 245. Arthur Mann (n.d.), in transcribing the above (MS11201, pp. 144–144b, NRO) notes that "I cannot understand how anybody could <u>on a violincello constructed and tuned in the ordinary way</u> bow with his left hand and finger with his right".

Figure 9. "The Musical Phaenomenon". Illustration in *The London Magazine*, 1779, showing Crotch's well-lit left hand and forearm to demonstrate his particular musical skill. There are three states of this image, which also circulated as a separate print. The variations are in the captioning, colour of paper on which the print was produced, and slight changes to the curtain in one version with barely-discernible variations in hatching. The portrait itself remains unchanged.

Crotch turned to the left seated at a double-manual organ with his feet resting on a footstool. As with the print brought to England by the Mozart family, this print was also separately produced and sold in music shops ahead of the family's visits to various towns and cities, acting as both a promotional tool and a way of making extra cash.

> A large organ is placed upon the centre of the room, against the wainscot; it is raised upon a stage about two feet from the floor, and a semicircular iron rod is fixed to it as to secure him in his seat and separates him from the company. An arm chair is placed upon this stage, and in it a common very small matted chair which his mother fastens behind with a handkerchief to the other, that he may not fall out, for he is a wanton, and full of antick tricks in the short intervals from playing. A book is placed before him, as it was a musick book, and strangers in a distant part of the room may mistake it for such; but it is no more than a magazine or some other pamphlet with an engraved frontispiece; this he looks at and emotes himself with the figures in the plate, while he is playing any tune, or striking into his own harmony. In short, he laughs, prattles and looks about at the company, at the same time keeping his little hands employed on the keys, and playing with so much unconcern that you would be tempted to think he did but know what he was doing. He appears to be fondest of solemn basses, and church music, particularly the 104th psalm. As soon as he has finished a regular tune, or part of a tune, or played some little fancy notes of his own, he flops and has the pranks of a wanton boy; some of the company then generally give him a cake, an apple or an orange, to induce him to play again ... unless you touch the pride of his little heart by telling him he has forgot such a tune, or he cannot play it, this seldom fails of producing the effect and he is sure to play it with additional spirit. After playing more than an hour, he desired to be taken down, and to have a piece of chalk, he then entertained himself and the company with drawing outlines on the floor ... (*The London Magazine and Gentlemans Monthly Intelligencer*, April 1779, pp.; cf. also Burney *Account*, p. 198)

The engraving provides a case where a pictorial item is best understood in terms of the text which it illustrates: whereas images of children or others at keyboards, and all other images of Crotch in his early years, including two silhouettes (see for instance Figure 7), usually show both hands, in this print only his left arm is shown, brightly lit, in celebration of the young child's unusual musical facility with his left hand. The writer concludes his article thus:

> We forgot to observe that if any person plays a tune he never heard with the right hand on his organ, he will put a base to it with his left hand; that he will name every note you strike on an organ or any other instrument, and he always knows if anyone plays out of tune.

CROTCH THE INFANT ARTIST

To illustrate his left-handed drawing as a child, with a comment that it had become "more spirited" by this time, Crotch has attached within the text of his memoirs two small pencil drawings, linear sailing rigs, dated in ink

"Edinburgh Sept. 1781" and "June 15th 1782, Sunderland" (Figure 10) (MS 11244, NRO 1783, unpaginated). Burney's earlier observation had recorded him as having a "love of drawing windmills, ships and violins", and boats and windmills are also shown in his drawing books on the floor in two prints, that by James Fittler commissioned by the child's mother and dedicated to the local Norwich MP, Sir Harbord Harbord (Figure 11) and the "Muse and Pegasus" print (Figure 3). The painting of small linear watercolours of boats can also be seen to have continued until his death, illustrating his life-long interest in the weather, cloud formation and tides (Figure 12).

Interestingly, in a further charming watercolour (Figure 13) done in an album when on holiday in 1844 (MS 11070, NRO), a rather naïve sketch of a "Sunday painter" type and not of the quality of his work held in national collections, a small child appears, perhaps in fancy dress and wearing an over-large hat, waving a sword in her left hand—an unconscious act on behalf of the artist? Domenico Angelo had, in his *School of Fencing* (1787, p. 80), suggested that

> I am of the opinion that a fencing master should accustom his scholars to fence with both hands; (that is to say), that when the pupil has learnt to handle his foil well with the right hand, he should be exercised with the left hand. This practice will be found hard to every body, but with a good will and by taking pains, you may attain to a degree of perfection which will be advantageous to yourself, and will do honour to him that teaches.

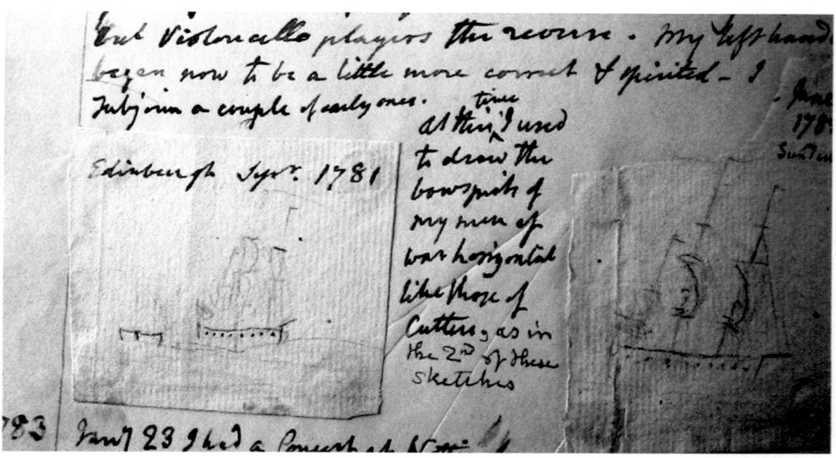

Figure 10. Two pencil drawings of boats by William Crotch, dated by him in ink 1781 and 1782. He notes "My left-handed drawings began now to be a little more correct if spirited—I subjoin a couple of early ones". Norfolk Record Office, MS11244.

Figure 11. (also Figure 14) William Crotch by James Fittler, 1778. In this print, commissioned by his mother, Isabella, the child's drawings are shown lower left, and show his affinity at an early age with sketching boats and windmills (see also Figure 3). On the right, among the musical trophies, is a lyre reminiscent of the instrument depicted by the sculptor Louis-Francois Roubiliac for the famous marble statue of the composer George Frederic Handel. The statue, made for and exhibited at Vauxhall Gardens in 1738, is now in the Victoria and Albert Museum. The music over William's arm is fictive. The print is noted as being "Publish'd according to the Act of Parliament, May 12th, 1779, by Mrs Crotch, near St. James's Street, Piccadilly".

Perhaps with his vivid youthful interest in theatrical productions Crotch would have enjoyed this publication (1787). Here, with this small drawing, he himself has also illustrated unconsciously the early ideas of Plato, who also

Figure 12. Schooners drawn by William Crotch, 1840. From a sketch book, Norfolk Record Office MS11080. [All figures can be viewed in colour in the online version of the journal.]

"advised against handedness training in any form and instead recommended methods for enhancing ambidexterity" (Harris, 2003, p. 100), enjoying this one aspect of his early life under which he himself had control, as a child from a working family blessed also by no interference from nannies.

Figure 13. Watercolour by William Crotch showing a small left-handed fencer in fancy dress, 1840 (see detail). Norfolk Record Office MS11080.

AN INFANT SELF-PORTRAIT WITH MUSICAL INSTRUMENTS

Schomberg describes Crotch at their first meeting in 1783 as having been curled up in a corner of a sofa with one of the publisher Newbery's popular little books for children, the story of *Robin Goodfellow*. Crotch's own first "musical comedy" on this subject at the age of six is accompanied by small drawings of musical instruments.[8] He has "updated" (Figure 14), complete with feathered hat, the engraved portrait of himself by Fittler (Figure 11), one of the earliest printed British images of celebrity which, as well as recording his infant fame, functioned as today's family or promotional photograph, being passed around to those associated with the child and family, including his patrons. Here, the six-year-old has surrounded himself with musical trophies—a violin, cello, harpsichord in good perspective, an organ and flute or flageolet—on all of which he performed, and he has also added, within an escutcheon or shield, three lyres, creating his own heraldic device. While his decoration of the letters forming his name run right to left, the bows of both cello and violin are set left to right. Although drawn a couple of years later than his outlines of instruments as first described by Barrington, here his image of the cello also provides an example of his execution of sound-holes (f-holes) in the form of an S and reversed S, the latter to better effect.

He may also have been introduced to a further popular book for infant children, *The Drawing School for Little Masters and Misses* by Master Michael Angelo (Richard Johnson), published in 1773, which was designed to teach them the rudiments of drawing, with sketches to be copied and drawing tips, with the idea of fostering artistic development of "prodigies". As the musical community hoped to find an English Mozart, this book aimed to contribute to "produce artists equal to those of Italy". The fact that learning was to be undertaken "without the assistance of a teacher" reflects both Locke's ideas of "fusing amusement with instruction" and Rousseau's ideas of learning by discovering—another "self-taught" approach. While there is no mention of handedness in the text, the frontispiece (Figure 15) shows an engraved portrait of His Royal Highness Prince Edward (Edward Augustus, Duke of Kent and Strathearn (1767–1820, father of Queen Victoria), his left hand prominently holding a book. Again incorporating the style appropriated from a biography of a "famous man", not dissimilar to William's image of himself, this portrait also makes use of a stone monumental frame. Here though, it is the engraver who may have transferred the image in reverse after a drawing, painting or circulating print of the young prince; a portrait of the

[8] *Robin Goodfellow or Fairy land [and Fortunio]* written by W. Crotch. Holograph n.d. ms. 51 p. With incidental music for the plays. Ms. note on cover: Comedy by Dr Crotch at 6 years old. m.b. (Arblay, F. d').

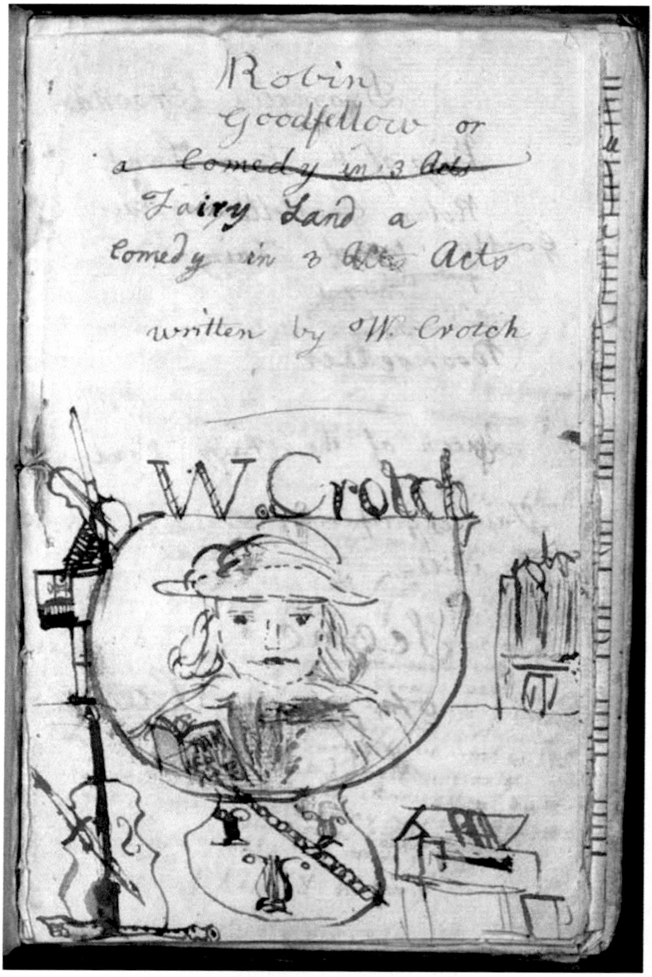

Figure 14. Frontispiece drawing with self-portrait by William Crotch for his musical comedy *Robin Goodfellow*. Fanny D'Arblay (Burney) papers, Berg Collection, New York Public Library. 6.5 × 4.4 ins. Courtesy of The New York Public Library.

prince in the Royal Collection, attributed to Francis Cotes, ca. 1768, show him as a baby holding flowers in his right hand.

A PORTRAIT OF SAMUEL WESLEY, 1778

Alongside the two portraits in the Royal Academy of Music's Duke's Hall of William Crotch as a child, one by John Sanders (1778) and the other by Sir

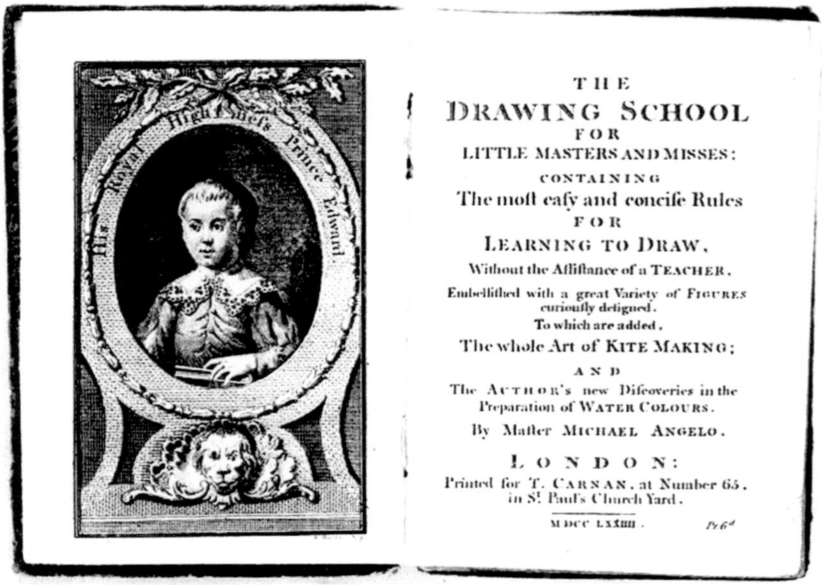

Figure 15. Engraved frontispiece to *The Drawing School for Little Masters and Mistresses* by Master Michael Angelo.

William Beechey (1785), is a portrait of Samuel Wesley by the evangelical artist John Russell (1777), later Crayon Painter to George III and the Prince of Wales.

Russell's portrait shows Wesley composing (Figure 16). He is clothed in a "suit of court scarlet" and handsome buckled shoes, and he is posed in the style of an elegant young gentleman amid fine gilded furnishings, in front of an organ. His hair is natural and fashionably shoulder-length, and he gazes out, his head slightly inclined towards the work he is writing, with the biblical text of the music, Psalm 39, published in the same year—"*Anthem Solo—I said that*" ... [I will heed my ways, lest I sin with my tongue; I will set a curb on my mouth] positioned to offer the text and its meaning to the viewer. This is also conveyed by the position and gesture of his left hand, and he holds a quill in his right. A bound copy of his work inscribed *Ruth, an Oratorio by Samuel Wesley aged eight* years (British Library Add 34997 8 Sept. 26 Oct. 1774, presented by Samuel Wesley to William Boyce), lies propped against the desk—the artist has rotated this object showing it as portrait, instead of its actual landscape shape. Russell's experiment with grand design could also be explained as celebratory, with the concurrent publication of the child's first keyboard sonatas Op. 1, in late 1777, and it may also have had a "pre-emptive" commemorative aspect to it as well.

Figure 16. Samuel Wesley by John Russell, oil on canvas, 1777. His oratorio *Ruth*, the manuscript of which is in the British Library, stands propped up against the desk. Here he is shown composing his anthem to words from Psalm 39, published in the same year. The text shows the words "I said I will take heed to my ways". Duke's Hall, Royal Academy of Music.

Samuel came from a well connected but not wealthy background and, of the eight children of the hymn writer Charles Wesley senior and his wife, Samuel was the youngest of the three who survived, and between him and his sister there were seven years and many deaths (Kassler & Olleson, 2001, pp. 3–6).

John Russell in his treatise *Elements of Painting with Crayons* (1772) suggests to the artist that:

> in making choice of a good subject ... he should be directed in his choice by the opinion of the most experienced Artists, who all recommend the Study of the Antique and other approved Plaister Figures previous to the drawing after living models ... to draw from a living Figure without having first studied the antique is no less absurd than to attempt to understand the Classicks without a previous knowledge of the Rules of Grammar. (Russell, *Elements*, p. 9)

In his writing he also shows concern for the "general sway of a figure", to "preserve the centre of gravity; which is that line always perpendicular from the pit between the Collar-bones to the Heel of the Foot on which the Figure rests", with an asterisked note that "It must be remarked that all graceful Figures stand on one foot only" (Russell, *Elements*, p. 14).

THE BRISTOL PORTRAIT CALLED SAMUEL WESLEY

A portrait hanging in the music room in the former Wesley family home in Bristol shows a young male violinist, a pleasing child of about eight, with a large violin held in playing position in his right hand and a bow in his left. Slightly-built and dressed in a scarlet suit, he stands in front of organ pipes looking at the viewer, his dark eyes and long hair contrasting with his white frilled collar and the decorative buttons on his coat and waistcoat (Figure 17). The portrait hangs in the house where Samuel spent his early childhood and where his mother, Sally, provided his earliest music education, teaching both himself and his organist and composer brother Charles junior (1757–1834) to play the harpsichord. A portrait of Charles at the keyboard, also by John Russell, hangs on an adjoining wall.

The child's large violin may have been depicted as such to exaggerate his own cleverness by making him appear younger than he was. This is not unusual in that Mozart, when in London, was said to be a year younger than his actual age, a ploy later used by Liszt's father. The painting, whose provenance is not however known, is thought to have been procured by Edward Lamplough, a London underwriter and deputy-chairman of Lloyds, who was largely responsible financially for the acquisition of Wesley's New Room Chapel in Bristol along with many furnishings and other items, in the 1920s. The chapel had been sold by the Methodists in the early nineteenth century. Any documentation concerning the purchase of the painting, if there was any, appears to have been lost, and it has not been possible to examine the rear of the work for old sale or gallery labels (personal communication from Dr Peter Forsaith, Coordinator, Methodist Centre, Oxford, responsible for the Centre's archives, library and art collections). It has been suggested, however, that this particular portrait may also be by Russell.

Figure 17. Portrait called Samuel Wesley, artist unknown, oil on canvas. Charles Wesley House, Bristol. Reproduced with kind permission of The Trustees of John Wesley's Chapel (The New Room), Bristol; the image was provided through Dr Peter Forsaith at the Oxford Centre for Methodism and Church History, Oxford Brookes University.

The handwriting of both Samuel and Charles Wesley Jr was examined a few years ago with the idea of trying to establish whether either brother was left-handed in the hope that it would help to establish the identity of the child holding the left-handed violin, but the results proved inconclusive (personal communication from Professor Philip Olleson, Nottingham University, 2008).

A PORTRAIT OF WILLIAM CROTCH, 1785

Sir William Beechey's portrait of Crotch (Figure 18), painted in Norwich, was hung at the Royal Academy exhibition in that same year. A notice in *The Bury and Norwich Post* recorded that "Our modern Tinteret's pencil is now engaged on a portrait of the musical wonder, Master Crotch, for the next Exhibition at Somerset House". William is depicted seated in an elegant dark green, gold-braided chair, composing, a quill in his right hand, deep in thought and looking upwards for inspiration. Organ pipes are just discernible at the rear. In contrast with the gentlemanly Samuel, he is posed with his legs athwart and he appears involved in his own world. Here Beechey has used this informal pose as a representation of how children actually behave. The child's long hair falls softly around his white collar and

Figure 18. William Crotch by Sir William Beechey, oil on canvas, 1785. Painted around his neck, hanging on a blue ribbon, is a sketchily-drawn representation of a medal. An organ is to the rear and a cello lies on the floor to his right. There is no reference to his violin, although the concert programme (Figure 6) shows that he was still playing the instrument in public in this year. Here he is shown, probably for aesthetic reasons, composing with his right hand. Duke's Hall, Royal Academy of Music.

pale face, and he wears a peach suit with a decorative pink sash, soft peach slippers with white hose and a white wide-collared shirt with a frill, clothing which he may have worn for a performance. No text is visible on the leather-bound scores, nor musical notation. Unusually for Beechey, neither background nor instruments seem to be finished. Perhaps, however, the barely-observed cello lying on the floor to William's left shows the influence of Sir Joshua Reynolds and the idea that perfection is to be found in "leaving out particularities and retaining only general ideas" (Reynolds, *Discourses*, pp. 57–58). William's face reflects the evocation of the passions and prevailing cult of Sensibility. The image also evokes a feeling of transience, a boy on the edge of adolescence and passing childhood, posed though as still not aware about the gentlemanly presentation of his limbs. That same year Crotch was taken up to Cambridge (as assistant to Dr John Randall, the professor of music) to be turned into a "scholar and a gentleman", and formal lessons were begun both in composition and academic studies, also allowing him exposure to musical performance at the university and opportunities for his developing his interests in astronomy, ballooning and fireworks (he moved to Oxford University in 1788 to begin his degree studies).

Around William's neck hangs a representation of a shiny medal on a blue ribbon, and here Beechey has painted the child's own choice of something which he cherished (MS11244, NRO, 2 June 1780. Crotch recalled that he used to wear it around his neck). The small silver medal (Figures 19 and 20), probably purchased initially as a blank, was presented to Crotch by Dr Alexander Hunter, the Edinburgh-born physician at the York Dispensary from its foundation in 1788 and founder and first physician of the York Lunatic Asylum. It is unique in that its decoration is fully the subject of the engraver's needle—that is, the design is neither cast nor struck. The obverse is inscribed with a legend from Book V of Ovid's *Metamorphoses,* DEDIMUS SUMMAM CERTAMINIS UNI—"We gave our best singer to the contest", a reference to the muse Calliope and her part in a music competition (Book V of Ovid's *Metamorphoses.* See http://www.ovidio.org/liber5.txt, lines 337–40) with, in the centre, within the double border, a lyre (here slightly elongated) which she played as she sang. Engraved on the reverse is the text A. HUNTER MD TO MASTER W. CROTCH AETATIS V 1780.

WESLEY AND CROTCH AND THE BRISTOL PORTRAIT

In considering Russell's portrait of Samuel and Beechey's of William, showing each male child depicted as a composer instead of an "artisanal" instrumentalist—reflecting the idea of composition as being a creative and

Figure 19. Medal presented to William Crotch when aged 5 in 1780, by Dr Alexander Hunter, York. Obverse, set within a black-painted wooden mount, and visible on both sides. The reverse carries the engraved inscription A. HUNTER MD TO MASTER W. CROTCH AETATIS V 1780. Norfolk Record Office, MS33211.

Figure 20. Detail of the medal showing the elongated lyre and engraved inscription.

imaginative process—both artists seem primarily concerned with beauty, nobility and pictorial line in the design of their paintings, with the well-lit faces of each of the child conveying ideas of intellect and inspiration. Both Beechey and Russell employ the idea of the right hand as the active source of creation. As a young composer, it is likely however that Crotch may have used his left hand, as he would have for "memoranda", drawing and probably composing, as an adult (see Figure 1).

Returning to the portrait of the left-handed child in Bristol, painted near waist-level on the left is a small medal (Figure 21) showing a similar elongated lyre within a double-border, hanging on a blue ribbon as in the Beechey portrait, its image similar to Crotch's medal (Figure 20). The child's clothing is stylistically more ca. mid-1780s than that worn by boys ten or so years earlier.

If the painting came from the Bristol area, it is easy to see how it could represent either child—the Wesleys had a home there, but William Crotch was present in Bath and Bristol for long periods in both 1783 and 1784, when he was about eight to nine years of age. Both children played the violin—Samuel Wesley rather brilliantly by Barrington's account—and facially it could be said to look like either child, both at this age with dark hair and of slight build. It is plausible, however, that the painting represents William Crotch rather than Wesley. Taking into account the unique left-handedness, the child violinist must have warranted some fascination for recording. If it is indeed Crotch, it may be that the artist

Figure 21. Detail showing the medal around the waist of the portrait of the left-handed child violinist. As shown in the Beechey portrait, the ribbon is blue in colour, more so than in this snapshot.

was John Sanders, who seems to have worked closely with William's parents to mark various stages of the child's development—his first portrait (exhibited RA 1779 and also now at the RAM), the painting of him with a Muse and Pegasus (as Figure 3, lost) and a further painting exhibited as *William Crotch, the Musical Boy* (lost, but exhibited RA in 1784. No. 174), which could indeed be this one. While Arthur Mann suggests that the third painting is the small oval (artist unknown) now in Norwich Castle, that appears to be an infant of around three, and is therefore out of sequence for the paintings created by Sanders (Mann, n.d., NRO, MS11207). Sanders himself lived in Bath for many years, dying in Bristol in 1825, and the painting could have remained with him, accounting for its presence in the Bristol area. In 1806 Crotch, on inquiring of Sir William Beechey about the whereabouts of the portrait mentioned above, was told by the artist that "he had painted over it" (MS11244, January 1779, unpaginated), so it was not unusual for an artist to hold onto a work, or find that they didn't have a market for it—Beechey himself presented it to the RAM many years later (*Freeman's Journal and Daily Commercial Advertiser*, Dublin, May 6, 1833). Crotch also notes in his memoirs against a date of January 1779 "The first letter from home is dated 2nd and mentions Mr Saunders who did three portraits in oils of me but I believe not likenesses as the prints from them are very unlike each other. That with the muse behind me seems to have been ye best". While prints of two of the paintings exist, no known print of the third is known. Further investigation of the canvas and paintwork by an appropriate conservator would be important to confirm this as a work by Sanders, however, and the portrait may have been by another artist altogether, and previously undocumented.

There is though a definite facial resemblance to Crotch's self-portrait at the age of 26 (Figure 22), where he can also be seen to be sketching left-handed, glancing slightly upward as though into a mirror. Against the date of January 1779 in his memoirs, as a footnote Crotch adds that, whereas in 1779 he had "blue eyes, flaxen hair and a fair complexion", he records with an asterisk that in 1788 he had "dark [crossed through] brown or grey eyes, straight black hair and a dark complexion—'I was very thin'". He also related that he had been breeched when in Edinburgh (July 1781), when he then "put on scarlet jacket and trousers" before returning to London, clothing worn presumably for performances.

Identifying the instrument in the Bristol painting poses some difficulty. The violin is Amatise (in the style or pattern of an instrument made by a member of the Amati family), seen in the golden-coloured varnish and edgework with its delicate hooked corners. Its pegs show that it is strung for a left-handed player; the peg for the E string visibly upper left-most. Crotch's descriptions of the 1783 instrument as being "no more than a dancing-master's kit", and references to the "small" or "diminutive" instrument, would probably not work here, unless it related to the sound it made—that is, as it was made for a domestic space, it would not quite fill a room with other instrumentalists present. While violins and musical instruments often presented a challenge for the artist, here the bow is well-painted, and it is suggested that it is of the London maker, John Dodd, ca. 1780 (personal communication, David Rattray, Instrument Custodian, Royal Academy of Music).

In a letter to John Sainsbury, compiler of *A Dictionary of Musicians* (1824), when many contributions were written by the individuals themselves or by those intimately known to them, mention is made in the entry relating to William Henry Cutler (1792–1827), a later prodigy, that he played when young on "that little Amati violin which was once Dr Crotch's", acquired by

Figure 22. Self-portrait in ink on paper by William Crotch, titled in his hand "Myself by Myself" and dated "1801/1775 aged 26". He appears to be drawing left-handed, while glancing upward at his reflection. Reproduced with kind permission of the Norwich Castle Museum and Art Gallery.

Cutler's family from the London violin dealers, J. Betts (MS Euing R.d.85/58, Glasgow University). An inquiry to the present holder of Betts' workshop books has unfortunately not resulted in a response. Merlin and other eighteenth-century London makers such as John Betts did indeed use patterns from instruments by famous makers for the British market. Samuel Wesley, however, was known to have played a Cremonese violin as a child. That is not to say, however, that Crotch did not play on other instruments, nor occasionally borrow one from those trying to teach him.

PATRONAGE AND PENURY

The economics of Crotch's family life meant that, without in his infancy a long-term patron, his family would not have afforded the money for lessons for music nor art. His comments on picking up lessons from various orchestral leaders, wherever he happened to be, and encouragement by others to change sides with his bowing arm, must have been affected as much by this aspect of his life, as well constantly being on the road. Certainly his mother was in penury at times, for example the *Bath Chronicle* of 29 April 1784 records that she was on bail for debt, so the responsibility of the child and his education must have been a terrible financial burden. A further advertisement in Bath, Thursday 14th May 1784, carried an appeal for the child's concert on 19th May with the line "Master Crotch will do himself the honour to wait on the Nobility and Gentry in person, to solicit their assistance, and he will perform to the utmost of his powers to please them at the Concert" (*Bath Chronicle*). It must also have been difficult for the many regional and other players he met to understand his predilection for playing his violin in the style of a cello and with his left bowing arm, although it does appear that attempts were made to help him with playing "on the left shoulder".

In a letter to Sir James Lake, Burney writes (25 May 1783),[9] when the child was eight, of "unfortunate little Crotch" ...

> ... I have always lamented his situation, without seeing the least Possibility of amending it; as this is not an age for the *solid* Patronage of uncultivated Genius any further than by transient admiration & and immediate gratification of curiosity. The Persons who have had the managem & Guidance of this wonderful Child must inevitably have checked & impeded the progress of his reasoning as well as Musical faculties. But who, in a free Country, has a right to take a Child from his Parents without consent or ample indemnification ... Mrs Crotch wd doubtless have been glad to have transferred to such a Patron the superintendence of her son's Education; but having been long maintained, though often miserably, by his premature Talents, it is natural to suppose that she wd be unwilling to part with him, merely for his own sake, without thinking of *herself*, & the loss of profit & importance she shd sustain by placing him in other hands. If therefore any great

[9] Excerpt from pp. 362–364 from "Letters of Charles Burney" edited by A. Ribeiro (1991), by permission of Oxford University Press.

> nobleman were disposed to patronize the boy, by taking him into his house or being at the expense of his board & Education elsewhere; (a species of patronage at present very difficult, I fear, to be found;) if he did not likewise support the whole family, my opinion is that he wd not be allowed to adopt or appropriate the Boy. Our sovereigns of the Tudor Race exercised a power of impressing singing boys, for the service of the Chapel Royal, & I believe this Tyranny extended to the Dean & Chapter of cathedral till the beginning of the last Century; & hard as such a prerogative might fall upon worthy & fond parents, it might have been happy for little Crotch if he had been taken from his vulgar & foolish family many years ago.

He continues some lines later:

> Indeed the boy discovered very early that his understanding was superior to those abt him, & therefore he not only despised their orders but acquired a habit of forwardness & disobedience to all kinds of admonition. Whether his own reason as yet has corrected this early defect I know not; but it is much to be feared that the admiration & applause wch his great natural but artless attempts publickly acquired for what nothing but infancy wd make wonderful, have rendered him as much satisfied wth his own imperfections in performance, as contemptuous of all such instructions as his weak & vulgar mother or her connections cd. supply ... I know not the place of their residence; & indeed have not time, consequence or abilities to take the whole upon myself, however my fervent affection for the boy & admiration of his great natural powers, & intellectual Capacity may incline me to wish it. When his health is well established If I can chalk out such a line for his future conduct & the further pursuit of his Musical Studies as, under the unfavourable circumstances of his situation may be practicable, it will afford me very great satisfaction ...

A gifted but spoilt child whose time was spent mostly in the company of highly educated adult males, Crotch was also troubled by the expectations which were made of him, especially at a time when British musicians were trying to establish themselves as a profession. Schomberg seems to express Diderot's description of the "rag-and-bone men" of music. Crotch records the following paragraphs written by Schomberg, against which he himself has scrawled in the margin "Oh no":

> The patronage of Dr Burney and the attentions of his family are very fortunate circumstances let me tell you. The name of Burney naturally brings up the subject of mere musicianer [underlined by Crotch in his transcription] in which I have often dwelt in letters and conversations. Compare him with P2XYZ and some others than you and I know in the musical line. Why I will tell you. The one is a scholar and a gentleman, respected by all and welcome wherever and whenever he appears. The other ignorant of all letters except the XXXX of XXXX, awkward and therefore bothersome to genteel company as soon as their instruments are shut up in their cases. Mrs Burney expresses herself about you like a mother. (MS11244, NRO, 1787, p. 59)

> And ought we not say too, farewell Robinson Crusoe, balloons ... soldiers and puppet shows, and welcome Latin, Greek and the best English writers? Most assuredly ... I here come to my old theme of mere musicians. Dr Burney can do both, Jackson of Exeter can do both ... Avison, Rameau and many others.[10] Pray then why not may Wm. Crotch do both? I can find nothing in our law books or in the Roman law books nor in the University statues that prohibits an attempt at this sort. You cannot think, Wm., what pleasure it gave me this morning when we breakfasted at Mr Cowper's chambers to find you so improved as you really are in your general manner and deportment, and in this Mr Cowper agreed with me. (MS11244, NRO, June 1787)

Schomberg's further comments on the subject relate to the prospect that the child, as a man, could otherwise end up teaching country ladies, with some occasional playing with friends—Crotch noted against a date of 1787 "I cannot help thinking that tho' a gentleman and a scholar may be a musician, it cannot be necessary that a musician should be a scholar, tho' he ought in manners to be a gentleman" (MS11244, NRO, 1787, p. 61).

DISCUSSION AND CONCLUSIONS

Infant prodigies are, by their very nature, rare, and left-handed infant musical prodigies are inevitably rarer still. It does therefore seem somewhat of a coincidence that the two greatest English musical prodigies of the period were born within a decade of one another. Left-handedness is probably too simple a term for the handedness of Crotch, who for writing and drawing at least was equally capable with both hands. But that Crotch played the violin and the cello in eccentrically self-taught ways, with the bow held in the left hand, seems indisputable (and in the process raises many questions about why stringed instruments are strung the way they are).

Although Samuel Wesley is said to have, in 1974, "taught himself the violin assisted for six weeks by 'a soldier'" (Kassler & Olleson, 2001, p. 22), he had first-hand contact with many of the master performers in London through his well-educated family and their wide social circle of friends and colleagues, in contrast to Crotch's family, with his father a master carpenter. Crotch does, however, stress on the first page of his memoirs the wide-ranging general interests of his father, which he in turn came to share, and his remarks about his parents are understanding of their problems in the handling of his own young life. Much more problematic is the idea of Wesley's left handedness, which would seem in large to be dependent on the evidence of the Bristol portrait, and yet, as this paper

[10] Dr William Jackson of Exeter, Dr Charles Burney, Charles Avison of Newcasle—"scholar musicians"—and the French composer Jean-Philippe Rameau. As well as his gaining of better manners, the improvement in Crotch's regional accent was also commented on by Dr Schomberg.

shows, that portrait is more likely to be of Crotch, particularly given the evidence of the medal and the child's pose and clothing. In some ways therefore it is indeed too much of a coincidence that there were two left-handed musical prodigies within a decade, and probably only one of them was left-handed.

As well as concerns for his technique as Crotch developed as a performer, the sight of his playing also seems to have disturbed those musicians around him, coinciding with new pressures to be formally taught to play *properly* (i.e., right-handed) to allow for growth of his facility, and to solve the problem of his instrument. The facility to bow with the right hand would also have been considered as helpful for playing within a group. When put under some pressure, however, his formal studies on this instrument were given up to concentrate instead on general musicianship, compositional and keyboard skills. Crotch seems to have been both proud and fascinated to have been able to use both of his hands, perhaps stretching these abilities by further training himself and experimenting with their use—so a case of both nature and nurture—and his comments seem to support the idea that he was not personally discouraged by his family regarding his use of his left hand nor his general ambidexterity.

It is not known in which hand Crotch composed his memoirs. Certainly in two opposing pages from December 1835 and January 1836, the text seems to have been in one hand on one page, and in the other on the opposing page (MS11244, NRO, pp. 140 and 141). At the time he was suffering from erysipelas, for which he was treated by Sir Benjamin Brodie, and he may indeed have been prone when recording his notes (Figures 23 and 24).

Finally, in considering Crotch's adult drawing, much influenced by the German drawing master and musician Dr John Malchair (1730–1812), with whom he studied following his own appointment at Oxford,[11] it is clear from many drawings and watercolours, including those available for viewing in digitised collections of the Royal Academy of Music (watercolours, 1838), Norwich Castle Museum and Art Gallery, Tate Britain and the British Museum, that he continued throughout his life to sketch left-handed, as evidenced in particular by his diagonal shading, sloping backwards.[12] This is visually illustrated in a painted portrait of the silver-haired and elderly Crotch, set against a landscape and gazing at the viewer, well wrapped in a heavy overcoat and scarf-collar, where he can be seen to hold an implement which appears to have a knib at one end and a brush at the other, in his left hand, with an open drawing book supported by his right hand (Figure 25).

[11] Colin Harrison with essays by Susan Wollenberg and Julian Munby (1998), *John Malchair of Oxford, Artist and Musician* (p. 37). Oxford: Ashmolean Museum.

[12] See entry on Crotch. Anne Lyles and Robin Hamlyn (1997). *British Watercolours from the Oppé Collection* (p. 186). London: Tate Gallery Publishing.

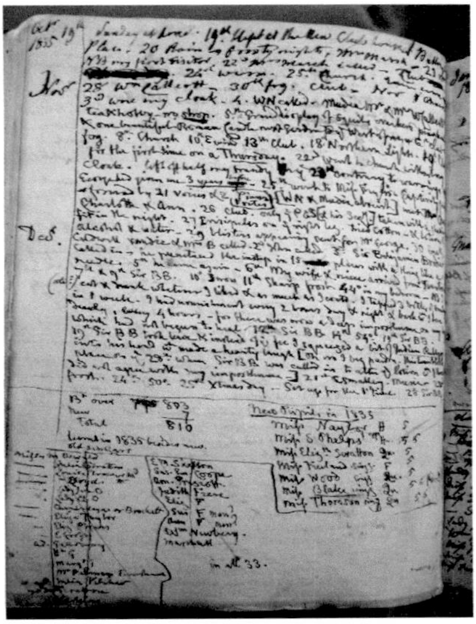

Figure 23. William Crotch Memoirs, left hand page 140, October 19th, 1835—end December 1835. Norfolk Record Office, MS11244. This covers a period of many weeks and Crotch includes, in note form, the onset of erisipelas [erysipelas] on his right leg. He records visits and treatment by the eminent physiologist and surgeon Sir Benjamin Brodie, whose important work included his treatise *Pathological and Surgical Observations on the Diseases of the Joints* (1818). Norfolk Record Office, MS11244.

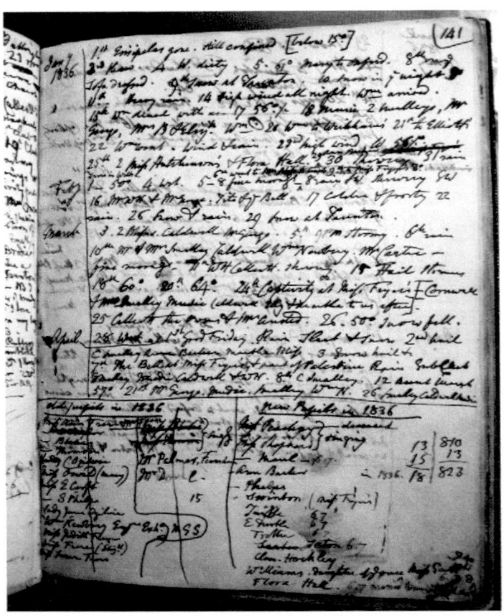

Figure 24. William Crotch Memoirs, right hand page 141, January 7th, 1836. He notes in the first line "Erisipelas gone, still confined ...". Norfolk Record Office, MS11244.

Figure 25. William Crotch sketching in a landscape setting. Artist unknown, oil on board, undated. Well wrapped-up, he holds a drawing book in his right hand and, in his left hand, what appears to be an implement with a knib at one end and a brush at the other. Reproduced with kind permission of the Norwich Castle Museum and Art Gallery.

REFERENCES

Anderson, E. (Ed.). (1989). *The letters of Mozart and his family.* London, UK: Macmillan Reference Limited.

Angelo, D. (1787). *The school of fencing with a general explanation of the principal attitudes and positions peculiar to the art.* London, UK: printed privately.

Barrington, D. (1770). Account of a very remarkable young musician. In *Philosophical Transactions of the Royal Society,* Vol. 60, December, p. 54, XIII.

Barrington, D. (1781). *Miscellanies.* London, UK: J. Nichols, sold by B. White [etc.].

Burney, C. (1779). *An account of an infant musician.* London, UK: Philosophical Transactions, pp. 183–206. Published also in the *Annual Register* the same year; slightly altered shorter version published in the *Gentleman's Magazine* and also as a separate volume. Reproduced in the *Norwich Mercury,* 15/01/1780.

Burney, S. (1779–1790). British Library Egerton 3691, Folio 15. Extract: Eg. 3691, 3692. Barrett Collection. Vols II, III (ff. 177, 196 including journal-letters, from Susanna Burney Phillips to Frances d'Arblay); Vol. II, circ. Dec. 1778–4 Dec. 1781; Vol. III, 3 Dec. 1787–4 Dec. 1795.

Cadogan, W. (1748). *An essay upon nursing, the management of children, from their birth to three years of age. By a physician. In a letter to one of the governors of the Foundling Hospital. Published by order of the General Committee ...* London, Printed for and Roberts. *English Short Title Catalogue. Eighteenth Century Collections Online.* Gale Group. Retrieved September 21, 2008, from http://galenet.galegroup.com/servlet/ECCO.

Crotch, W. (undated but ca. 1835–1847). Memoirs compiled by him from his own letters. With a sketch of himself by John Constable. MS11244, Norfolk Record Office.

Crotch, W. (undated). *Robin Goodfellow or Fairy land [and Fortunio]*. Ms. 51 p. With incidental music for the plays. Ms. note on cover: Comedy by Dr. Crotch at 6 years old. m.b. (Arblay, F. d'). In collection of 271 letters to various members of the Burney family.

Crowley, F. (November 1934). "A Letter from Helvetius about Mozart", *Huntington Library Bulletin*, No. 6, pp. 170–171.

Cutler, W.H. to John Sainsbury. MS Euing R.d.85/58, Glasgow University.

Foxley, B. (Ed.) (1911, 2007), Rousseau, Jean-Jacques 1757–(1760). *Émile*. London, UK: Read Books. Retrieved September 21, 2008, from http://books.google.com/books?id=ynG0B5a_NrkC&pg=PA104&dq=emile+rousseau+%2B+barefoot&ei=CB3hSImvM4zaigHF8_TnDg&sig=ACfU3U2jeun8MuVRbC2gSGrZMFiW-YaVUg.

French, A., Wright, M., & Palmer, F. (1985). *John Joseph Merlin: The ingenious mechanick. Exhibition catalogue:* Iveagh Bequest, Kenwood House. London, UK: Greater London Council.

Harris, L. J. (2003). What to do about your child's handedness? Advice from five eighteenth-century authors, and some questions for today. *Laterality, 8* (2), 99–120.

Hill, J. (writing as Juliana-Susannah Seymour) (1754). *On the management and education of children*. London, UK: R. Baldwin.

Jackson, T. (Ed.). (1872). *The Sermons of John Wesley*. "On the Education of Children" (Sermon 95, 18c). Retrieved from http://wesley.nnu.edu/john_wesley/sermons/095.htm

Johnson, R. (writing as Master Michael Angelo) (1773). *The drawing school for little masters and misses*. London, UK.

Kassler, M., & Olleson, P. (2001). *Samuel Wesley (1776–1837): A source book*. Aldershot, UK: Ashgate.

Kroeger, K. (1988). John Valentine; eighteenth-century music master in the Midlands. Notes, (Music Library Association), second series. 44. *No.*, *3*, 444–455.

Lichtenberg, G. C. (1780). *Vermischte Schriften* (Vol. 5, pp. 258–266). Gottingen, Germany.

Locke, J. (1692). *Some thoughts concerning education*. New York: P.F. Collier and Company, 1909–14. Digitised: http://www.bartleby.com/37/1/

Lyles, A., & Hamlyn, R. (1997). *British watercolours from the Oppé collection*. London, UK: Tate Gallery Publishing.

The London Magazine or Gentlemans Monthly Intelligencer (April 1779). "Account of the Musical Phaenomenon with his portrait after a drawing from the life" (Vol. 49). London, UK: R. Baldwin.

Mann, A. H. (n.d.). Extra Notes to the Memoirs of William Crotch. MS11211, Norfolk Record Office, UK.

Mann, A. H. (n.d.). Notes on Pictures of William Crotch. MS11207. Norfolk Record Office, UK.

Mann, A. H. (n.d.). *Göttingen Pocket Almanac*. Typed transcription from German into English, pp. 258–266. MS11092, Norfolk Record Office, UK.

Norfolk Chronicle. June 15, 1782.

Robert, R. W. (Ed.). (1997). Sir Joshua Reynolds. *Discourses on Art*. Paul Mellon Centre for Studies in British Art. London, UK and New Haven, USA: Yale University Press.

Reiro, A. (Ed.) (1991). *The letters of Charles Burney*. Vol. 1, 1751–1784. Oxford, UK: Clarendon.

Starobinski, J. (1991). The concept of genius in the 18th century. Mozart and the Enlightenment: The Mystery of Genius. *UNESCO Courier*, July, pp. 18–21. Retrieved September 21, 2008, from http://findarticles.com/p/articles/mi_m1310/is_1991_July/ai_11102234

Twining, T., & Twining, R. (1887). *Selections from papers of the Twining family*: A sequel to "The Recreations and Studies of a Country Clergyman of the 18th Century", the Rev.

Thomas Twining, Some-time Rector of St. Mary's Colchester, p. 245. London, UK: J. Murray

Warton, J. (1746). *Ode to Fancy.* Retrieved September 21, 2008, from http://www.poemhunter.com/poem/ode-to-fancy/

West, M. I. (Editor and translator) (2003). Ode to Hermes. In *Homeric Hymns, Homeric Apocrypha, Lives of Homer*, LCL 496. No. 4, pl49, lines 439–50. London, UK: Loeb Classical Library, Harvard University Press.

LATERALITY, 2010, 15 (1/2), 253–269

Eclectic lefty-hand: Conjectures on Jimi Hendrix, handedness, and *Electric Ladyland*

Stephen Christman

University of Toledo, OH, USA

An analysis of Jimi Hendrix's guitar playing and song writing is presented in light of the effects of his mixed-right-handedness on motoric and conceptual processing. It is argued that (i) his mixed-handedness allowed him greater integration of the roles of his left and right hands in guitar playing and (ii) his right-handedness conferred specific benefits in playing a left-handed guitar. In terms of his song writing, the greater interhemispheric interaction (and consequent greater access to right hemisphere processing) associated with mixed-handedness is argued to characterise aspects of his lyrics and vocal delivery.

Keywords: Handedness; Interhemispheric interaction; Musical instruments; Rock music; Musical ability; Musicians.

I always thought of [Jimi] as just coming from outer space, because he was just so different. He just came from such a left-field place.

Robbie Krieger

Alongside his musical contributions, Jimi Hendrix left an enduring legacy of visual iconography, ranging from his trademark afro and bandanna to his practices of playing the guitar behind his back and setting it on fire. One of the most salient aspects of Hendrix's visual legacy was the fact that he played guitar left-handed. From Paul McCartney to Kurt Cobain (who, like Hendrix, was from Seattle and died at age 27, and who once said, "I'm gonna be a superstar musician, kill myself and go out in a flame of glory, just

Address correspondence to: Stephen Christman, Department of Psychology, University of Toledo, Toledo, OH 43606, USA. E-mail: stephen.christman@utoledo.edu

The author is indebted to Russell Reising, Professor of English at the University of Toledo, for providing the initial inspiration to write this paper. The extensive and constructive commentary on an earlier version of this paper provided by Chris McManus, Bruno Laeng, and Lutz Jancke is also gratefully acknowledged.

DOI: 10.1080/13576500902953815

like Jimi Hendrix"), left-handed guitarists have long stood out, with the necks of their guitars pointing in a different direction from everyone else's. Left-handedness has intrigued, perplexed, and sometimes disturbed humans since time immemorial, and Hendrix's left-handed guitar playing constitutes a powerful part of his public image. This paper examines the influence of Jimi Hendrix's handedness on two aspects of his art. It will be argued that his handedness played a vital role in both his innovative guitar-playing techniques and in his often unconventional approach to song writing, using examples primarily drawn from his classic 1968 album, *Electric Ladyland.*

While the full details of Hendrix's handedness are not known, it appears that he was neither strongly right-handed nor strongly left-handed. Contrary to popular lore, Hendrix was clearly *not* left-handed in the traditional sense of the term: he wrote, ate, and held the phone with his right hand, while he threw, combed his hair, and held cigarettes with his left hand (Noble, 1995a). However, Shapiro and Glebbeek's (1992) authoritative biography of Hendrix makes it clear that Hendrix thought of himself as a left-hander (e.g., in Hendrix's own words, "I was left-handed", p. 37), so it is likely, although undocumented, that he was forced to switch to writing with his right hand, a common practice in public schools in the 1950s. For what it's worth, Hendrix's right-handed writing posture was non-inverted, and he operated his foot pedals with his left foot.

The key point here is that Hendrix did not appear to be *strongly* handed. In an extensive series of papers, Christman and colleagues have argued that distinguishing between strong- and mixed-handers may be more useful than the traditional left- versus right-handed classification (e.g., Christman, Bentle, & Niebauer, 2007a; Christman, Henning, Geers, Propper, & Niebauer, 2008; Christman, Jasper, Sontam, & Cooil, 2007; Christman, Propper, & Brown, 2006; Christman, Propper, & Dion, 2004; Jasper, Barry, & Christman, 2008; Jasper & Christman, 2005; Kempe, Brooks, & Christman, 2009; Niebauer, Christman, Reid, & Garvey, 2004; Propper & Christman, 2004; Propper, Christman & Phaneuf, 2005; Propper, Lawton, Przyborski, & Christman, 2004).

In the parlance to be used in this chapter, Hendrix would be classified as "mixed-handed". An unpublished analysis from my lab of Edinburgh Handedness Inventory (EHI; Oldfield, 1971) scores for 1636 participants yielded a median score of 80 (with the overall range being –100 to + 100), which has been used in the research cited above as a median split to divide samples into roughly equal-sized groups of mixed- and strong-handed people. An EHI score of 80, used as the upper bound for the mixed-handed classification, is obtained if a participant indicates performing just a single activity (out of the 10 listed on the EHI) with their non-dominant hand. Thus, strong handedness is defined as consistent use of the same hand for all 10 activities. Moreover, the same unpublished analysis indicates that over

75% of left-handed males are classified as mixed-handed using the above criterion. Accordingly, given Hendrix's right-handed eating and phone holding and his left-handed throwing and hair combing, the current paper will assume that Jimi Hendrix was a mixed-hander. While, as noted above, Hendrix identified himself as a left-hander, the fact that he wrote with his right hand would lead him to be classified as a right-hander by accepted neuropsychological practice. It also worth noting that his handwriting was legible and stylish enough to warrant being made into its own font, Axis Bold (published by Letraset), suggesting a high level of right-hand dexterity. Accordingly, the current paper will provisionally assume that Hendrix was a mixed-right-hander.

Both biological and behavioural evidence supports the view that degree of handedness (mixed versus strong) is more important than direction (left versus right). For example, genetic studies of both humans and non-humans indicate that *degree* of lateral preference (strong versus mixed) is more heritable than *direction* (left versus right) of lateral preferences (e.g., Collins, 1985; Morgan & Corballis, 1978). As Morgan and Corballis (1978, p. 270) concluded, "It is difficult to find clear-cut examples in which the direction of an asymmetry is under clear genetic control. By contrast, it is much easier to find examples in which the degree but not the direction of asymmetry is under genetic control." Behaviourally, studies that divide people into three handedness groups (i.e., strong left, mixed, and strong right) routinely find that the strong left- and strong right-handers resemble one another, while it is the mixed-handers who stand out (e.g., Barnett & Corballis, 2002; Christman, 1993; Niebauer, 2004; Niebauer et al., 2004; Porac, 1993). The mixed-handed Jimi Hendrix certainly stood out.

It is first necessary to address one particular myth about Hendrix's guitar playing. It is a commonly held misconception that Hendrix played a regular right-handed guitar that was simply turned upside-down, with the strings consequently in a reversed order (i.e., higher strings above, lower strings below). This is not true: there is ample photographic and biographical evidence that Hendrix reversed the strings on the right-handed guitars that he played left-handed so that the strings were in the "normal" order (Hendrix also regularly removed and reversed the nut so that the strings would fit properly and proper intonation was ensured). Thus, Hendrix fingered chords in the same basic manner as other guitarists. It is also worth pointing out that Hendrix apparently never used any open tunings, playing all of his songs in the standard E-A-D-G-B-E tuning (although he regularly tuned his strings down a half step to E♭-A♭-D♭-G♭-B♭-E♭ in order to fit in more readily with horn sections and to allow the strings to be bent more easily).

Hendrix's mixed-handedness has two important specific implications for his pioneering guitar ability. The first involves his ability to coordinate the activities of his left and right hands, and the second involves the specific mechanics of a right-handed person playing a left-handed guitar.

GUITAR PLAYING: INTEGRATION OF THE LEFT AND RIGHT HAND ROLES

In regard to Hendrix's ability to synchronise the motions of his two hands, research shows that mixed-handedness is over-represented among players of string instruments (Christman, 1993) such as guitar and violin, an instrument that Hendrix played briefly as a child. This reflects a fundamental difference in brain organisation between strong- and mixed-handers: mixed-handedness is associated with increased interaction between and integration of the left and right sides of the brain (e.g., Christman, 1993, 1995, 2001; Christman et al., 2004, 2006, 2007a; Christman, Jasper, Sontam, & Cooil, 2007b; Jasper & Christman, 2005; Propper & Christman, 2004; Propper et al., 2005). The increased interaction between the left and right sides of the brain presumably arises from the fact that the corpus callosum, the bundle of nerve fibres connecting the two sides of the brain, may be significantly larger in left- and mixed-handers (e.g., Moffat, Hampson, & Lee, 1998; Westerhausen et al., 2004; Witelson, 1985; Witelson & Goldsmith, 1991).

As each side of the brain controls the opposite side of the body, this means that the greater integration between the left and right sides of the brain in mixed-handers is associated with greater integration of the right and left hands. Since the actions of the two hands need to be tightly synchronised while playing guitar (i.e., the timing of the left hand fretting and right hand picking must be closely coordinated), this confers an advantage for mixed-handed guitar players. Conversely, keyboard instruments require a certain amount of decoupling and independence between the left and right hands, which requires independence between the processing of the left and right sides of the brain; accordingly, strong handedness (left *and* right) is over-represented among keyboard players (Christman, 1993). Aggleton, Kentridge, and Good (1994) also reported a similar over-representation of non-right-handers among string players.

A hallmark of Jimi's guitar style involved his ability to integrate the actions of his two hands in terms of simultaneously using his right hand to fret the strings and his left hand to pluck the strings and manipulate the pickup selector and the tone, volume, and tremolo (i.e., whammy bar) controls on the body of the instrument. It is important to note that the fact that Hendrix played a right-handed guitar upside-down (as opposed to simply playing a left-handed guitar) meant that these controls were located above the strings instead of below, making it easier for him to manipulate them with his right and left hands while playing.

Although manipulation of the control knobs and switches is obviously possible on normally played right-hand guitars, the knobs are generally intended to be adjusted in between songs as opposed to while playing (indeed, the control knobs are normally placed below the strings precisely to make them harder to access, thereby avoiding inadvertent contact with the controls while playing).

About the only disadvantage that Hendrix faced with his unusual guitar set-up was the fact that the cutaway in the guitar body where the neck joins the body hampered access to the top reaches of the fretboard. However, Jimi was able to overcome this problem thanks to his unusually long fingers and his double-jointed thumb, which he used as a fifth fretting finger. Nonetheless, the left horns of Hendrix's guitars were often partially worn away as a result of his repeatedly striking the guitar with his ring as he played on the upper frets.

Thus Hendrix's ability to coordinate the actions and timing of his left and right hands was enhanced both by the mechanical set-up of his guitar and by the increased bimanual coordination allowed by his mixed-hander's brain and its increased interhemispheric interaction. Hendrix regularly employed techniques such as striking a sustained note or chord, then using his right hand to operate the tremolo arm (i.e., whammy bar) while his left hand manipulated the volume control and pick-up selector, allowing him to generate otherworldly howls, shrieks, and siren-like sounds on the guitar.

Hendrix's version of 'The Star Spangled Banner', recorded at Woodstock, features perhaps the most dramatic examples of his ability to tweak the controls of his guitar to create amazing sounds. Other examples of Hendrix's sonic inventiveness can be found on his album *Electric Ladyland*. 'Voodoo Chile' features some nicely understated use of the tremolo bar towards the end of the guitar solo preceding the organ solo, continuing on through the guitar accompaniment of the organ. The final measures of this song also feature an example of Hendrix striking a sustained note and using the tremolo bar to go back and forth between a B and a D, while simultaneously twiddling the tone control to modulate the tone of the guitar. An example of Hendrix's flicking back and forth between different pickups (which both alters the sound of ongoing sustained notes and creates a percussive click) is found during the final 16 measures of 'Voodoo Chile (Slight Return)'.

Perhaps the most impressive and representative example of his bimanual coordination on *Electric Ladyland* is found in the opening bars of 'Still Raining, Still Dreaming', where Hendrix uses his right hand to play an intricate series of bends and slides, while his left hand, in between plucking the strings, uses the pickup selector to switch back and forth between the treble and bass pickups. On top of all this, Hendrix also uses his left foot to manipulate a wah-wah pedal in tight synchronisation with the guitar playing. The result is one of the more impressive evocations of a human voice produced on a guitar.

The ability to coordinate and integrate the actions of his left and right hands was a critical foundation of Hendrix's sonic experimentation and exploration. And his ability to put together his two hands extended up his arms: films of Hendrix playing his guitar reveal a poetic choreography of his arms, as his left arm glides up and down the neck tapping and tweaking, while his right arm dances around the fretboard, bending and hammering strings.

GUITAR PLAYING: RIGHT- VERSUS LEFT-HANDED GUITARS

The second key implication of Hendrix's right-handedness for his guitar-playing style lies in his unorthodox decision to play guitar left-handed. Evidence suggests that Hendrix chose to play the guitar left-handed because he simply found it easier. Indeed, Hendrix wrote and ate with his right hand, and the case can be made that Hendrix may have had better basic hand skill and dexterity with his right than left hand.

The story of how the ostensibly "right-handed" Hendrix came to play a guitar left-handed is worth recounting. Hendrix's father, Al Hendrix, described in his autobiography how Jimi first started playing guitar (Hendrix, 1999). Jimi spent his early childhood transforming cigar boxes into guitars, trying to get music out of a one-string ukelele, and using a broom to play air guitar. He finally convinced his father to buy him an old right-handed acoustic guitar from a neighbour for $5. Jimi played this guitar in the traditional manner at first, but then one day his father saw Jimi changing the strings and starting to play left-handed. His father asked why he was playing the guitar left-handed and Jimi responded, "I find I can play left-handed easier than I can right-handed." As Hendrix described in an article that appeared in the March 1967 issue of the now defunct magazine *Beat Instrumental*, "I didn't know that I would have to put the strings the other way [around], but it just didn't feel right. I can remember thinking to myself, 'There's something wrong here.'" (p. 38). This quote seems to point at two different aspects of his initial experience at guitar playing: "it just didn't feel right" appears to refer to fretting the neck with his left hand, and "There's something wrong here" appears to refer to the fact that the strings are in the wrong order when one simply turns a right-handed guitar upside-down in order to play left-handed.

Why would someone who wrote with his right-hand and was given a right-handed guitar spontaneously decide that playing it left-handed would be easier? One argument is that, historically, what was originally a "right-handed" guitar has evolved into a "left-handed" guitar (and vice versa), as the more demanding aspects of guitar playing have switched over the centuries from the right to left hand.

When the predecessor of the modern guitar was being developed in fifteenth-century Spain, it was tuned to an open or quasi-open tuning and had a wide neck, making the left hand's role the very simple one of playing individual melody notes (while the open strings provided the harmonic accompaniment). In addition, the strings were composed of cat-gut (which is actually made from the intestines of sheep, not cats), a substance more pliable and easier to fret cleanly than modern steel strings. The complicated role fell to the right hand in the form of intricate finger-picking patterns, arpeggios, and rest stops. As the guitar developed over the centuries, however, the relative difficulties of the two hands' roles reversed in four important ways.

First, guitars gradually moved to the standard E-A-D-G-B-E tuning. The advantage of this tuning is that it enables a guitarist to play songs in a wider range of keys, allowing them to play with other musicians more readily (guitars in open tunings are generally restricted to playing in a single key). The disadvantage, however, is that now even the simplest of melodies require three or four fingers to be fretting the strings throughout in order to provide the proper harmonic accompaniment. Second, in order to provide a brighter, crisper sound, make the instrument easier to tune, and help prolong string life, modern guitars (with the partial exception of classical guitars) use steel strings, which require greater effort and precision to fret. Third, guitars were originally played by plucking strings with individual fingers of the right hand, but modern styles of guitar playing generally involve the simpler method of strumming the strings with a plectrum. The finger motions involved in finger picking require finer motor control than the wrist-based motions involved in strumming. Finally, early guitars (as well as modern classical guitars) featured a wide neck to accommodate the space between strings necessary for finger picking. As modern guitar-playing styles evolved towards a reliance on using a plectrum, the neck has become progressively narrower, leaving the fingers of the left hand less room in which to move around.

Thus the left hand's role evolved from fretting a single, easy-to-fret string at a time on a spacious neck, to fretting three or four metal strings at a time on a significantly narrower neck. At the same time, the right hand's role evolved from an intricate activity in which the thumb and three or four fingers regularly plucked strings, to holding a small piece of plastic and more or less just moving the whole hand up and down. Although playing with a plectrum can involve great speed and precision, the motions are generated by more proximal wrist and arm muscles instead of the more distal finger movements, thus requiring less dexterity.

Evidently, when Hendrix first picked up a right-handed guitar and noticed that "it just didn't feel right", he intuitively realised that he might be better off using his presumably more dextrous right hand on the fretboard and his presumably less agile left hand to strum the strings. Consequently, part of Hendrix's superlative guitar style reflected the fact that he was able to use his agile right hand for difficult fretting patterns (such as his masterful use of hammer-ons, pull-offs, and string bending), while his left hand handled the more basic and less demanding activities of plucking, strumming, and manipulating the whammy bar and volume knob. At the same time, his mixed-handedness meant that the two sides of his brain could easily coordinate and integrate his left and right hand actions. Moreover, his extensive use of hammer-ons, pull-offs, and trills meant that his right hand could produce notes on its own, freeing his left hand to manipulate the guitar's controls.

By simply following his own gut feeling, it appears that Jimi grasped that a right-hander might be more comfortable playing a modern guitar in a "left-handed" fashion. Jimi, however, may not have been unique in this regard. For example, Mark Knopfler, the guitarist from the band Dire Straits, and Steve Morse, guitarist for the Dixie Dregs, are both left-handers who started playing right-handed guitars after realising it would be easier to use their "good" left-hand for the demanding task of fingering the strings rather than the easier task of plucking and strumming.

For what it's worth, the author is a left-hander who started playing a right-handed guitar because there was one in his house. I initially felt that I should be playing a left-handed guitar but quickly realised that I was quite comfortable using my left hand on the fretboard; by the time I finally had a chance to try a left-handed guitar, it felt very awkward. It should be noted that the overwhelming prevalence of right-handed guitars makes it an easy choice for left-handers. In contrast, Jimi Hendrix is one of the very few guitarists who wrote with the right hand to spontaneously settle on playing a left-handed guitar. A recent book on left-handed guitars details a handful of other right-handers who play left-handed guitars (Engel, 2006).

Interestingly, a similar framework has been applied to piano playing. In piano playing the more demanding role of playing the melody is usually handled by the right hand. Not surprisingly, therefore, left-handers find it easier to play a reversed keyboard in which the higher notes are on the left side (Jancke, 2002; Laeng & Park, 1999). More pertinent to the current argument that Hendrix's mixed-handedness led to greater interhemispheric interaction is the observation that a highly skilled left-handed pianist who is able to play normal and reversed keyboards with equal proficiency showed left versus right hemispheric dominance for musical perception versus production, respectively (Jancke et al., 2006), suggesting that increased interaction between the left and right hemispheres may play a role in unusual musical talent.

It is worth noting that Hendrix could, when necessary, play a right-handed guitar upside-down *without* restringing it (meaning that the fingerings for chords needed to be mirror-imaged). For example, back in 1960 when he was in high school playing with The Rocking Kings at a local club call "Birdland", his guitar was stolen and he reportedly just turned another guitar upside down and proceeded to play along with a slow blues number (Noble, 1995b). Similarly, Paul Kossoff, the late guitarist from the band Free, once recalled Hendrix walking into the British music store where he was working. There weren't any left-handed guitars, so Hendrix simply took a right-handed Stratocaster, turned it over so that the low strings were now at the bottom, and began playing a passable version of his song 'Little Wing' (Lescroart, 1977). Finally, Hendrix also played Noel Redding's right-handed, un-restrung bass guitar upside-down for an overdub track on 'All Along The Watchtower' on a day when Redding was not at the studio. The fact that bass playing requires fewer chords made this an easier feat than it would be on the guitar (moreover, chords on the bass often involve only two strings).

A final comment is in order concerning hand skill in musicians. While it was argued above that Hendrix may have had more dexterity with his right hand, it should be noted that early musical training leads to a diminution of left versus right hand differences in fine motor control (Jancke, Schlaug, & Steinmetz, 1997). This means that, with early enough training and enough practice, anyone, left- or right-handed, could learn to play left- or right-handed instruments with comparable proficiency. However, the fact that Hendrix did not play guitar on a regular and serious basis until the age of 15 suggests that the relative skill of his left and right hands was not dramatically affected by his guitar training.

SONG WRITING

With regard to song writing, Hendrix's mixed-handedness again provides two important influences. First, given (i) the evidence reviewed above for greater interaction between the left and right sides of the brain in mixed-handers, and (ii) the fact that language and rhythm processing are lateralised to the left side of brain while the processing of melody and harmony is lateralised to the right side (Gates & Bradshaw, 1977), the possibility is raised that mixed-handers may have an advantage in integrating the lyrics and melody in song writing; that is, mixed-handers may be better able to put the "right" words with the "right" melody such that the syntactic and emotional aspects of the lyrics are tightly integrated with the phrasing and contour of the melody line.

It may be no coincidence that 'All Along The Watchtower', the hit single from *Electric Ladyland*, was written by Bob Dylan, another mixed-handed songwriter. It should be acknowledged that specific details about Dylan's handedness are as murky and hard to come by as other details of his personal life. On the one hand, there are literally hundreds of websites devoted to left-handedness that confidently proclaim Dylan is left-handed (although few provide any supporting documentation). On the other hand, photographic evidence clearly shows that Dylan writes with his right hand. For example, a book-length collection of pictures of Dylan in his early years shows him writing lyrics and signing autographs with his right hand (Feinstein, Kramer, & Marshall, 1999). However, the same book depicts Dylan in other one-handed activities, such as making unilateral gestures and smoking cigarettes, and these activities seem to be evenly split between his left and right hands. Also, when Dylan plays harmonica without using the holder around his neck, he holds the harmonica with his left hand. Accordingly, the current paper is willing to cautiously assume that Dylan is mixed-handed.

Hendrix's song-writing style is very free and natural, his lyrics sung with an ease and spontaneity reminiscent of ordinary speech. While Hendrix often complained about the inferior nature of his singing voice, there is no doubt that his vocal delivery more than made up in rhythmic and emotional expressiveness what it lacked in purely tonal qualities. This characteristic of his singing may have arisen in part due to the increased interaction between the left and right sides of his brain. While talking is under the control of the left side of the brain, singing is controlled by the right hemisphere (Gordon & Bogen, 1974).

Since the two hemispheres operate in a more integrated manner in mixed-handers, this suggests that the singing style of mixed-handers may be prone to comprise a mixture of spoken and sung vocalisations, akin to a technique developed in classical music by Arnold Schoenberg and called "Sprechstimme" in which the lyrics are spoken at approximate pitches instead of being sung at exact pitches (in musical notation, Sprechstimme vocals are denoted by the use of *x*s on the musical stave, in place of the traditional elliptical note markings). Thus Hendrix's vocal style is neither purely melodic, like in most pop singers, nor is it primarily spoken, as in much of today's rap music. Rather, his style is characterised by a fluid integration of left-hemisphere-based speaking and right-hemisphere-based singing.

Certainly, Hendrix's vocals on *Electric Ladyland* features an abundance of Sprechstimme-like stylings. One of the most prominent examples is found on 'Burning Of The Midnight Lamp', in which over a third of all the words are spoken/sung in the Sprechstimme style. Other notable examples are found in

'1983 …', in which portions of the first and second verses and the entire third verse are half spoken, half sung, and in 'House Burning Down', in which conversational lines from the first ("He just coughed and changed the subject and said, 'Er, ah, I think it might snow some'") and second verses ("He shouts retired and disgusted so we paint red through the sky") are delivered in the Sprechstimme style.

It is unlikely that Hendrix's use of Sprechstimme was completely conscious and under his control. It more likely arose as a natural by-product of his attempt to mask his self-perceived vocal deficiencies with a more speech-like delivery. For example, in the fourth verse of 'Voodoo Chile' Hendrix sings the first appearance of the phrase "Jupiter's sulphur mines", and yet a few moments later delivers the same phrase Sprechstimme style. In many ways Hendrix used Sprechstimme vocals as a means of providing spice and emphasis to his vocals in the same way that he used whammy bar and trill techniques to enhance his guitar playing.

A related phenomenon involves Hendrix's extensive use of vocal interjections, such as 'yeah', 'well, all right', 'mm mm', 'hey', and 'ah', which are sprinkled liberally through many of the songs on *Electric Ladyland*. While such interjections contribute little if anything to the lyrical content and themes of his songs, they clearly add to both the rhythmic and emotional impact of Hendrix's vocal delivery. It is interesting to note that such common and automatic phrases like 'yeah' and 'hey' are typically produced by the right, not the linguistically dominant left, side of the brain (e.g., Code, 1997). Hendrix appeared to truly sing with both sides of his brain.

Another important manifestation of Hendrix's fusion of speech and song involves the way that the phrasing of lyrics fuses with and often takes precedence over the melody. In typical pop songs the metric structure of verses and choruses are fairly rigid and invariant: for example, the melody line and number of syllables per line vary little if at all from verse to verse. It is as if the melody is dominant, and the lyrics must fit into the rhythmic structure dictated by the melody line. In Hendrix's songs, on the other hand, the melody line is often subordinate to the phrasing of the lyrics.

As a representative example, consider the syllabic structures of the verses from 'Voodoo Chile' as shown in Table 1. This song employs a traditional blues structure in which an initial couplet is repeated once, followed by a third concluding couplet. As Table 1 makes clear, there is virtually no consistency in the number of syllables per couplet either within or between verses, as the phrasing of the lyrics guides the melodic and syllabic structure, instead of the other way around. In Hendrix's songs, left brain words and rhythms are dynamically integrated with right brain melodies.

The second influence Hendrix's mixed-handedness on his song writing involves magical and ambiguous aspects of his lyrics and melodies. Research

TABLE 1
Number of syllables per couplet for the five verses of 'Voodoo Chile'

	Verse 1	*Verse 2*	*Verse 3*	*Verse 4*	*Verse 5*
Couplet 1	15	18	13	20	15
Couplet 2	13	16	16	20	15
Couplet 3	21	28	21	19	28

has shown that mixed-handers have higher levels of magical thinking (Barnett & Corballis, 2002). Magical thinking refers to beliefs in paranormal forms of causation, such as belief in UFOs, ESP, and astrology. Hendrix's propensity towards magical thinking is illustrated by his lifelong belief in voodoo that he evidently picked up during childhood visits with relatives in Georgia. As he put it, "Voodoo stuff! You think that sort of thing is rubbish 'till it happens to you, then it's scary. There's different things they can do, they can put something in your food, or put some little hair in your shoe. I saw it. If I see it happen or if I feel it happen, then I believe it" (Fairchild, 1994). Hendrix's voodoo beliefs, of course, formed the foundation for lyrics to the song 'Voodoo Chile'. Hendrix also felt that UFOs followed him around, and that his life was once saved by a UFO in Woodstock, New York in 1965 (Knight, 1992).

The higher levels of magical thinking in mixed-handers arise from the fact that the left side of the brain is responsible for maintaining our current "status quo" beliefs about the world, while the right side acts as a sort of "devil's advocate", looking for inconsistencies in left hemisphere belief systems, and forcing an updating of those beliefs when necessary (Ramachandran, 1995; Ramachandran & Blakeslee, 1998; see also Gazzaniga, 2000). Thus, because of their increased amount of interaction between the two sides of the brain which allows the right side to more efficiently act on and update left hemisphere-based beliefs, mixed-handers are more flexible in their thinking, are more likely to engage in divergent and lateral thinking (i.e., "thinking outside the box"), are more open to persuasion, and are more likely to readily update their beliefs, for better or worse (Christman et al., 2008; Coren, 1995; Niebauer, Aselage, & Schutte, 2002; Niebauer et al., 2004). Hendrix's lyrics reflected the general openness to new ideas, from science fiction to psychedelic utopianism, that arose in the 1960s.

The songs on *Electric Ladyland* explore an often bizarre and fantastic world populated by references to "electric love penetrat[-ing] the sky" ['Have You Ever Been (To Electric Ladyland)'], trips "on a eagle's wing" beyond "the outskirts of infinity" where he receives "a venus witch's ring", and "arrows made of desire from far away as Jupiter's sulphur mines" ['Voodoo Chile'], a road that "rambles on for a million miles" ['Gypsy Eyes'], "giant pencil and lipstick tube shaped things", and a machine that makes it possible "to live and breathe under water, forever" ['1983 … (A Merman I Should Turn To Be)'], "Neptune champion games", smiling mermaids, and "Atlantis full of cheer" ['Moon Turn The Tides … Gently, Gently Away'], "a giant boat from space land[-ing] with eerie grace" to take "all the dead away" ['House Burning Down'], and standing "up next to a mountain" and chopping "it down with the edge of my hand" ['Voodoo Chile (Slight Return)'].

It should be noted here that many songwriters during the 1960s were similarly focused on mystical and science fiction themes, so Hendrix was by no means unique in this regard. However, given that roughly half the population is mixed-handed, it is possible that mixed-handed songwriters like Hendrix were responsible for the lion's share of mystical lyrics.

Mixed-handedness is also associated with an increased tolerance of ambiguity (Garvey & Niebauer, 2003), which characterises much of the lyrical and musical content of *Electric Ladyland.* Examples of ambiguity in the lyrics include the reference to floating "in liquid gardens way down in Arizona red sand" and being "a million miles away at the same time I'm right here in your picture frame" ['Voodoo Chile'], and "everybody's on fire but I'm snowin' in a cold blizzard" ['Long Hot Summer Night']. The title of Hendrix's song "If 6 was 9" is another nice example of ambiguity.

Electric Ladyland also features prominent examples of musical ambiguity. The most prevalent is Hendrix's use of the tonally ambiguous Dominant 7#9 chord (often referred to in rock circles as the "Hendrix Chord"). The 7#9 chord consists of a tonic root, major third, perfect fifth, minor seventh, and an augmented ninth. Examples of this chord (in the key of E) are shown in musical notation (showing the full version) and guitar tablature (showing the version Hendrix typically played, dropping the perfect fifth interval) in Figure 1.

The ambiguity of this chord derives from the fact that it contains both a major third interval (E – G#) and a minor third interval in the form of the augmented ninth (E – G). Thus, it is not clear to the ear whether this chord

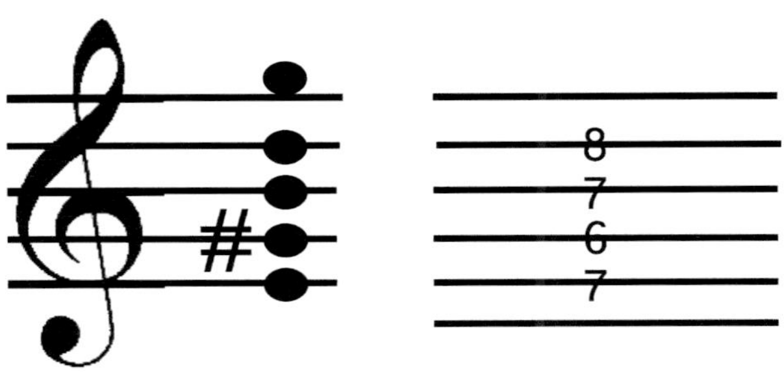

Figure 1. The Dominant E7#9 chord, shown in both traditional musical notation and in guitar tablature.

should be heard as a major chord or as a minor chord. Furthermore, altered dominant seventh chords like this are typically used to resolve to a tonic minor. However, Hendrix often uses this chord as a tonic chord itself, leading to a chronic state of tonal ambiguity as the chord simultaneously relieves musical tension by returning to the tonic key and increases tension by its implicit pointing to an unplayed alternative tonic chord. Notable appearances of the "Hendrix chord" on *Electric Ladlyland* include 'Crosstown Traffic', where it appears behind the "*do do do*s" of the chorus and during the second verse, the final chorus of 'Voodoo Chile', the chorus of 'Come On (Let The Good Times Roll)', and at the end of each verse quatrain in 'House Burning Down'. For a nice discussion of the roots and history of this chord's use in popular music, see Everett (2002).

Hendrix was also fond of suspended chords, especially the sus2. The sus2 chord is characterised by a tonal ambiguity arising from the fact that the sus2 interval introduces two competing fifth intervals, one based on the tonic and the other based on the dominant. Finally, Hendrix's guitar playing on the song 'Come On (Let the Good Times Roll)' by New Orleans bluesman Earl King is at times based on using the cycle of fifths, which has a jazz-like effect of introducing transient uncertainties about the tonal centre of the song.

It is worth noting a few other general ambiguities associated with Jimi Hendrix. He cut his musical chops playing African-based rhythm and blues styles, yet found his largest audience playing rock'n'roll for European whites. His biggest hit, 'All Along The Watchtower', was a heavy metal-like treatment of Dylan's sparse, acoustic original—Zak (2005) has written an ambitious essay comparing the evolution and nature of Dylan's versus Hendrix's versions of 'All Along The Watchtower' that the interested reader is recommended to consult. There was a dramatic contrast between Hendrix's flamboyant persona onstage and the more thoughtful and introspective musician in the recording studio. His public persona was often characterised by a touch of sexually ambiguous androgyny. Even the spelling of his name, Jimi Hendrix, is an ambiguous play on the more conventional spelling "Jimmy Hendricks".

One final aspect of Hendrix's musicianship bears mention. One of the implications of the increased interhemispheric interaction in mixed-handers is that it may give such individuals enhanced conscious access to right-hemisphere-based processing. It is well established that the right hemisphere is superior at processing nonverbal environmental sounds (e.g., Schnider, Benson, Alexander, & Schnider-Klaus, 1994). This may help to account for the wide variety of nonverbal environmental sounds that permeate *Electric Ladyland*, from the sound collages of '... And The Gods Made Love' and 'Moon, Turn The Tides ... Gently Gently Away', through the use of a home-made comb-and-waxed-paper kazoo to augment the opening guitar of 'Crosstown Traffic', and the frequent presence of guitar and microphone feedback in songs like 'Voodoo Chile', to the mysterious underwater chime-like sounds during the guitar solo and bird-like sounds at the very end of '1983 . . . (A Merman I Should Be)'.

SUMMARY (SLIGHT RETURN)

Jimi Hendrix's mixed-handedness, and the ensuing enhancement of interaction between the left and right sides of his brain, resulted in a synergetic confluence of factors that led to both his groundbreaking style of guitar playing and the engaging and provocative nature of his songs and lyrics. Perhaps the most important aspect of the current paper, from the perspective of handedness researchers, is the argument that modern "right-handed" guitars are better viewed as left-handed guitars in terms of the relative motor demands on the two hands, and that Hendrix's superlative guitar abilities arose from the fact that he played a "left-handed" guitar and was thus able to use his more dextrous right hand on the guitar's fretboard.

A common theme in this paper has revolved around the fact Hendrix's mixed-handedness was associated with increased integration of the left and right sides of his brain, which in turn enabled him to integrate the actions of his left and right hands while playing guitar, to integrate the lyrics and melodies of his songs, and perhaps even to integrate the older blues and R&B traditions with the emerging folk, rock, and psychedelic sounds of the sixties, creating what Hendrix deemed "a mixture of rock, freak-out, blues, and rave music" (Shapiro & Glebbeek, 1992, p. 129). Nigel Kennedy, a classical violinist who recorded an album of Hendrix covers performed by an eight-piece classical ensemble, once remarked, "I think that that's what's interesting about Hendrix – the lateral consciousness that he has. I think integration in music is really what makes originality" (Noble, 1995b, p. 36).

REFERENCES

Aggleton, J. P., Kentridge, R. W., & Good, J. M. M. (1994). Handedness and musical ability: A study of professional orchestral players, composers, and choir members. *Psychology of Music*, *22*, 148–156.

Barnett, K. J., & Corballis, M. C. (2002). Ambidexterity and magical ideation. *Laterality*, *7*, 75–84.

Christman, S. D. (1993). Handedness in musicians: Bimanual constraints on performance. *Brain and Cognition*, *22*, 266–272.

Christman, S. D. (1995). Independence versus integration of right and left hemisphere processing: Effects of handedness. In F. Kitterle (Ed.), *Hemispheric communication: Mechanisms and models*. Hillsdale, NJ: Lawrence Erlbaum Associates Inc.

Christman, S. D. (2001). Individual differences in Stroop and local-global processing: A possible role of interhemispheric interaction. *Brain and Cognition*, *45*, 97–118.

Christman, S. D., Bentle, M., & Niebauer, C. L. (2007a). Handedness differences in body image distortion and eating disorder symptomatology. *International Journal of Eating Disorders, 40*, 247–256.

Christman, S. D., Henning, B., Geers, A. L., Propper, R. E., & Niebauer, C. L. (2008). Mixed-handed persons are more easily persuaded and are more gullible: Interhemispheric interaction and belief updating. *Laterality, 13*, 403–426.

Christman, S. D., Jasper, J. D., Sontam, V., & Cooil, B. (2007b). Individual differences in risk perception versus risk taking: Handedness and interhemispheric interaction. *Brain and Cognition, 63*, 51–58.

Christman, S. D., Propper, R. E., & Brown, T. J. (2006). Increased interhemispheric interaction is associated with earlier offset of childhood amnesia. *Neuropsychology, 20*, 336–345.

Christman, S. D., Propper, R. E., & Dion, A. (2004). Increased interhemispheric interaction is associated with decreased false memories in a verbal converging semantic associates paradigm. *Brain and Cognition, 56*, 313–319.

Code, C. (1997). Can the right hemisphere speak? *Brain and Language, 57*, 38–59.

Collins, R. L. (1985). On the inheritance of direction and degree of asymmetry. In S. D. Glick (Ed.), *Cerebral lateralisation in nonhuman species* (pp. 41–71). New York: Academic Press.

Coren, S. (1995). Differences in divergent thinking as a function of handedness and sex. *American Journal of Psychology, 108*, 311–325.

Engel, J. (2006). *Uncommon sound.* Bruxelles: Left Field Ventures.

Everett, W. (2002). Detroit and Memphis: The soul of *Revolver.* In R. Reising (Ed.), *'Every Sound There Is': The Beatles'* Revolver *and the transformation of rock and roll.* Cornwall, UK: Ashgate.

Fairchild, M. (1994). [Liner notes accompanying *Jimi Hendrix: Blues* CD.] New York: MCA Records.

Feinstein, B., Kramer, D., & Marshall, J. (1999). *Early Dylan.* Milan: Bullfinch Press.

Garvey, K., & Niebauer, C. L. (2003). *Cerebral laterality and ontological sophistication: Strength of handedness predicts cognitive complexity.* Paper presented at the 2003 Meeting of the American Psychological Society, Atlanta, GA.

Gates, A., & Bradshaw, J. L. (1977). The role of the cerebral hemispheres in music. *Brain & Language, 4*, 403–431.

Gazzaniga, M. S. (2000). Cerebral specialization and interhemispheric communication: Does the corpus callosum enable the human condition? *Brain, 123*, 1293–1326.

Gordon, H. W., & Bogen, J. E. (1974). Hemispheric lateralisation of singing after intracarotid sodium amylobarbitone. *Journal of Neurology, Neurosurgery, Psychiatry, 37*, 727–738.

Hendrix, J. A. (1999). *My son Jimi.* Seattle, WA: AlJas Enterprises.

Jancke, L. (2002). The case of a left-handed pianist playing a reversed keyboard: A challenge for the neuroscience of music. *Neuroreport, 13*, 1579–1583.

Jancke, L., Baumann, S., Koeneke, S., Meyer, M., Laeng, B., Peters, M., et al. (2006). Neural control of playing a reversed piano: Empirical evidence for an unusual cortical organisation of musical functions. *Neuroreport, 17*, 447–451.

Jancke, L., Schlaug, G., & Steinmetz, H. (1997). Hand skill asymmetry in professional musicians. *Brain and Cognition, 34*, 424–432.

Jasper, J. D., Barry, K., & Christman, S. D. (2008). Individual differences in counterfactual production. *Personality and Individual Differences, 45*, 488–492.

Jasper, J. D., & Christman, S. D. (2005). A neuropsychological dimension for anchoring effects. *Journal of Behavioral Decision Making, 18*, 343–369.

Kempe, V., Brooks, P. J., & Christman, S. D. (2009). Interhemispheric connectivity supports foreign language vocabulary learning. *Psychonomic Bulletin & Review, 16*, 480–485.

Knight, C. (1992). *Jimi Hendrix: Starchild.* New Brunswick, NJ: Inner Light Publications.

Laeng, B., & Park, A. (1999). Handedness effects on playing a reversed and normal keyboard. *Laterality, 4*, 363–377.

Lescroart, J. (1977). *Rock guitarists, Vol. II*. Saratoga, CA: Guitar Player Books.

Moffat, S. D., Hampson, E., & Lee, D. H. (1998). Morphology of the planum temporale and corpus callosum in left handers with evidence of left and right hemisphere speech representation. *Brain, 121*, 2369–2379.

Morgan, M. J., & Corballis, M. (1978). On the biological basis of human laterality. II: The mechanisms of inheritance. *Behavioral and Brain Sciences, 2*, 270–277.

Niebauer, C. L. (2004). Handedness and the fringe of consciousness: Strong handers ruminate while mixed handers self-reflect. *Consciousness & Cognition, 13*, 730–745.

Niebauer, C. L., Aselage, J., & Schutte, C. (2002). Interhemispheric interaction and consciousness: Degree of handedness predicts the intensity of a sensory illusion. *Laterality, 7*, 85–96.

Niebauer, C. L., Christman, S. D., Reid, S. A., & Garvey, K. (2004). Interhemispheric interaction and beliefs on our origin: Degree of handedness predicts beliefs in creationism versus evolution. *Laterality, 9*, 433–447.

Noble, D. J. (1995a). Lefty matters. *UniVibes, no. 17*.

Noble, D. J. (1995b). Nigel Kennedy on Jimi Hendrix. *UniVibes, no. 18*.

Oldfield, R. (1971). The assessment and analysis of handedness: The Edinburgh Inventory. *Neuropsychologia, 9*, 97–113.

Porac, C. (1993). Hand preference and the incidence of unilateral hand injury. *Neuropsychologia, 31*, 355–362.

Propper, R. E., & Christman, S. D. (2004). Mixed- versus strong-handedness is associated with biases toward "Remember" versus "Know" judgments in recognition memory: Role of interhemispheric interaction. *Memory, 12*, 707–714.

Propper, R. E., Christman, S. D., & Phaneuf, K. A. (2005). A mixed-handed advantage in episodic memory: A possible role of interhemispheric interaction. *Memory & Cognition, 33*, 751–757.

Propper, R. E., Lawton, N., Przyborski, M., & Christman, S. (2004). A naturalistic assessment of sleep architecture as a function of handedness using a home sleep monitor. *Brain & Cognition, 54*, 186–197.

Ramachandran, V. S. (1995). Anosognosia in parietal lobe syndrome. *Consciousness and Cognition, 4*, 22–51.

Ramachandran, V. S., & Blakeslee, S. (1998). *Phantoms in the brain*. New York: William Morrow & Company.

Schnider, A., Benson, F. D., Alexander, D. N., & Schnider-Klaus, A. (1994). Non-verbal environmental sound recognition after unilateral hemispheric stroke. *Brain, 117*, 281–287.

Shapiro, H., & Glebbeek, C. (1992). *Jimi Hendrix: Electric gypsy*. New York: St. Martin's Griffin.

Westerhausen, R., Kreuder, F., Sequeira, S. D. S., Walter, C., Woerner, W., Wittling, R.A., et al. (2004). Effects of handedness and gender on macro- and microstructure of the corpus callosum and its subregions: A combined high-resolution and diffusion-tensor MRI study. *Cognitive Brain Research, 21*, 418–426.

Witelson, S. (1985). The brain connection: The corpus callosum is larger in left-handers. *Science, 229*, 665–668.

Witelson, S. F., & Goldsmith, C. H. (1991). The relationship of hand preference to anatomy of the corpus callosum in men. *Brain Research, 545*, 175–182.

Zak, A. J. III (2005). Bob Dylan and Jimi Hendrix: Juxtaposition and transformation – "All along the watchtower". *Journal of the American Musicological Society, 57*, 599–644.

LATERALITY, 2010, 15 (1/2), 270–288

A Left Handed Compliment: A newly discovered, early nineteenth-century lithograph by John Lewis Marks

I. C. McManus

Division of Psychology and Language Sciences, University College London, London, UK

Janet Snowman

Royal Academy of Music, London, UK

A newly discovered, early nineteenth-century lithograph by John Lewis Marks (b. ca. 1795–1796, d. ca. 1857–1861), entitled *A Left Handed Compliment*, is described. In this humorous print a young boy is using his left hand to draw the face of an elderly woman who is his grandmother, and she is shocked at the boy's suggestion that he will, "just see if I can't touch off your old Phizog left handed". The source of the joke about the left-handed compliment is obscure, but more than likely it is sexual in origin. Glued to the verso of the print are early versions of two prints by Robert Seymour (1798–1836), the illustrator of Dickens' *Pickwick Papers*, suggesting a possible link between Marks and Seymour. From the hatch patterns on the Seymour engravings, it appears that Seymour may himself have been left-handed and perhaps therefore the butt of the joke. An alternative possibility is that Phizog is a reference to Dickens' later illustrator whose pseudonym was Phiz. It is also just conceivable that the young boy is Marks's own young son, Jacob. The print can be placed in the context of a scatological English vernacular humour that extends from Shakespeare through to Donald McGill and into the present day.

Keywords: John Lewis Marks; Left-handed compliment; Lithograph.

Address correspondence to: Professor Chris McManus, Division of Psychology and Language Sciences, University College London, Gower Street, London WC1E 6BT, UK. E-mail: i.mcmanus@ucl.ac.uk

We are very grateful to Lauren Harris for his comments and thoughts on the interpretation of this print, to John Martin for his very helpful recollections of John Taylor, and to Anthony Griffiths and his staff at the British Museum.

DOI: 10.1080/13576500903201800

Figure 1. The recto of *A Left Handed Compliment* by J. Lewis Marks. To view this figure in colour, please visit the online version of this Journal.

In 2006 one of us (JS), at a sale of antique prints and ephemera in London, discovered the print of size 239 mm (height) × 192 mm (width), that is shown in Figure 1. The print is a hand-coloured lithograph, the image and the hand-drawn lettering being typical of that technique (Gascoigne, 2004). Entitled, at the top, "A LEFT HANDED COMPLIMENT./N°. XII", in the bottom left-hand corner it is signed on the block, "J.L.M.", and in the bottom right-hand corner, also on the block, is "3^{d} Col^{d}" (presumably, "threepence coloured"[1]). The text at the bottom, that is clearly handwritten, reads, "Now Granny, sit still; and I'll just see if I can't touch off your old Phizog left handed [.]/Mercy on us Child! what could put such an idea into your head?". There is no date on the print, and no obvious sense of the context in which it would have been published, although it would seem compatible with the early 1830s.[2] The print was sold to JS by John Martin of Mayfly Ephemera and Books, who subsequently told us that the former owner was John Taylor, who could be described as "a true ephemerist", who had amassed a large and rather miscellaneous collection, said to be "three truckloads", which was left to John Martin after John Taylor's death. In Martin's own words,

> The story of John Taylor is a somewhat sad one. He came from a well-to-do family in Yorkshire and travelled much before World War II (and I recall he was born in 1912). Before the war, I believe he worked in advertising before being called up. He served in the Royal West Kent Regiment and was wounded badly; although the physical wounds healed, he never recovered from what was clearly shell shock. The rest of his working life was spent as a porter in the Travellers Club [in London's] Pall Mall. He did not relate well to people and never married. His abiding passion was the pursuit of printed trivia—ephemera collectables. He was very knowledgeable about the subject. He lived with his collection, which was never organised, in a garret in Notting Hill, choosing but few creature comforts. He died in 1992. The collection, which was more in the nature of a personal accumulation, is largely dispersed now.

The print is glued on to a sheet of thin, cheapish, bright yellow paper, on the verso of which (see Figure 2) have been glued two seemingly unrelated and unsigned prints, which are etchings[3] by Robert Seymour (1798–1836) (Heseltine, 2004), whose fame now rests mainly on his illustrations for the first part of Dickens' *Pickwick Papers.* Both images have been slightly cropped, and neither image has anything on its verso. The images are entitled *Peter Simple's Foreign Adventure No. 1*, and *A Musical Festival.*

---

[1] At least one other of Marks' published prints, number 8 in his *Military Costumes* series, of 1831 ("Enniskillen or 6th"), has "1^{D} plain" in the lower left corner, and "Price 3^{D} col^{d}" in the lower right corner (see www.sandersofoxford.com/images/stock/8927.jpg). Other prints by Marks give the price of two pence coloured. The first reference in the OED to "penny plain and twopence coloured style" ("Originally used with reference to prints of characters sold for toy theatres, costing one penny for black-and-white ones, and twopence for coloured ones") is from 1854. A much earlier use of the phrase is in the toy theatre prints published by William West in the early 1800s as "penny plain, and twopence coloured" (Robinson & Powell, 2004, p. 10). Somewhat surprisingly, the first reference to the phrase in *The Times* is as late as Dec 15th 1880 in an article on Christmas Cards.

[2] We are grateful to Anthony Griffiths for this opinion.

[3] Seymour was originally a wood engraver (Engen, 1985), around 1827 he learnt copper engraving (Maidment, 1996), and from 1830 onwards he was using lithography (Heseltine, 2004).

Figure 2. The verso of *A Left Handed Compliment* showing the two prints by Robert Seymour, both of which have been slightly cropped. To view this figure in colour, please visit the online version of this Journal.

Individual prints from *Sketches by Seymour* were published by Richard Carlile between 1834 and 1836 (Maidment, 1996).[4] After Seymour's tragic, early death in 1836, the sketches were published in book form with appended text and verses in five volumes as *Seymour's Sketches: Illustrated in Prose and Verse by Alfred Crowquill* (Seymour, 1838), Crowquill being the pseudonym of Alfred Forrester, with editions appearing until at least 1878, when they were steel engraved.[5] The full text of an undated version is available online at www.gutenberg.org.[6] Although the Carlile prints are

[4] For examples of the Carlile plates see www.pbagalleries.com/search/item_img.php?acq_no = 173410 where it is clear that the typography is different from the versions in the book, and there are also two images on a single printed sheet. The BM catalogue has a copy of *Peter Simple's Foreign Adventure No. 1*, described as an etching, catalogued as 2006,0929.40, dated 1834–1836 and of size 130 × by 107 mm. See www.britishmuseum.org/research/search_the_collection_database.aspx. The BM does not appear to have a copy of *A Musical Festival*.

[5] See http://www.antiqueprints.com/proddetail.php?prod = f9529.

[6] See www.gutenberg.org/files/5650/5650-h/p4.htm#Odd17%20Peter%201 and www.gutenberg.org/files/5648/5648-h/5648-h.htm#Odd27%20Musical for versions of the images discussed here.

similar in content to the same titles in *Seymour's Sketches,* the typography in the two versions is different and there are also minor differences in the images, suggesting that those in *Seymour's Sketches* are in a later state.[7] The versions on the verso of *A Left Handed Compliment* are presumably those of the Carlile or perhaps an earlier edition.

How the Marks and Seymour prints came together is not clear. One possibility is that the yellow paper is from a nineteenth-century commonplace book,[8] and that they were either acquired from a chapman, or were a printer's commonplace book. The fact that the Seymours are cropped through their printed matter, and the yellow paper does not extend beyond the edge of the Marks print, except in the rounded top corners, along with the Marks print being cropped very slightly (the "d" of "handed" is incomplete), suggests that some previous owner, probably in the nineteenth century, had wished to frame *A Left Handed Compliment*, and cared little for the Seymours attached to it. The importance for the present paper is that the Seymour images and *A Left Handed Compliment* were presumably all at some time in the hands of a common source, either a seller of prints, a collector of prints, or perhaps someone involved in the London printing world of the late 1820s or more likely the 1830s. A later owner presumably did not recognise any interest in the Seymour prints, since they have been cropped.

A Left Handed Compliment was identified as being by J. Lewis Marks, the initials "J L M" being consistent with other prints by him, as also was the style of the lettering, and in 2007 the print was seen at the British Museum by Sheila O'Connell, the author of *The popular print in England* (O'Connell, 1999), and the attribution confirmed. The museum has an extensive collection of other items by Marks from 1814 to 1832, although it is difficult to estimate the extent of his total output, not least because, as a note in the BM collection says, unsigned works published by him always seem actually to have been etched by him. However, the Museum collection does not include a copy of *A Left Handed Compliment*, and neither did this print seem to be a part of any series in their collection.

---

[7] Some of the 1838 edition images have an inscription at the bottom saying either, "Etched by H. Wallis from a sketch by Seymour" or "Eng.^{d} by Ha. Wallis from a sketch of Seymour's". It is possible therefore that Wallis also added to some of the other etchings, which are presumably by Seymour himself.

[8] For a good example of a late eighteenth- or early nineteenth-century scrapbook with a number of political and other cartoons, see the "Green Marble Scrapbook" at http://www.crcstudio.arts.ualberta.ca/heritage/index.php. For histories of the social context of prints and caricatures, see George (1959b, pp. 174–177) on the role of print shops, and George (1959a, pp. 257–260) on the rise in the early 1830s of the coloured lithograph, and of scrapbooks.

J. Lewis Marks, as he is usually known (or sometimes JL Marks or Lewis Marks; the J has been said to stand for 'John'[9]) has been described as one of the most radical of the late Georgian political caricaturists who attacked the Prince Regent who was subsequently to become George IV (Press, 1977). Marks's radicalism is well seen in a cartoon from 1819, "The massacre at Peterloo! as a Specimen of English Liberty" (Bayly, 2004). However, while Marks as a caricaturist, cartoonist and illustrator makes his presence readily visible in a host of illustrations over perhaps two decades, as an individual he is extremely elusive. The website of the National Portrait Gallery in London merely says of him, "J.L. Marks (floruit 1814–1832)" with no information on dates of birth or death, and on the internet, the Davidson Galleries have him as "fl. c. 1800–1830".[10] The NPG's date of 1814 is compatible with a set of etchings dated at 1814, entitled *Something concerning Nobody. Edited by Somebody. Embellished with fourteen characteristic etchings.*[11] Other works of reference are mostly silent (with the *Oxford Dictionary of National Biography* making no mention of Marks, despite having entries on James Gillray, George Cruikshank and Robert Seymour). The extremely brief, seventeen line entry in the *Dictionary of British Cartoonists and Caricaturists* says only that he flourished, "1814–32", appearing as a designer in 1814,[12] and a publisher of political caricatures in 1817, and that his last, "trenchantly pro-Reform" prints appeared in 1832 (Bryant & Heneage, 1994). Contrary to those sources though, the dealer Marilyn Pink has items by him dated 1836, and images such as those at www.arthouseonline.co.uk/e1.htm are clearly signed and dated on the plate as May 1st, 1837, and as well as that, in 1839 there are theatrical images.[13] Finally, the very fine image by Marks of the fire at the Tower of London,[14] on October 30th, 1841, and published from Long Lane, Smithfield, shows that he was still active into the 1840s. Amongst the very limited biographical information available is that Marks published from several

[9] The only source which seems to suggest this is the recent reprint of *The Adventures of Paul Pry and His Young Friend in London*, which is dated to 1835, and attributed to John Lewis Marks (Marks, 2007).

[10] As will be seen, the 1800 is not possible.

[11] http://www.skreb.co.uk/caricature.php The sepia etchings were published in London by Robert Scholey. However a similar set of etchings are sometimes attributed to George Moutard Woodward, although he died in 1809.

[12] George (1959a, p. 263) describes him also as, "Publisher of theatrical prints (Toy Theatre) by himself . . .". These may be the undated toy theatre sheets published by Marks in New York (see http://www.nypl.org/research/lpa/the/pdf/theweyhe.pdf).

[13] See http://www.dramatispersonae.com/ST.htm. Also http://www.catalogue-host.co.uk/mallams/oxford/2007-03-09/lot_8?prev_page=illustrations%2c%20page%201%20of%203&prev_url=%2fmallams%2foxford%2f2007-03-09%2fillustrations_1. The quality is distinctly less than that in the earlier prints, and it may be that Marks is only the publisher of these images.

[14] The image can be seen at the website of the Bridgeman Art Library in New York (http://images.bridgeman.co.uk/cgi-bin/bridgemanImage.cgi/600.GHL.86290.7055475/6089.JPG).

London addresses, including "17 Artillery Street, Bishopsgate", "Sandy's Row, Bishopsgate", and "No 37, Princes St, Soho". In 1850, Marks was publishing children's books such as *Puss in Boots* and *Blue Beard*, the back cover of which says "A GREAT VARIETY/OF/CHILDREN'S BOOKS;/ PAMPHLETS/THEATRICAL/CHARACTERS/CARICATURES,/PRINTS/ PLAIN AND COLOURED/ALWAYS ON SALE/AT/*J. L. Marks, 91, Long Lane/Smithfield*",[15] an address at which Todd's *Directory* suggests Marks was printing from 1836 to 1857 (Todd, 1972).

Census records are now readily available on the internet, and a search of census records for 1851 finds a John Lewis Marks, aged 55, and hence born in about 1796, described as a "victualler and publisher", living at 2 Long Lane, Aldersgate, with his wife Sarah (aged 45), and children Maria, Benjamin and Mary, aged 18, 15 and 8. Two years earlier, on Oct 20th, 1849, the license for the Portland Arms, in Long Lane, had been transferred to a "John Lewis Marks".[16] The 1841 census has a record for "John Marks", aged 45, described as an Engraver, living at 91 Long Lane, St Bartholomew the Great, with his wife Sarah, aged 35, and nine other members of the Marks family, Rachel, Jacob (himself described as an engraver), Isaac, Hannah, Maria, Louisa, Nathaniel, and Benjamin (aged 19,15,14,12,10, 8, 5 and 3), as well as a three-day-old son as yet unnamed; whether all of these are John and Sarah's children is not stated, but is possible. A search of London marriage records found that a John Marks married a Sarah Tibble at St George's, Bloomsbury, in 1836, but it is unclear if this is our Marks, although it could be. There is no record in the 1861 or subsequent census for any John Marks of the right age living in London, and the Portland Arms at 2 Long Lane was now being run by a Peter Jupp.[17] A search of nineteenth-century death records found no obvious candidate for John Lewis Marks, and although several John Marks were found, none were of the right age. Probably what can be concluded is that Marks lived from 1795 to 1796 to somewhere between about 1857 and 1861.

Marks was clearly a prolific illustrator, and was also very inventive, his "The progress of Boney !!!"[18] of about 1817 being one of the earliest strip cartoons, which is notable not only for its imaginative use of stick figures (Kunzle, 1973), but also for Marks's love of exclamation marks (albeit he

[15] http://www.cts.dmu.ac.uk/AnaServer?hockliffe+1195+hoccview.anv. The website also comments that "William B. Todd's *A Dictionary of Printers* locates Marks at this address from 1836 to 1857". For a more complete list of children's books see the back page of http://www.archive.org/details/markshistoryofa00londiala.

[16] "Transfer of Licenses", *The Era (London)*, Oct 28th, 1849, issue 579. (Available online from the British Library's *Nineteenth Century British Library Newspapers.*)

[17] As in the 1859 *Post Office Street Directory*, although in the 1852 *Post Office Street Directory* the Portland Arms is still listed as "John L. Marks".

[18] See www.flickr.com/photos/deathtogutenberg/423202004/in/set-72157600003169123/

was not alone in that). Although *A Left Handed Compliment* is subtitled, "N°. XII", it is not clear whether this is the twelfth in a series of illustrations of left-handed compliments, or is twelfth in a more general series. What does seem to be clear, though, is that Marks and others did publish series of themed prints, of which this is likely to be one. Others of Marks' series include *Illustrations of Plays* (of which number 17 is in the British Museum), *Military Costumes*, and *Double Entendres*.

A major interest of *A Left Handed Compliment* is what it tells us about the perception of left-handedness at the beginning of the nineteenth century, and an immediate question of interest concerns the handedness of Marks and also Seymour. The handedness of an artist can usually be determined in drawings by looking at the hatch marks made when shading, these typically running from bottom-left to top-right in right-handers (/////) and from bottom-right to top-left in left-handers (\\\\\). A good example of the hatchmarks of an undoubted left-hander can be seen in the drawings of Adolph Menzel (Maaz, 2008). An important complication arises when prints are being made. Traditionally prints such as wood cuts, wood engravings, etchings and the like, are made by making marks on a surface and the ink is then transferred from the surface to the paper, with the result that marks on the surface become mirror-reversed on the paper (and artists from the Renaissance onwards have evolved techniques for the reversal of images—see Bury, 1996). The important implication for present purposes is that on any such print the hatch marks of a right-hander, particularly since hatch marks are the most automatic of the marks used in representation, would slope in the opposite direction to that on a pencil or other drawing (i.e., they would slant \\\\\). A further complication though, that cannot be ignored, is that some engravers used a mirror while working, to help in reversing the image.

A subtle but important complication arises with lithographs. In their simplest form, as invented by Alois Senefelder in Munich in 1796, a lithographic image is drawn onto a stone (or metal) block, and the image becomes reversed when ink is applied and the block pressed against the paper. However, Senefelder also developed what is known as "transfer lithography", in which the drawing is first done on a sheet of specially prepared paper which is then pressed against the stone, transferring the image to the stone, so that the image is then transferred to the paper; for a good history of the importance of the technique, see Twyman (2001). The double contact process means that the image on the sheet of paper is printed without left-right reversal. The technique was first mentioned briefly in English in the 1816 edition of Bankes' *Lithography* (Twyman, 1976). As Raucort (1820, p. 27) later explained, in the 1820 English translation of his *Manual of Lithography*, "The necessity of reversing both writing and drawings on the stone, has made the use of [transfer] paper indispensable to all those who are not in the habit of writing reversed". The commercial advantages of transfer lithography were enormous, for as Bryans (2000) says, it, "solved the difficulty of printing picture and text separately", particularly for complex printing such as of music, of maps, of non-Roman characters, of scientific diagrams, and of large amounts of text within images, since the artist or illustrator did not have to be able to write or draw in a mirror direction, with its high likelihood of error. Large numbers of illustrators therefore used transfer lithography, so much so that even though Senefelder's monograph was not published until 1818, "he reported that transfer lithography was already popular with jobbing printers for handwritten lettering ..." (Gascoigne, 2004, 20.a). Marks undoubtedly produced lithographs from at least 1818, his *Found it out; or, a German P- humbuged*, saying at the bottom, "Inv.d Drawn & Printed from stone! by J.L.Marks No.2 Sandy's Row Artillery St. Bishopsgate".[19] There is however no clear evidence that he ever used transfer lithography.

In *A Left Handed Compliment*, the hatch marks around the right hand side of the grandmother's dress, in the chair back, and at the back beneath the clock are all running from top left to bottom right (\\\\) (see Figure 3), which in a drawing would be typical of the marks drawn by a left-hander. Assuming that the print is a conventional lithograph (and expert opinion suggests it is not a transfer lithograph), then the print would have been reversed in the printing, and so we can probably conclude that Marks was right-handed, and therefore is probably not making some veiled personal comment on the treatment of left-handers in society.[20] Intriguingly, however, the cross-hatchings in the Seymour wood engravings that somehow came to be attached to the back of *A Left Handed Compliment*, can be seen to run in large part from top right to bottom left (////) (see Figure 3), as would also seem to be the case in other Seymour engravings. The implication, since the engravings would have been reversed, is that Seymour may well have been left-handed.[21] Given also that it seems likely that Seymour and Marks would have known one another in the close world of radical Georgian publishing (and Seymour and George Cruikshank were certainly close friends (Heseltine, 2004)), then Marks may have been making some sort of comment on Seymour's handedness.

[19] See also *Bess and her R-l humbug* of 1818 (BM Satires 12992).

[20] A potential problem is that not all of the hatch marks in Marks' drawings are consistent. On the British Museum website, some of the early images of 1817 and 1818 appear to show //// hatches (e.g., BM 12876, 12990, 12991, 12992, 12989, which are between 1817 and 1818, whereas several of the *Doubles Entendres* series of 1832 seem to have \\\\ hatching.

[21] The assumption is of course that Seymour engraved these images himself. Some of his earlier prints were however wood engraved by George Dorrington (Engen, 1985, p. 233).

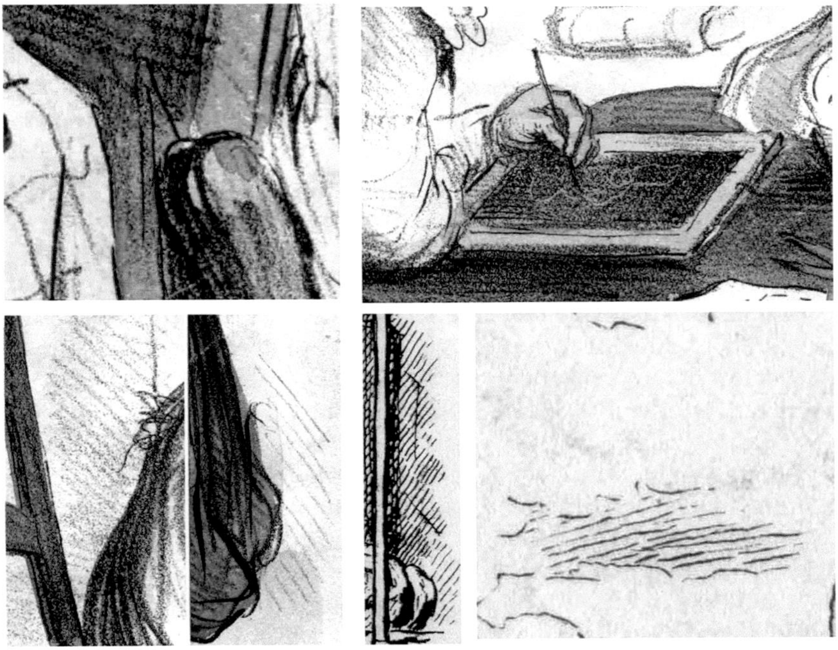

Figure 3. Anti-clockwise from top right: details from *A Left Handed Compliment* (the slate and drawing instrument; the needle held in the left hand through the stocking; hatching from beside the chair back; and hatching beside the grandmother's dress); and hatching from Seymour's *A Musical Festival*, and *Peter Simple's Foreign Adventures, N°. 1*. To view this figure in colour, please visit the online version of this Journal.

The phrase, "A left-handed compliment", is only first described in the Oxford English Dictionary as coming from 1881. Earlier usages are however easy to find, and there was a cartoon in Punch in 1853 entitled *A left-handed compliment.*[22] The first usage of the phrase in *The Times* is on April 27th, 1791:

> The MAJESTY OF FRANCE, with all that divinity supposed to hedge a King, could only procure a feat on the LEFT hand of Mons. Le President—with all the subsequent VIVE LE ROI's! of the National Assembly, surely this was but at best a kind of LEFT HANDED compliment. (Spelling modernised)

Although the next usage in *The Times* was not until June 25th, 1847, those two usages bracket Marks's print, and other early nineteenth-century examples can readily be found in archives such as Google Books. Searching *Eighteenth Century Collections Online* finds but a single use of the phrase, which is from 1768, in William Donaldson's novel, *The life and adventures of*

[22] http://www.john-leech-archive.org.uk/1853/left-handed-compliment.htm

Sir Bartholomew Sapskull, Baronet (Donaldson, 1768), where the King grants the right to have Concord on a coat of arms, but it is felt that because "she is placed on the sinister side, that Concord was intended as a left-handed compliment" (p. 104). A search of *19th Century British Library Newspapers* and *19th Century UK periodicals* finds, for instance, uses in *The Liverpool Mercury* of March 28th, 1823 and Dec 31st, 1824. The phrase itself seems to be uncomplicated in general,[23] for as Ira Wile says, "No one can mistake the irony of the reproach in a left-handed compliment" (Wile, 1934, p. 42) (although unfortunately Wile says nothing about the origins of the expression). Occasionally the ironic or sarcastic reversal of the normal meaning of a phrase, is compounded, as in both examples above, with the added effect of a more literal use of left or right. We can probably conclude that in the early decades of the nineteenth century the phrase was being used in its modern sense.

The most mysterious part of *A Left Handed Compliment* concerns the nature of the compliment itself and the grandmother's shocked response. The young boy is clearly drawing on his slate with his left hand, and the faint image on the plate is compatible with the drawing being of the grandmother. The grandmother herself has her left hand inside a stocking which is being darned, that being a typical way for a right-hander to sew or darn. In a nice touch, the very fine needle can also be seen to be held, through the sock, by the left hand (see Figure 3). Clearly the boy has said or intimated something that has shocked the grandmother, causing her to throw up her arms, and she says, "Mercy on us Child! what could put such an idea into your head?". What that idea is though, is less than clear. The boy has said, "Now Granny, sit still; and I'll just see if I can't touch off your old Phizog left handed". We presume that this is a family scene, and that drawing the grandmother would be easier if the model stays still (but then she probably would have been still if she were darning). The tricky bit is the expression, "I'll just see if I can't touch off your old Phizog left handed". The inclusion of "left handed" perhaps implies that although the boy is drawing with his left hand, that may not be the normal way in which he draws, and therefore the drawing will not be as good as usual. If so, though, it is difficult to see why the grandmother is quite so shocked. However, just as "left-handed" means a reversal of normal proprieties and an inversion of sense and relationship, as in

[23] However an additional usage of the phrase, both literal and metaphorical, is also found repeatedly in the reports in, say, *Bell's Life in London and Sporting Chronicle* of June 1st, 1828, where of a prize fight between pugilists it is reported, "Each stopped a left-handed compliment" (presumably a left hook to the jaw); a similar usage occurs 20 years later, when the same periodical reports, "Martin … delivered a good left-handed compliment on his [opponent's] brow" (*ibid.*, Oct 1st, 1848). This usage does not seem to be in the *OED*. It also bears mention that the same sources often also refer to the face as the "phizog".

"left-handed compliment" itself, or in a host of other expressions such as a left-handed marriage (a morganatic marriage), a left-handed wife (a concubine), a left-handed sugar-bowl (a chamber pot), a left-handed cigarette (one containing marijuana), a left-handed bricklayer (a freemason), or simply "left-handed" (a term for homosexual), so it might be that in *A Left Handed Compliment* something similar is happening.

The earliest entry in the OED to "Physog" is to F. Grose's *Lexicon Balatronicum* [subtitled: A Dictionary of Buckish Slang, University Wit and Pickpocket Eloquence]: "Physog, the face. A vulgar abbreviation of physiognomy". And there are then frequent uses throughout the nineteenth century. "Physiognomy" was also in frequent use throughout the eighteenth century, Eighteenth Century Collections Online finding it in 3546 works, 97 of them being within the first decade, and interest in it going back many centuries earlier. "Physiogonomy" was also used, in examples in the OED from 1483 to 1603, as is itself a term for "A representation of a face; a portrait".

Physiognomy as a pseudo-science was popular from ancient through mediaeval times, and perhaps reached its heyday in the eighteenth century, with the publication of Johann Kaspar Lavater's *Physiognomische Fragmente zur Beförderung der Menschenkenntnis und Menschenliebe,* published between 1775 and 1778, and translated into English in 1789 as the *Essays on Physiognomy designed to promote the knowledge and the love of mankind.* Given Marks's reference to Phizog, it is intriguing that in many ways both of the faces in *A Left Handed Compliment* could have come from Lavater's *Physiognomy* (and perhaps have been adapted by Marks for that very purpose). The grandmother is remarkably similar to the third figure on Plate 77 of Lavater[24] (see Figure 4), for which the text says,

> The most accurate female housewifery: the forehead entirely feminine; the nose indicative of household discretion; the eye sharply attentive; the mouth kind, but strictly economical; the undulation of the jawbone as effeminate as possible; all the wrinkles express good sense, confined within a small domestic circle.

Indeed the grandmother is, in some ways, a stock figure who appears in many contexts (and see for instance G. M. Woodward's "The dutiful grandson" of 1792,[25] or George Cruikshank's "The age of intellect" of 1828, or indeed for that matter, the Old Woman in the plate entitled *The Bumpkin* in volume 3 of *Seymour's Sketches*). The first decade of the nineteenth century saw British artists looking back to small-scale seventeenth-century

[24] The figures are taken from Digital Lavater at www.newcastle.edu.au/department/fad/fi/lavater/, and are based on the 4th edition of Lavater's *Essays on Physiognomy*, translated by Thomas Holcroft, London, ca. 1844.

[25] A copy is in the National Archive, catalogue D5459/2/3/1. See www.nationalarchives.gov.uk/A2A/records.aspx?cat =026-d5459&cid =-1&Gsm =2008-06-18

Figure 4. Centre: Post card by Donald McGill (obtained from en.wikipedia.org/wiki/Image: McGill_betting.jpg), along with (top right and top left) details of the heads from *A Left Handed Compliment,* showing the similarity in the expressions. Bottom left and right show two of the physiognomic heads from Lavater, which have been left-right reversed from the original to match better the two figures in *A Left Handed Compliment*. To view this figure in colour, please visit the online version of this Journal.

Dutch domestic works (Solkin, 2008, pp. 37–77), and genre paintings such as David Wilkie's "The Cut Finger", Thomas Heaphy's "The Family Doctress" and James Northcote's "The Village Doctress" all feature elderly women wearing similar bonnets and, in the case of the latter two paintings, with glasses perched on their noses, of a type which both Seymour and Marks have here satirised.

In contrast, Marks's boy, while not quite looking lascivious, does look up to some sort of mischief with the strange position of his tongue and his ruddy face. He could well be a younger version of the first figure on the same plate (see Figure 4), for which Lavater says,

> Corrupt rudeness, and malignity, contemning morals. Natural power degenerates into obstinacy, in the forehead. Affection is far distant from this countenance. Insensibility usurps the place of courage, and meanness the seat of heroism. Alas! what must thy sufferings be ere thou shalt be purified equal to thy original destination! The thing most pitiable in this countenance is an expression of the conscious want of power to acquire the degree of malignity it may wish, or affect to possess.

An additional twist on Phizog is that it is also close to the nineteenth-century expression "phiz-gig", defined in Partridge as "An old woman dressed young", but also, which becomes relevant with the meaning of "touch off" (see below), as "A pyramid of moistened gunpowder, which, on ignition, fuses but does not flash" (Partridge & Simpson, 1973). "Phiz-gig" isn't in the OED.

Finally, while discussing "Phizog", it surely bears mentioning that the most well known of Dickens' illustrators, Hablot Knight Browne (1815–1882), used the pseudonym Phiz throughout his career, starting while working on the *The Pickwick Papers* (published 1837) (Patten & Lester, 2004). In 1836, although only aged 21 and running his own studio, and after Robert Seymour committed suicide in 1836, it was Dickens who suggested that Browne become his new illustrator. Browne, who was clearly very talented as a young man and whose father was also a talented artist, had lived mostly in London, and for a while attended the Life School in St Martin's Lane. Again, given the small world of London illustrators, is it possible that the talented young man in Marks's drawing relates to the artist who was to become Phiz? One detail which may support that interpretation is that "Phizog" in the print's caption is capitalised, suggesting that it is meant to be associated with a proper name. Although the standard story for Phiz's pseudonym is that the name went harmoniously with Dickens' own pseudonym of Boz (Patten & Lester, 2004), it is perhaps possible that the artist named himself Phiz, or perhaps was so named by his friends, because of his talents as a "phiz-maker"—a "maker of grimaces", although grimaces made not with the face but with the pencil. As Jane Cohen has said, "the old humorous, colloquial abbreviation of physiognomy [was] an appropriate pseudonym for one who excelled in capturing facial expressions with a few deft strokes" (p. 63). If a young Browne is indeed being referred to, then a crucial detail is that Browne would appear to have been right-handed (as shown, for instance, in the hatching of the pencil sketches in Cohen (1980, pp. 92–93). If a young Browne is indeed featured in *A Left Handed Compliment*, then his normal handedness has presumably been intentionally reversed for some humorous purpose.

The phrase "touch off" is an interesting one. Although originally used in the sense of firing off a cannon or musket, by the mid-eighteenth century the OED shows it was also being used in the sense of "representing exactly", a meaning clearly germane to drawing, and also in the sense of taking the measure of someone so that they can be conned, which may perhaps relate to the intentions of the boy in the picture. Given the ways in which prepositions subtly modify verbs in English it is not surprising that "Touch off" is also closely allied to "touch up", for which three meanings are given in the OED. "To improve, finish, or modify by adding touches or light strokes", is clearly related to touching off a likeness. The second meaning includes, "to rouse the emotions of", and the third meaning is explicitly sexual, coming from Grose's *Dictionary of the Vulgar Tongue*, of 1785, where it is defined as, "to touch up a woman; to have carnal knowledge of her", and Partridge defines it as, "to caress intimately in order to inflame (a person to the sexual act)". The closeness to "touch up" suggests that "touch off" may also have sexual connotations, perhaps allied to setting off an explosion, such as that of an orgasm, a usage that later appeared in Nabokov's novel *Ada or Ardor*, where the author talks of how an encounter might "touch off internal fires".

The drawing in the picture is being made on what looks like a slate of the sort used by children in school. One might therefore expect that the writing instrument would be chalk, but this instrument appears to be dark in colour, and quite thin, and may therefore be a slate pencil, which also leaves a pale line on the slate.[26] In the present context, the sexual connotations of the instrument cannot be ignored. "Pencil" is, of course, derived from the Latin *peniculus*, which means a little penis, and according to *Grose's Dictionary*, a nib or neb, is "the slit of a pen", and figuratively is, "the face and mouth of a woman; as, She holds up her neb: she holds up her mouth to be kissed" (and "slit" as OED also says, is itself a slang term for the vulva). Finally, it is possible that the drawing medium is meant to be an engraving plate, covered in a black ground to make the image more visible, and the thin instrument is an etching needle. Is it perhaps possible that the compliment is being paid to a fellow left-handed engraver, who might be Seymour? That the drawing is indeed on an engraving plate might be supported by the picture on the rear wall, which looks remarkably like an image of the grandmother, but with black lines on white (i.e., either printed or drawn with pencil on paper), which may be an earlier work by the boy (and hence the reference to, "*Now* Granny sit still, ..." (our emphasis).

Throughout this article the implication has been made that Marks had included an explicitly sexual sub-text to *A Left Handed Compliment*. That suggestion is supported by an awareness of a growing market at the beginning of the nineteenth century in obscene images, both politically motivated, and also simply for their pornographic value. In an influential historical article by McCalman (1984) entitled "Unrespectable radicalism: Infidels and pornography in early nineteenth-century London", it is interesting that although he is not mentioned by name in the article, Marks was responsible for three of the seven plates illustrating the piece. One print of circa 1820 shows Lord Conyngham discovering that his wife was the mistress of the King (see also Colligan, 2005); a second dated June 1820, ironically entitled "Chastity!" showed the Prince Regent seated on the laps

[26] See http://www.nebraskahistory.org/images/oversite/store/catalog4/slate-pencil.jpg and also en.wikipedia.org/wiki/Slate_%28writing%29, where it says that a slate pencil "is a rod made of soft slate, soapstone, or pressed clay, which makes a thin white line on the slate".

of two skimpily glad, buxom women; and a third, which was anti-clerical as well as anti-Royalist, was dated April–May 1821 and showed Lady Conyngham having her left breast squeezed by a tonsured George IV who promises her absolution. (A further cartoon by Marks featuring Lady Conyngham can be found in Kaellgren (1992), and a detailed account of the Queen Caroline affair can be found, along with another engraving by Marks of George IV wanting to be proclaimed a cuckold so that he could then obtain a divorce, can be found in Hunt (1991)). As the McCalman article says, "during [1820–1821] London's radical and gutter presses had poured out salacious prints, pamphlets, songs and chap-books, many of them lampooning the sexual habits of the Prince Regent", where it is made clear that cartoons inspired by political radicalism, particularly during 1820–1821 in the face of the sexual scandals surrounding the Prince Regent, were bordering into the below-the-counter world of frank pornography (McCalman, 1984). Including sexual content or innuendo in *A Left Handed Compliment* would not therefore have been out of character for Marks, whom the print historian Dorothy George described as being, amongst his contemporaries, the "least hampered by considerations of propriety" and possessing "a seeming love of vulgarity for its own sake" (Bryant & Heneage, 1994).

A final intriguing possibility, which was stimulated by finding the census records for Marks, is that *A Left Handed Compliment* is precisely what it seems to be—a charming domestic scene, faithfully recorded, in a household where books were certainly being read. The census records of 1841 show that Jacob Marks, the oldest child in the household, who was by then already recorded as an engraver by trade[27] was then 15 years old, and hence in 1831 or 1832, when *A Left Handed Compliment* was produced, would have been about five or six years old. If so, then perhaps the boy in the picture is indeed Marks' own son—a son who later clearly had at least some talent for drawing—who perhaps was already drawing on a slate, and perhaps drawing his grandmother. And maybe he was indeed left-handed. And as is often the case in families, perhaps the child had innocently produced his double entendre, and the father recorded the scene as a family joke.

Taken overall, *A Left Handed Compliment* is an intriguing image, with its connections to Marks and those other great illustrators Robert Seymour and Hablot Browne. It can also be seen as being in a tradition of risque, saucy images with sexual overtones, often relying on words or phrases having alternative meanings, that within popular British culture culminated in the saucy seaside postcards of Donald McGill (1875–1962). The example of

[27] A search of the later census records finds no evidence for Jacob Marks, and certainly not for anyone of that name whose trade was engraver. It seems probable therefore that he did not have a career that followed in Lewis Marks's footsteps.

McGill's work that is shown in Figure 4 and was used in McGill's obscenity trial in 1954, has many of the same properties as *A Left Handed Compliment*—the young, apparent innocent on the left, using an expression rich in sexual double entendre, and the expression on the face of the older man on the left which is reminiscent of the grandmother, both of whom clearly know enough to recognise the ambiguity of the statement; and of course the viewer also recognises the ambiguity, for thence comes the humour. In his famous essay on McGill, George Orwell commented that,

> ... at least half of McGill's post cards are sex jokes, and a proportion, perhaps ten per cent, are far more obscene than anything else that is now printed in England. Newsagents are occasionally prosecuted for selling them, and there would be many more prosecutions if the broadest jokes were not invariably protected by double meanings. A single example will be enough to show how this is done. In one post card, captioned "They didn't believe her", a young woman is demonstrating, with her hands held apart, something about two feet long to a couple of open-mouthed acquaintances. Behind her on the wall is a stuffed fish in a glass case, and beside that is a photograph of a nearly naked athlete. Obviously it is not the fish that she is referring to, but this could never be proved. ... [J]okes exactly like McGill's are the ordinary small change of the revue and music-hall stage, and are also to be heard on the radio, at moments when the censor happens to be nodding. ... In the past the mood of the comic post card could enter into the central stream of literature, and jokes barely different from McGill's could casually be uttered between the murders in Shakespeare's tragedies. That is no longer possible, and a whole category of humour, integral to our literature till 1800 or thereabouts, has dwindled down to these ill-drawn post cards, leading a barely legal existence in cheap stationers' windows.

Several of Marks's prints makes Orwell's point exactly, his 1816 print entitled "THOSE THAT WISH TO SEE A FULL MOON! MUST VISIT HYDE PARK ON A WINDY AFTERNOON".[28] A corpulent young lady in the park stands with her back to the wind, which is blowing the cloth of her dress tightly against her outstretched buttocks, to the shape of full moons, while the comments from various onlookers are invariably ambiguous with their emphasis on flatus, one emphasising the point by saying, "What a rude wind this is ...". Likewise, the British Museum has a series of prints entitled *Doubles Entendres*, of which there were at least six. Number two (BM 1951,0411.4.59) shows a young girl reaching up to take a pear from a tree, and, shockingly for the day, revealing her ankles and calves. The print is titled, "WHAT A FINE PEAR.", the ambiguity being rather over-emphasised by pear being spelled "PAIEAR". The same basic joke was still

[28] See http://www.michaelfinney.co.uk/caricstock.htm#J%20Lewis%20Marks where the print is identified as BM12842.

being used in the film *Carry on Doctor* (1967), where a character seeing the large-breasted Barbara Windsor eating a pear, comments, "Oh you've got a nice pear!".

A Left Handed Compliment is, we believe, a part of that same vernacular, exuberantly scatological, literary stream which is found in abundance in Shakespeare, and is still a live part of oral culture, seen particularly well in stand-up comedians, and which thrives on sexual ambiguity and pornographic punning, in this case perhaps also with some personal humour directed at an associate of Marks. That the ambiguity itself derives from alternate readings of lateral references means that the humour itself is well described in several senses as "left-handed".

REFERENCES

Bayly, C. A. (2004). *The birth of the modern world, 1780–1914: Global connections and comparisons.* Oxford: Blackwell.

Bryans, D. (2000). The double invention of printing. *Journal of Design History, 13*, 287–300.

Bryant, M., & Heneage, S. (1994). *Dictionary of British Cartoonists and Caricaturists, 1730–1980.* Aldershot, UK: Scolar Press.

Cohen, J. R. (1980). *Charles Dickens and his original illustrators.* Ohio: Ohio State University Press.

Colligan, C. (2005). The unruly copies of Byron's *Don Juan*: Harems, underground culture, and the age of mechanical reproduction. *Nineteenth-Century Literature, 59*, 433–462.

Donaldson, W. (1768). *The life and adventures of Sir Bartholomew Sapskull, Baronet. Nearly allied to most of the great men in the three kingdoms. By somebody.* London: J. Williams.

Engen, R. K. (1985). *Dictionary of Victorian Wood Engravers.* Cambridge, UK: Chadwyck-Healey.

Gascoigne, B. (2004). *How to identify prints: A complete guide to manual and mechanical processes from woodcut to inkjet* (2nd ed.). London: Thames and Hudson.

George, M. D. (1959a). *English political caricature 1793–1832: A study of opinion and propaganda.* Oxford, UK: Oxford University Press.

George, M. D. (1959b). *English political caricature to 1792: A study of opinion and propaganda.* Oxford, UK: Oxford University Press.

Heseltine, M. (2004). Seymour, Robert (1798–1836). *Oxford Dictionary of National Biography,* [http://www.oxforddnb.com/view/article/25180, accessed 30 May 2008].

Hunt, T. L. (1991). Morality and Monarchy in the Queen Caroline Affair. *Albion: A Quarterly Journal Concerned with British Studies, 23*, 697–722.

Kaellgren, C. P. (1992). Lady Conyngham's Silver Gilt in the Royal Ontario Museum. *Burlington Magazine, 134*, 368–374.

Kunzle, D. (1973). *The early comic strip: Narrative strips and picture stories in the European broadsheet from c. 1450 to 1825.* Berkeley, CA: University of California Press.

Maaz, B. (2008). *Adolph Menzel: Radikal, real.* Munich: Hirmer Verlag.

Maidment, B. E. (1996). *Reading popular prints: 1790–1870.* Manchester, UK: Manchester University Press.

Marks, J. L. (2007). *Marks's Adventures of Paul Pry and His Young Friend in London (1835).* Whitefish, MT: Kessinger Publishing, LLC.

McCalman, I. (1984). Unrespectable radicalism: Infidels and pornography in early nineteenth-century London. *Past and Present, 104*, 74–110.

O'Connell, S. (1999). *The popular print in England*. London: British Museum Press.

Partridge, E., & Simpson, J. (1973). *Routledge dictionary of historical slang*. London: Routledge.

Patten, R. L., & Lester, V. B. (2004). Browne, Hablot Knight [pseud. Phiz] (1815–1882). *Oxford Dictionary of National Biography, Oxford University Press, 2004* [http://www.oxforddnb.com/view/article/3675, accessed 1 June 2008].

Press, C. (1977). The Georgian Political Print and democratic institutions. *Comparative Studies in Society and History, 19*, 216–238.

Raucort, A. (1820). *A Manual of Lithography, or Memoir on the Lithographical Experiments made in Paris, at the Royal School of the Roads and Bridges; Clearly explaining the whole art, as well as all the accidents that may happen in printing and different methods of avoiding them* [Translated by C. Hullmandel]. London: Rodwell and Martin.

Robinson, D., & Powell, D. (2004). *William West and the Regency Toy Theatre*. London: Pollock's Toy Museum.

Seymour, R. (1838). *Seymour's sketches. Illustrated in prose & verse by Alfred Crowquill [pseudonym of Alfred Henry Forrester]*. London: H. Wallis.

Solkin, D. H. (2008). *Paintings out of the ordinary: Modernity and the art of everyday life in early nineteenth-century Britain*. New Haven, CT: Yale University Press.

Todd, W. B. (1972). *A directory of printers and others in allied trades, London and vicinity 1800–1840*. London: Printing Historical Society.

Twyman, M. (1976). *Henry Bankes's Treatise on Lithography; Reprinted from the 1813 and* 1816 edition with an introduction and notes. London: Printing Historical Society.

Twyman, M. (2001). *Breaking the mould: The first hundred years of lithography*. London: The British Library.

Wile, I. S. (1934). *Handedness: Right and left*. Boston, MA: Lothrop, Lee and Shepard.

For Product Safety Concerns and Information please contact our EU representative GPSR@taylorandfrancis.com Taylor & Francis Verlag GmbH, Kaufingerstraße 24, 80331 München, Germany